Gold &
Spices

Gold &
Spices

THE RISE OF COMMERCE IN
THE MIDDLE AGES

Jean Favier

Translated from the French by
Caroline Higgitt

HM

HOLMES & MEIER
New York/London

Published in the United States of America 1998 by
Holmes & Meier Publishers, Inc.
160 Broadway
New York, NY 10038

First published under the title *De l'or et des épices: Naissance de l'homme d'affaires au
moyen âge*, copyright © Librairie Arthème Fayard, 1987. Bibliographical additions for
the English translation copyright © 1998 by Holmes & Meier Publishers, Inc.

Book design by Lynne Arany
Maps by Christopher Brest
Typesetting by Coghill Book Typesetting, Chester, VA

This book has been printed on acid-free paper.

Library of Congress Cataloging-in-Publication Data

Favier, Jean, 1932–
   [De l'or et des épices. English]
   Gold & spices : the rise of commerce in the Middle Ages / Jean
Favier ; translated from the French by Caroline Higgitt.
     p.   cm.
   Includes bibliographical references and index.
   ISBN 0-8419-1232-7 (cloth : alk. paper)
   1. Europe—Commerce—History. 2. Europe—Economic conditions—To
1492. 3. Middle Ages—History. 4. Merchants—Europe—History.
I. Title.
HF3495.F3813   1998
382'.094'00902—dc21   98-14166
                                                        CIP

Manufactured in the United States of America

CONTENTS

MAPS

Gold & Spices

Introduction

*H*umanity is defined by its horizons—horizons, with their waves and crests, that are sometimes perceived and at other times only imagined, sometimes earthbound, at other times the stuff of dreams. These horizons give each one of us a sense of the scale, and limitations, of our needs and abilities. One horizon we accept; the other remains ever beyond our reach. One is sterile while the other is fertile; one is real while the other remains an ideal. Both are relative to the moment and to our state of mind. These encircling horizons define people and things, opportunities and obstacles.

The boundaries of these horizons can be pushed back by our intelligence. All it takes is the creative impulse, which is expressed in acts of daring or enterprise. Necessary, too, is that immediate grasp of reality which demonstrates not only what is possible but also how much effort is required to obtain a desired outcome. Thus individuals create their own horizons, which lie at the point where necessity ends and ambition begins.

This book takes as its point of departure those horizons that determined the advance of the individual and the group. This expansion, made possible by the new forms of trade and methods of finance, gave rise to new markets and increased exploitation of resources, opportunities as varied as the spheres of influence created by geographical diversity. As generation succeeded generation, the map of economic relationships reflects this effort of the will to extend the world beyond its originally perceived limits.

Traders now had to take into account new realities that were foreign to their natural horizons. They had thus to overcome two interdependent components in their fear of the unknown and the need to overcome it: time

1

and space. It was no less important to master those objectives, which depended more on inventiveness than on imagination. Intuition is not on its own enough: provided that it fulfilled the double condition of being both precise and up-to-date, information also played an important role for the successful merchant or banker. As always, the old questions applied: where, which way, when, how? To these the merchants had to add the fundamental question: what? Those familiar with trading routes on sea and land knew very well that the question "when?" would often be answered by another question, "where?" and, inevitably, "which way?"

As the horizons of time and space expanded, selling what one had and buying what one intended to sell ceased to define economic exchange. Opportunity became no longer a matter of chance—simply selling what one happens to have—becoming instead the object of choice. It was a matter of obtaining what was available and knowing what could be sold in one place, and not in another. People no longer bought what was there simply because it was there, nor did they sell what they had transported just because it was available. A new factor now appeared on the scene: the entrepreneur or businessman. Here was someone who could anticipate, react, seek out, and choose. He took responsibility: in short, he made decisions.

From the spice merchant to the shipowner, from the market to the bank, from the craftsman's forge to the emergence of vertical integration in the textile industry, the routes were many, arrived at through collective attitudes to economic realities and determined by the unique abilities of the individuals involved. Confronted by the outside world, as by colleagues and neighbors, cooperation and competition began to emerge, expressing themselves differently depending on local traditions and horizons. One's reaction to the world will vary depending on whether one looks out on the open sea or at the enclosing slopes of a valley. We do not perceive others in a port or market town, where a world of strangers passes, in the same way as in a local market where inhabitants have known each other for generations. Individualism, competition, publicity—all appear in one guise in Genoa and in quite another in London; they have one meaning in Florence and quite another in Lübeck.

No less than the unpredictable harshness of the elements and obstacles of nature, the weight of history bears down on humankind. Dangers at sea, violent storms, and hostility in foreign parts will always affect the ever uncertain relationship between the group and the individual, whether found in his environment by birth or by choice. The same is true of the individual's relationship to the state, which may take the form of the city in the eyes of its citizens or of the prince in the eyes of his subjects.

Given the infinite number of variables—political, economic, social, even climatic—affecting the interaction between the individual and the group, even behavior that passes for admirable among some people may be seen as deplorable by others. In a study of the gradual emergence of modern commerce, therefore, we need to be able to explore every nuance that hints at innovative developments, despite the fact that the connection between innovators and later developments is not always clear. The rejection of the new is often merely an expression of the pragmatism of a particular milieu that feels no need for it, just as the new is often no more than the result of a local response to a very specific necessity. At each stage in this history it is useful to move about from one place to another, taking care, however, not to fall into the trap of false extrapolation. The Baltic is not the Mediterranean, and the Atlantic is not some compromise between the two. The alum trade has nothing to do with that of salt, while the market for Gascon wine—Bordeaux—is in no way similar to that of Beaune.

Our idea of economic activity, its resources and zones, its short-term profits and its long-term outcomes, is determined by political context, intellectual milieu, and traditions of individual development. To say "he is a merchant" does not place a man or describe his role in the city. What is true for Paris may not be so for Florence, Seville, or Danzig.

It becomes essential also to master the means—whether material, financial, or, particularly, human—of knowledge and action. Rough estimates had sufficed when it was simply a matter of setting aside grain from the year's harvest, and when prices were set on the local market according to the supply and demand prevailing at the precise moment of the transaction. To exploit distant markets—both supplying and buying goods—it was necessary to speculate on the morrow's contingencies, plotting deals where the complexity of objects and the multiplicity of sources offered a range of alternatives. Now distance and exchange were measured in months and years, and an immediate and subjective assessment of the situation was no longer adequate. It was one thing to raise the price of rye when the supply was scarce or to lower the price of wine after an unusually abundant harvest; it was quite another to know, in Florence, which Russian skins would sell the following winter to the furriers of London, or to anticipate, in Bruges, whether or not the scarcity of wool exported from England would result in cloth merchants on the Continent accepting the rise in price or making do with the cheaper but inferior wool of the merino sheep bred in Castile.

For the future businessman finally to break out of the limitations of his workshop and horizons, he needed to take control of the unpredictable nature of the world around him. This unpredictability can be understood as the complex dynamics of the economic climate. It was becoming increasingly necessary for merchants to coordinate their activities—with the exception of those who deliberately decided to act independently, in full awareness of the risks they were running. Those who managed to make use of these tendencies rather than be dominated by them were to meet with the greatest success.

Herein lies the art of playing the market rather than simply being a player within the market.

Knowing what would be required tomorrow and what would increase in value the day after that, be it credit or wool, tax-farming or the need for arms, was soon to become the basis of all trade—in other words, speculation.

Intelligence, experience, and information can all reduce the element of chance, but they can never entirely eliminate the risk that justifies profit—at least in the eyes of both the theologians who endlessly debated the subject and the clients who paid for it. All the energies, astuteness, and solidarity of the traders were dedicated to minimizing its effects. The quest for profit was to engender other types of speculation, each with its attendant risks.

In this world that had expanded to the size of a continent—and that would soon be bigger still—it was becoming apparent that financial caution was restricting if not actually preventing trade, though only the solitary operator was at a real disadvantage. He remained confined to his workshop, market, or stall. He had no place in the money market of Bruges or in trade with Egypt. Thus we see that the development of trade came about just as much through the management of people—by the creation of new organizations of professionals, burghers, or nations—and through the ability of these groups to act in concert, encouraging all those involved, whether actively or passively, to initiate and to invest. The benefits were reaped by those who knew how to free capital from its sterile inactivity and who could coordinate their activities in a fruitful balance of talent and responsibility.

As the domains of business expanded until they could be called economic zones, the tendency to specialize became more marked. Activities began to diversify as the range of products increased. Just as a pewterer could not do the work of a potter, so a man competent to distinguish between the ten qualities of pepper available on the market in Alexandria might not be able to do the same in Champagne for the hundred types of wool arriving from a variety of towns and villages.

It began also to be possible to distinguish the different functions within an enterprise through the various contributions of capital, labor, competence, and organizational ability. Many different skills were required to organize the technical processes carried out by some twenty artisans in the production of a piece of cloth, to adjust from one day to the next the movement of the three-sided monetary exchanges that could produce cash in one place and credit in another, to ship a cargo, to decide on the placing of new investments, or to keep oneself informed on an hourly basis of the rumors circulating in the capital or town. Different roles were similarly played by those who knew whether it was wiser to invest profits from a successful artisan workshop in animal stock or to divide available funds between the equipment of a mill and a public loan, those who had the ability to refine the bookkeeping methods of a concern, the initiative to find mules for a convoy, or the persuasive powers of a stallholder to convince a hesitant customer.

A time was to come when capitalism was to be defined by this separation of the economic spheres of finance, management, and production. At the same time, it provided an answer to the internal needs of an economy faced with increasing diversification by offering to the successful enterprise a means to achieve a kind of universalism.

One could argue endlessly about the use of the word *capitalism* by the historian of the Middle Ages. It is now over twenty years since one young medievalist, Fernand Braudel, was severely reprimanded for doing just that. But at least, unlike Espinas and some others, he did not put it on the cover of his latest masterpiece. We should be clear about one thing: medieval capitalism resembles only very slightly the system of wealth production analyzed in the last century, for an industrialized society, by Karl Marx. Here, as elsewhere, we should not be misled by words: the reality that they conceal is always related to a particular time. Ancient Athenian democracy has nothing to do with the America viewed by de Tocqueville, any more than the Roman dictatorships have with those of our century. Capitalism in the thirteenth or fourteenth century is clearly not that of the industrial era.

And yet, by separating the functions of an enterprise and drawing the nonproductive classes into a personal involvement in business, the medieval businessman had, nevertheless, helped the economic world over a particular hurdle—that of the limitations to freedom of action imposed by the individual operating alone. The name we give to this process—medieval capitalism, the birth of capitalism, or the origins of capitalism—is unimportant. Circumlocutions are simply preliminary precautions, not something to fight over. The important thing is that we accept that the epoch of the Tuscan companies is not that of the great industries of the Ruhr; the first is a distant anticipation of the second.

Technical industrial progress, it is clear, would not have led to much had there not been a similar development of the intellectual tools by means of which the businessman was able to manage markets as well as his own affairs, devise operational structures and analyze the management of his enterprise, and observe and measure fluctuations in the economy. In order to make choices and gamble on the chances of the morrow—from peddler to businessman, tradesman to banker, from the eleventh to the fifteenth century—the world of trade had to perfect systems for dealing with rates of exchange and payment for transactions and services rendered. In order to progress, it had to establish procedures for obtaining credit suited to the times and, particularly, to the requirements of moral theology and canon law. Legal bases for these enterprises had to be created appropriate to the needs of trade, not to the needs of the feudal lords and the rural economy from which most of the nobility's income was derived. Last, in order to transact their commercial and banking activities, businessmen had to invent a method for both continual monitoring and final balancing of their accounts.

The techniques born as a result of these needs, engendered in their turn by growth, would be those of our modern system of economic relations. The last three centuries of the Middle Ages introduce not only the notion of monetary transfer but also trade in commercial bills and letters of exchange—in other words, paper money and financial credit.

Different forms of speculation also appeared or reappeared during this period: purchases on credit, leased monopolies that were the basis of the greater part of the wealth of the Medici and Fugger families, loans to princes, and the fixing of exchange rates at future fairs. Risk, inherent in all speculation, stimulated the ingenuity of businessmen. Having learned to analyze an anticipated risk, they began to protect themselves from the effects of chance, taking the first timid steps in setting up a system of shared risk and compensation that would eventually become the basis of insurance.

Historians have to select their vantage points and evidence, but we do not, for all that, have an entirely free hand. In every case, out of the multiplicity of situations and perspectives examined by the historian, we are dependent on the sources. The businessmen we know best are those who have left us their account books and letters, those who thought it wise to go to a notary, those who devoted time to setting down for others the fruits of their own experience. When Francesco di Marco Datini decided to leave all the documents relating to his trade and banking activities to the hospital he had founded in his hometown of Prato, he had, without realizing it, ensured that he would be quoted here more frequently than any other businessman. Others may have been equally able, but not all were so concerned with posterity.

It is, however, true that the organization of documentary records is an aspect of the organization of work, and it may be that these actors in our history deserve to be remembered. A lack of documentary evidence usually indicates inefficiency, although the contrary—an excess of papers—is not necessarily a proof of productive efficiency. If we accept that the state of the sources is often in itself indicative, then the historian who is obliged to follow the path traced by the available sources is not, for all that, led by chance. The place given in this book to a few towns and a few people is not determined merely by the existence of some five to eight centuries of preserved archives; it is a place that remains today in living memory, earned by those protagonists in the economic game who forged the tools of economic life and the methods by which it evolved. By the same token, it is not the intention of this book to give a general picture of marketplaces, or to provide a list of the most successful stock exchanges and markets. The origin of commerce is a story of the formation and development of one or several types of businessmen.

There emerged types—in all the diversity described here—who were as able to adapt their ways of thinking to the realities of the economic world as to act collectively within social organizations created by others and for others.

The social and intellectual outcome begs the question: Did businessmen really exist in the later Middle Ages? Could it not be that there were simply people and business, in as many different varieties as there were climates and markets?

There are several answers. And these answers give shape to the businessman, in whatever country we find him. But the questions remain the same, whether in Cádiz or in Novgorod. They all point to the same search for the greatest profit with the least risk, the same desire for growth in the face of the competition. Businessmen are basically the same the world over: they strive to be the best informed today, so that tomorrow they can find what is known to all by the name of Fortune.

Orval, 2 August 1987

ONE

Horizons

A New World

*E*urope was not a creation of the Roman conquest. Nevertheless, during the reign of Pepin the Short in the eighth century, the horizons of the economic world, like those of the political world, still followed the lines of the Roman Empire. The Mediterranean countries remained more or less intact, although, from the third century, migrations from the steppes to the east were beginning to cause some problems. Constantine reinforced this unity around two poles: Rome and Constantinople. Though shaken by the first rumblings of the Arab conquest, it was revived for a time by Justinian. In the seventh and even the eighth centuries an Eastern presence was as marked in Gaul as in Italy and Spain. "Syrian" merchants were to be found not only in the ports along the Mediterranean coast but also inland in towns as far apart as Paris and Lyons, Bordeaux and Orleans. Eastern religions had invaded the West: Mithraism with its dualistic belief in good and evil, and Christianity with its mystery of redemption. The earliest forms of Western monasticism were influenced—in Marseilles, Hyères, Lérins, and Arles—by ideas borrowed from the tradition of religious communities in the East. The West was introduced to the monastic rule of the Egyptian St. Pachomius through St. Jerome's translation, while Caesarius of Arles, whose rule was written around the year 500, took his inspiration from practices introduced from the eastern Mediterranean into Lérins a century earlier. The political ideas of St. Augustine, the Berber bishop of Hippo in Algeria from 398 to 430, renewed intellectual life in the Latin world. Berber law was not so very different from Theodosius's simplified version of Roman law.

All this time merchants had continued to travel to and fro along the trade routes of the West. They brought back with them from further east both luxury goods and the decorative motifs that ornamented these objects. Byzantine ivories and Syrian silks introduced new symbols and images that the West adopted and incorporated into its own culture. Although Ireland, the guardian of the Latin forms of scholarly culture during the period of the invasions, was able to restore part of the Western heritage of the Roman Empire to the Continent, merchants, monks, and pilgrims brought back to Western Europe tales and objects from the "new Rome"—Constantinople—and its colonies in neighboring Egypt and Syria. In Italy we find sunflower motifs in the openwork balustrades—the "chancels"—of its sanctuaries. Lions and sphinxes begin to appear among the animals depicted in the art of Christian Gaul. The grave, bearded face of the Christ in the mosaic depiction of Saints Cosmas and Damian in Rome seems to have come straight from the steppes in the wake of the Ostrogoth Theodoric. Theodulf, the friend and adviser of Charlemagne and bishop of Orleans, was similarly influenced by Byzantine art in his choice of a Greek cross plan and mosaic decoration for his priory of Germigny-des-Prés.

The East was also in contact with the countries lying to the north, the Europe of furs and timber, made easily accessible by the great rivers that flowed into the Baltic. Northwestern Europe lay far off the routes taken by these traders, and there were few contacts between the northwestern European peninsula and a world to the east that for the Mediterranean countries was close and everpresent. Even when the Lombards reached Italy, the Franks invaded Gaul, and the Goths Spain, the world's horizon was no different from that known to Tiberius, Trajan, and Septimus Severus.

Charlemagne was to construct a very different Europe. In a few decades the seventh-century Arab conquest had imposed an entirely new kind of unity on the world that stretched from the shores of the Persian Gulf to the Atlantic coast of North Africa. Once the Mediterranean had represented a road and a means of communication; now it became a barrier. The life-blood of towns like Narbonne, Marseilles and Barcelona was cut off. Meanwhile, Austrasia was emerging as the dominant power in the Frankish world. From the sixth century this area, bounded by the rivers Meuse, Moselle, and Rhine, became the center of political and religious innovations. The Franks, of course, expanded as far as Italy and made forays into Spain in the time of Charlemagne, but it was in Germania that they achieved the greatest measure of success. The strengths and ambitions of this empire, with its capital in Aachen, showed that it was essentially part of continental Europe. A revitalized Christianity, spreading out from Mainz and Fulda, further united the empire. The old trade route down the Rhône valley to Marseilles and the Mediterranean was superseded by passes over the western Alps that placed Austrasia and Lombardy in more direct contact. A great slave market was established in Verdun at the time of the mayors of the palace, where slaves from England and the Slav countries were unceremoniously sold off to masters from all over Europe and particularly from what was by now Islamic Spain.

By the early eighth century the Mediterranean had ceased to be a unifying factor. Before long it came to represent a barrier. The split that, in the eleventh century, would make Byzantium the rival of Rome was the last and fatal blow to an empire centered on the Mediterranean. Because of her geographical position, and despite the threat of pirates, Italy was obliged to maintain commercial links not only with Byzantium, but also with Antioch and Alexandria, that would one day make the fortunes of Italian ports. Trade between northern Europe and the Arab world was carried on by way of Russia. As for the rest, Europe was content to operate within the Continent. The common horizon of Europeans was henceforth that of Europe.

Events combined to reinforce the cohesiveness of this continental Europe that, with the Norman conquests of the eleventh century, drew into its sphere first England and then Sicily. A powerful movement of spiritual and political unification resulted, finding expression in turn in Cluniac monasticism, the Gregorian reform, the military *Reconquista* of Islamic Spain, and finally in the Crusade—successfully designed by the papacy to be undertaken as a common effort—at the end of the eleventh century. Even if the Holy Land was the focus of rivalries and internal quarrels of European Christendom, the conquest, defense, and loss of the holy sites were, and continued to be, a common goal uniting Europe as well as a shared political and financial burden.

Western Europe had not yet seen the end of invasions: still to come were the Normans in the ninth and tenth centuries and the Hungarians in the tenth, not to mention the Saracens who were still making their presence felt on the borders of the Mediterranean, from Sicily, by way of Provence, to Andalusia. Deep insecurity prevailed, exacerbated for many by the breaches of that political unity apparent in the Frankish kingdom. In the face of immediate danger, local control triumphed over an impossible global strategy. The empire of Charlemagne and Charles the Bald had neither the strength nor the means of communication needed to provide real government in difficult times. The horizon contracted still further. The only effective political unit now became the county, formerly the district administered by a count, the king's official representative. Everyone supported the count in his pretense that the county belonged to him. When danger threatened, a count on the spot was worth more than a distant king. Occasionally the boundaries of the political unit expanded when the count extended his control over several counties. In this way were formed the territorial principalities and duchies that prefigured future political units. Sometimes things went the other way, when lords who controlled castles or villages did to the count what he had done to the king. The day of the independent castellan was not far off.

Roads and Rivers

The trade routes that were to give rise to a new economic Europe—rich in potential and energy—were created within the confines of these relatively narrow and essentially continental horizons. Transport was a decisive factor: without roads or rivers there could be no movement of men, merchandise, or information.

The major part of the network of Roman roads had long since fallen into disuse, disappearing under mud and reeds, even if small sections—recognizable by their carefully laid blocks of stone—survived. They had not simply been allowed to fall into disrepair, they had been deliberately abandoned. These strategic routes had been constructed by and for the legions to ensure rapid communication between the garrison towns that were joined by the straight lines so characteristic of the Roman network of roads, traces of which are still visible today on maps or in aerial photographs. It followed that the Roman road builders were oblivious to any geographical obstacles in their paths—something that the merchants unfortunately could not ignore with their heavy wagons—just as they were entirely uninterested in providing routes to less important centers. Those whose business it was to buy and sell could not afford to neglect clients in such places. The merchant was not in a hurry to reach the end of his journey. He could do better business by following the simple paths—established by local custom, social relations, and farming practices—from town to town and village to village, instead of taking the imperial roads so ill fitted to his needs. Traveling at this more leisurely speed, it was easier to go around a hill than to try to climb it, and the opportunities for trade were correspondingly greater.

The merchant's road was, then, a simple path, sometimes hard and dusty, in other cases muddy and wet. Although pitted with deep ruts, the road would otherwise be unmarked; the merchant could easily lose his way or sink into the marshy ground. Here the packhorse came into its own. Although it could carry little more than a hundredweight, such an animal could heave itself out of the mud and carry its pack of goods well out of the dust where its master walked. A wagon could carry more. These heavy four-wheeled vehicles traveled in convoys transporting heavy loads such as salt, wheat, stone, and wood. Although there were many regulations limiting the amount that could be carried by one wagon—the towns of southern Germany generally imposed a ceiling of sixteen hundredweight*—the majority of merchants were quite prepared to risk exceeding the limit. It was not unusual to find wagons carrying one and a half tons; on the other hand, a wagon that sticks in the mud represents a lost load, and a wagon team traveled slowly. The faster two-wheeled cart was fine in good weather for

*Trans. note: Throughout the text non-metric units refer to medieval usage; metric units are the modern equivalent.

the merchant carrying goods over short distances, but the risk in taking such a vehicle any distance was out of all proportion to the value of the merchant's time.

The only other possibility was to travel by water—an ideal method were it not for the well-known attendant risks. Boats were, without dispute, the best form of transport for heavy goods and, costing six or seven times less than road transport, not to be ignored. Furthermore, shipping was for a long time the only method of transporting barrels that did not result in breakage or leakage caused by the jolting of the wagons. Without a waterway there would have been no wine. A vineyard without a nearby river was confined to producing wine only for the local market.

The waterways were passable only if they were constantly maintained, for nature is ever ready to snatch back its rights. Weeds and bushes would invade not only the banks but also the watercourse, blocking the channel, while the curtains of trees and tall grasses growing up around the towpath would also deflect the wind that should have filled the boatman's sails on the Eure:

> The river is much encumbered with trees, reeds, and grasses and very low in water, which is why the boats and vessels on the said river cannot catch the wind nor use their sails to drive them forward. Thus men have to pull them from the land with ropes.

The slightest mishap could block the waterway for a considerable time: one barge jammed across the river could bring all traffic to a halt. It was a simple matter to block the river deliberately: in 1324 the seneschal of Guyenne had stakes driven into the main channel of the Garonne in order to stop the "French" boats. Throughout the Middle Ages, the state of the waterways was to represent one of the major preoccupations of rulers after a period of unrest.

It was apparent to all that the failure to maintain the waterways spelled the ruin of their livelihood. They did not wait for a royal decree to go and clear the water weeds or burn off the reeds on the towpath. But the king had powers that extended beyond the local horizon: only he could authorize or command dredging work that overrode the rights of the local lords through whose lands the river ran. And only he, while naturally requiring the towns to make sizable contributions, could facilitate the financing of measures that went beyond the normal capability of local communities. In one year, 1455, barely two years after the end of the war between France and England, the leading citizens of the Vendée tried to organize the dredging of the waterways around Luçon, while Charles VII improved the navigability of the Eure upstream of Nogent-le-Roi as far as Chartres so that it could accommodate boats up to 120 feet long and 18 feet wide. These fine barges could easily transport anything from thirty to sixty tons.

At the same time the harbor formed by the basin of the Marne and its tributaries was reopened to small seagoing ships. By the end of the fifteenth century it was possible to take a simple boat up the Loir as far as Châteaurenault, up the Clain to Poitiers, and up the Sèvre to Niort. Other rivers that were usually navigable were the Yonne as far as Auxerre, the Seine up to Nogent, and the Oise as far as Compiègne. It was possible to take the Loire as far as La Charité and even Roanne. The Cher was navigable only as far as Saint-Aignan, but with a small boat it was easy enough to reach Bourges along the Auron. At the right time of year Toulouse could be reached without difficulty up the Garonne—though the water level remained low in Languedoc for a considerable part of the year—while supplies of wood and stone were floated down from the Pyrenees on rafts. In Germany the Oder was navigable, even upstream of Frankfurt an der Oder almost as far as Oderberg.

On the upper reaches of a river, where navigation was more difficult, boats were replaced by rafts. On the Adige, although boats easily reached Trento, rafts were able to go as far up as Bolzano.

Even when nobody was deliberately hampering the free flow of traffic, the waterways were navigable only at certain times of the year. This annual cycle was marked by periods when the water was low, frozen, or full of drifting ice after the thaw. In summer the boats would scrape the bottom; with the exception of the lower Seine between Harfleur and Paris, the Seine basin was effectively closed to shipping between June and September. In winter the problems were of a different order: boats might be trapped in the ice or prevented by the swollen waters from passing under bridges, the swirling ice floes and melting snow hurling them against the piles or causing them to crash into watermills. If the rivers of southern Europe were of little real use in the summer, those of the north were useless or dangerous from December to February. It was a lucky man who could anticipate the date of the freeze or the thaw; no two winters are ever the same. The wise merchant was prepared for it, and the one who had enough foresight to prevent his capital from lying idle for two months, immobilized by ice or drought, was always more successful than the merchant for whom a sudden drop in temperature was a disaster. A fundamental difference divided one from the other; the seasons were merciless to those who lacked the means or the intelligence to diversify their activities.

Even more than for a wagon, it was essential for a boat to have a return cargo. It was a simple matter of the division of costs: the boat's overhead, the boatman's wage, the hire of towing horses. It was important to avoid using the boat for only half a round trip. One-way routes were less advantageous than those around river networks where it was possible to take advantage of the natural resources of the region. A boat traveling downstream to

Rouen could transport wine from Burgundy or the Paris area, bringing back upstream fruit or hay from Normandy. On the great northwestern rivers—the Meuse, Moselle, and Rhine—wine and wood traveling upstream would pass salt and North Sea fish coming down.

It was all too easy to seize control of a waterway. Even the most insignificant lord or the least daring brigand could board a barge as it passed under a bridge or berthed for the night. Thus it is not surprising that, as state power increased in importance, tolls began to multiply, ostensibly for the services provided by those who ensured a safe passage for shipping and maintained the waterways. The nature of the network of waterways made it very open to increases in taxes levied in exchange for the right to pass through certain tollgates. These tolls represented both a customary tax and a form of extortion. In 1325 there were at least thirty-one tolls on the Garonne between Toulouse and Bordeaux. A little later there were fifty tolls on the Rhine, and by the end of the fifteenth century the number had gone up to sixty. Between Hungary and Venice in the 1500s, the Fugger copper trade was bearing some 30 percent of the fiscal and related charges. During this period a cargo of salt traveling from Rouen to Chartres by the Seine and the Eure would pay in tolls a sum that in total came to slightly more than the price paid for the salt in Rouen.

No less than road traffic, river traffic was hit by war. Even if it was not entirely blocked by a sunken boat, the merchant was well aware that when soldiers were around it was easier to conceal a cart than a boat. It was hard enough to change roads; changing rivers was impossible. Troubled times, whether real or imaginary, made trading in heavy goods difficult, and it was the larger towns that felt the effects. In an area crawling with soldiers, it was easier to carry a piece of cloth than three casks of wine.

Whether the cargo was cloth of gold or millstones and the transport a cart or a boat, it took a very long time. A carrier did well to average 30 or 40 kilometers a day over several days. It was perfectly normal for the journey from Paris to Toulouse to take three weeks. From Paris to Rouen took three days. Pegolotti found nothing unusual in a journey from La Rochelle to Nîmes—600 kilometers—taking seventeen days. In 1350, Barthélemy Bonis of Montalbin and his fellow pilgrims, unencumbered by merchandise, took only twenty-two days to travel from Avignon to Rome, but this was in the middle of summer, and travelers on horseback move faster than carts.

Even barring accidents, it was impossible to calculate the time a journey would take. The Alpine passes were out of the question in winter. Someone setting off from Paris in February might take two months to reach Toulouse. There was no way of knowing if a load of merchandise was delayed, and the owner could count himself lucky if everything arrived according to plan. Of course, the merchant was well aware that the carrier would readily explain away the time spent in the inn drinking hot wine by blaming it on the marshy ground.

This slow speed of travel was ill suited to the need for up-to-date information. It soon became possible, though expensive, to hire a messenger who, unencumbered by heavy loads, could travel swiftly, changing horses at each stop.

On the seas, ships confined themselves to a cautious coastal trade where Genoa was no more than a week's sail from Marseilles. In good conditions, with a calm sea and a favorable wind, a ship could cover sixty to a hundred miles a day—five times as far as by road—but at the price of a very round-about route. If we add to the time taken for the sea journey itself the days when the ship could not put out to sea and the delays in chartering a ship and forming the convoys, shipping always worked out cheaper in terms of cost but never in terms of speed. Whether trading by sea or by land, the merchant required, above all others, the virtue of patience.

Coastal trading was always the better choice when the political situation made the land routes hazardous or, more simply, where the coast was mountainous. To travel from Barcelona to Trebizond across the Mediterranean and the Black Sea was infinitely preferable to taking the mule tracks along the mountainous coastlines and the dangerous routes through the Balkan countries. Similarly, it would have been unthinkable to compete overland with the sea route from the Channel to the Baltic by way of the North Sea, which transported without too many mishaps heavy goods such as salt, wine, wheat, fish, and wood.

The quantities shipped remained relatively small, generally on the order of twenty to thirty tons, although occasionally as much as three or four hundred tons. On the other hand, the need to call at ports and the periods of inactivity in the winter were a costly burden for merchants choosing the sea routes. Even when a cargo arrived safely at its final destination, the cost of risking their all on the high seas was never far from their minds.

Supply and Demand

Trading remained purely regional for a long time, even as late as the thirteenth century. The limits of a merchant's trading were determined—as were his horizons—by the type of transport used; by the amount of capital made available by surplus agricultural production or the growth in revenue from land; and, not least, by the traditional relationships that had gradually emerged in the process that made the towns the center of attraction and influence. The geographical origins of the townspeople and their networks of family relationships determined both their clients—the suppliers and purchasers—and their workforce, which sometimes needed the assistance of paid intermediaries. We have the example of a merchant of Toulouse who is in constant correspondence with his compatriots installed in Rodez or Montaubin, while a successful Parisian citizen is the obvious partner for his cousins in Rouen. Before trading with the outside world, Florence at first looked no further than its own *contado*. Genoa and Venice made sure of an inland base, while Barcelona extended its sphere of activity as far as the outskirts of Montpellier. Bruges was the chief port of Flanders long before it came to be seen as the hub of trade for northwestern Europe.

The geographical contraction of trade naturally led to the substitution of one product for another. Wax candles replaced oil lamps in regions outside the olive-growing areas. While nut oil was a suitable replacement for culinary needs in countries without olive trees, the limited use that was made of lamp oil, even in churches, meant that it became an exotic luxury item. Papyrus became similarly rare, and parchment—made of the skin of a sheep tanned and treated to take and preserve ink—came into general use in the chancellery. It was introduced into Merovingian Gaul around 670, in Italy after 715, and in Germania about 730. Only the papal chancellery insisted on the continued use, until the mid-eleventh century, of papyrus—of very inferior quality—from Sicily.

The first and most essential trade in this new Europe, where regional spheres of interest were growing up around the first economic metropolises, determined by the siting of their river basins and type of hinterland, was the supply of food and everyday necessities. A fertile countryside could feed the town whose development was due to the profits from the countryside's surplus. The town could find customers in surrounding regions for the products made by its newly established craftsmen—tools or clothes—and could take advantage of opportunities for investment through a variety of forms of credit or purchase.

The extent of regional contacts was determined, above all, by the degree of attraction exercised by the town. In addition to being a consumer of foodstuffs produced in the country, it represented a source of employment. With its facilities for communication, the population of the surrounding region as well as agricultural profits grew. As speculation in agriculture increased and the need for manpower in the towns became more urgent, the economic region was enlarged. This progressive expansion had another effect: it introduced a hierarchy among the different urban centers. The peasant became a citizen of the small neighboring town rather than the distant metropolis, while the population of a large town like Paris added to its small number of original inhabitants—to have lived there for three generations was considered a long time—simple laborers arriving from Bourg-la-Reine or Le Bourget together with a number of petty notables who had left Auxerre, Troyes, or Évreux in the hope of improving their fortunes. In this way, areas of production and supply were built up. Small centers specialized in particular goods—Muret for the blue dye made from woad or Gaillac for wine—with local merchants providing a market to keep a town like Toulouse supplied.

The provision of food was not a one-way process. Distribution throughout the region encouraged an exchange of goods. Wine from neighboring Argenteuil, Clamart, and Chaillot, as well as from Beaune and the Orleans and Auxerre regions flooded into Paris. But the capital could not consume all this wine, and convoys of boats laden with casks of red or white wine left the port at Grève for regions where wine was scarce, such as Artois, Picardy, and Normandy in the vicinity of Rouen and Saint-Lô. Boats carrying wine in one direction went back upriver to the capital and on to Burgundy and Champagne with their cargo of herrings from the fishing ports on the Channel, cereals from Normandy and Valois, fruit from the lower Seine, and timber from the banks of the Aisne.

The same system of exchanging goods established itself in the Po Valley where, as early as the seventh century, the merchants of Comacchio—prior to the Venetians—traded fish from the Adriatic and salt from the coast of Romagna for wheat from the plains of Lombardy.

Another example of such exchange is that of Danzig—the modern Gdansk—where the sea meets the basin of the Vistula. From Lvov to Cracow, inland Poland delivered the products of its mines—particularly copper from the Carpathians—together with the luxury goods, silk and spices, brought by Italian traders to Cracow by way of the Black Sea to the great Baltic port. Prussia sent rye, collected together at the important market at Torun, while Masovia supplied timber. These goods encouraged sea trading between Danzig and Lübeck, Bruges and England. By the fifteenth century this had extended to Holland, Brabant, and even Scotland. In exchange, Danzig imported not only salt—a fleet of some fifty ships was dispatched to Bourgneuf every year—and wine from Gascony, bought in London or Bruges, but also cloth from Flanders and Brabant. Such merchandise stimulated trade both along the inland waterways of Prussia and Poland and across the sea to Sweden, Finland, and Latvia. Merchants from Danzig set up in Lithuania, particularly in Kovno, to provide a collection point for the wax and furs so highly valued in the West. Others went as far as Lvov, where they traded amber, leather, and even herrings with the Venetians and the Genoese who had come from the Crimea or the Bosphorus.

We can see the same thing happening as early as the eighth century on the North Sea coast and along rivers like the Elbe and Schelde, where the Frisians dealt in wheat from the Rhineland, Moselle wine, and Frisian cloth. Similarly, the Irish Sea was crisscrossed with ships carrying Breton salt and Gascon wine, tin from Cornwall and lead from Poitou.

Trade in the local raw materials, so essential to the developing trades, was carried out within a similarly regional framework. The cloth maker in Toulouse would obtain his wool from Commingues, Bigorre, Béarn, and even Aragon. He bought his woad in Lauragais or Albigeois. Sometimes this accumulation would lead to exports to more distant destinations. A London merchant might sell wool from English flocks to the Flemish weavers, while iron from the Asturias would be sold by the Cantabrians to England, Brittany, and Normandy. The Hanseatic city of Novgorod exported furs and wood obtained in the lands around the White Sea to ports on the North Sea like Lübeck and Bruges.

The citizens of Bordeaux and La Rochelle began to set up as professional middlemen between wine producers and merchants who—sailing from Bayonne, the Basque country, Brittany, or England—would transport this wine to Bruges, Bristol, Southampton, London, or Hull.

Supplying the needs of the town and accumulating goods for trading in the town were the two types of development that defined the regional limits of investment and hence of economic power. In the twelfth, and indeed often in the thirteenth, century the businessman of the day was not prepared to venture beyond the limits of his personal experience of economic realities. The flocks owned by the middle classes in the Toulouse region were to be found in the pastures between the Garonne and the Tarn. Those belonging to the people around Barcelona grazed in the Ebro Valley, between Aragon and western Catalonia. The early purchase of land, more usually in the form of a simple manor than a lordship, rarely ventured beyond the limits of safe investment and investment for prestige . Even the most adventurous had a rather narrow perspective. The horizons of their world went no farther than the distance walked in a few days by their grandfathers to become townspeople, or that they themselves traveled to collect hay for their horses or linen to make sheets. Not surprisingly, those with access to good roads took a longer view than those separated from the main routes of communication by inhospitable tracts of land. Social space was defined as much by the quality of roads as by economic development.

New needs that were to have far-reaching consequences began to make themselves felt, which encouraged exports from particular regional markets. The fishermen of the North Sea needed their supply of salt renewed annually for each fishing season since fish did not keep well. To economize on salt would be to risk being left with barrels of rotting fish. While it was always possible to obtain this precious commodity by boiling seawater, it was much easier to rely on that produced by natural evaporation on the salt marshes of the Atlantic coast. The fishermen on the rocky coastlines of the western Mediterranean were of much the same opinion when they looked to salt pans in the flat coastal regions of Provence and Languedoc.

At about this time, the towns of northern Europe, where developing industry brought with it more buying power, were becoming less content with the local ales supplied from the local countryside. For both its taste and its medicinal qualities, everyone wanted wine—and not just any wine. Although it was obtainable locally from the vineyards of Cotentin, Artois, and even Kent, the people of Bruges, Ghent, Lille, London, Southampton, and Lübeck traveled to get their wine in sunnier climes, and preferably in those wine-growing regions easily accessible by water. The vineyards of Aunis and Gascony were fortunate in this respect. Before long, despite the need to use an overland link between two waterways, Paris was to import wine from Beaune and Saint-Pourçain-sur-Sioule.

When beer brewed with hops—infinitely superior to the rustic *cervisia* first introduced by the Gauls—became widespread toward the end of the fourteenth century, it was too late to change an established habit. With the exception of a few regions such as Flanders, wine was to remain the preferred drink of countries lacking in vineyards. It was to prove to be one of the most important elements in international trade.

The development of secondary industries, in particular woolen cloth, created other needs with far-reaching implications for the future. The greater the demand, the further afield the producers had to cast their nets. Whole cargoes of English wool had to be imported for the Flemish weavers. Competition and the pursuit of quality led to the use of a greater range of colors, based on dyes made from exotic plants that could not necessarily be found growing in the fields around the sheep pastures. The blue dye from woad known as *guède* in Picardy was identical to the *pastel* used in Lauragais, while the madder used in Lille could equally well come from Arras; but whether in Lille or in Paris, Ypres or Rouen, nothing could replace saffron, cochineal, and purple. And the dyers could do nothing without the mordant alum, which came originally from Castile and later from Asia Minor and eventually from Tolfa in Italy.

At the same time the Italians realized that it would be advantageous to get hold of some of this beautiful cloth, made of wool of a quality not to be matched by the Alpine and Apennine sheep. It was in Florence that an organization was set up to develop the industry and market its products. It was to be known by the name of the road where it was first established: Calimala. The Florentines bought the thick, velvety Flemish cloth, so well suited to the generous flowing robes fashionable at the time, and applied a secondary process to it, introducing more subtle colors and special finishes. A day was to come when the Italians, in an attempt to economize on imports from Flemish spinning and weaving mills, started to seek out substitutes, personally going to fetch raw wool from beyond the Alps and eventually from overseas.

One merchant's horizons might be no more than another's backyard.

For Marco Polo the Elder—eldest uncle of the more famous Marco who visited the court of Kublai Khan—those horizons embraced the international trade being carried on in Constantinople, the ships traveling up and down the Bosphorus, and the caravans that traveled from the steppes of Asia to those twin gateways to the West, Genoa and Venice. For his younger brothers, Matteo and Niccolò—the latter the father of Marco the Younger—the horizons stretched no farther than the small neighboring port of Soldaia, in the Crimea. This port had no other purpose than to supply Constantinople and a few other towns in Asia Minor with wheat from the surrounding countryside, salt from the salt lakes, and fish from the local fishing grounds. Although separated by only a few days' sail, the Crimea and the Bosphorus were worlds apart.

As Europe grew in wealth, from around the year 1000, an increase in population matching that in agricultural productivity—and, consequently, profits from land—began to manifest itself. One of its consequences, felt in the royal court as well as in the towns, was a new need to mark the social differences between the classes. This could be achieved by eating, dressing, or building in a different way from the local peasants. Although they had always had a place in the life, religious worship, and adornments of the rich and powerful, from the eleventh century onward luxury goods such as ivory, silk, and spices were increasingly in demand as an outward demonstration of the owner's strength, wealth, and success. As people once again began to undertake long journeys—pilgrimages and crusades being the most notable examples—there came into fashion a certain exoticism that was to be an enduring characteristic of the ruling classes.

These new needs revived trade in the Mediterranean and were to make Italy's fortune. This time it was no longer a matter of allowing a few colonies of Syrians to arrive, as they had done in the sixth century, bringing the products of Asia to the West. Now it was Europe, and particularly Italy, that took the initiative and traveled through the Black Sea to Antioch and Alexandria in Egypt to meet the caravans bearing silks from China and spices from India. Since luxury was an important element in court life, and the court a symbol and means of asserting political power, the rivalry between the great families was closely linked to that between the supplying cities. Everything conspired to push up demand. From the eleventh to the twelfth century, there was a rapid movement away from casual peddling to an established trade and permanent routes.

The opening up of trade in the Mediterranean satisfied another need: more than other Western countries, Italy needed maritime connections. This desire to take to the high seas was, on the one hand, a consequence of the geography of a peninsula with poor roads, mountainous terrain, and few inland waterways. With only a few exceptions, such as Naples, the ports lay with their backs to the mountains and had little access to the inland areas. To escape the Florentines, the Pisans had only the sea, and even that was receding, since the original Roman port was no more than a memory and now Porto Pisano was silting up in its turn. To break out of her isolation Genoa had only her fleet. Venice could expect nothing from her terra firma. Palermo, Syracuse, Bari, and Rimini had a single raison d'être: they were ports. Geographical necessity forced Italy to look outside; it was indicative of the talents of the different governing bodies that they were able, in their different ways, to use this necessity to the great benefit of their cities.

These towns, whose extraordinary density was an inheritance of antiquity but whose proximity gave them a dynamism paid for dearly by incessant and onerous conflicts, were able to expand on a scale commensurate with their new urban vitality only by conquering new trading routes and markets, adventuring on the sea and gaining a foothold in faraway ports of call, commercial colonization, and sometimes (as Venice demonstrated both in Europe and in the East) armed conquest. Well before the start of the Crusades, Italian sailors had proven their worth on interminable expeditions of *Reconquista* against Islam. It was at sea and beyond that they became involved in conflicts that would never have been tolerated closer to home. Lack of unity among the Christians present in the Holy Land was to cost the Latin world many a setback in the East.

Economic Space

As the eleventh and twelfth centuries progressed, important and more diverse economic routes opened up. Merchants could now use a combination of sea and overland routes, or of road and river, in order to achieve that vital material balance so important for trade of having cargoes traveling both out and back.

Most important, as much in terms of the value of goods as of political considerations, was the network of sea routes between Italy and the Near East shared between the commercial fleets of Pisa, Genoa, and Venice. Once the Pisans had been relegated to second place—from about the middle of the thirteenth century—and after Antioch lost, along with any control over her hinterland, any interest in relations with central Asia, Genoa and Venice now occupied well-defined positions. The Venetians were preeminent in Alexandria, meeting place of trade routes from southern Asia, the Arab world, and India. The Genoese sphere of influence was centered on the trading posts established on the Black Sea in Trebizond and the Crimea at the end of the caravan routes from central Asia, the so-called Silk Road (see Map 1).

The events of 1204 temporarily upset this equilibrium. Venice had encouraged the crusaders to take Constantinople, seeing what proved to be

Map 1. Principal Sea Routes in the Mid-Thirteenth Cent

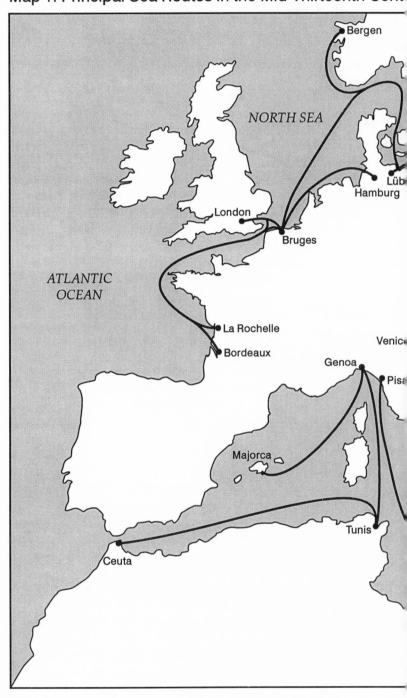

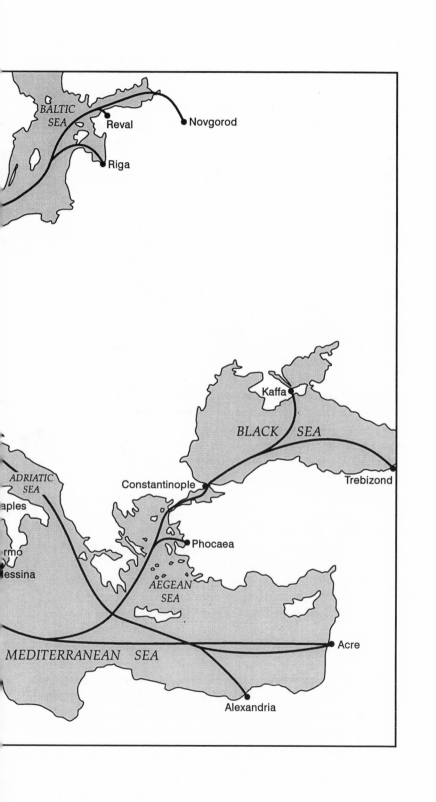

the short-lived Latin empire as an essential part of their commercial plans. The fall of Emperor Baldwin II—a Courtenay—and the return of the Byzantine Empire under Michael Paleologus in 1261 sounded the final knell for Venetian illusions in the East. The realism of the Genoese won the day. Venice had to be content with her domination of the market in Alexandria, even though, after 1250, the power of the Mamelukes had brought an end to the longstanding policy of tolerance toward Christians that had been of such benefit to the Rialto merchants.

Industrial growth in the West gave rise to an important new trade in alum, an essential ingredient in the dyeing of woolen cloth. Although the Venetians were able to obtain supplies from Egypt and Syria, the best alum came from Asia Minor, and the fortunes of the Genoese were greatly increased by their almost complete monopoly of the supply.

While they could travel to the East to fetch spices, silk, alum, or dyes, the Italians were disinclined to let others come to collect goods from their ports. A genuinely transcontinental movement of goods was born of this desire on the part of the Italians to do their own marketing. The products of this trade with the East had to be redistributed to the northwest. Furthermore, a return cargo had to be found, whether it was cloth bought in Bruges or wheat taken on at Tunis or Bône, Seville or Cádiz. Leaving the major sea routes for the more important ports, the Tuscan businessmen soon cornered their own markets and routes on the Continent. Their regular presence—almost permanent from the thirteenth century onward—represented an important element in the development of towns such as Troyes, Lagny, Provins, and Bar-sur-Aube, towns in Champagne with big fairs that, during the twelfth and thirteenth centuries, came to be central to European trade. It was here that deals were struck between the Italians, on one side, and the merchants of Flanders, Brabant, and, of course, France, on the other. Here, too, following on the commercial transactions, financial links were established that were in time to become distinct from trade in goods, and that were to continue in Champagne well into the fourteenth century, when trading in merchandise had long since declined.

Other routes opened up in response to demand from northern and northwestern Europe. This area had long been active in regional trading and exchange on an enormous scale, from the Irish Sea to the Caspian through the Baltic and along the great Russian rivers. At the heart of this activity were the Scandinavian merchants and navigators who together with the emerging bourgeoisie of the German ports looked toward similar horizons. Those men who initiated the new trading enterprises of the early thirteenth century were the same who would take control of the management of business and the political interests so intimately linked with it. It was they, too, who took on the financial and material organization of trade.

Political union with the Angevins in the early thirteenth century, at the very moment when the Plantagenet King John was losing Normandy, favored the establishment of the important regular trade in wine from Gascony to England. It was to increase, and upset, the supply to other countries in northern Europe—which went via Bruges as much as via the English ports—of wine that had previously come, in lesser quantities, from the vineyards of the Seine, the Rhine, Anjou, and Aunis. The fortunes of Bordeaux and Southampton were to play an important part in this trade that, from the time of St. Louis, was to represent one of the major currents on the economic map of Europe.

The salt trade had long retained its regional character, a result of the widely separated centers of production. As long as the heat of the Mediterranean sun multiplied the salty marshes on the coasts of the Adriatic, Provence, or Languedoc, and salt from the Atlantic marshes could supply the needs of neighboring countries, there seemed to be enough rock salt for those more northerly regions where the climate made the systematic exploitation of sea salt—except through the use of inconvenient boiling cauldrons—impractical. Inland Europe was supplied with salt from the Alps and the Jura, from Bohemia and Romania, while salt from Lüneburg was already enriching the Lübeck merchants who exported it as far away as Scotland, Scandinavia, and Russia.

But it was expensive to mine this salt, and it was not produced in sufficient quantities. The increase in tonnage of the merchant ships was to change the equation. It was now possible to make Atlantic salt available to fishermen who supplied the markets of Riga and Novgorod. Fishermen in Bergen could use it to preserve their fish harvest and thus export it. Trade by sea was established in the second half of the fourteenth century. From Bourgneuf and Guérande, great fleets streamed out every year toward the North Sea and the Baltic. Internal disputes in the Hanseatic League hastened this tendency, and towns like Riga, Revel (or Tallinn, as it is known today), and Danzig were able to break away from the trade in Lüneburg salt monopolized by Lübeck.

Carrying wine, salt, or Flemish cloth in one direction, ships plying these new trading routes obviously did not wish to return home empty. Instead they became involved in the internal trade of the towns of England and Germany. Thus the growing power derived from improved ships also contributed to the increasing diversification of Hanseatic trade.

The Hanseatic League, a commercial organization of German towns and their marketplaces, stretched from Cologne, London, and Bruges in the West to Riga, Bergen, and Novgorod in the East. Dominated in the thirteenth century by the recently established patriciate of Lübeck, it had created a commercial structure made possible by a remarkable network of seaports.

It had easy access to Scandinavia, the British Isles, and Flanders. The Weser, Elbe, Oder, and Vistula, and their tributaries, allowed it to penetrate deep into the heart of Germany and Poland. The League traded in fish from Sweden and Norway, wax and furs from Prussia and Russia, beer from the Baltic ports, and copper from Sweden and Hungary. The fortune of the Fugger family at the end of the fifteenth century was owed to Hungarian copper. Iron came not only from the Alps and the Carpathians but also from the schist of the Rhine massif. Beech, oak, and pine came from Masovia, ash and yew from the Carpathians, wheat from Poland and Prussia. With a western base in Bruges and a strong presence in town markets and at the fairs of Flanders and Champagne, there was no part of the Continent that the Hanseatic businessmen could not reach.

During this period, the Order of Teutonic Knights in Königsberg controlled the trade in amber, which was collected on the Samland peninsula. The final link of the chain was completed when Cracow was liberated from the Mongol threat. In the fourteenth century the town became the hub of the trading routes that linked the countries to the north with those of the Mediterranean. From Champagne to Poland and from Gotland to Amalfi or Kaffa (once Theodosia), a new economic region was taking shape (see Map 2).

Bringing together an extraordinary gathering of merchants of very different origins and interests, the great fairs were to play a decisive role in the expansion of economic horizons. We know that Italian merchants were coming to these fairs as early as 1080, because Gregory VII complained about the treatment they received in Philip I's small royal domain between Paris and Orleans, where they were frequently robbed. The world outside, the world of "foreigners," now seemed less like a hostile bloc surrounding the locals. The strangers had become visible and comprehensible, because they were present in all their diversity.

The fairs in Champagne, held once or twice a year in each of the four towns of Troyes, Lagny, Provins, and Bar-sur-Aube, had originally been no more important than those held elsewhere; it was the astuteness of the counts of Champagne that made all the difference. Merchants would go there, rather than elsewhere, because they knew that they and their goods would be safe, because they knew that the count of Champagne would take as a personal affront any interference with the interests of people who came to the fairs. They could rely on this protection both on the journey to and away from the fair. The fairs were provided with a police force, judicial powers, and safe-conducts, together with the necessary equipment—well-maintained covered markets, accurate weighing scales, and strictly regulated weights and measures. Such provisions were guaranteed to promote confidence and attract traders from outside. An "officer in charge of fairs" (*garde des foires*), first mentioned in 1174, was there to ensure the smooth running of every aspect of trade, while the court would guarantee the execution of contracts presented to it. This security and its attendant advantages were well worth the journey. The success of the Champagne fairs can be attributed solely to this intelligent policy of applying public order to business.

Because common origins created common interests and internal competition that it was obviously advantageous to contain rather than display to others, the merchants began to organize themselves into groups. All those coming from one town or country formed an easily identifiable group, sometimes even a "nation," endowed with its own institutions. The diversity of the economic world was no longer just a vague impression, obtained from stories of adventure and the existence of other languages. For the people who talked in figures—prices and quantities—it now appeared as a measurable and structured reality. They learned how to take the measure of Florentines, Sienese, or merchants from Piacenza.

The king became involved, which contributed to the international influence of the Champagne fairs from the 1230s onward. It was Philip Augustus who granted the royal "safe-conduct" to the merchants traveling to Champagne. From the moment they set foot in the kingdom to the moment they left, they were under the king's protection. To attack a merchant "attending the Champagne fairs" was verging on high treason.

The count of Champagne had played his cards well. Both he and the king, no less than the merchants, profited from the arrangement. Even with a very low rate of taxation, clearly designed to encourage trade, the six fairs represented a major source of income in the Champagne region. By 1284 when the countess of Champagne, Queen Jeanne of Navarre, married the future king Philip the Fair, the fairs were one of the mainstays of Capetian economic policy. The route through France was by now seen as the normal western link between the Mediterranean world centered in Italy and the countries to the north of Bruges.

The economic map around 1250, nevertheless, had its weak spots. The predominance of trade by road and by the still incomplete network of waterways meant that the inevitable slowness of travel was further complicated by an alarming increase in the number of charges to be paid and risks to be taken. Tolls were set up along the roads. There was a charge to cross over a bridge or under a bridge, another for entry into a town or for docking at the landings in river ports. Moving goods this way was just about possible with expensive merchandise: in the fifteenth century 60 percent of the price of the wine taken from Burgundy to Hainaut went for transport costs and taxes. For heavy goods it was a major disincentive. To look beyond the usual horizons in order to supply provisions for a distant region hit by a bad harvest meant providing them at a price that was hardly acceptable to the

Map 2. Principal Continental Routes in the Mid-Thirteen

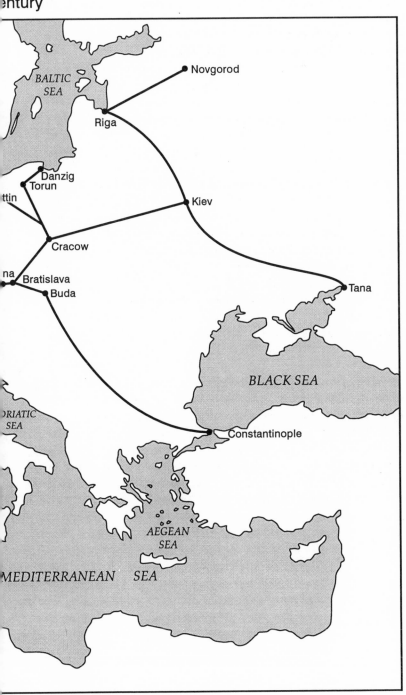

BALTIC SEA

Novgorod

Riga

Danzig
Torun

ttin

Kiev

Cracow

na
Bratislava

Buda

Tana

BLACK SEA

DRIATIC SEA

Constantinople

AEGEAN SEA

MEDITERRANEAN SEA

consumers. Thus economic complementarity, or mutual suppply, did not function effectively except in those few regions surrounding river basins or a well-established network of roads.

This kind of time span tied up both capital assets and manpower to a degree that was rapidly becoming unacceptable. The problem was that goods do not transport themselves, and the merchant was rarely so trusting as to allow the carter to travel on his own. There were decisions to be made en route, and the merchant could not rely blindly on someone whose only expertise lay in hauling carts or harnessing horses. On the other hand, very few merchants could afford to accompany a convoy of stone, wood, or wheat—a journey involving an absence of several months—without charging extremely high prices.

No less serious in its implications for the economic balance of Europe was the relative isolation of central Europe. The Alps formed a barrier that was not easily crossed by convoys of wagons—except to the west by the Mont Cenis and the two St. Bernard passes and to the east by the Drava Valley and Moravia. While it benefited the French markets, such as Champagne or Chalon-sur-Saône, and those of the great ports on the middle Danube, like Vienna and Budapest, it delayed development in the region of the upper Danube and the Rhine, cut off as it was from Italy and her ports open to the East. The Rhine was thus relegated to a regional role in the redistribution of goods, a form of trade for which it was ill equipped because of its few outlets onto the North Sea. A large delta such as that of the Rhine was ill suited for the construction of ports. Although Augsburg's industrial potential was able to develop as a result of new mining techniques and new methods of treating minerals, its influence could reach no farther, at this time, than middle Germany. It seemed that there was a vast detour around the European market. Despite its wealth and particularly its mineral resources, the geographic heart of Europe was ignored by the major currents of trade. The straight Roman road had been abandoned when it ceased to be of use in daily transactions. To transport the volume of goods now in demand by a direct route seemed more difficult to imagine than ever.

TWO

Opening the Way

*E*xpansion seemed to have reached an impasse, horizons closed off and capacity limited. And then, suddenly, in the 1250s, everything began to change. This occurred at the very moment that one of the most serious crises yet experienced by the European economy was looming, and when statistics available to us—particularly in relation to agricultural prices and land rents—begin to show the first signs of a general winding down of energy; yet it was at this time that technological innovation and intellectual progress joined in bringing about developments that would postpone this decline. The result was two centuries of demographic growth and an expansion in rural economies that had important consequences for the towns.

The Art of Navigation

For a start, things were happening in the naval shipyards. From the galley of antiquity to the caravels that would cross the Atlantic, ships had been continually evolving. In the three or four centuries that mark the close of the Middle Ages, constant collaboration between the experience and imagination of shipbuilders and sailors led to the construction of safer and faster boats that could better cope with bad weather or unfavorable winds, carry heavier loads, and adapt more easily to the various cargoes that might be available in different ports. Ships were asserting their dominance as by far the best means of transport for heavy goods such as wheat, wine, salt, alum, timber, or raw wool.

Some ships were still rowed. These were principally the light galleys still used, in time of war, by the maritime powers to lead their expeditions and, at all times, to protect their merchant ships from threats such as the

Barbary pirates or fleets from rival towns. There were also countless ten- or twelve-oared boats that carried the greater part of coastal trade along the shores of Prussia and Liguria, on the Irish Sea and the Adriatic. They were easy to handle and reduced the overhead of sea transport, putting it within the reach of even a modest shipowner. This was a boat that slipped easily through customs controls, remaining until very recent times the most effective instrument of tax fraud.

In the Baltic and North seas the lighter sailing ship became, from the twelfth century, more important than the larger seagoing rowed boats, in which the weight of the rowers and supplies needed to sustain them exceeded that of the cargo. In the Mediterranean, on the other hand, the large galley with twenty or thirty rows of three rowers was still being used as late as the fifteenth century for profitable speculative sea trading since speed was often more important than tonnage. It was the perfect vehicle for the competitive spice or silk trades, while its maneuverability made it the ideal machine for sea battles. No other vessel could equal its ability to outwit pirates—Christian or Barbary—outstrip pursuers, or penetrate blockades. The Provençals, Catalans, Genoese, and Venetians remained faithful to them for many years, despite the occasional "accident":

> As the nobleman Ser Martino da Mosto, our governor in Cyprus, has paid 213 hyperperes and 5 carats in order to buy back some of the men from our galleys on the La Tana voyage who were shipwrecked in dangerous seas and for various expenses made in relation to this event, expenses amounting to about 71 ducats, it has been decided by the Grand Council that he may make this payment and that the accounting officers should receive it in the account of the aforementioned Martino da Mosto.

Nevertheless, the sail had the edge in almost every instance that heavy goods were transported and speed was no extra advantage. More money was to be made by carrying a larger cargo of wheat, salt, wine, red herrings, wool, or wood than by being weighed down with drinking water, biscuits, and dried meat. The sail used was a large square canvas that could be rotated in all directions and adapted to all winds. During the twelfth century it had been adopted by the northern *nef,* in the thirteenth century by the Frisian *kogge.* During the same period it could been seen on the mast of the *szkutas* that sailed up and down the Vistula and on the large two-masted merchant galleys from Venice, Genoa, and Florence. The larger the boats became, the bigger the wind surface of the sail.

The rowed galleys indicated a valuable cargo, while broad sails meant a cargo of heavy goods. From the narrow *cog* of the thirteenth century to the larger *hoeker,* flat and big-bellied, of the mid-fourteenth century, the capacity of the boats continued to rise. As early as 1190 some 150 ships were able to transport Richard Coeur de Lion's entire army, complete with horses, to the East. In the fifteenth century, the Genoese or Venetian merchant galleys with a hull forty meters long and five wide could, like the northern *hoeker,* carry a load of two or three hundred metric tons, infinitely greater than the ten or twenty tonnes that were the maximum load carried by the boats and *esquifs* of the Breton coastal traders or the Languedoc and Provençal barges. At about the same time a more complex three-masted rigging gave the Iberian caravel—quickly adopted by the fleet of the Germanic Hanseatic League—and the Genoese carrack or nef a maneuverability and speed that were soon to bring the New World within reach of European traders. A caravel was able to carry as much as four hundred tonnes, and a carrack up to a thousand. The upper limit of the tonnage it was possible to transport had by now effectively been reached. Many trades, like the Venetian salt trade, were to suffer from competition between ships of small and large tonnage.

Looking at the figures, one comes to appreciate the immensity of the investment in shipping. Associations, combining capital and sharing risks, became increasingly necessary for those wishing to acquire the means to embark on a venture as significant as sea trading. An early form of capitalism was born of this development, quickly overtaking the small boats whose owners were the captains and whose crews consisted of no more than ten to fifteen men. The great ships of the late Middle Ages needed crews of fifty or a hundred. It was little wonder, then, that state investment came to be involved in shipping. Like "La Serenissima," as the Venetian state was known, the king of France and the duke of Brittany, princes and important officials, all became shipowners. Lesser men who wanted to participate went into partnership.

The search for a greater capacity that would not at the same time interfere with the handling of the ship was assisted by technical progress. Most important of these innovations was the introduction, in the thirteenth century, of the "stern rudder"—turning on an axis at the stern of the ship—a marked improvement on the lateral rudder that was little more than an oar on a pivot. At the same time, ship designers were attempting to resolve the problem of making the hull watertight. This became a matter of urgency in the fifteenth century when, in an attempt to lighten the hulls, they began to be carvel-built, replacing the old-style clinker-built ships. The new hulls were easier to maintain but needed a watertight covering that added unacceptable extra weight.

Another major problem concerned navigation away from the coastline in overcast weather. When close to land it was possible to navigate not only by natural features but also with the aid of landmarks deliberately constructed to provide sailors with easily recognized and aligned reference points. The church tower of St. Peter at Rostock was built to a height of 132 meters for the sole reason that it be visible thirty miles from land. Once away from the coastline and on the high seas, it was an entirely different matter. The ship that could ride out stormy weather, or advance against adverse winds thanks to its sophisticated sails, lost any advantage it might have if it then strayed off course. At best, time was lost; at worst, the ship and the cargo. Any mistake could drive a ship onto the rocks or enemy coasts. The sailor who took soundings at the prow of the ship with a knotted rope weighted with a stone was invaluable in the shallows; but he was not much use out at sea when he had to take soundings to know if they had reached the spot where, experience had shown, it was time to change course.

A compass was therefore vital. It was all the more essential because the art of navigation was not yet able to take advantage of the advances in theoretical astronomy being made in Western Europe. The astronomical tables drawn up in Paris around 1327—misleadingly known as the Alphonsine Tables, because their authors believed that the credibility of the tables would be greater if they attributed the work to the wise king of Castile, Alfonso X—were of little use in practical navigation. The ship's captain had neither the ability nor the material conditions for observation that might have enabled him to take more accurate astronomical readings with which to establish his position and chart the routes taken on the high seas.

The navigator was forced to rely on the compass. Introduced into the Mediterranean by the Arabs, the water compass was in common use by the twelfth century. It consisted of a magnetized needle inserted into a short piece of reed that floated on the surface of a glass of water. The early fourteenth century saw the appearance of the modern compass with its system of pivots that ensured the horizontality and sensitivity, and thus the accuracy, of the compass.

Although the compass soon became normal equipment for the Italian sea captains, many sailors in the north continued to do without it well into the fifteenth century, using the trade winds to guide their ships. Such journeys were, however, generally confined to coastal trading rather than sea crossings. In the North Sea and the Baltic, the difficulty was not so much finding the route as keeping to it. The Italians, by contrast, were able to make use of the new compasses to set out without excessive risk straight for the ports of the Channel and the North Sea. With a compass, Gibraltar no longer marked the boundary between two different maritime worlds.

Progress in navigation was immediately translated into a change in the scale of distances. Wool from Southampton could now be transported in thirty or forty days to Porto Pisano by Florentine galley, and the same was true for salt from Cyprus by Venetian nef. Gascon wine reached London in ten days. There were, of course, many variables: Alexandria was three weeks from Venice in calm weather but three months on a bad trip when as much time could be wasted waiting at the quayside as at sea.

The merchant's horizons and calendar altered radically. A strong ship with its rudder suitable for maneuvers less dependent on the wind, and possessing a sure method of charting its course even in cloudy weather, meant freedom from the onerous servitude of coastal trading. Hitherto only for the daring, and often at a cost that was scarcely commercial, the high seas were now open to all. It was now possible to ignore the restrictions—lasting longer in the Baltic than in the Mediterranean, but too long in any case—imposed by the wintry weather that had forced shipowners to offset the depreciation of their floating capital with income accumulated only in the summer season. Even if still limited, the possibility of winter navigation ensured a better return on their maritime investment and thus persuaded businessmen not to fear this type of financial arrangement. As an additional advantage, the costs of transport were reduced accordingly. Another consideration for the merchant involved in long-distance trading was time. Previously, during the winter, he had been forced to pay rent and employees' wages and yet see his stocks, capital, and transactions lie idle. Now he could benefit from a shorter fallow season.

The concern to exploit to the full both men and ships led to some ingenious arrangements. The Hanseatic traders, for example, removed their ships from the Baltic and the North Sea, where they would have been immobilized for several months, before winter set in. The same ship that would crisscross the northern sea routes from June to October could be found among one of the convoys setting off, in November, to collect salt from Bourgneuf. The salt was loaded in January and February, when the worst storms were raging off the coast of Brittany, and the ships then set off for Bruges, Lübeck, or Revel (the modern Tallinn) between April and July.

Taking full advantage of such seasonal factors, a ship might lie in port only when taking on a cargo. Over a period of thirteen years, the nef owned by the Genoese Paolo Italiano made the journey between Genoa and London or Bruges fifteen times. During a period of seventeen years, his compatriot Lorenzo Bandinella traveled eleven times to the North Sea and twelve times to the East.

New Merchandise, New Routes

Those merchants who were best able to spot a profitable cargo were the ones to reap the most benefit from the new forms of transport. The maximum cost for a long sea voyage—from Italy to Flanders or from Egypt to Italy—was 10 percent, compared with the 30, 50, or even 60 percent it cost to transport goods by land over a medium distance. In the late fourteenth century, purely and simply to encourage land trade in heavy goods, now increasingly carried by sea, transporters even agreed to charge according to the value of the goods carried. From Italy to Flanders, alum and woad cost six or eight times less to transport than the precious cochineal and the irreplaceable saffron but was twice as expensive as the returning raw wool, and three times as much as tin from Cornwall, which appears normally to have cost less than 3 percent to transport. Given these prices, the business world—transporters and transported—agreed that the size of a ship was more important than its speed.

It followed that trade in a single product was not practical. In order to pick up a sufficiently large cargo, particularly for the return journey, it was necessary to call in at more than one port. A ship delivering alum to Bruges would then go on to pick up wool in Southampton. If there was an opportunity to complete its load with some iron, fruit, or wine, it would be quite prepared to put in at an Iberian port. A ship that had just delivered a cargo of cloth to Alexandria might, if there was nothing for immediate loading in Egypt, move on to Khios to collect alum to supply the textile industries in Flanders or Tuscany. Trade conducted on an annual cycle, where with luck costs were balanced by profits, more than made up for the loss of the old specialization. This the large-scale merchants willingly sacrificed to those who were happy to specialize and would not change—the small traders.

Keeping pace with these developments was an expansion in the intellectual horizons of the investor. These were people who, as a result of an economy that was less and less dependent on surpluses in agricultural produce and the price of grain, were now in possession of capital that could be used far away from the areas of primary production that, a century earlier, had been seen as the most profitable.

Capitalism had been born. We use the word in the sense it had for the Middle Ages, which has nothing to do with the economic and social conditions of the industrial era. A new activity involving people and capital—finance—was emerging, and becoming quite distinct from political and technical innovations. This was in a different league from the financing of land clearance, where one person offered the land, another the tools, another the seeds, and a fourth the labor. Such activities had no further repercussions, being concerned only with someone's land and its dependents. Here profit, in the form of direct revenue, was simply an indication of the value of the estate. It was quite another matter to invest in infrastructures and medium-term ventures in which the financier had no direct contact with the actual product. Because capital was now available—profits from regional trade, cottage industries and the first textile industries, and even the emerging public services—it became possible to finance the exchange of goods over a period of six months or a year. Long-term financing was made feasible by means of the delayed reinvestment of profits made in distant markets. Financial support was made available for shared shipyards—for example, at the ports of Lübeck, Genoa, and Paris—and for the construction and outfitting of the new large-tonnage ships. The businessman was beginning to set his sights on more distant goals.

Multiple financing was not a one-way activity. Capital was invested in long-distance cargoes, but the investor diversified. Emergent capitalism incorporated the notion of spreading risk, in order to minimize the risks of business in general and, in particular, those involved in that most hazardous of ventures, maritime trade. While providing security for the more cautious, this arrangement had the advantage, for the more adventurous, of enabling them to take calculated risks, such as longer journeys, dangerous convoys, speculative cargoes, and out-of-season trading as well as activities that gambled on political change.

Although horizons might be extending to embrace the whole of the exploitable world, it was still the case that, for the individual, they were not constant, being defined by the cycle of possible business. By now, in many cases, business was subject to an annual cycle. The Hanseatic ships, forbidden by the League's strict safety regulations from setting out to sea in the winter, could hope to make the journey to Novgorod or Bergen only once a year, and the same went for the trip to the salt marshes on the Atlantic coast. Favored by the climate as well as by geography, the Italian ships had a more flexible calendar; in a single year, the Genoese Oliviero Doria's ship made three trips, to Marseilles, Corsica, and Elba. But for anyone with more ambitious goals, such short-term voyages were impossible. A ship from Genoa leaving at the end of winter for Bruges or London would rarely return before the autumn. From Venice, it was practically impossible to fit in the same journey between one winter and the next. Since it was necessary to spend eighteen months on a voyage, a Venetian ship would call in at more ports and diversify its trade.

The rhythm of the seasons of production adapted to this annual cycle of sea trade. This was the case both for the fleets collecting salt—from Venice for Cypriot salt, from the Hanseatic ports for salt from Bourgneuf or Setubal—and for those loading wine at Bordeaux and La Rochelle.

This newfound ability to control equipment and long-term ventures, both financial and technological, encouraged the opening of routes that were equally new. It was a development that was radically to alter established patterns of trade in Europe (see Map 3).

In the high Alpine valleys, a concerted effort by local landowners and village communities to improve roads through the passes, previously used only by local people and their mules, made them passable to wheeled vehicles. Thus, in the second half of the thirteenth century, the routes over the Simplon and the St. Gotthard were opened up to major traders, piercing the central Alps that had once formed an insurmountable barrier between

Map 3. Principal Sea Routes in the Fifteenth Century

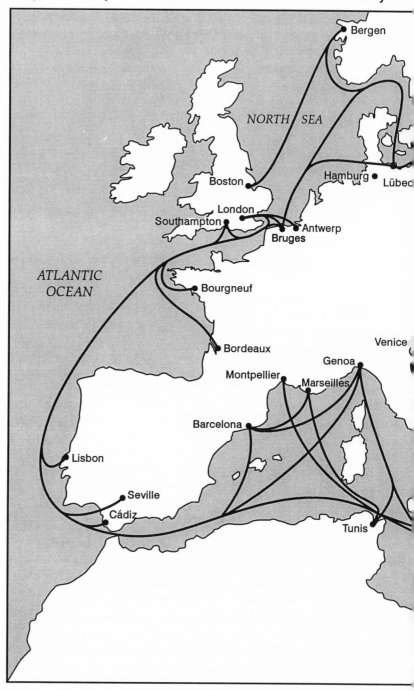

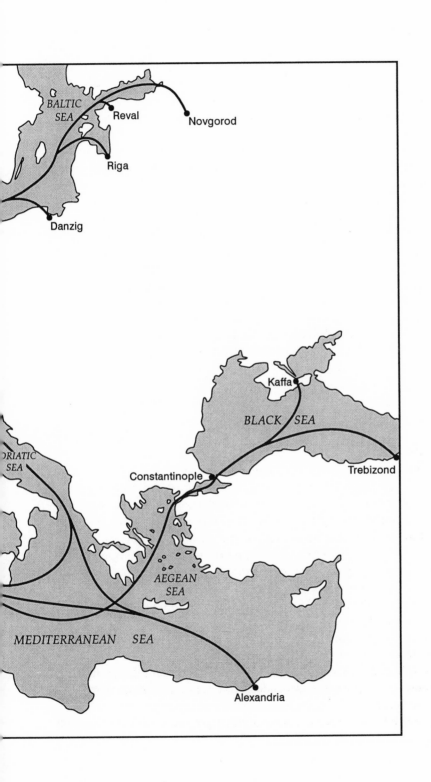

the heart of Europe and Lombardy and that had reduced Switzerland to a mere backwater. The Simplon Pass provided a direct route between the Po Valley and the upper Rhône connecting the Piedmont and the Valais, linking Turin and Milan to the south with Berne and Basel on the other side. The St. Gotthard connected the Ticino with the continuation of the Reuss and opened the way from Milan to Zurich and Constance. The long-established political and religious center of Milan, whose importance lay solely in its control over northern Italy, found its hitherto inconvenient geographical location much improved by the opening of these two passes. On the other side of the Alps other towns, such as Stuttgart, Augsburg, Regensburg, and even Nuremberg, also benefited from the new situation; the Rhine, Elbe, and Weser no longer led, to the south, to a dead end.

Eastward movement was further encouraged by the new route—maintained by the Milanese—over the Splüngen and San Bernardino passes, linking Valtellina with the shores of Lake Constance, and, even more important, by the development of direct trade between the Trentino and the German Danube by way of the Tyrol and the Brenner Pass.

The opening up of routes through the central Alps was soon to have a prejudicial effect on what had hitherto been the main route, over the western Alps. Trade over the Great St. Bernard collapsed. The Mont Cenis Pass, still used as a link between Savoy and the Dauphiné on one side and the Piedmont on the other, as well as more generally for east-west relations between Italy and France, was to lose all importance in anything but local trading. It was able to recover some of its importance only in the fourteenth century when it became an important element in the political unity of the state of Savoy and subsequently one of the routes giving access to the trade growing up around the Lyons fairs in the fifteenth century.

The decline of the western passes was symptomatic of a more general tendency: all north-south trade routes were shifting. From the beginning of the fourteenth century the Champagne fairs were to suffer from the effects of the change every bit as much as the old trading routes of Western Europe. Now the vital role of providing a regular meeting place for merchants active in Western Europe—one that neither Basel nor Regensburg was able to take on—moved to Paris. All routes now led to this capital of a French kingdom with a fully institutionalized structure. From now on, it would be in Paris that all business deals were set up and concluded. With such a town—whose population had grown in three generations from about 50,000 to some 200,000 according to a tax census carried out in 1328—only a few hours away by road, it was hard to see what could remain for the Champagne fairs, whose commercial role depended on a periodic coming together of people and business.

The new interconnected road network emerging in the period 1270–1300 was to undergo some further minor changes, generally in response to political events. The legacy of the Hundred Years' War was a widespread sense of insecurity that was not conducive to economic risk taking. After 1350, merchants tended to favor routes well away from battlefronts, marching armies, or the pillaging of soldiers. The eastern routes to the south, including the Rhine, sometimes benefited. In the following century, the Hussite movement that caused Bohemia to erupt into a bloody war in the 1420s similarly drove commercial traffic off the main route through central Europe linking Nuremberg, Prague, and Breslau (the modern Wroclaw) toward the northern route that was, from the fifteenth century, to bring great wealth to Leipzig.

Another alteration to the map was the result of disputes within the Hanseatic League, whose member towns could keep their commercial grip on the trading ports of the North Sea and the Baltic only as long as they maintained a close unity and total confidence in the vital trading center of Bruges. The slow political and economic disintegration of the League toward the end of the Middle Ages, apparent from around 1475, left two beneficiaries: the rival centers of England and Holland. Between them they contributed to the ruin of Bruges, already being overtaken by Antwerp. This is not to say that Antwerp simply replaced Bruges and that Brabant supplanted Flanders, or that English or Dutch traders stepped into the shoes of the Hanseatic merchants. The entire balance of trade in northern and northwestern Europe had been upset. Cloth industries, less restricted by the stifling industrial protectionism that inhibited new developments, were able to profit from the crises that spelled the end of the luxury cloth industry in the great towns of Flanders. Brabant, Holland, and England gained at Flanders' expense.

As this same cloth industry developed across the Netherlands it upset the preexisting balance of the market in basic commodities, making new demands, in particular, on the cereal-producing countries. The effects of this demand were felt chiefly by the plains of Germany and Poland, conveniently accessible from the Baltic. The Russian plains, already supplying wheat using the Oder and the Vistula, began increasingly to turn to the traditional products of the Carpathian mines—iron, copper, lead, and silver.

The horizons of the English businessman had expanded very suddenly when, toward the end of the thirteenth century and the beginning of the fourteenth, the new financial and technological advances in sea trading, together with a number of other innovations, made direct long-distance voyages a possibility.

The first to venture out were the Genoese. Nicolozzo Spinola reached Bruges in 1277. It was a Genoese ship that first reached England the following year. For the new textile industries growing up in the towns of Italy, this meant that there was now direct access to English wool. What had been prohibitively expensive by road, with the cost of transport and tolls, now became economically possible. Italy seized her opportunity. By 1298 the Genoese shipowners had enough clients to ensure a regular link with Bruges and London. Fifteen years later, and despite the handicap of a considerably longer distance to sail, Venice was to imitate Genoa's example. But Venice was doubly disadvantaged in Flanders in comparison with Genoa, for Genoa had a monopoly of the alum trade. It would take another century—1374 to be precise—before La Serenissima was able to send more than the occasional ship to Bruges.

Even though it was considerably less important than the trade brought by the Genoese and their Florentine clients to Flanders and England, trading activity on the Atlantic around Gibraltar increased. Portuguese, Basque, and even Breton traders began to appear in the Mediterranean.

It would seem, however, that the textile industry in Florence and Milan had already started to expand at the end of the thirteenth century, before the opening of a regular shipping route through the Straits of Gibraltar. If we are to believe Pergolotti, who describes the trade routes of the 1320s, English wool continued, for some time to come, to be transported across western France. Packed into two-bale sacks, the wool was first loaded onto boats that, while robust enough to brave the Channel and the Atlantic, were also small enough to sail up the Dordogne as far as Libourne. It was then transported by mules, loaded with a bale on each side, through Cahors and Albi as far as Montpellier and Aigues-Mortes. It soon became apparent that the journey from Libourne to Aigues-Mortes cost seven times as much as the journey from London to Libourne. These figures were more than enough to justify a move to the sea route around the Iberian peninsula.

The success of these ventures by sea stimulated new ambitions among the Florentine merchants, hitherto obliged by their position halfway up the Arno to depend on intermittent and costly treaties with the port of Pisa. The fate of the Florentine textile industry—not only of the *Arte di Calimala* involved in the secondary treatment of the cloth but also of the *Arte della Lana* (Wool Guild) that produced it—now depended on obtaining an independent supply of raw materials. The Florentines saw all too clearly that without free access to English wool—the only high-quality wool available in medieval Europe—their industry would be wiped out by competitors who were able to take advantage of the ships from Genoa and Venice.

Faced with the only other possibility, that of giving in to Genoa's conditions, Florence preferred to fight. The first objective was to gain free trading rights at the port of Pisa. The ultimate objective, finally obtained in 1406, was nothing less than the conquest of Pisa, followed up, in 1421, by the capture of the Pisan port of Livorno. The face of Italian trade was to change radically from this time. Florentine galleys appeared in Barcelona in 1422 and in Bruges in 1425. By 1428, trade from Tuscany represented one-quarter of the total trade in and out of Barcelona.

Forty years later, two Florentines living in Rome—Lorenzo de' Medici (later known as "the Magnificent") and Giovanni Tornabuoni, then in charge of the Rome branch of the Florentine company headed by Piero de' Medici—successfully bid for the right to extract alum from the papal mines at Tolfa. This new supply had providentially become available just as the supply from Phocaea began to be threatened by the Turkish advances in Asia Minor. The Medici, and later another Florentine family, the Pazzi, thus had no difficulty in finding a market for Italian alum as far away as London and Bruges.

The opening of the Straits of Gibraltar to long-distance shipping had far-reaching consequences, and not only for the Champagne fairs, which had been hit as much by this opening as by the new route over the St. Gotthard Pass. It was obvious that most trade between Italy and northwestern Europe would now bypass France. In fact the seagoing convoys did more to create new trade than they did to supplant old trade. The traditional Italian exports to France were, for the galleys from Genoa and Florence, never anything more than make-weights. The month it took even the fastest ship to get from Genoa to Southampton meant that they could not seriously compete with the packhorse carrying pearls, swords, spices, and cloth of gold. On the other hand, the link between the two seas meant the arrival in Italy of wool—and later cloth—from England, tin from Cornwall, and canvas and fustian from France and Flanders. The Mediterranean ports began to receive shipments of tuna, caught off the Moroccan coast by Castilian and Portuguese fishermen and preserved in oil for the delight of both Italian and English customers, who were no longer satisfied with the traditional salted fish. The North Sea ports began to witness the arrival of alum from Asia Minor, cotton from Egypt, oils and soap from Andalusía, and cochineal, a red dye, from Portugal.

The new sea routes reflected and partly accounted for huge changes in the commercial map as the centers of economic activity were being reorganized. A day was to come when Italian businessmen were in evidence everywhere. They had come to stay. With the exception of the Hanseatic ports, where northern merchants used strict regulations to defend their monopoly, Italians overtook the local merchants. The Genoese and the Tuscans dominated major trade, with its attendant financial traffic, along with the broader new horizons. The local merchant had to be content with the local view.

The Italian Takeover

In the first decades of the 1300s, when no one could yet be sure of the durability of the new trends, the richest Parisian was a recent arrival,

Aguinolfo degli Arcelli of Piacenza, soon known as Gandoufle d'Arcelles. During the same period the world of significant financial speculation—or prevarication, as it could be termed—was dominated by two Florentine brothers born in San Gimignano of the Guidi de Franzesi family. Albizzo and Musciatto—Biche and Mouche Guy—advised Philip the Fair on both monetary policy and diplomatic relations with the warring factions of central Italy. "Mouchet" was the second richest man in Paris after Gandoufle, while *sire* Pierre Marcel, a true Frenchman, was only the third. Tote Guy, nephew of Biche and Mouche, was the "merchant of Enguerran de Marigny"—his business adviser, counselor, and secret agent.

A century later, after the merchants of Lucca had divided the European markets among themselves in order to avoid unnecessary competition, and when the Rapondi had a hand both in the financial affairs of the Avignon papacy during the Great Schism and in the international affairs of the Parisian market, we find that the head of the family and of the family firm, Dino Rapondi—Dine Raponde—is also counselor to the duke of Burgundy, Philip the Bold. Philip had the difficult task of attempting to strike a balance between the economic interests of his county of Flanders, whose links with England for the supply of wool were still strong, and those of a French kingdom whose relations with England were more complex and could not be reduced to a simple matter of the supply of raw materials.

The strength of the Italians—beginning with the Sienese in the thirteenth century and later the Florentines, Lucchesi, and Genoese—was due in great part to their success in acting as a group. They already had tried out the methods and experienced the advantages of this collaboration when acting as advisers in apparently local organizations like the Champagne fairs. The Lucchesi were probably the only group, in the space of one generation at the end of the fourteenth century, to have successfully limited competition between compatriots. The Sienese, Florentines, Genoese, and Venetians were, and would remain, prey to rivalries that were aggravated by reports abroad of conflicts dividing families, clans, and factions at home. In London as in Avignon, a Guelph remained a Guelph, and a "white" Guelph was still the sworn enemy of a "black" Guelph. Throughout the West, the loyalties of the great financial companies that ensured the movement of funds collected by the agents of the Apostolic Chamber lay with Guelph and Angevin policy. When the Guelphs lost their power in Florence after the Ghibelline victory of 1260, a Guelph power base—and a significant one—still existed, although not in Florence itself: the Guelph bank. However strong such factional rivalry became, still the Florentines never failed to unite in the face of the foreigner. Whether from Bruges or Venice, a foreigner was a foreigner.

The success of the Italians also depended on the extent of the trading activities that stretched from the Black Sea to the North Sea, passing by way of Cádiz and Seville (long preferred by the Italians to Lisbon and Oporto) and through that extraordinary trading center, Avignon, the seat of the papacy until the late fourteenth century. The greater the choice of markets with available capital, the more a businessman would prosper. The Genoese or Florentine businessman always had some contact in the Crimea, Catalonia, or England—be it a partner, customer, or supplier—who could obtain credit or pay off a loan. With London and Bruges now the destination of a direct route, expeditions by Italian ships brought not only merchants but also clients and collectors of information. After a mere half century, the great Florentine companies were in a position to finance the buying of wool in England for their industrial offshoots with money raised from the taxes imposed on the English clergy by a papal collector, who could see the inconvenience of actually sending bags of gold and silver coins to Avignon or Rome. Instead, for the tithes and annates paid by the English, Portuguese, or Polish clergy, the papal treasury received gold and silver obtained for the same companies through supplying the papal court—a client with a considerable purchasing power.

Thus the Italian businessmen who, thanks to their many contacts, could obtain loans all over Europe were in the best position to take over the money market and appoint themselves its bankers. For over a century their position was never seriously challenged. Their head start in the late thirteenth and early fourteenth centuries seemed to be irreversible. Non-Italians seemed incapable of finding the intellectual weapons that only the Italians seemed able to forge: banking, accounting, partnerships, insurance. The world was the Italians' horizon. For the rest, this Italian horizon was the world.

There was more than one way of approaching the world. While others went out to seek it, some waited for it to come to them. In Paris as in Bruges, the world could be measured by the accents overheard on the quay or at the inn. The Parisian could hear not only the accents of Rabelais's Limousin schoolboy, the student of law from Normandy, the theologian from Picardy, the cleric from Brabançon, and the Scotsman, but also those of the merchant from Saint-Lô who came every year for his wine, the apple and pear growers from lower down the Seine, in Paris to deliver the produce of their orchards, or the quarryman, Clément de Glan, from Lizy-sur-Ourcq who came every three or four months with a boatload of paving stones, sewage outlets, millstones, and tombstones. Here, too, he might encounter the wealthy Tuscan financier and the Genoese spice merchant with a specialty in luxury goods, a *consul* from Conques or Albi in Paris to attend a court case involving his town, a Breton lawyer acting for his master the duke, a bishop from Champagne well known in the corridors of power, or a soldier from Navarre in the service of the king of Navarre, who in the fourteenth century was cousin to the king of France.

Passive as this view of the world may have been, it was one to which each man brought his own experience and attitudes. A Florentine and a Genoese merchant might encounter each other for the first time in Paris. It was the same in Bruges, where, without leaving port, one could travel as far as the banks of the Duna or the Bosphorus. The merchants of Bruges traveled less and less, but they kept their ears open, and their role in business was as important as their knowledge of the world that came to their door in the shape of foreign merchants.

It was left to others to carve out new routes, settling down for a period or establishing a colony. The merchants from the great Italian ports—and, after 1420, the Florentines as well—were rivals in the exploitation of the East, but they all experienced the same difficulties. Although the position of the Venetians in Constantinople had become more difficult after the collapse in 1261 of the Latin empire born of the Fourth Crusade, the Venetians were present in all the markets of the Near East. Their particular interest in Alexandria and the route from there to India did not prevent Giacomo Badoer from trading in Anatolia around 1440, nor the Bembo brothers, half a century later, in Thessaly. During this period the Genoese controlled from Khios the redistribution of alum from Phocaea, ran the trade of Byzantium, and were forging new links with North Africa. Both the Venetians and the Genoese were forced by the advancing Turks to make a gradual retreat. Their trading posts collapsed one after another. The last to go, in 1475, was the Genoese market of Kaffa in the Crimea, while Egypt cut off any regular trade with the Christian world for a long time to come.

It was the Italians who created and operated the banking system that extended throughout continental Europe. The Sienese were the first on the scene, in the thirteenth century, shortly followed by the Florentines, and eventually, in the fourteenth century, by others from Lucca and Asti. They were more than capable of taking advantage, when the opportunity occurred, of speculative investments involving land rents and taxes owed to princes and towns. "Bétin Cassinel" from Lucca and the Florentine Donato Brunelli shared with the Peruzzi the farming of taxes from Philip the Fair's mints. A century later, in the Paris of 1420, we find "Augustin Ysbarre"—one of the Sbarra family of Lucca—organizing and running the association of sixteen French money changers and merchants who held the lease for all minting done for the Burgundian rulers. For a while, in the fourteenth century, the Florentines Bardi and Peruzzi did well by advancing credit to the king of England, Edward III. The tax imposed on exports of wool, which would then finance the voyage to Flanders, was their security. As it turned out, they were to pay dearly for their privileged position in the English wool market. Similarly, the Genoese "Jean Sac" and his compatriots the Spinolas advanced credit for financing the Parisian administration of Henry VI and his regent Bedford on the security of the taxes paid into the exchequer at Winchester. Their services ceased to be of any use in the Parisian market after the victory of Charles VII.

From the fourteenth century, the Florentines, Venetians, and Genoese competed with one another for the rights to exploit the mines of central Europe. In Poland, Hungary, and Transylvania the extraction of ore was often controlled by Italian companies. Following the discovery of alum at Tolfa, the Medici, Pazzi, and one or two other families succeeded each other quite naturally in the management of a trade that was vital to European industry.

Toward the end of the fourteenth century, an end to opportunities in the East in combination with an inconvenient geographical position on the Mediterranean caused Venice's horizons to contract. In carving out her territorial empire, she had laid the basis of her policy of sovereignty in the thirteenth century. By the fifteenth century, Venice ruled over a territory that embraced the hinterland as far as Brescia, Bergamo, and Friuli, in addition to Dalmatia, Ragusa, Cattaro, and Durazzo, most of the markets of Epirus and Morea—in the Peleponnese—and the Ionian islands, among them Corfu and Cephalonia, to the Negrepont—Euboea—and most of the Aegean islands, especially Naxos, and finally Crete. Cyprus was added to this list in 1489. But this very greatness was proving to be an impossible burden.

While Venice was buying Cyprus, the Genoese were seeking new markets to the west. The Vivaldi brothers never returned from their Atlantic expedition of 1291, but the Genoese, who used Cádiz as their main port on their westward sea voyages, had reached the Canary Islands in the early fourteenth century, while their successors went on to discover, in 1418, a wooded island that they named Legname (Italian for "timber"). Later it was to be known as Madeira. A few years later their compatriot Antonio Malfante reached the Touat oases in the Sahara. It was, however, to be a Florentine, Benedetto Dei, who, at the end of the fifteenth century, would get as far as Timbuktu.

There were Genoese and Florentines in Africa and on the Atlantic, all searching for a direct route to the gold of Sudan. They were to be found also in Spain, trading in the wine, sugar, and silk that were so much in demand north of the Pyrenees. The merchant of Prato, Francesco di Marco Datini, sold salt from Languedoc—particularly from Peccais—up and down the Rhône, as well as wine from Majorca in Bruges. Florentine and Genoese companies made Seville one of the financial centers of Western Europe, its wealth derived both from exploitation of the raw materials of Andalusia and from Seville's role as a port of call where increasingly large numbers of goods, brought by sea from both north and south, were bought and sold.

Both by sea and on land the Italians had many competitors. Merchants from Barcelona looked on the western Mediterranean as their own private

Catalan pond. They were to be found in Naples, Palermo, and Cagliari. They had established themselves in Tunis. The spice route was reversed for them, becoming the Catalan cloth route. They bought Tartar slaves in Naples and African slaves in Tripoli. They sold Sardinian doeskin in Sicily. Even if it meant selling linen from Alexandria in Tunis, they would import Algerian linen into Aragon, along with coral from the coasts of Sardinia or Tunisia.

Merchants from Marseilles, meanwhile, were performing a difficult juggling act, between a trade with Rhodes from which they were for the most part excluded and a local coastal trade where they suffered from the proximity of Genoa, enjoying none of the advantages offered to Montpellier by the king. Although they also dealt in coral from Tunis, they could not hope to compete with the large-scale operations of their Italian rivals. Nevertheless, they were able to carve out a not insignificant niche for themselves as inshore traders along the coast from the Ligurian Riviera to Catalonia and even as far as Valencia, the sea route being the best for trade in this region, given the geography of the land.

Although the Andalusían businessmen were little inclined to travel north, there had, nevertheless, been Spaniards in Harfleur on the Seine estuary since the beginning of the fourteenth century. Now Seville and Cádiz, chief beneficiaries of the opening of a route between the Mediterranean and the North Sea, began to take on a role not dissimilar to that of Bruges. With so many ships stopping off in the two busy Andalusían ports, the variety of goods bought and sold was almost infinite. Seville became the most important European market for gold from the Sudan as well as leather and cochineal dye from Morocco. In addition to the local fruit and oil, Cádiz could offer mercury that went to Bruges, where German entrepreneurs bought it to add to silver ore. As the Spanish began to colonize the islands of the Atlantic, Seville was to become, in the fourteenth century, the chief European market for sugar.

While Italy, reviving memories of the ancient Roman Empire, began to take over the Mediterranean as its own economic kingdom, the Hanseatic League exploited its de facto monopoly in the north. Since the 1150s it had progressively eliminated all competition with the exception of the Teutonic Order, which continued to export amber, wax, and furs to Flanders. It did not, however, seek to expand beyond this protected domain. With only a few exceptions—for example, the Hildebrand brothers and Sievert Veckinchusen who, in 1407, established their partner Peter Karbow at the head of a branch set up in Venice to conduct large-scale trade with Bruges and Lübeck, the annual excursion to collect Atlantic salt, or the presence of a few Hansa merchants in Seville—the League's merchants confined themselves to an area that extended from Novgorod and Bergen in the north to Bruges and reached eastward along the German and Polish rivers as far as Cologne and

Cracow. But these were well known, and the Hansa's horizons, already embracing the whole of northern Europe, comprised enough contacts elsewhere—in Bruges, London, and Venice—for a Lübeck merchant to see the world on a European scale.

Nuremberg, on the other hand, was expanding its field of action. Nuremberg merchants were seen at the Champagne fairs in the thirteenth century and in Italy during the fourteenth century; during the fifteenth century, they were active on the shores of the Baltic in competition with the Hanseatic merchants. By the end of the fifteenth century, businessmen from Nuremberg were accepted as citizens of Lübeck.

Nuremberg merchants made serious inroads into Hanseatic trade on land. As a southern extension of the new—but rapidly becoming essential—axis formed by the great continental road passing through Frankfurt and Leipzig, skirting the Thuringian Mountains and the mining districts of Saxony, Nuremberg established itself as a crossroads for trade from upper Germany, which here branched off beyond Franconia toward Hesse, Bavaria, and Austria. Thus an international market, previously lacking, emerged for the redistribution of products from central Europe. Important businessmen from Nuremberg could be found during the fifteenth century in places as far apart as Geneva, Lyons, Warsaw, Seville, and Brescia.

Other centers began to grow in importance. Frankfurt started to develop its own trading links, while Augsburg profited from developments in the new metal industries that, with new methods for separating and refining metals, in particular the silver contained in copper ore, opened up hitherto unsuspected possibilities for the mining regions and for those who used the metals, previously small artisans. The income gained from mining made by the count of the Tyrol, Frederick IV of Habsburg, nicknamed "Frederick of the empty pockets," was, in about 1425, some 7,500 Rhenish florins a year. Around 1480, his son, "Sigismund the Rich," was receiving as much as 80,000 florins. The merchants of Augsburg did not fail to take advantage of this opportunity. It was a stroke of genius on the part of Jacob Fugger when he obtained control, by dint of substantial advances to the count and his successor, of the Tyrolean silver industry. He went on to take over the Hungarian copper mines.

Leipzig's fairs were becoming important, and by the end of the fifteenth century the town was able to stand on its own without the assistance of Nuremberg. Merchants from Augsburg, such as the Welser family, had branches in Lisbon. And the "Great Company," the *Grosse Ravensburger Gesellschaft*, with its eighteen bases and branches set up from Bruges to Geneva and from Pest to Valencia, did not hesitate to present itself as a rival to the Medici family. For all that, Ravensburg, where it had its headquarters, never became a significant economic center.

Map 4. Principal Continental Routes in the Late Middle Ages

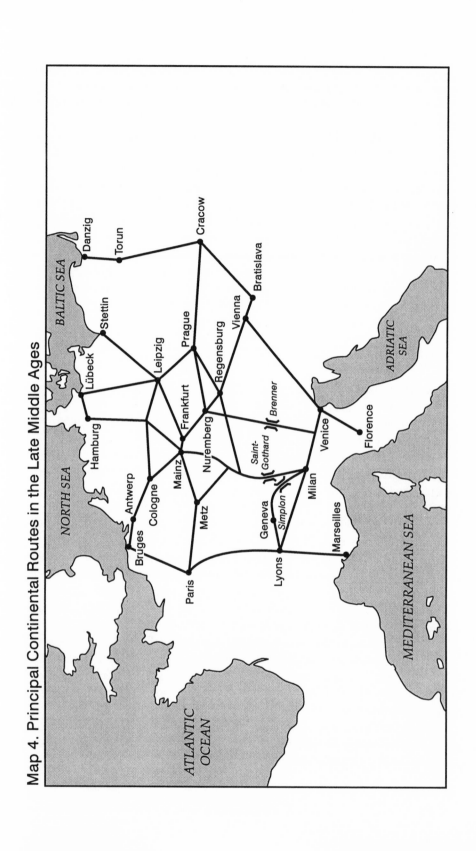

During the 1450s, at a time when Jacques Coeur was trying to establish a presence for French galleys—over which he had the monopoly—in the Mediterranean, and when the entire world was beginning to carry out business in Antwerp or Lyon, Augsburg was attempting to conquer new markets in Europe. If it did so, it was largely through the help of the emerging Fugger family. At the same time the Genoese were looking toward Africa, the Atlantic, and for a sea route to India and China. The normal horizons of commerce now extended not only to the known world but also to worlds yet to be discovered.

A gulf was opening up between the merchant who saw no further than procuring supplies for the towns and was wary of anything but the most controlled forms of speculation and the merchant who could buy and sell anything and everything in any market. Depending on how successful he was, the first might become a munitions officer, a tax-farmer, an important citizen, or a shopkeeper. The second, both banker and shipowner, was, in addition, to become involved in affairs of state. Sometimes the next generation might become princes, as was the case with both the Fugger and Medici families. Their horizons continued to be as wide as the world.

The result of evolving attitudes as much as of technological innovation, the expansion of the economic horizon was to make its consequences felt in every sphere. The greater distances covered and the increased tonnage of ships meant that it was no longer possible to leave arrangements for return loads to be made on the spot and left entirely to the initiative of the captain or traveling merchant. It became necessary to plan ahead for round trips by sea. Trading began to involve not a two-way but a three-way exchange, a development that was to play a major role in the money market, which is to say, in the development of banking.

The greater geographical distances meant that operations took longer. Capital was immobilized and so were men. Henceforth it became virtually impossible for one person to operate alone. The pooling of cargoes and finance became essential. Such integration could operate horizontally through the grouping together of similar enterprises or vertically by the inclusion of complementary enterprises. It appeared, paradoxically, to be the simplest answer to increased risk. Together with this sharing of investment, another response to the increased risk involved in the longer distances and increased tonnage was credit, which effectively represented an early form of insurance.

Another effect of the raising of economic sights was the increasing distinction made between transporting merchandise and methods of payment. Agreements were organized independently, no longer transacted on the spot or simply in relation to current supply and demand, product by product, in specialized markets.

Eventually and, as time passed, increasingly, the fortunes of the different groups were to diverge according to their commercial and geographical choices. There were those who persisted with trade in the East, such as the Venetians, or men like Jacques Coeur, who was three generations too late in his understanding of the economic map. There were those who diversified their enterprises in different directions: Genoa, active to the last in the Black Sea, but already present in the Atlantic archipelagoes; or Rouen, already looking further afield without neglecting her traditional role in trade in the Channel and the North Sea as well as the Seine Valley. And there were others who deliberately chose to break new ground. Lisbon and Seville were two such cities. It was already possible to see which of these paths would lead to the great economic fortunes of the modern world.

Horizons had expanded, but not everyone had contributed equally to this development. More important, some people understood the opportunities of the moment and, more successfully than others, foresaw those of the future.

THREE

Learning About the World

Knowledge of the world was easy to attain in a period when markets were expanding on a limited and local basis, when foreign merchants seemed more like new immigrants than travelers, and when a businessman rarely encountered anyone but those people—always the same—whose language and customs he already understood. Things changed as the economic world began to expand, from the mid-thirteenth century through the first decades of the fourteenth, as a result of new developments in technology and the opening up of new trade routes. As merchants from Florence, Lucca, and Marseilles began to do more business with London, Seville, Genoa, Barcelona, Bremen, and Leipzig, they became increasingly aware of the need to understand foreign environments and adapt to different markets and methods of trading.

Any training the businessman received was inevitably sporadic and incomplete, since the need for such training depended on a person's view of his particular situation. The merchant who was content to travel twice a year from Auxerre to Paris to sell two or three casks of the Auxerre wine that was so popular in the best inns felt quite able to cope with his world. The merchant who traded with half of Europe had a better understanding of how much there was to learn and understand, together with a greater desire to communicate and pass on this useful knowledge.

The Schoolroom and the Marketplace
The merchant received his principal schooling on the job. Nevertheless, there was a role for the teacher who could give instruction in the rudiments of reading, writing, and arithmetic. Such skills were fundamental to any

further learning. The merchant was more than ready to pay out of his own pocket for his assistants and eventual successors to return to the schoolroom. Training was given by whomever was available—the local priest, the lawyer, perhaps a hard-up student or a former student.

A few hours a day or a week was enough, but the wiser employers took this schooling seriously, even when it consisted of no more than the occasional lesson from a village schoolmaster. One such teacher, Master Guillaume de Villon, the chaplain of Saint-Benoît-le-Bétourné, brought the young François de Montcorbier to live in his own home. Like his fellows, he saw such children—whether living in or out—as useful unpaid servants whose duties included lighting the fire, carrying water, and serving at mass. Many contracts of apprenticeship specify the number of free hours that an employer would grant to his apprentice in order to allow him to attend lessons with the local notary. Butchers sent their apprentices to school during Lent, when abstinence from meat meant a quiet period for their trade.

Even if it was only a matter of middle-class snobbery, the better-off merchants preferred lessons to be taught at home by a tutor. A mere cobbler like Azémar Couronne of Toulouse did not think twice about engaging a student from Albi for a whole year to teach both his son and himself "science and polite manners." The young man had to pay six francs for his meals; it would appear that the opportunity of free lodging in a university town was not to be sneered at. In this case, his employer even promised to supply free candles so that he could continue his own studies in the evening.

It was not long before proper elementary schools began to be set up in response to demand from the petite bourgeoisie. The larger Italian towns had schools as early as the end of the thirteenth century; the Florentines even sent their daughters to them. By the next century there was hardly a town in Europe without a school. In 1336, we find the inhabitants of the small town of Decize in the Nivernais anxiously trying to replace a teacher who could not keep discipline in the class—he was even allowing them to play at dice!—with another who had the added merit of being not only a good teacher but also a local boy. Decize required only the rudiments, and it is to be feared that the good schoolmaster would not have had the chance to introduce his students to the legal documents, so essential for the merchant, or the use of an abacus, infinitely more complex than the three piles of counters that sufficed to teach the four basic operations of arithmetic. The children of Bruges or Marseilles, who, beginning at the age of five or six, went to school for two to four years must have made better progress.

Of course, in France as in Germany, the public scribe was always available for the peasant who came to market, or for the journeyman or chambermaid who needed a letter written or read. The merchant did not need such services. Keeping his own accounts and reading his own letters, he was learning the importance, no matter how modest his endeavors, of prudence and confidentiality.

In Florence, Genoa, and Venice they expected rather more from their schools than did the people of Toulouse, Marseilles, or Leipzig. Although in France and Germany a child spent only a few of his or her younger years at school, Italian merchants kept their children there until the age of fourteen or fifteen. In other words, instruction in mathematics was not confined to the four basic operations but embraced algorithms, or the application of predetermined rules to problem solving. The techniques of accounting were acquired at the end of this apprenticeship, allowing Italian businessmen to dispense with the use of professional accountants. They would have a bookkeeper, but the responsibility for the organization and updating of accounts lay with the businessman and his partners.

One reason for the lasting superiority of the Tuscans, Venetians, and Genoese over other long-term markets such as Bruges, London, and Barcelona was to be their ability to do their own accounts. The key to speculation lay in knowing how to calculate compound interest and the capitalization of interest, to judge the rates of commission on commercial stock, and to calculate the value of a single loan out of a group of bonds falling due at different dates.

Inevitably the businessman had to deal with complex calculations and fractions: the Louis XI "crown," for example, was minted in 1474 at a rate of 72 coins from each mark of a metal alloy of $23\frac{7}{8}$ carats—fine gold is 24 carats—for a legal value of 30 sous 3 *deniers tournois* or, in other words, 363 *deniers*. Similarly, the silver *guénar* struck in 1389 at a rate of 74 to a mark of a metal alloy of 5 *deniers* 12 grains—$5\frac{1}{2}$ out of 12 deniers—of a silver that was not even fine silver, but the so-called "king's silver" of $^{11}/_{12}$; in other words, $5\frac{5}{12}$ of $^{11}/_{12}$. And that was when the mintings were all based on the same mark. The merchant who had to go off in search of an accountant every time he needed to change money was clearly liable to lose his profit in the business if he found one, and to be cheated if he did not.

Whether Florentine or Venetian, the schools also taught some basic economic geography. The pupils learned about the different marketplaces and what was bought and sold where. The rudiments of commercial law, which underpinned every deal, were also taught. The drawing up of a contract was and would remain a job for the lawyer, but it was the merchant's job to discuss its terms.

The schooling of the Italian businessman even included a basic language training that was to save valuable time in later years in far-off marketplaces. A brief study of humanism meant that the young Florentines had to read a little Latin at school through the works of Virgil, Seneca, or Boethius. Of more practical value were the rudiments of Italian and Flemish taught in the Hanseatic port of Lübeck or the northern French *langue d'oil* learned by young Italians—the southern French *langue d'oc* was clearly considered too similar to Italian to be worth studying—to ensure that they would not be cheated on the quayside in Bruges, at the London customs, or at the Champagne fairs. The Flemish notary Brunetto Latini chose to write his encyclopedia of c. 1260, *Li livre dou trésor,* in the *langue d'oil,* and it was used in 1298 by the Pisan notary Rusticello for his *Devisement,* the adventures of a Venetian traveler, one Marco Polo, whom he had met by chance and to whom the book has always been subsequently attributed.

The essentials of these disciplines, however, could only be taught on the job. Apprenticeship was decisive in this process. In the workshop or office, everything known to those who passed through was imparted to the child. Son, nephew, or contracted apprentice—it was all one; the apprentice was often a relative and the contract of apprenticeship made the child part of his new family. He learned how to deal with people and with merchandise, how to recognize different qualities, and how to determine prices. He discovered local usages and heard others speak of far-off customs. In this way he was being prepared for that essential moment in his life at the age of twelve or thirteen when the wise businessman would send him on his first sea voyage.

When the Florentine Buonaccorso Pitti set off from his home on the Arno in 1372 at the age of eighteen, it was with the expectation of gaining practical and varied experience. It was not until 1396, when he was thirty-two, that he finally returned to his hometown for good. In the intervening period, he had been to France, England, Germany, and the Netherlands. He visited London twice, Bruges five times, and Paris fifteen times, traveling by all possible routes. He saw Mainz, Heidelberg, Munich, Buda, even Zagreb.

The Venetians Niccolò and Matteo Polo had much the same idea when they set out again for the East in 1271. These two merchants, in no way extraordinary, had already traveled from the Crimea to Mongolia ten years earlier along one of the caravan routes that kept the West supplied with precious silks. This time, as they set off again for deepest Asia they took with them their son and nephew Marco, a boy of seventeen. Niccolò and Matteo had been youngest sons, and they were acting as befitted the younger members of a family whose head, Marco the Elder, after living for so many years in Constantinople at a time when the Venetians had benefited from so many privileges, now stayed at home in Venice in order to see to the continuity of the family business.

The three Venetians were to be away for a quarter of a century, having more than once lost sight of the original aims of their journey. They became involved in diplomacy and acted as representatives of Christendom at the court of the Mongol khan. The latter asked them to investigate the workings of the administration in the remoter corners of his empire. They were drawn into the management of taxation, and Marco Polo more than once inspected the imperial tax collectors at Hangzhou. They even went to India as ambassadors of the khan.

Marco, for some three years, became a high-ranking official of the Mongol empire. He was governor of Yangzhou on the Yangtze delta. Well provided for with income, rank, and a title, he could quite well have stayed in China permanently, if it had not been for the fact that he never forgot either Venice or the family business in which, when the time came, he would have to take his place.

And so they returned to Italy. On their way out to the East they had used only continental routes, across Armenia, Persia, and the Gobi Desert. They saw Tabriz but missed Mosul, Bukhara, and Samarkand. On the way home they wanted to try the sea route, probably to save time. The emperor offered them the opportunity and the means: they would accompany a Mongol princess as far as Persia, where she was to be married. Thus they embarked, probably from Quanzhou, then called Zayton. They put in on the coast of Indochina, passed the point of the future Singapore, sailed around Sumatra and then Ceylon. Long months of sailing along the coast of Malabar—the western coast of India—and then along the Persian coast of the Indian Ocean brought the three Venetians to Hormuz, where they finally left their ship. Traveling overland directly northward, they arrived at the southern end of the Caspian where lay the route they had taken on the way out. Once again they missed Baghdad, a sore point with Marco when he came to narrate the story of his travels (see Map 5).

By now the Polos were at Trebizond. They were lucky to escape unscathed, for the Venetians were no longer the blue-eyed boys on the Black Sea. Unfortunately, the Genoese confiscated the greater part of the merchandise that, ever the good traders, the Polos had not neglected to collect, both in China and in India.

From this point the journey became more rapid. A boat took them to Constantinople and another on to Venice. After a journey lasting three years, two years of which had been at sea, they were finally back on the Rialto in 1295.

They had been away for a quarter of a century. The young man who had left in 1271 was now forty-one. This marked the end of his travels, although he lived for another thirty years. In business circles he passed for a man of experience, but his adventures brought him neither rank—for he arrived home at a time when the ranks of Venetian society were already closed—nor prestige in the Venetian markets, since he had little to show for his time in China and he had lost all the goods he was carrying on the journey home. There was much interest in his travels, but few were inclined

Map 5. Marco Polo's Journey

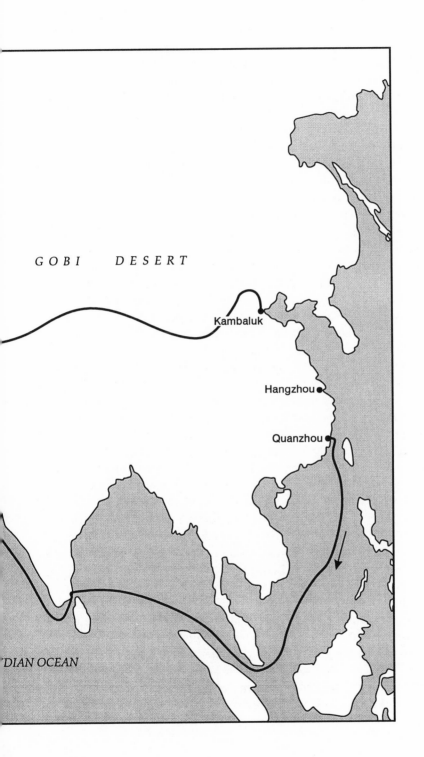

GOBI   DESERT

Kambaluk

Hangzhou

Quanzhou

DIAN OCEAN

to follow his example. He had been to Kambaluk—later Peking and now Beijing—and traveled the length and breadth of Asia, but he was not the only Westerner to arrive there.

The younger members of the Hanseatic merchant families, meanwhile, were traveling between Flanders and Russia, attending the fairs in Skåne, visiting Gotland, or setting up in Riga. Between the ages of twelve and twenty, Hans Wessel of Stralsund made no less than seven major sea voyages—one a year. Jacob Fugger spent a year at the *Fondaco dei Tedeschi* in Venice, between giving up thoughts of a career in the Church in 1478 and taking up permanent residence in Augsburg in 1479. On a more modest scale, the younger members of merchant families from Rouen often took cargoes down the river to Paris for a father or older brother. Guillaume Le Moine, a merchant who bought large quantities of "French" and Auxerre wine at the Grève market, decided in 1462 that in future he would no longer entrust the cargoes to a third party but rather to his son Robert, known as Robinet. During the same period, Enguerran Le Page, a rich merchant dealing in hay and firewood, transferred the job of accompanying his boats to the capital from his usual carriers to his son-in-law Maulin Lozère and later to his son Pierre Le Page. Thus the future businessmen of Rouen had the opportunity to get to know a different place, to be introduced to the family business, and to gain some experience of the laws and practices governing the activities of the Parisian port at Grève. For the rest of their lives they would know how to make use of the respectful but influential concierge of the Hôtel de Ville.

As merchant society became established it began to make travel a condition for the young people, not least because a traveler was of real value to the whole group. He was their informant, correspondent, and even agent. His eventual return would be the guarantee of his loyalty. The quality of his service when away would justify the confidence placed in him when he came back to settle. So it was very much in the general interest when, in 1380, the Lübeck company of *Bergenfahrer* (the Bergen travelers), adopted statutes that defined two categories of merchant: those based in Lübeck, the *Borger to Lübeck,* older and more experienced; and those still of an age to make sea journeys, sailing frequently to Bergen or elsewhere, the *Copgeselle to Bergen,* or "companions in Bergen." The economic function of both groups took on the importance of a civic role.

Though less rigorously enforced, because their horizons were more varied, the great Tuscan families acted in a similar way, entrusting to the younger members, their sons or younger brothers, the management of the family's interests at the great fairs on the other side of the Alps and in the permanent markets that were established later. At the beginning of the fourteenth century, Giacomino—known as Mino—di Scricca of Siena, son of a prior of the same city, was the permanent representative in Paris for the Galliani society, a group of thirty-two Sienese merchants united, for the most part, by close family ties. The Rapondi of Lucca sent members of the family to Paris, Bruges, and Avignon. The eldest, Dino, moved on from Paris to Bruges, while his younger brother Andrea set up a branch in Avignon before leaving it in the hands of his brother Filippo. When the latter returned to Bruges his nephew Giovanni was sent to Avignon in his place. In this way all the members gained experience of both the family business and the diverse horizons of the European market.

The Book

The businessman was tight-lipped on matters that might be of use to his competitors. It would be of little benefit to broadcast his success in business by stressing opportunities or ways of saving time or money. Those who did recount their experiences usually did so only for the benefit of their partners, relatives, or successors. Although the tales of the traveler who had finally returned home—as the Tuscan or Venetian almost invariably did—enlivened or bored many a winter's evening, it was unusual for the businessman to think of publishing them, as was the habit of diplomats or soldiers. A Villehardouin or a Joinville might seek to defend himself, or boast of his exploits, by recounting his experiences in the Crusades. In order to celebrate the spread of the true faith and to encourage others to continue the good work, the Franciscans Pian Carpino and Guillaume de Rubrouck both published books: the former his *History of the Mongols,* a history combined with an account of his own adventures; the latter an *Itinerary,* a valuable travel guide for use by future missionaries. The merchant was little concerned with such things; he was not inclined to give away trade secrets. This is not to say that he did not indulge in the pleasures of self-congratulation or of pretensions to authorship. He would reveal his experiences, but only so long as it was to his advantage to do so.

Thus, with the semiprofessional help of Rusticello of Pisa, Marco Polo put on paper his *Devisement du monde,* a book written in French that is more a traveler's yarn than a commercial itinerary. His chief preoccupation is to amaze rather than to inform, and the merchant's natural interest in figures appears only in his systematic recourse to exaggeration. The public was not deceived, and the book by Rusticello and Polo was soon nicknamed *The Million:* "For one shipload of pepper going to Alexandria or elsewhere in the Christian world, a hundred or more come to this port of Zayton." But the figures were vague, and a reader might seek in vain for information more precise than "great quantities of goods," "innumerable marvels," or "great riches." There is nothing of any real value on the topics of production or trade. For example: "There are many great ships in Hangzhou, which sail to and from India and other foreign parts, taking and bringing back merchandise of all kinds that the city values most."

Polo is as eloquent about what he did not see as what he did see. His description of the Mongol empire, its administration, finances, and system of social and political relationships, which allowed him to dazzle his readers with incredible tales—about the postal system or paper money—and to give himself a role that was not only exotic but also important, is of much greater interest than his dull description of the trading centers of China, India, and Persia. It was the intention of the author of the book—Rusticello, not Polo—to make the *Devisement* more like one of the great romances of antiquity, with their fabulous tales of chivalry and adventure. Marco Polo, the businessman, was careful to reveal nothing about his trading activities except that which was common knowledge. Between the wonders and the trivia, he keeps his real experiences to himself and is silent on facts and figures that might have been useful.

Not everyone had the Venetian's talent, and no one had such a tale to tell. But the detailed information and practical observations that emerge in the course of a narration often give interest to texts that initially lack the appeal of *The Million*.

And then there were those whose decision to write the history of their city was prompted by patriotism. This gave them ample opportunity to describe the world that they had visited and observed in the course of doing business. Thus we find in the writings of Guido Mossaldi, Giovanni Frescobaldi, and Donato Vellati notes for the instruction of young Tuscans setting out on their first voyage. A merchant in the *Arte di Por Santa Maria,* the silk guild, Dino Compagni is an excellent informant about the concerns of a Florentine businessman in the 1330s. Equally valuable for what it tells us of Florence at that time is the evidence provided by Marchione di Copo Stefani, son of one of the partners of the Acciaiuoli company. The most stylish description of the European markets, as well as of Bruges during the period 1302–7 and Florence thirty years later, has been left to us by Giovanni Villani, who worked with the Peruzzi family and later with the Buonaccorsi. For anyone wanting to travel to Flanders, however, a description of the economic situation at least a generation out of date was probably of little use. It succeeds better as a literary work than as a practical guide. Perhaps a useful introduction, but certainly not a business handbook.

Such accounts were even less common outside Italy. The chroniclers—once a Villehardouin and a Joinville, now a Monstrelet or a Commines—were more often men attached to the court looking back over their past careers than informed observers of economic affairs. And professional men of letters rarely rose to a global approach to phenomena and systems. Nicolas de Baye and Clément de Fauquembergue, secretaries to the Paris

Parlement during the first half of the fifteenth century, note in the margins of their minutes the state of the weather, the level of the river, the thaw, war and peace, but never the habits of the boatmen or the·weights and measures officer at Grève. The daily round was not of interest.

The desire to instruct is not apparent in their remarks any more than it is in the gloomy observations of the anonymous author of *Journal d'un Bourgeois de Paris*. Thought to be written by a cleric, Jean Chuffart, it records the price of broad beans and cabbages. But while giving us yesterday's price, Chuffart says nothing of the privileges granted to Parisians or the restrictions imposed on people from outside. He writes for himself, not to instruct.

The only writer with a deliberately educational intent is the anonymous author of the *Ménagier de Paris*. This elderly citizen set out his advice to his young wife in the 1390s so that she would serve him well in his life and be a worthy wife to another husband when he died. But business is business and the house is the house. The young wife had to know how to run the household of servants, deal with the linen and cooking, supervise household expenditures, chase away flies, and look after the planting and harvesting of the kitchen garden. All that she needed to know about her husband's business was that he came home tired after a day's work and deserved all her attention:

> Men have the task of caring for all that is outside, and to this end they must come and go, running here and there in the rain, wind, snow, and hail, now wet, now dry, now sweating, now shivering, badly fed, badly shod, in bad lodgings and in an uncomfortable bed.
>
> And yet all this does him no harm because he is comforted by the hope that his wife will take care of him on his return and the thought of the ease, joys, and pleasures that she will provide for him, or have the servants provide, taking off his shoes before a good fire, washing his feet, making ready fresh stockings and shoes, good food, good wine, serving him well, treating him well as the master, comfortably bedded in white sheets and nightcap, covered with good furs and satisfied with other joys and pleasures, private and amorous, of which I will say no more. And on the next day, new clothes and linen.
>
> Certainly such services make a man love and desire to return to his home.

The writer advises his wife to be a "good secretary": to keep her husband's secrets. It is true that this has more to do with his faults than his business. Of the latter he deliberately does not breathe a word in the advice he gives to the mistress of the house. A few years later, the misogynistic author of the *Fifteen Joys of Marriage* boasts of how he keeps his wife apart from his professional life. Clearly, in France, we are very far removed from the world of the Florentine who sent his daughters to school. We are a long way, too, from the small world of the shopkeeper, where women had an important place.

So the merchant did not place much importance on the instruction to be gained from travelers' tales or memoirs. His methodical mind and taste for practicalities led him to prefer more direct information. If he wanted to relax, he would turn to a chivalrous romance. But if he wished to be instructed, he would make use of a good manual, simply arranged in order to provide, at different stages of his life, either basic professional training or a convenient encyclopedia in which to find names, figures, and precise information about trade and customs.

The *Tariff or Notice of Weights and Measures* compiled in Venice during the 1300s was still a useful reference for specialists more than a century later, as was the *Book of the Sea* written a little later in Flanders and given a further lease of life at the end of the fifteenth century with a translation into Plattdeutsch that was still widely available well into the sixteenth century, even when so much had changed in the world of the merchant and the sailor. At the very least the *Book of the Sea* remained a precious repertoire of the tides, depths, and known hazards of the sea routes.

Numerous proper encyclopedias were constantly updated and recopied before the invention of printing. Many of the works that claimed to be new were in fact nothing more than a reworking of an older text. Among the very earliest of such works, usually Italian, we find three dealing with similar topics but providing a variety of different pieces of information, depending on the firsthand experiences of the author and his chances of checking and investigating his facts.

Giovanni di Antonio da Uzzano's *El libro di mercatantie a usanze de' paesi*—still in print in the eighteenth century!—and the *Libro di mercatantie et usanze de paesi* by Giorgio di Lorenzo Chiarini lagged behind the work offered by one of the directors of the powerful Bardi company, Francesco di Balduccio Pergolotti. His *La pratica della mercatura,* revised and updated over a period of fifteen years after each new journey or experience, was explicitly intended to perpetuate the superiority of the Bardi family and the efficiency of their agents. For the convenience of the latter, the work contained arithmetical tables to help with complex calculations—in particular of interest and exchange rates. Pergolotti was content merely to copy down the tables that were widely available in schools and various small scholarly manuals, such as that by Leonardo Pisano, commonly used by many merchants. Similarly, Pergolotti provides information gleaned from other sources on ways of calculating repayment dates or the details of a journey by land or sea. With the help of the "dominical letters," for example, it was possible to work out what day of the week a certain date fell on, or the dates of Easter, needed by the businessman in order to know on which dates the fairs connected with Easter or Whitsun would fall and how many months it would be before the next movable feast day.

Pergolotti drew on his personal experience, on the other hand, when he drew up a balance sheet of production and trade for each market he had visited or with which the Bardi had dealings. He enumerated the 188 different types of spices available on the market; he provided a description of the towns and their commercial infrastructure; and he furnished lists of local weights and measures and their rough equivalents. The currencies circulating in the different markets were obviously of interest to him: he describes, judges, and evaluates them. Nor does he fail to provide practical information about formalities, taxes to be paid, and the cost of using intermediaries:

> If you come with your merchandise to the port of Écluse and do not unload, you can go on your way as you please, without unloading or paying any dues. But if you unload a single bale of your cargo, you will have to pay taxes on the whole of your goods still on the ship.
>
> The toll rights at Écluse and Damme belong to the same lord. So, if you unload at Écluse and want to sell there, you will pay the dues at Écluse; but if you do not want to sell there and prefer to take your merchandise from Écluse to Bruges, you will pay the dues at Damme if you have not already paid it at Écluse.

He even provides information on bank exchange rates, noting the rates charged for changing money and the period of time—the usance—customarily allowed between the drawing and paying of a bill. Despite the objective nature of his work, Pergolotti does not deny himself the odd anecdote or digression that might serve to illuminate the daily life of distant markets for the future traveler.

Communications

Such information would have been rather inflexible had there not also been, day after day, information flowing in via a network of communication that the merchant rightly considered to be a priority. In order to influence the money market or the supply of provisions, to take advantage of opportunities and get ahead of the competition, agents were needed to provide information to their head office from abroad, or to the company's branch offices when at home, where information converged regarding new customs or changing tastes, supply and demand, the price of pepper or gold thread, or up-to-date figures on the exchange rates. They needed to know, before their rivals, about variations in monetary rates or the arrival of a ship or the wreck of another. The winner was the merchant with the best network of well-placed contacts and the speediest communications—the one who knew before anyone else and who, for several days or even only for several hours, was the only one to know whether the morrow would bring war or peace, famine or plenty. The farsighted businessman was the one who was never caught by the imposition of a new tax or ruined on the whim of an Egyptian sultan.

One of the strengths of the Hanseatic League was its shared information. Even when the competition was weak, the merchants constantly exchanged messages. It was essential not to be caught unawares by events in other markets, where the Hanseatic League was able to maintain its position only by satisfying the clients' needs. Thus we find the merchants trading in Riga alerting their colleagues in Lübeck in 1458 that the Russians were more interested in price than in quality and that there was more demand for the light English cloth than for the opulent Flemish woolen fabrics.

An importer in Bruges and his buyer in Torun or Novgorod would feel badly let down by their informants in Paris around 1380 if they were left unaware of the new fashion for dark furs. It was true that, at court, people continued to wear the light-colored miniver for a long time to come, and it was still much prized in the mid-fifteenth century; nevertheless the preferred fur was now sable. This radical change in male fashions, or at least the increased pace of change that relegated the use of squirrel to ceremonial clothes, may have had something to do with the arrival in Paris of the young Isabelle of Bavaria and her German followers in 1385. Half a century later, the same development affected women's clothing. Between these two dates—and the members of the court of Burgundy from Lucca certainly had something to do with it—we see how black lambskin from Italy became one of the most fashionable furs at the court of Philip the Good. At the end of the fourteenth century it once again became fashionable to wear furs from wild animals: the silvery winter fur of the lynx and the black sable.

The businessman had to know these things. There would come a moment when it was pointless to buy up a load of Siberian squirrel fur and highly advantageous to get hold of Prussian sable. At another time a shrewd merchant might look elsewhere than in the Baltic.

There was always the possibility of a slump. There was also the more common problem of an unprofitable investment. Fashion meant high prices. Between 1350 and 1400, the average price of miniver in Paris fell by 40 percent, and by 50 percent in Avignon. The price could also vary from one year to the next by as much as 30 percent. In three months during the summer of 1384, 396,087 skins—377,000 of which were squirrel—arrived at the port of London; it is easy to understand how a purchasing error in Torun, Danzig, or Novgorod meant missed profits or unsalable stock. An observant and well-connected informant represented money.

Similarly, when a change in fashion to more tightly fitted clothes and an influx of silk in the fifteenth century, combined with the increasing comfort of the homes of the wealthy, almost destroyed the textile market in wealthy towns among the upper classes, news traveled from Bruges to

Lübeck that furs from the north—a commodity that hitherto had been very safe—might not be a good investment. It might be cold in Novgorod, but the important thing to know was whether the people rich enough to wear fur had better-heated homes in Paris or in Brussels.

The Tuscans were among the earliest to set up an information network. Their strongly united companies with their subsidiaries and branches, combined with the extra solidarity derived from agreements negotiated between companies and towns, meant that several times a year something very like an economic bulletin arrived on the banks of the Arno, providing information about the latest changes in fashion, piety, or artistic trends, of use to those involved in speculative ventures. The well-informed negotiator would know the right moment to sell cloth of gold from Lucca, alabasters from England, a Virgin of the Seven Sorrows or a Mystic Marriage of St. Catherine. The agent in Paris would have been congratulated for predicting in his letters to his employers in Florence—written at the time when efforts of the duke of Burgundy, Philip the Bold, and the king of England, Richard II, seemed to be pointing to an end to war—that the probable peace and a possible alliance between France and England would come about only if sealed by a royal marriage. If the king of England was going to marry a French princess there would be great festivities: better to stock up in Paris with jewels than with weapons.

These letters not only contributed to the education of the young merchant, whether he read them or furnished them with descriptions of what he saw daily—becoming a means to manage business, just as states used diplomatic envoys to manage their affairs—but also guaranteed the internal cohesiveness of the enterprise, the coherence of its commercial policies, as well as its financial equilibrium. From the humblest Parisian merchant receiving information from his nephew in Rouen or from his agent delayed in Auxerre to the company of twenty branches receiving news in Genoa, Florence, or Asti from all over Western Europe, the need was the same: to coordinate their activities in the full understanding of risks taken here or profits acquired there, and with full confidence in their representatives on the spot.

It was in the matter of risk, even more than in that of opportunity, that the businessman needed to be alert to the political situation. All trade with distant markets inevitably involved, sooner or later, advancing credit—loaned or discounted—to princes. In the 1330s this was the absolute condition of the privileges granted to the Italians in the London wool market. For the merchants from Tours in the 1470s, these were the terms of privileges granted in the Lyons market or for the speculative activities involving income from royal revenues. Banker to popes and princes, the businessman always had to pay close attention to a letter that warned him of a possible rival or a change in political circles—a dismissal, a promotion, or a scandal. The Peruzzi's agent in Rhodes, in 1338, was glad to have been warned in time of the rout of the English in Flanders; he was able to take precautions to limit a panic among depositors who were well aware that the company was heavily involved in financing the expedition. The Italian in Avignon at the time of the Great Western Schism was thankful to his correspondent in Rome who had alerted him to upheavals in the Church. When a canonical dispensation was needed to trade with the infidels, it would be better to keep one's papal options open.

Information was easily obtained. Agents, partners, contacts, and middlemen in the foreign markets were called upon, as were relatives and friends locally, for any information that they might hear or see. One can easily imagine the advantages enjoyed by those with permanent access to the heart of political decision making: the senatorial families of Venice, the patricians of Lübeck, or the financiers who advised the king—Biche and Mouche for Philip the Fair, Pierre des Essarts for Philip VI of Valois.

Getting the news from place to place was less easy. Verbal and written news generally traveled together. The traveler would gladly carry a few letters, if he did not have to deliver them until he had transacted his own business and taken time off to relay the most precious news to those close to him. Sometimes this was openly and honestly made a condition of the arrangement. Those who depended on news relayed by others were inevitably the last to hear it. But an ideal courier was not always available. A rider carrying an urgent missive and well provided with fresh mounts could sometimes cover a hundred and fifty or even two hundred kilometers a day, but the cost of such a messenger was, more often than not, beyond the reach of the average merchant, being reserved for princes. And the prince was well aware of the risk he took if he used only one route for an important message. Sometimes the messenger would get no further than the first turn in the wood.

It was no wonder, then, that the business world was much interested in establishing a common communications network. From the twelfth century onward, messages could be sent more or less regularly between the Italian towns. In the following century, when the Champagne fairs were at their peak, the Florentine *Calimala* guild dispatched a courier in both directions at the start and at the close of each of the six fairs. By the fourteenth century, this seemed insufficient to the businessmen who wanted to speculate more specifically on the fluctuations in the market caused by the interaction between trade and politics. In 1357, seventeen Florentine companies united to form a common organization, the *Scarsella dei mercanti fiorentini*, which ensured a weekly service between Florence and Avignon by way of Genoa in some twelve to fourteen days. Avignon was a collection point for information from most of Europe, and certainly from north of the Alps.

This scheme would not have been financially possible if the *Scarsella* had carried only the mail of its members. Other companies were able to make use of it, too, but in the knowledge that their mail would be delivered only one or two days later than that of the seventeen founder members. Nevertheless, a small businessman knew that mail entrusted to the *Scarsella* still arrived before anything given to a carrier or a friend traveling in that direction. Although they would miss opportunities, it was better than the alternatives.

The Florentines were not unique in this. During the fourteenth century, Barcelona set up a system of public messengers that was open to merchants whenever private interests did not interfere with the collective interest. Provided that they paid the right price, the inhabitants of Barcelona could use the system for their private letters:

> I, Francesc de Peramola, courier and citizen of Barcelona, agree and promise to you, Miquel de Manresa and Johan de Lobera the younger, merchants and citizens of Barcelona, by firm and legitimate stipulation, that in the fifteen days counting from the twelfth hour of the night of this present day, I shall go to Bruges by way of Montpellier and the city of Paris, to deliver for you in the said towns and cities the letters that you will entrust to me.
>
> I will not carry nor accept any other letters except yours during the period of my journey in these regions.
>
> If by any chance I do not accomplish this journey in the time stated, I promise to return, reinstate, and render to you everything that was given to me relating to this journey except the case in which I was delayed by a just impediment.

The courier Peramola was to receive thirty-four Aragon florins with a bonus of another four for each day saved if he reached Bruges in less than fifteen days. At such a price, the letter sent on 14 March 1418 must have been something very exceptional. Normally a Barcelona merchant was content to add his letters to the general mail even at the risk of a change of itinerary or delivery date. The courier Ricardo Dalamanya, for example, postponed his departure from Malines for six écus. He even agreed, for this price, to delay by two days his regular delivery to Barcelona. He who paid the piper called the tune. In an attempt to stamp out such abuses, the Council of Barcelona in 1444 limited to twenty-four hours any "advantage" to a single individual that was prejudicial to the business affairs of the town as a whole.

During the same period, the Hanseatic League set up correspondence offices that performed a double function: writing letters for those who needed such a service and sending the letters. The parish priest of St. Peter's in Novgorod specialized in such work. In London, three clerks were appointed to this task by the Hanseatic merchants. The desire for a better service became general. Montpellier established a regular link with Toulouse,

Marseilles, and a few other towns in its area of commercial dealings. Dijon similarly had a messenger service to Paris and Bruges.

This did not mean that news traveled fast. Even if not delayed it would take three weeks for a letter to go from Paris to Genoa. It was only slightly quicker—sixteen to eighteen days—from London to Barcelona, while Florence to Bruges took at least twenty to twenty-five days in favorable weather. As for correspondence between London and Venice, delays recorded during the fifteenth century vary from twenty-three to fifty-one days.

At this kind of speed, the unexpected was more likely to occur. The longer the journey, the greater the likelihood of accidents, unfortunate encounters, and chances of delay. It was always advisable to send the same letter by two different carriers, and even by two different routes. Bills of exchange had to be numbered. Even when storms and Barbary pirates could be avoided, long journeys required special care. The Venetian Andrea Barbarigio sent no fewer than seven copies of one letter to his agent in Acre.

By the fourteenth century, no longer content to work in the dark, a merchant was devoting a significant part of his time to his business correspondence. The letters of the Veckinchusen brothers in the quite modest archives of their Baltic branch office in Revel run into hundreds. But the best collection of letters revealing the activities of a businessman are those exchanged between 1364 and 1410 between the merchant of Prato, Francesco di Marco Datini, and his agents in major trading centers such as Barcelona, Valencia, Avignon, Genoa, and Pisa. There are 125,549 letters, two-thirds of which date from the decade 1395–1405!

At the peak of Datini's career—one that, it should be stressed, did not approach in level and volume those of some of the great Florentine businessmen—the correspondence amounted to nearly 10,000 letters a year. There was a constant flow of information: 15,604 letters from Florence to Pisa, 5,652 letters from Pisa to Florence. No wonder Datini's Florentine agent in Avignon complained: "What with reading and answering letters, it takes up half our time!"

In their advice to merchants both young and old, the manuals offered fixed facts and figures that were sometimes out-of-date. Correspondence gave information that was up-to-date but often limited to one particular instance. The letters related what was being shouted or whispered in the marketplace and stalls. Communication in one market was thus at once a prerequisite for an effective communication network beyond the seas and mountains and, more simply, for business in that same market. Success in the marketplace depended on the merchant's ability to adjust to the local situation.

Partners and Middlemen

Unfortunately, once on the spot, neither the manuals nor the eagerly perused letters can have been of much help to the German finding himself in deepest

Russia, the Italian stepping off his ship in London, or the Catalan setting foot for the first time on African soil. His fellow countrymen would have extended only a moderately helping hand, for the newcomer would in too many respects represent the competition for them to pass on the best advice. Marco Polo's silence about the existence of the many Venetians and Genoese who had preceded him, and whom he encountered across the trade routes of China and at the court of Kublai Khan, stems from his desire to make himself seem important and to present his expedition as another of the many "marvels" of his story. It also reflects his relative isolation.

The first problem to be solved was one of language. It was a daily preoccupation, even if sometimes more important than at other times. Dino Rapondi, Philip the Bold's banker and counselor, passed the major part of his life in Paris and Bruges. He eventually began to sign his name as "Dyne Raponde," gallicizing it just as had the great spice merchant "Henri Orlant," who kept a shop for luxury goods in Paris during this period and whose real name—Enrico Orlandi—was long since forgotten. Much greater difficulties were faced by the Solingen armorer, Albert Cherf, who arrived for the first time in Paris in 1456 to sell iron and bronze spades, scythes, and sword blades. One wonders how he had learned enough French to manage among the other traders. So far as the Polo brothers were concerned, we should not forget that they would have encountered twenty or thirty different languages on their journey through Persia and China, languages that no teacher in Venice could have taught them.

Of course, businessmen were not the only ones who had to adapt to other languages. Giovanni di Andriolo Guadagnabene, a cleric from Piacenza in Italy, was equally at a loss when, in 1381, he was appointed papal tax collector in Portugal. It would be curious to know how the four Italians fared who succeeded each other in the same post in Poland between 1391 and 1408. All royal administrations had to face up to this problem when they gave up exclusively local recruitment. The jurist Gérard de Courtinne, who ended his career as bishop in his hometown of Soissons, had been successively a student in Montpellier, a judge in Nîmes, and then ambassador in Aragon, Castile, and finally England. University teachers would undoubtedly have taught in Latin, but litigants in Nîmes and courtiers in London would certainly not have used the language of the *Codex* and the *Digest* in their daily lives.

Apart from the rudiments—of French in the larger Italian towns, of Italian and Flemish in Lübeck—we find little indication of any instruction in the living languages. If any merchant returning home from abroad set up as a teacher of foreign languages for the benefit of his nephews we have no evidence of it. The apprenticeship seems to have been served on the spot. What does seem likely is that these medieval travelers had a very good ear and a facility for picking up new languages. A little would have had to go a long way, and many successful careers must have relied on people's ability to convey their needs in sign language.

So it is easy to appreciate how necessary middlemen must have been to a much-traveled merchant. Present at the various marketplaces, they were there to help him and to check up on him as well. They often held an official position in trading, defined by the public authority in agreement with the local trade organizations. Like sworn brokers, they guaranteed the honesty of transactions, the quality of the products, and the conformity of prices. From the point of view of the marketplace and the opportunities of each trader in general, they formed a barrier between visiting foreigners and the local merchants. Generally optional, but difficult to bypass, their intervention was sometimes obligatory, particularly in cases where the outsider wanted to use public equipment and premises such as the port, the measures, or the covered market. To unload a ship or measure a barrel required the appearance of the public official appointed to the job. Those most likely to complain about the need to use these "swallowers"—as those who supervised the unloading of wine were known—or the onion measurers at the port in Paris were people like the wine grower from Bourg-la-Reine or Chaillot, and not the real foreigners who were quite pleased to find labor, an introduction, and a guarantee awaiting them on arrival.

There seem to have been two types of middleman, combining two services—reception and advice. The "hosts," the innkeepers, were mainly people who provided accommodation, but the inn also served as a depot for stranded travelers or for those who intended to return at a later date and wished to leave some unsold goods there until their next stay. Nor were the innkeepers averse to becoming involved in such dealings. They sometimes allowed credit. They advised and warned foreigners. They introduced them to other people and sometimes even entered into partnership, putting some of their own money into their client's business.

Alongside the innkeeper, and sometimes in competition with him, was the broker, typically the specialist in this area. In Paris there was a broker in wine, in grain, or in horses. In some other markets, such as Toulouse, one broker was in charge of a street or a neighborhood.

Less strictly assigned to a particular product or area, the broker in Barcelona might deal at the same time in wool, saffron, silk, wax, leather, fish, oil, cheese, iron, coral, hemp, and nuts. Apparently holding a higher status in the Barcelona marketplace than the "neck brokers" who dealt with inshore fishing for sardines and other modest merchandise, the "ear brokers" also dealt in rented property as well as fulfilling the function of what would today be known as a matrimonial agency. A successfully arranged marriage earned the broker five sous if the dowry was less than fifty *livres*. There was a proportional deduction for dowries more than that amount, and he only received one sou per fifty *livres* if the dowry exceeded three hundred *livres*.

Although a specialist, the broker was only a middleman, and he was almost always forbidden by statute from any personal involvement in business affairs. As an expert appointed by the authorities, municipal or royal, it was his job to bring together buyers and sellers, but nothing more. Many towns forbade brokers from trading at the same time in the goods that they handled. If a Parisian broker had too much wine in his own wine cellar, or if his brokering was earning little during a difficult trading period, he had to resign temporarily from his office in order to carry out a deal in competition with those whom he usually assisted and looked after:

> Today (23 February 1420) Pierre Musnier, wine broker, has been given leave of absence so that he may work as an innkeeper and retail wine in view of the high cost of living and also so that he can keep and earn his living and that of his wife and children, provided that, during the period he carries out such business, he shall not exercise his office, under pain of losing the said office.

In more liberal Barcelona, where it was possible to trade without a broker, he was allowed to pursue a variety of activities, including keeping a tavern, hiring out slaves, and even shipping.

Whether as broker, sworn seller, inspector of weights and measures, gauger, measurer, or counter, with jurisdiction over corn, wine, cloth, nuts, firewood, or coal, the middleman provided the traveler with advice that was all the more welcome, since the responsibilities of convoys and far-off markets were often entrusted to the young and inexperienced members of the business or even to mere agents. The decisions involved in buying and selling were much helped by advice obtained on the spot.

There was just one disadvantage in this system, and that was one of scale. However experienced, the broker gave, or was supposed to give, the same advice at the same time to all his clients. Thus the greatest benefit was always reaped by the merchant on the spot or represented by a partner who was both competent and involved personally in the business. In other words, once again, the bigger concerns benefited, particularly when the establishment of branch offices made it possible for local initiative—now given an increased degree of financial autonomy—to react immediately to unexpected fluctuations in the market. When the Rapondi's interests in Avignon were managed by Andrea Rapondi, or those of the Medici in Bruges by Tommaso Portinari, decisions no longer depended on the broker's recommendation. The latter confined himself to his role of informant while the businessman used the information as he wished.

Innkeepers and specialized middlemen knew the market. They knew who sold what, when, and where. They collected up-to-date news. They ensured the continuity of the market. And they had the linguistic abilities that the newcomer so sorely needed. In Barcelona, where brokers were obliged to work in pairs, the rules prescribed that one of the two should know how to read and write. Interpreters in business conversations, they were also specialists in technical vocabulary, for it is one thing to know how to ask the way and quite another to find one's way around specialized terminology. The same fish or cloth might have a different name from one town to another, while the same name was often used for different commodities.

The middleman was a servant, but also an inspector, and the majority of municipal regulations made a variety of activities obligatory for the sole purpose of exerting some influence over the market. Extensive measures were sometimes taken to ensure that foreign merchants did not carry out their business alone: in Livonia, for example, it was forbidden to teach the Slav language to nonmembers of the Hanseatic League. Thus a translator had to be present at all transactions.

A foreigner who, in exchange for an illusory service, was forced to conduct his business through such intermediaries would clearly feel somewhat inhibited. Foreigners visiting Paris were required to "take French company," in other words, to form an association with a Parisian citizen if they wanted to bring any kind of merchandise into Paris along the surrounding waterways—the river basin of the middle Seine and its tributaries, and particularly the ports and the bridges of the capital. In the majority of cases, this amounted to halving the profits. Forced to bear, in return for only half the profits, the total initial investment and all the risks associated with loss or poor sales, the foreigner found himself in a very disadvantaged situation vis-à-vis his Parisian rival. It was one thing when the "French companion" was a relative or represented a useful connection, or when, with his greater knowledge of the place, the customs, or the clients, he could offer real help. It was quite another matter when a foreign merchant who knew the Grève market well was obliged to take on at random some local citizen who could offer him neither help nor advice, or when the clerk and the concierge at the Hôtel de Ville got together to offer their services and, for a price, were prepared to recommend absolutely anyone for absolutely anything.

When the business partnership was genuine, and the tasks were really shared, the middleman could be a useful cog in the commercial wheel. The "innkeeper-fishmongers" of the Caux region in Normandy, and those of Dieppe in particular, fell into this category. They contributed to financing the fishermen's boats through "contracts of partnership." They saw to the payment of taxes and dues to the lord, particularly by the wholesale buyers from Rouen, Amiens, and Paris. In return for half the profits, they dealt with every aspect of marketing. Since the fisherman did not have to deal with selling his fish himself, he had more time to spend at sea. It was money well spent. As an official, the innkeeper-salesman had sworn to defend the king's interests, but also those of the seaman. A middleman of this kind had an important economic role. To use his services was more a matter of delegation than a constraint.

On a larger scale, the "woolmen" held a similar place in 'the English wool trade. As intermediaries between the producers and the foreign buyers, chiefly Italians, these woolmen were sometimes themselves producers. Their knowledge of new developments in the wool market was to contribute, as did their financial investment, to the development of the home cloth industry. Involved in many economic sectors, and with their own premises where they could pursue a variety of commercial activities, they were anything but small specialized middlemen. In London they might be cloth merchants, but they were also haberdashers, spice merchants, and furriers. They were businessmen who played their roles in the industrial cycle, which was to invest, manage, and organize. As much wholesalers as middlemen, they came to dominate trade. By the fifteenth century, those who set up in the wool counties of the Cotswolds would be people of consequence.

Even when the buyer was in direct and constant contact with the producer—the monasteries, for example, had their regular clients—nobody would be so foolish as to underestimate the woolmen. Their knowledge of the available products was well known. Their ability to lay their hands instantly on the quantities required was appreciated. They knew their way around the fifty-one different qualities of wool—not to mention those from the northern counties—that featured on price lists during the late Middle Ages. However well he thought he knew the country and its goods, a foreigner would get lost. Using the woolman was a good investment.

Practical knowledge, then, could be acquired only in the shop or in the marketplace. Handed down from the elder to the younger merchant or from the local expert to the traveler, professional knowledge was nothing without the opportunity to examine the goods. Even the most expert trader would not know how to distinguish among the eight different kinds of cotton known as Pegolotti—cotton from Syria, Byzantium, Apulia, Calabria, Sicily, and Malta, white cotton thread, and colored cotton—unless he had handled it or had the help of a local expert. He would not manage any better even in a modest market like Narbonne, which offered cloth from Arras, Bruges, Saint-Omer, Chartres, Reims, Figeac, Cahors, Albi, and Lerida, as well as from Narbonne itself. All these types of cloth were taxed according to four different rates. Anyone trying to manage alone would be sure to be cheated.

Nothing could ever be taken for granted by the merchant seeking knowledge of the world in order to exploit its resources and needs. Arriving in

Paris for the fifteenth time, the Florentine Buonaccorso Pitti encountered, in a capital governed for the young Charles VI by his uncles, a market that differed in every way from the one he had known so well in the Paris of Charles V. Between the ages of eighteen and thirty-two, Pitti had traveled all over the world, in war as well as peacetime. No manual could have prepared him for the changes that would take place between the date of his first departure in 1373 and that of his final return home to Florence in 1396.

The businessman traveled to become informed, to trade, to make contacts, and to establish his own people abroad. The less successful merchant would join a convoy, charter a ship, travel with his wagon. His profit would be smaller but of the same nature. The convoy or the ship would have the added advantage of offering opportunities for companionship with others like himself. As the long journeys unrolled, these travelers could pool their valuable experience for the benefit of the group.

The best of all meeting places was the fair. In a known place on a fixed date, the fairs were periodic gathering places for the merchant community. From one fair to the next, merchants met again and again, continuing conversations begun at the previous fair. They got to know new people, a son who had succeeded his father in the business or was about to, an agent who was setting up on his own, a hitherto insignificant merchant who was poised to break into the market. They learned who had gone out of business, who had died. The opinion of each about everything combined to form the opinion of all about each one.

It was to the Lendit fair in June 1395 that Charles VI's treasurer came in search of the extra furs needed to celebrate both the peace and the marriage of Isabelle of France and Richard II of England. This was to be the golden opportunity for two merchants from Tournai and Mons who happened to be there seeking business. And it was at the Mid-Lent fair at Compiègne that this same treasurer, realizing that he had not placed a large enough order, issued an appeal for more furs. It was the business of the successful importer to hear his words and write to his agent without delay.

This was the lesson that the medieval businessman learned from attending the fairs: here were opportunites to be seized and information to be gleaned. The two went together. The merchant who did not attend lost his chance to compete in the market.

FOUR

Privileges

*T*he world of business had little to do with that reflected in and ruled by the law of the feudal jurist. Though very different, the almost-Roman Law used by Italian judges and notaries and the customary law of northern and western Europe, strongly marked by its barbarian roots, had one thing in common: they both predated the expansion of urban centers and institutions.

Business and Public Power

The businessman emerged from a feudal and rural background governed by customary law. Foreign to a system of social relations based on cultivation of the land and organized in a pyramid of landed and personal rights dominated by vertical bonds, the businessman stood outside the institutions provided by feudal custom as well as those governing lands held in exchange for payment in money, service, or kind. He was governed neither by the rules of chivalrous society nor by those of the peasant world. The exchange of protection for personal service, the mutual but unequal solidarity of those who gave and those who owed, the inheritance, de facto and then legal, of situations and bonds—none of these had any more meaning for the businessman setting out across the high seas than for the artisan who had no resources except his own talent and abilities. It would be a long time before such people were considered part of normal society. Their activities would lie essentially outside the law of the jurists, taught in the faculties of civil and canon law.

This is not to say that the public powers had no concern for those involved in commerce and banking. Whether in the form of a ruler or the councils of city-states, the state was always there, initially as guarantor of the support it gave to and recognized in economic activity. No one lived without privileges in a period when everyone had his or her rights, and privileges were simply adaptations of the law to the specific needs of particular social groups.

Privileges were those recognized customs or promulgated statutes that defined constituent bodies and situated them in the larger world. Towns had their own highly complex privileges. Thus Paris was able to obtain for its merchant companies the monopoly of all commercial navigation on the Seine and its tributaries between Nogent-sur-Seine, Sens, Compiègne, and Vernon. The others, "outsiders," from Cologne or Rouen or even nearby Bourg-la-Reine, had to take "French company" or, in other words, enter into more or less fictitious partnership with a Parisian citizen who thus made a small profit without taking any risk. Similarly, in Southampton, citizens were exempted, after 1189, from paying the "custom," or duty, imposed on other merchants.

Privilege had no muscle unless the public authorities guaranteed its benefits and punished any infringements: in Southampton, as in Paris, this was a matter for royal justice. Thus a right to monopolies was established, founded in part on concessions or confirmations obtained from the prince and partly on the precedents resulting from litigation and attempts to infringe the privileges.

Although they arose independently in different places, these privileges tended to be of the same order, giving cohesion and a legal foundation to the *métiers* in France, to the "crafts" in England, and to the *arti* in Tuscan towns. Since they normally governed the internal organization of these associations, the privileges approved by public authorities could, for their benefit, shape the law that regulated their relations, both individual and collective, with others.

Not that the chief function of such a "privilege" was to give this or that person some exclusive right. During the Middle Ages, "privilege" meant "order," not "advantage." It put each person in his or her allotted place; to step out of it was to violate the public order. A prince who breached that order, or allowed it to be breached, would no longer be fulfilling the function that legitimized his power, just as the independent city-state, in so doing, would lose the consensus that enabled it, however temporarily, to exercise the prerogatives of state.

Privilege was the only basis of a law of business founded on the more or less spontaneously granted concession of a public power. This authority might predate the economic group or have emerged from its ranks. Thus it played a part in forming the nature of the de facto social body. When he speaks of "all those who attend the fairs of . . . ," the king of France or the count of Flanders is defining a hypothetical group to which a law can be applied. A privilege granted to all merchants "going to the Champagne fairs and returning from them" clearly highlights how much of an anomaly the merchant was in medieval society: it was up to the merchant, and him alone, to register as one of the beneficiaries of a privilege, thus coming under the law.

This could mean protection under the law. A privilege granted by Henry II Plantagenet was just this for the Cologne merchants who came to the port of London in 1157. Those who went to the fairs had to obtain a "safe-conduct," and the one issued for the Champagne fairs, supported and later—since the early thirteenth century—ratified by the king himself, seemed particularly attractive to the merchant. To attack a merchant and his goods on the road to Champagne was to offend the king's own person. Ambitious or important merchants sought safe-conducts that offered effective protection during the period of the fair, together with reliable justice should anything go wrong. It is easy to see how the value of a safe-conduct and the success of a fair depended to a considerable extent on the ability of the judiciary to make its authority respected.

Instead of privileges, we also find the opposite, something that was equally important in establishing the legal foundations of the business world. Thus Louis XI, concerned with promoting the success of his fairs in Lyons, issued a decree on 20 October 1462 forbidding his subjects from attending the fairs in Geneva:

> We order that henceforth no merchant or any other person of our kingdom may go or take their merchandise or goods to the fairs that are held in Geneva.
>
> And also that no other foreign merchants shall, having been to the said fairs or returning from them, carry any goods or merchandise through the confines of this our kingdom, for whatsoever reason, pretext or action, on pain of losing their goods or merchandise that may have been taken to or brought from the said fairs and of a discretionary fine.

More often, the privilege was concerned with matters of taxation. This was entirely a matter for the state, which decreed both the levels of taxation and any individual exemptions. It is hardly necessary to repeat that such exemptions were in no way favors, their aim being to attract or consolidate any trade considered necessary to the "public good." Inevitably the small trader paid the price for the bigger merchant who was considered more desirable. This was the method used by the king of England to encourage the Italian importers of English wool to come to England, as well as the Hanseatic merchants whom the English preferred to see carrying on their business in London rather than in Bruges. Again, in these two cases, it was a matter of exempting the Italian and Hanseatic merchants—in the face of a certain amount of xenophobic antagonism from the English merchants, jealous of the favored treatment being given to their rivals—from a system of indirect taxation recently set up by the king himself. In other cases the privilege went further, placing those benefiting from it outside a common law even when it was firmly established. One can see from these examples the degree to which custom stood in the way of economic development.

Just how inappropriate the system could be can be seen in the case of the laws of *aubain* and *reprisals*. *Aubain* was the right to confiscate the goods of a foreigner who died unexpectedly when away from home. It dated from a period when the word *aubain* referred to an uprooted peasant, unattached to a lord or estate, a fugitive, or an unknown person. He had no rights and was forbidden to marry freely or to leave the little he possessed to his children. The right of *aubain* was one of the little perks enjoyed by the lord; any profit he made from the confiscated belongings of a dead stranger compensated in part for what he lost on those men from his estate who ran away to live and die elsewhere. It was unlikely that any businessman would accept the principle of such an uncertain form of taxation.

The lord understood quite well that to seize the goods of a traveler who died on his journey would assuredly mean the death of that trade route. And we are not talking just of the well-established merchant with a family and personal estate; this was even less wise when the new systems of partnership and shared capital meant that the goods carried by a partner or even an employee were owned by the group. Whether big or small, what company would have agreed to place part of its assets at the mercy of the accidental death of the agent accompanying the wagons or managing the warehouse in which the goods were stored before sale?

The development of public power was opportune, facilitating a new status for the outsider. The city-states intended to be the sole arbiter of who would participate in economic activities. While the sovereigns took over the right of *aubain* and any profits from it, it was chiefly in order to rationalize this legal discrimination, applying it on the scale of a whole kingdom. Clearly there was all the difference in the world between a vagrant passing through a rural lord's estate and a merchant traveling through a kingdom with its eye on the broader horizon. From the thirteenth century, even as the right of *aubain* seemed to be receiving further reinforcement in customary law, this expression of a rural and somewhat inward-looking society was allowed, by mutual agreement, to fall into disuse, insofar as businessmen traveling or living abroad were concerned. The suppression of the right of *aubain* was to be central in the many negotiations between princes and between towns. Collective privileges were offered instead.

Agreement was reached in a similar way on the matter of the rights of salvage, which allowed the owner of the shore to take possession of anything that might wash up after a shipwreck. Anything that sank out at sea was obviously lost, but the majority of ships rarely sailed far from shore and most wrecks occurred when ships were thrown against the rocks. There were often cargoes to be salvaged, particularly anything that floated. Salt was washed away in an instant, bales of wool in less than an hour, but barrels of wine and herring floated for several hours. Merchants were prepared to pay a good price for the right to rescue them.

> If the men or the merchants of the kingdom of Norway in the country of Flanders, or the men of the country of Flanders in the kingdom of Norway, are victim of any shipwreck, we desire that they may be allowed to recover and possess, or have recovered and repossess, their wrecked ships with all their goods, for as long as they do not believe them to be lost.
> The bailiff who will be there, in Norway or in Flanders, must, in the case of a shipwreck, protect and defend the shipwrecked men, their ships, and all their possessions from all annoyance and all spoliation, on pain of punishment according to the severity of the crime or the negligence.

Before long it was the turn of the right to *reprisals*, known as the rights of marque. If a man from Barcelona committed some crime or left a debt in Toulouse, in the absence of a judge, and bearing in mind that it would be very costly to go to court in Barcelona, *reprisals* were taken from another citizen of Barcelona who happened to be in Toulouse. It was up to the latter to prove that the blame was not his but that of his fellow citizen. He would have to return to Barcelona to be reimbursed—or to obtain justice. This was another instance of the continuation of a law from an earlier period when foreign debts were unusual. By the time they had become the rule, the right of *reprisal* could effectively paralyze men and business. Sovereigns were only too aware of this situation and were cautious in the number of letters of marque that they signed. Collective privileges and negotiations between cities often brought such practices to an end, through an awareness of "national" solidarity and the benefits of replacing *reprisals* with mutual representation. The debtor's fellow countryman would no longer tolerate the bad behavior of others. He would instead take over the defaulter's interests. There was always a place for solidarity, but in a contractual legal framework, and between merchants of good faith.

It was less easy to abolish the right of salvage. The Hanseatic League was eventually allowed to recover its wrecked or sunken cargoes, normally the property of the owners of the various riverbanks and seacoasts; but it involved endless disputes to establish that a cask washed up on the beach had originated in a Hanseatic ship or to estimate the cost of the delay elapsing between shipwreck and compensation. Indeed, the dangers of the sea brought about as many conflicts as opportunities, and it seems that there was bad faith on both sides.

The Group and the Market

A privilege did not place the individual outside the group; it merely placed him in another group, defined by a collection of privileges other than those of common law. Personally and financially protected, exempted from the usual taxes and customary laws that would have ruined him if they had been in operation in every marketplace where he traded, the businessman attempted to establish his own rights and his own justice. When he was away from home, an exemption from the local justice allowed him to settle matters with his counterparts that concerned only them. In Paris as in Bruges, the Lombards handled internal matters themselves, a tacit agreement often taking the place of privilege. The medieval judge's role was, more than anything, that of arbitrator, and the best way to avoid the local judge was to leave him out of conflicts within the group of foreigners. Sometimes, as at the Champagne fairs, such communities—the Italians or the Hanseatic merchants in Bruges—would obtain the right to judge their nationals openly.

As proper courts of law began to be established within the business community, it was in everyone's interests to have them recognized by the public authority. The highest court in the system, the trade tribunal, became an essential cog in the wheel of public justice. Thus we find, in Florence, the *Mercanzia,* a judicial court established at the beginning of the fourteenth century by the "Major Arts"—the six great guilds representing international trade, the cloth industry, and banking—that dominated the city's governing council, the *Signoria,* appointing its *priori,* and the army for which it chose the *gonfaloniere.* A stone's throw from the *Palazzo della Signoria,* the *Mercanzia's* building, with its austere facade ornamented with the crests of the *Arti,* took up an entire side of the square. This was a far cry from tacit understandings. The Florentine businessman's legal system was an institution, and one that was visible to all. This was to be true also of the *Curia di Petizion* in Venice.

Outside the city-states, and with a smaller degree of autonomy, were special courts such as that operated in Paris by the provost of merchants and his four magistrates. They had jurisdiction over everything relating to the privileges of the town as well as its association of those involved in river trading, the *Marchandise de l'eau.* Fraud in the sales place or in the timetable, disputes relating to contracts or prices, or arguments over quantity and quality, whether or not satisfaction had been obtained from the royal court at the Châtelet, were all matters for the court of merchants that had its headquarters in the *Maison aux Piliers* on the Place de Grève. If unsuccessful, however, it was to the king's normal judicial system—in the Parliament—that the litigant would have to appeal; ultimately it was royal authority that would or would not uphold the merchants' decision. This could lead to a situation where the same man of law was simultaneously performing the functions of town procurator and king's procurator before the court of the provost of merchants.

Guarantor of the privileges it granted and of the everyday realities it confirmed, the public authority sometimes became involved in the organization of trade, even participating at times. This was the case when the state—the prince or the town—created or strengthened monopolies, or when a more or less interventionist policy channeled or limited new ventures, or forced the business world to follow a particular line of investment or relations.

Such interventions were already in evidence in fourteenth-century France. The tax authorities became involved in the commercial distribution of salt, which was essential to the preservation of meat and fish. This had always been a free trade, given that anyone could buy or sell salt, that no corporate body was involved that might act for the benefit of a group, and that decisions about purchases at the salt pans and transport to the consumers depended on the judgment of the merchant alone. But it was the king who fixed prices. By the middle of the century, no one still believed that this restriction was justified by the need to prevent speculation. It was also the king who got his officers—the *grènetiers* who looked after the warehouses (*greniers*) where the precious salt was stored—to administer a system that fixed the order in which stock deposited in the warehouse by the different merchants could be sold, the so-called paper turn. A free market had become highly controlled. The new regulations proved to be sufficiently popular with the consumer to protect the salt tax from serious attack by reformers in the 1350s, and again around 1410. Even when the salt tax was increased, the people realized, for once, the advantages to be had from state intervention.

A very different kind of monopoly, but one that was equally strict, was that of alum. This trade, in Genoa, was the object of concessions and state tax-farming. The importance of alum, the only good-quality mordant that could be used by the wool industry, is well known. Without it the dye would not take and the wool would lack suppleness. Unfortunately, alum came from Phocaea in Asia Minor, a Genoese possession since 1346. Nothing changed until 1462, when a source of alum was discovered at Tolfa near Civitavecchia. It was to make the fortune of the papacy and the Medici family.

The Commune of Genoa was determined to profit from, but not to become a trader in, alum. Thus it leased out the rights to exploit the precious mineral, from its mining in Phocaea to its sale by the tradesmen of Bruges or elsewhere. Thus different companies became involved in this business—the Cattaneo and the Doria families, followed by the Draperio company in the mid-fifteenth century. A lease obviously implied a monopoly. The successful bidder won it and cut out the competition. We should not assume, however, that these decisions were freely made. Sometimes it was not the highest bidder but the best connected who won, and bidding had as much to do with influence as the regulation of prices.

The state's involvement in the alum market was the exception, not the rule, in Genoa. To the depths of their souls the Genoese remained individualists. In Venice, by contrast, *dirigisme,* or intervention, ruled. The Council of the Republic openly regulated business affairs, introducing state measures to ensure both legal and material security. As the economy prospered, this collective interventionism, an expression of the solidarity of the great merchants in foreign markets, from Alexandria to Bruges, became ever more pervasive. It came to a peak in the fifteenth century, during the 1420s and '30s, when Venetian prosperity was at its height, before running out of steam through lack of vision. Although it brought greater security in the short term, this state intervention eventually stifled a business environment where everything was played out inside the high walls of the Senate, where agents of the republic decided commercial policy and where a network of contacts and family relations led to the creation of a patriciate that, in 1297, was frozen in place by the *Serrata del Consiglio.* This was the time when the noble families, fiercely resisting the rise of ambitious outsiders, closed their ranks. It was the Senate that prescribed the kind of ships to be used, having them built in a state arsenal that employed some two thousand workers. Galleys and galleasses were hired out to merchants who wished to participate in this or that trade. They even had to accept the tonnage chosen by the Senate, which also dictated the date of departure and itinerary of the convoy. In short, to trade in Venice was to finance a part of Venice's trade.

It is true that the Venetian Senate, like the Genoese Grand Council, consisted of those same great merchants who financed business; that collective decisions were informed by collective information; and that the experience of everyone involved contributed to such decisions. Interventionism inhibited private ventures, but not the individual's contribution. A system in which membership in the group that managed the system and profited from it was restricted to the closed ranks of the patrician class was obviously privileged. But this was far from being a public power that could impose an external standard of fiscal and commercial guarantees. The Venetian guarantee was mutual: the state and business were one and the same.

Organization and regulation often went hand in hand with privileges. The public authorities liked to channel a particular trade into a "staple"—the place where a body of merchants had the exclusive right to purchase certain goods for export—in order to simplify and control its activities, and to ensure that the right taxes were paid. This system of staples for the sale and purchase of goods, with obligatory centers for financial deals and regulations, was reassuring to some but restrictive to others. It had very real advantages for the local wine growers, allowing them to benefit from a movement of trade that they might not otherwise have attracted. The repercussions of the system for the retail trade and service industries were also of considerable significance, as the innkeeper and haberdasher were well aware.

The siting of a staple was fiercely disputed. The price for winning and keeping it was the price of the prince's favor. In Paris the Place de Grève, which hitherto had shared with the Halles the trade in wines from the Ile-de-France and Burgundy, did not finally become the staple for French wines until 1413. Loire wines continued to be sold near the windmills of the Temple. Later, in 1491, Maximilian punished the merchants of Bruges, who were showing too much of a taste for independence, by depriving them of the papal alum trade to northern and eastern Europe and transferring it to the staple at Antwerp. The continental staple for English wool, still shared among several towns in the thirteenth century, had only just become fixed in Saint-Omer in 1313 when it was transferred, in 1315, to Amiens. Reestablished in Saint-Omer in 1320, it was then sited in Bruges in 1325, only to be completely abolished in 1326. For twelve years the staple for exports was to be in England itself, before Edward III reestablished it in Antwerp in 1338. Two years later he moved it back to Bruges. In 1353 it was back in England. Ten years were to pass before it reappeared in the new Plantagenet port on the Continent: Edward III established it in Calais in 1363. It was to stay there until 1558.

We can only guess at the deals and persuasion that lay beneath the surface of these continual changes, but we know something about the cost of the privileges that exempted this or that individual from the staple. In order to collect supplies of wool directly from England, the great Italian companies of the 1330s offered Edward the unlimited credit that was to lead to their eventual ruin.

When a staple was established, resistance was organized:

In the year of grace 1331 on the Saturday of the feast of St Bartholomew, at about the hour of Prime, in the house where the *echevin* [deputy mayor] of the commune of Saint-Jean d'Angély meets, in the presence of *sire* Pierre Boisseau, mayor of the said commune, and several citizens and officials of the said commune, the aforementioned mayor declared:

"Sirs, it is true that the people of Flanders have much harmed, wronged, hurt, and injured our people, you and the merchants of this land, and that they wish to make and keep many unwarranted usages that would be to the great damage and prejudice of the people and merchants of this land. Therefore we have written about this to the people and merchants of Bordeaux, Libourne, and La Rochelle.

"And it has been ordained and agreed that from each place, that is to say from Bordeaux, Libourne, La Rochelle, and Saint-Jean d'Angély, wise men will travel from here to Flanders and will call upon the people of Flanders to put aside and return to their former state the things mentioned above.

"And if they will not do this, the two representatives of each place mentioned above will go into the presence of the men of Bruges, who have promised to our people and merchants of this country to show them favors and courtesies, openness and freedom if we would move our staple to Flanders.

"And they will get the count of Flanders to agree and consent to this, and they will obtain good privileges and freedoms and will have them ratified by the king our lord."

They knew how to strike a deal. The citizens of Saint-Jean d'Angély were well aware of the price they would have to pay, and took upon themselves a tax of ten *deniers* per barrel of wine from the next wine harvest. But they knew the weapon that they could use: they could themselves move the staple for their exports of wine to Flanders. The people of Bruges, for their part, would understand exactly what they would have to grant in order to have such a market on their soil.

Interventionism and Its Constraints

The businessman could, then, expect a lot from the state but, with the exception of a few trading states, such as Venice and Lübeck, he was not quite part of it. Above all, and in all their endeavors, protagonists in the world of trade were part of the horizontal network of mutual relationships among partners who were equals in law, if not always in fortune. These relationships defined the group and gave it its shape. The closeness of ties varied. The artisan and shopkeeper were part of this network and would not have wished to remain outside it. The merchant—a businessman who manipulated financial as well as commercial dealings and who organized industrial life as well as the trade map—was less closely restrained, finding it quite easy to limit the effects of those constraints over which he had no power.

If the rigor of the corporate straitjacket was felt anywhere, it was Paris. But as trade began to expand in the capital of the last Capetians, the important merchants of the Place de Grève were increasingly able to escape from this grip. In Toulouse an organized trade like that of the spice merchants, importers of luxury goods from the Orient and elsewhere, agreed that the regulations inscribed in their statutes should apply only to retail sales.

Climbing a step on the ladder of the business world, the London merchant could not exempt himself from membership in a guild. He was obliged to join a "craft" or "company." But the woolman could join whatever guild he wished: the drapers, haberdashers, or even the spice merchants. The great merchants did not let mere formalities get in the way of their initiatives. In the fifteenth century one of the richest merchants in London was officially a "mercer." Everyone knew what he really was.

The system worked in the opposite way in Florence. Intended to provide a framework for artisans and small shopkeepers, the *arti* rapidly became the vehicles by which the great commercial and banking companies obtained control of the *Signoria* and the Tuscan economy. The chief companies were brazenly represented in each one of the "Major Arts." The business world took advantage of this multiplicity of contexts to assert its diverse interests.

Avoiding the restrictions of the system did not mean leaving the group. Submitting to them did not mean that there was no profit to be had. All were interested in a common defense of their professional interests, and even in the "publicity" to be derived from a collective image of quality composed from each merchant's reputation and sanctioned by reciprocal controls.

Perhaps the best expression of the local solidarity of the group is to be found in its concern for the reputation of its products. Wherever it was sold, a product was identified first of all by its place of origin. Wine was from Beaune, salt from Bourgneuf, cloth from Brussels, and gold thread from Lucca. To make one slip in quality, one fraudulent sale, was to damage the reputation of all. Confidence, the essential requirement in long-distance trading and in purchasing on credit, was acquired at the price of consistency in quality. The group was all too well aware of it and was quick to condemn anyone stepping out of line. The fault would be remedied where possible; members were expelled if necessary. The large number of regulations, which seem to reflect actual practice, were more than anything the *arte*'s response to the absentminded or the lazy.

There was another side to this coin. This common struggle to maintain reputations was also a fight against innovation. As in the case of the luxury cloth trade of the Flemish towns, many small traders were reluctant to understand that tastes change with customers and that yesterday's quality may be tomorrow's rejects.

The need for a communal organization was most acutely felt by those who worked abroad. Whether passing through or established for a period, the foreigner prayed for a common defense to represent him before the local authorities and to protect him in the face of local competition. They had to be far from home to best appreciate the strength of the natural bonds that stemmed from common origins.

Everywhere that commerce was carried on abroad, groups were organized. The Florentine *Arte di Calimala* appointed consuls in both Pisa and the Champagne fair towns. In nonaffiliated towns like London and Bruges, the Hanseatic League set up its own centers for the defense and representation of its members. The English "merchant adventurers" had their own appointed protector in Antwerp from 1305, known variously as mayor, captain, or consul, whose constant function was to ensure that each merchant received the due privileges granted by the duke of Brabant. These same merchant adventurers had in Bruges, half a century later, a "governor" whose job it was to represent what was beginning to be generally known in the Netherlands as the English "nation."

The sense of solidarity was no less strong in opposition to other professional groups. This was particularly true of the small world of the shop and the workshop, so unlike the world of international trade with its mix of diverse merchandise and destinations. Technical constraints were enough to prevent a worker in pewter from making clay pots, or a wool fuller from attempting to make a doublet. They produced what they could make in a particular workshop, with the available equipment, tools, or abilities. Specialization was almost inevitable, and the collective work practices that were most in need of defense were those which separated one group from a neighbor that might wish to compete with it. Thus the Parisian money changers, experts in metal alloys—with their weights and scales—were disturbed to see the goldsmiths establish themselves and their forges on the "Pont au Change," the "Exchange Bridge"—in fact the Grand Pont, opposite the Châtelet—and begin to trade in precious metals. For a goldsmith, gold and silver were raw materials, not themselves articles of trade. In 1419 the money changers were able to persuade the royal provost to forbid any "exchange activities" on the part of their neighbors the goldsmiths.

An avowed intention of the professional organizations was to limit the effects of competition. Their surveillance was aimed, above all, at production taking place outside their framework along with unauthorized commerce. The group's protections involved advertising the places and hours of commerce and systematically comparing the goods offered for sale. Woe betide the person who tried to go it alone: as a potential threat to the stability of the market, he would find himself implacably excluded. Here again, what was true for the tailor who made his workers stay up late into the night—and precisely for this reason was impossible to regulate—did not apply to the banker who would keep to himself information about trends in the market in Alexandria or the solvency of the duke of Burgundy. The group was as restrictive for the former as it was necessary. Unnecessary for the latter, the restrictions seemed few. The loyalties of the Bardi and Medici families lay elsewhere than in the *Arte di Calimala*.

The Parisian goldsmiths were quick to complain about the difference in treatment given to their petty trading activities and to those of the great merchants who never got into trouble for changing coins. An official at the Châtelet had to listen to their protestations:

> I took myself to the said bridge in Paris and enjoined Jacquet Lescot, the constable, to guard it.
> The latter informed me that, on Saturday the 22nd day of July 1419, on crossing the said bridge, he had found several goldsmiths who had their

forges open, their green cloths on the counter and coins on them, and that people had stopped at the aforementioned forges, offering to sell them coins.

The said goldsmiths said that there were other goldsmiths, twice as rich as they, who were changing far more money than they were, such as the spice merchants, blacksmiths, and cloth merchants, and who never got into trouble for it.

For which admission, I sealed up the coins that were thus found and confiscated by the said constable.

Having emerged as an expression of the professional community, the group took on an increasingly social role, thus providing itself with a double protection. Its intention was that only the members of a clearly defined group should benefit from the privileges that they had acquired in common and, moreover, that only a certain number be admitted into the group to enjoy these privileges. This social and professional Malthusianism of a group whose structure, in the case of the money changers, was not well defined led to the closing down of businesses or to problems caused by the need to accommodate, in this case, interference from other local professions and family loyalties.

It was an easy matter to limit the number of those entitled to enjoy a privileged status. Paris limited the advantages of the *Marchandise de l'eau* to members of the city guilds; and we know that by the fifteenth century the examination, the masterpiece, and the banquet required from apprentices seeking promotion to "master craftsman" in most of the organized guilds were possible only for a very few, usually the sons or nephews of masters. It took a seven-year apprenticeship to become a boatman at the port of the Louvre, which meant having the right to ferry up and down between the Louvre and the Nesle tower. The ferryman who, in 1449, tried to justify his right to work did not attempt to give evidence of his competence or refer to his apprenticeship. He thought it more relevant to mention that his father had been a boatman too.

In the towns of the Hanseatic League the group enjoying commercial privileges grew ever more select. Until the definitive constitution of the League was drawn up in 1356, any businessman born in a north German town, or even a non-German town on the Baltic like Stockholm, would be accepted at any marketplace on the North Sea or the Baltic. After this date the Hansa towns admitted only citizens of the member towns. This was further restricted, the diet of 1434 even going so far—though not entirely successfully—as to say that only citizens born in a Hanseatic town could be admitted into the League. In this way, outsiders who had been made citizens were excluded, though their sons were allowed in time to enjoy the privileges of citizenship.

In London, rigorous segregation was the rule, the people being divided into three categories. The true Londoner, who enjoyed all the advantages and freedoms of the city, who could, if he saw fit, open a workshop or a shop, but who also had to bear the brunt of taxation, was the "citizen," or "enfranchised" man. In the fourteenth century he would have been a member of a "craft" or "mystery," in the fifteenth century of a "company" or "fellow-ship." These societies were particular about who was allowed to join: the Company of Mercers admitted only outsiders with a capital of at least one hundred pounds.

Alongside the citizen was the "alien"—strictly speaking, the foreigner—who nevertheless enjoyed a relatively comfortable existence. They did not possess the freedoms of the former, but they had those defined by the privileges of their "nation." They may not have been Londoners, but as members of the Hanseatic League or of an Italian company, they had status. If they could not belong to an organized "nation," it was better for them to move on.

The third category was that of the "denizens," or immigrants. Although English, and perhaps even Londoners, they had no rights of citizenship. They were considered "foreigners" in their own city. This heterogeneous mass, in which rich and poor rubbed shoulders, did not constitute a group. They had no common interests to defend, nor the means to defend them. Their only hope was that one day they might join the ranks of a "company" or get their sons into one. But their weakness gave them little ammunition to conquer the right to privilege. A decree of 1463 made this legal marginali-zation a physical reality: all "foreigners" were to be confined to one district of London—Blancheappleton, not far from Mark Lane. The banishment emphasized, and reinforced, the social barrier, which even the younger generation could not overcome. In London, as elsewhere, advancement could now come about only through the courts. The group had added a new weapon to its defenses against the newcomer.

The constraints of the group could lead to an out-and-out *dirigisme*, or interventionism. This found its fullest expression, certainly, in Venice; the most brutal in Lübeck.

Nationalism and protectionism combined in Venice. Only the big Vene-tian ships were allowed to put into port on the Grand Canal or in the lagoon. Only merchandise belonging to Venetians could be exported. Foreign merchandise could not be imported except when it was simply carried as a make-weight. State intervention meant that the Venetian merchant had no choices except that of what to sell. This meant, in practice, a free choice of destinations, terms of credit, suppliers, clients, cargoes, and quality, which made up for the lack of total freedom in matters of price. The Venetian businessman remained a merchant, never losing his sense of initiative.

The state monopoly was the same in Lübeck, at least in general outline. Foreigners did not have even the right to display their goods in the public market. In other words, they were completely in the hands of local competitors. If they imported goods, they were not allowed to reexport them: everything had to be sold on the spot. And, as part of the Hanseatic system that perfected the art of making the position of others untenable, foreigners were not permitted to buy retail. They were confined to unloading their cargo and getting rid of it as quickly as possible.

In most places, however, such regulations were little more than guidelines. Major traders enjoyed an internal freedom that artisans and smaller retail traders either did not have or did not want. The system was in place to control the flow of business, to ensure that taxes and dues were paid, and to restrict foreign competition without depriving itself of the foreign imports so necessary to customer satisfaction and financial stability.

Thus it was with England's trading relations. Exported from London, or even from Boston, Hull, or Ipswich, the wool intended for the continental staple (that is, for northern Europe rather than the Mediterranean region) was in the hands of the "staplers," merchants so specialized that they did not bother with organizing a return cargo. The money that they made in Bruges, Antwerp, or Calais could have been used to finance imports into England. But the staplers left this kind of activity to others, instead sending home their earnings in the form of letters of credit payable in England. However, the money was not always lost to the marketplace: the "merchant adventurers," who imported every kind of merchandise, could successfully invest the credit thus made available on the Continent, with the proviso that the sums due be payable in England through their agents, so that the stapler could reinvest them in his wool purchases as soon as possible.

The physical staple was both a constraint and a convenience. Financial regulation was another matter, since the wool vendor, when abroad, could not always find people prepared to accept a bill of exchange payable in England. The importers of wheat, wine, iron, or woad—the blue dye known in Languedoc as *pastel*—could find nothing to buy in the wool staple unless it was an established trade, as was the case in Bruges for some years in the mid-fourteenth century, in a large port with diversified resources. Usually the merchant had to balance his account, and it was in the major ports of Flanders or in the markets of the great Flemish fairs, especially at Berg op Zoom, that financial transactions took place that could settle the deals made at the nearby staple.

There is evidence that there was room for maneuver. Privileges, whether personal or more often collective, occasional or more or less permanent, gave many merchants the right to take English wool directly to their customers, or to go and collect it themselves from the countryside. The northern counties were able to export directly to the cloth mills of the Netherlands. The merchants of Berwick, a small town on the estuary of the river Tweed on the border between Scotland and England, were thus able to organize the sale of wool from Scotland and from the entire region between the Coquet and the Tweed. The merchants of Newcastle upon Tyne did the same for the wool between the Tees and the Tweed and for that produced in Northumberland, Cumberland, Westmoreland, and County Durham. This was a privilege with obvious practical value: to force the people of Berwick or Newcastle to travel via Bruges, or particularly Calais, would have been geographical nonsense as well as an invitation to fraud. Privilege was a way of maintaining royal control over exports. Fraud would undermine it.

And then there were those who came to England to buy the wool recognized by everyone in Europe as the best. The Italians took advantage of their rights to free access. In other cases, foreign merchants enjoyed what was clearly special favor, as when the duchess of York obtained from her son Edward IV export rights that allowed her quite simply to organize trade under advantageous circumstances entirely to her own personal profit. The king did not, of course, neglect his own interests: wool from the royal estates was normally exempt from the restrictions governing trade in the continental staple.

The "merchant adventurers" were able to ignore such restrictions. Trading in every kind of goods except wool since the thirteenth century, they traveled the world in search of merchandise. Similarly, they sold whatever they might have at that time wherever and to whomever wanted it. This trade expanded very rapidly. The adventurers' sphere of action extended first to the Netherlands and later to the Baltic, where Hanseatic merchants saw them, during the fourteenth century, as rivals to be reckoned with. They were just as happy to travel to Iceland as to Gascony. Although they gave up trading in wool in order to preserve their independence, they continued to trade in the woolen cloth that England still imported from Flanders and, by the fifteenth century, even in the cloth that England began to produce at home and to export. The merchant adventurers became involved in the cloth trade only because it was unrestricted. As it turned out, the success of the English weaving industry during the later Middle Ages was to make their fortunes and become, in some respects, their raison d'être.

These merchant adventurers—so called because they were prepared to take risks on less well trodden trade routes—nevertheless organized themselves into Italian-style "companies" whose level of trade was sufficiently high to support a new commercial venture, that of money changing, or banking. By end of the fifteenth century these companies had virtually fused into one. The "Company of Merchant Adventurers trading in Holland, Zeeland, Brabant, Hainaut, and Flanders" became the Merchant Adventurers' Company, one of the great financial powers of northwestern Europe on the eve of the Renaissance.

There was no market that was not, to some extent, regulated. One was obligated to enter into an agreement with a Parisian citizen belonging to a guild in order to obtain permission to carry the smallest cargo beyond the Grand Pont. This meant abiding by all the rules laid down by the *Marchandise de l'eau*—in other words, by Parisian businessmen—or at least obtaining permission from that body. The geography of Paris reinforced this segregation: even without organizing themselves into "nations," foreigners gathered together in their own special sites both in the Halles and in the other covered markets at Pontoise, Gonesse, and Beauvais. And the bakers of the Bourg Saint-Marcel sold their bread, as a group, on the Place Maubert. Suspicious of strangers—ready to identify them in order to apprehend them, anxious to organize them in order to keep better tabs on them—the group not only enjoyed privileges but also put up with restrictions in order to ensure its future.

The economy of Bordeaux, dominated by the ebb and flow of the wine trade, worked on an annual cycle. Thus the way to benefit the local producers was to make use of the calendar. This in turn required a system to make it work. As of 1241, the merchants of Bordeaux obtained permission from the king of England, in his role of duke of Guyenne, to be the sole exporters of wine until St. Martin's Day; merchants in the other towns of "Gascony" were not allowed to dispatch their cargoes until after 11 November. Henry III took little persuading at the time, since the privilege was explicitly directed against the Agenais, a region then belonging to the king of France. A few years later, however, this monopoly enjoyed by the citizens of the town of Bordeaux began to have an impact on the surrounding diocese of Bordeaux, which belonged in its entirety to the Plantagenet king.

The date was to vary. In the fifteenth century, Bordeaux moved it to 25 December. Not wishing to ruin the economy of his father's newly acquired territories, Louis XI was to change it to 30 November, thus striking a compromise between the demands of the citizens of Bordeaux and the needs of the inland wine growers. In fact, despite a relatively liberal trading atmosphere, this privilege meant that in some years wine from the surrounding countryside could not be dispatched to the markets on the Channel and the North Sea until after the winter storms. Bordeaux sold its wine in the autumn; the inland areas could sell theirs only in the spring. In the interim the wine had not improved, the cellars of Bruges and London had been filled, and the price of wine had dropped.

But all this did not crush individual initiative, or freedom of choice. Both could be found equally in a town fortified by its ancient traditions, such as Genoa, and in a newly expanding market such as Nuremberg. With the exception of the alum monopoly, Genoa's trade appears to have been more or less unfettered. A Genoese was free to trade in whatever merchandise he wished, with whomsoever he chose, under whatever conditions he considered to be the most advantageous. He alone bore the responsibility of failure. The administrative framework here was purely the result of a solidarity that had developed rapidly among Genoese merchants when they arrived in foreign markets. Unity was necessary abroad, in order to obtain and exploit privileges beyond the reach of an individual.

In Nuremberg, the traditional restrictions applying to business circles relaxed with the small town's rapid expansion. The fifteenth century saw their virtual disappearance. Foreigners were now allowed to remain in town for as long as it took to transact their business. Nuremberg citizens and foreign merchants could enter into partnerships as they wished. With the new diversity of business—industry as well as commerce and banking—handled and assimilated by ambitious economic operators, there was no longer a place for barriers, restrictions, and artificial balances. Those who had least benefited were the first to repudiate them. Still confined in a rigid corporate and protectionist straitjacket, the old monopolies were slow to realize that they were dying for want of air.

FIVE

Competition

*W*hile the merchants as a social group were deliberately closing their ranks in order to preserve and exploit their advantages, the problem of competition began to present itself on two levels. The first was that of the kingdom or of the town, or even the guild—the *arte* or corporation, *hansa* or "company." Despite their efforts, the merchant groups, whether large or small, found themselves challenged, outside the frontiers defined by their privileges, by other groups enjoying similar privileges. This is evident in the fierce and sometimes dramatic competition between Florence and Pisa during the thirteenth century or the struggle of the Florentines against Lucca during the fifteenth. During the same century, rivalry also existed between Bruges and Antwerp, and between Lübeck and Nuremberg, although competition between Paris and Rouen was long standing. Nor should we forget the parallel and hostile histories of the two Florentine guilds, the *Arte della Lana* and the *Arte di Calimala,* or the interminable cases brought before the *Parlement* in Paris involving the dressmakers, the doublet makers, and the drapers. The group stood firm against outside competition, but this competition had the effect of making the group still more exclusive. To lift the barriers would be to court its own destruction.

The second level of competition was, needless to say, that between individuals. Even though a member of a group, each person continued to seek to make more money than his neighbor. For all the legally enforced egalitarianism—quite widespread and with a noticeable effect on the customs of everyday life—in practice business drew its vitality from a very real sense of competition. The delicate play of restrictions imposed on this competition, and the extent to which this affected individual initiative and fortunes, is often what most clearly distinguishes one marketplace from another.

Free Competition

Egalitarian policies depend on the strength of collective constraints. In an individualistic society like that of Genoa there could be no question of such a policy. Only public authority is capable of prohibiting the formation of private monopolies or preferential patronage. It is necessary, furthermore, for this public authority to have the strength to act and for it to have the assent—or rather, the connivance—of the business community. One effect among others of such solidarity, egalitarianism could also lend itself to protectionism; and only a unified market could be protected.

This could range from detailed practical arrangements to major systematic policies. In Paris it went no further than holding a lottery for the allocation of stalls in the covered market. It was better to be near the entrance so as to be seen by customers as they entered, and everyone knew that the main thoroughfare in the hall was better for trade than the cross aisles or the corners. The organization of the Hanseatic League, on the other hand, was based on the principle of absolute equality for all citizens of the member towns. The Venetian Senate generally guaranteed to every merchant the advantage of the same public services—the state maritime armament—and identical economic conditions, which generated equal risks but little chance for initiative. It is hardly necessary to point out that this egalitarianism, while safe, represented a further impediment to trade: with the same opportunities and risks for everyone, it was impossible for the small trader ever to enter into the ranks of the international merchants. Egalitarianism leads to parallelism, which consolidates large fortunes but inhibits daring and reinforces mediocrity. One can see how this parallelism could be popular with those merchants who were already successful in a society where, with the closing in 1297 of the list of families eligible to sit in the Grand Council, the obstruction of individual destinies became institutionalized.

At the dawn of their trading history, the Tuscans had felt the advantages of free competition. Fabulous fortunes were built up in a few decades. The thirteenth century saw the rise everywhere of enterprises thriving in competition in markets that seemed infinitely expandable. Just as earlier in the eastern half of the Holy Roman Empire the Pisans, Genoese, and Venetians were masters of the sea and fierce rivals in the ports of Syria, Byzantium, and the Black Sea, so now Florentine and Sienese merchants found themselves side by side in the marketplaces of Western Europe and competing, without excessive difficulty, at the Champagne fairs, in Bruges, and in London. The great fortunes in Paris during the 1300s were those being made by Gandoufle d'Arcelles (Aguinolfo degli Arcelli) and Biche and Mouche. The Tuscans and their close neighbors in Piacenza and Siena found themselves having to compete daily with one another in the marketplace, but then there was still room for everyone.

Things moved quickly. Competition between the Tuscan companies—not just between towns—was already merciless even before the effects of the first crises of the fourteenth century began to make themselves felt. Rivals had to be eliminated. Biche and Mouche "Guy" were regarded by Philip the Fair as two of his most valued counselors, and they shamelessly exploited this position. They kept the best investments for themselves. They took over the royal mint. They took on the tax farm for the Champagne fairs. The firsthand information to which they had access in their position close to the king offered them many opportunities in commerce and banking. Their nephew Tote became personal business adviser to Enguerran de Marigny at a period when this man, whom jealous rivals saw as a kind of deputy king, was transforming diplomatic relations—with both the pope and the Flemish towns—in a sordid piece of continental horse trading. Not surprisingly, the presence of the Guidi family was to block the business ambitions of many Florentines in France.

Toward the end of the thirteenth century in Siena, and a little later in Florence, this internal competition would intensify. A cascade of bankruptcies followed: in Siena the Buonsignori in 1298, the Riccardi in Lucca in 1300, the Mozzi in Florence in 1301, the Franzesi in 1307—by which time Biche and Mouche were dead—the Frescobaldi in 1312, and finally the Scali in 1326. These collapses had financial repercussions. Confidence foundered. Still very closely linked to trading in goods since clients were the same and proceeds from sales were needed in order to dispose of cash on the credit market, banking came to a halt right in the midst of its successful expansion.

The Florentines reacted, but the price was a drastic overhaul of their activities. The crisis was the fault of competition: in order to restore confidence throughout Europe it seemed better to give it up. The new companies then being formed were to opt for cooperation to stave off mutual ruin. Markets were divided up, and bankers operated in concert.

Thus, in Avignon at the time of John XXII and Benedict XII—until 1342—the Bardi, Peruzzi, Buonaccorsi, and Acciaiuoli cooperated in the movement of funds collected throughout the Christian world by papal collectors. Each company operated within a clearly defined geographical area. Where several companies were present in one central marketplace, such as Bruges, they divided up their activities. This accord may have been only superficial, and we have no way of knowing whether each individual was in his heart of hearts equally delighted by this division of markets and profits. But everyone understood that this was the condition for survival. Later, after the banking crisis of the 1340s, the popes were more inclined to deal with a single company—the Strozzi, the *antichi* Alberti, the Guardi, and one or two others. The political split with Florence led the papacy to turn to a banker from Pistoia, Andrea di Tici. The Great Schism resulted in the installation of the Rapondi company from Lucca and finally the Piedmontese from Asti.

But during the period when papal funds were being tapped by a single company, the division was being made on a European scale. The Florentines and Lucchesi treated the pope's finances as just one more element in a global market that had to be shared out. In such an agreement, particularly obvious to the people from Lucca, a certain Dino Rapondi received, along with a marketplace in Bruges, the Parisian clientele of the duke of Burgundy, Philip the Bold, as well as of an Avignon pope forced by the crises in France and the Church to throw his lot in with the king of France.

One of the weapons of free competition was obviously that of secrecy. Even in markets where they attempted to constrain competition, there remained a lively rivalry. A sentiment of economic cooperation, which everyone understood as the best protection, was revived only in times of collective danger.

The fiercer the competition, the more secrecy was maintained. The Genoese concealed everything, even their itineraries. There was not a Genoese who would speak of his voyages or of his experience of foreign marketplaces. They were even suspicious of the notary, and there are many contracts that omit details about the ship's destination. Only the captain knew where they were bound. "Where they will decide to go," writes one notary. "Where God will lead them," writes another. On his return from his Atlantic crossing, Christopher Columbus behaved in a typically Genoese manner, leaving only the vaguest of indications for posterity.

The Venetians, by contrast, openly stated their cargoes and destinations, noting ports of call, describing voyages, and publishing memoirs. Marco Polo was only one of many. On the shores of the Lido words flowed freely. They saw no need to be cautious when everything was arranged by the state.

Secrecy had to be ensured. The structures of emerging capitalism reflected this preoccupation: it was important that not too many partners know the exact economic situation. The practice of paying interest on investments, which attracted and made use of capital coming from outside the company, effectively prevented the majority of partners putting up money from knowing about or managing their business affairs. A group of firms either under a collective name or consisting of affiliated branches made it possible to have a large number of partners, each of whom knew only a small part of the business. The Medici's director in Bruges, Tommaso Portinari, knew nothing about the status and enterprise of the Medici empire in other locations. Or rather, he knew only enough to be useful to him in the managing of his commercial and banking activities in Bruges. Like capital—more was found soon enough in Florence when Portinari got into financial trouble—information was compartmentalized.

The internal transmission of such information was, by contrast, given the highest priority, being seen as a necessary practice of the economic world. As a young merchant's mentor in business advised his pupil: Wait until the following day to give your colleagues and neighbors the mail that has arrived for them. Draw your own conclusions from the information first and think of others later.

Protectionism

When exercised collectively against outside competition, the solidarity of the local group tended to express itself in protectionist regulations that favored, channeled, and curbed its own activities. During the fifteenth century, measures against foreigners were institutionalized in the Hanseatic towns. The role of Bruges as a marketplace for the Hanseatic League was reinforced in the face of competition from the Dutch, when the influence of the fair in Delft spread far and wide, and ships from Amsterdam were to be found as far away as Norway. The reaction of the Hanseatic market was to close ranks. The Diet decreed in 1442 that cloth destined for the Hansa towns might in the future be bought only in Bruges. Three years later Bruges became the obligatory port for the export of all nonperishable goods. It was still possible to sell fish in Hamburg or Lübeck, but not furs or wood.

The closing of markets was obviously the most immediate weapon against foreign competition. But wise rulers generally restricted the use of such trade barriers to moments of crisis. At the peak of the monetary hemorrhage that was to force the devaluation of spring 1303, Philip the Fair went so far as to prohibit all exports of raw wool to the cloth towns of Hainaut, Valenciennes, and Maubeuge unless it was to be sold to French merchants. Similarly—though in the opposite direction—the Hanseatic League, whose ports on the North Sea were being threatened by Holland, was to close its markets in 1445 to all imports of cloth from Holland. As for England, eager to protect her nascent cloth industry, a ban in 1463 on the export of all raw wool allowed it to stockpile raw materials. Merchants were similarly forced to find outlets when, in 1484, imports of foreign cloth were forbidden.

Sometimes, with varying success, they even resorted to physical force. The English merchants demanded that Henry VI sink the Breton and Norman boats so that they could "rule the seas." A little less fantastic were the threats made by Charles VII between 1462 and 1464 that he would imprison and seize the goods of any French or foreign merchants setting foot in the Geneva fairs. In the circumstances, the supporters of Louis XI thought it better to direct business toward the fairs at Lyons.

Such networks of solidarity, anticompetition pacts, and protectionist barriers were created at all levels, even the most humble. The Parisian belt makers persuaded the king to close the gates of the capital to belts made in the neighboring town of Saint-Marcel, where the belt makers mixed lead, wood, shells, and other shoddy materials with the pure tin used exclusively by the Parisians.

Family alliances were called into play, favoring the acquisition of new clients and allowing a control over business or a concentration of capital that did not attract the attention of prying outsiders. Whether resident at Barcelona, Bruges, or Avignon, the Tuscan merchant would take a bride from his hometown. If he had left home without planning to return, he could still reinforce his solidarity with his compatriots in the face of foreign competitors through this family link. It was not only patriotism—unless this sense of business solidarity is an aspect of patriotism—that prompted the Lucchese living in Paris, "Geoffroi" Cenami, to marry Filippa, daughter of Dino Rapondi of Lucca. The well-known double portrait painted in Bruges by Jan van Eyck in 1434 of Giovanni Arnolfini of Lucca and his wife, Giovanna Cenami, from the same town, celebrates another such marriage.

It was not always possible to eliminate foreign competition. Legal monopolies and de facto takeovers are difficult objectives and fragile edifices. Driven by necessity, the merchants got together to control prices and reserve the best conditions for themselves. From the end of the thirteenth century the Venetians made combined purchases of pepper and cotton at the market in Alexandria. Half a century later in Trebizond we find the agent representing the Venetian merchants buying up, on behalf of all his compatriots with an interest in the business, the entire cargo of spices brought in by a caravan. Sometimes it was just a matter of meeting to discuss prices; another time they would sweep the market clean. The Genoese did the same, driving their competitors in the alum trade out of Phocaea to the centers of redistribution that were, for the East, the island of Khios and, in the West, the Bruges market.

It only needed a parallel market for an enterprise to be ruined. On the eve of a fish war, the Hanseatic merchants living in Riga were only too aware of this, living in fear of seeing the Dutch fleet arriving at the same time as their own. The price of salt would be halved.

It was a similar attempt to control prices that led the English merchants, in 1454, to demand that Parliament fix a maximum price for wool intended for export. The rise in raw wool prices outside England threatened the manufacturing costs of the young home industry. Freezing the price of wool for export would encourage the producers to sell on the local market. In this the interests of the great landowners, whose main product was wool, prevailed over those of the entrepreneurs, and Parliament refused their request.

There was also corporate protectionism, which operated simply within a single market where different guilds, often representing very different social classes within the same professional world, came into conflict. This was particularly obvious in the competition between those who procured and those who produced. Thus in the fur business the market saw a clash between the fur traders, who brought to Bruges and beyond the northern furs needed for the manufacture of luxury goods, and the furriers, who prepared the skins and produced the fashionable garments. For the client, both were equally useful and the art of the latter counted for as much as the former's skill in merchandising.

Furthermore, the matter could often be complicated by the fact that the client would supply his own furs bought outside the local market. Princes had their own "purveyors" who went to the source of supply and attended the fairs. When it was a question of supplying the court, it was up to the prince to define who should do what. A certain Thomassin Potier, future *fourreur de robes* to Louis of Orleans, first makes his appearance in the accounts of the princely households as supplier of precious furs to the court.

For all their mutual dislike, there were times when the two worlds of the merchant and the artisan were bound to overlap. Commanded by Charles V to pass judgment on the dispute in the fur business, his brother-in-law the duke of Bourbon did his best by forbidding all trading by artisans who did not pay the *hauban* paid by the fur merchants, but even the king's intervention made no difference. Although they were at least successful in limiting the buying of new furs by the artisans, no one could prevent a client from selling back to his favorite robe maker a fur of which he had tired.

The trade itself was divided. No sooner had the merchants managed successfully to prevent the artisans from trading in new furs when a new type of competition appeared, striking at the very heart of the market: the haberdashers, dealers in all that was necessary for a show of opulence and fashion, began to offer their clients precious furs. During the fifteenth century, they were offering bear, fox, otter, and ermine furs. It was useless for the fur merchants who, only yesterday, had been selling squirrel and sable to make a fuss about competition from someone who was offering goods over which they had not yet acquired a monopoly. As in the earlier dispute with the artisans, now it was the turn of the fur merchants to plead that the fur business presupposed some kind of technical knowledge.

In practice, the sole competitor was eliminated easily enough in the marketplace. And it was a fight with no holds barred. A merchant from the Auvergne, Regnardon of Clermont, was to learn this to his cost around 1380. In Paris to sell three bales of muslin, he knew perfectly well that the bigger Parisian drapers normally traveled to the Auvergne to obtain their supplies directly and that he was thus treading on the toes of an already established trade. He was careful not to duplicate their activities, however, and it was to them that he went to offer his goods. Thus at least they could not say that he was trying to take their clients away from them. We can imagine his astonishment when he found them offering him a lower price than what they normally paid in the Auvergne—ten francs a bale: "On the contrary, they offered him a great loss, so that he would never again be inclined to return to trade in the same merchandise." In other words, they wanted to put him off the whole business. But Regnardon was more than a match for them. This was February and mid-Lent was approaching—an important time for him with the mid-Lent fair at Compiègne. Off he went with his muslin, which he had no difficulty in selling to merchants from Tournai and Bruges.

The Parisians soon heard about this and were quick to inform the Flemish merchants that in the future they would be able to buy muslin cheaper direct from them, avoiding this roundabout route. For the moment it meant the big drapers' losing a certain amount of money on this rather unimportant trade in muslin, but it was worth it. The important thing was to stop this cheeky Regnardon in his tracks before he began trading by direct routes.

In the end it was the client who decided. Even if, as in the case of the Venetian Senate in 1424, the political authority declared that the technical competence of one was superior to that of another, and even if cases of fraud were invoked, as happened in the town council at Arras, regarding the poor quality of goods apparent only to the trained eye, there was nothing to prevent clients from making the final decision and choosing the goods that they preferred.

It was all a matter of clientele. It was easier to prevent an artisan from selling what he should not to the man in the street than to forbid the prince to order from a favored supplier.

Egalitarianism and Advertising

In the local market, competition was more easily contained. It was frowned upon to try to attract the client by any means other than the fair and open presentation of the products for sale. The client's free choice was based on his free judgment. All the professional statutes condemn soliciting and direct advertising. It was a serious infringement to seek out a client at his lodgings or to accost him on the road. Two Parisians, Jean Boucher and Simonet Grandin, were fined forty sous for delivering goods directly to some firm clients, scarcely making a pretense of offering them in the market:

> A large quantity of wool, which they had unloaded not in the marketplace but at the Hôtel de Carneaux, near the Mignon college, to which place had

come Regnault Jouault and Jean Le Maignen, merchants of Paris, to inspect and discuss prices, in contravention of the regulations.

Although, since this occasion, the said Boucher and Grandin have been enjoined to bring their wool in a cart to the covered market for such products, they did, a few days ago, past seven o'clock in the morning, bring the said wool to the market in a cart and, without stopping there, without even spreading it out and displaying it publicly, they sold it to the said Jouault and Le Maignen who had bought it from them and had it taken to their house and unloaded.

The stallholder compensated for being confined behind his stall by shouting louder than his neighbor, and there was nothing to prevent him from exhibiting an attractive servant girl. The "market wine" had a fixed price, while bribes and commissions were prohibited. A veritable army of officials and brokers kept a watchful eye on the market to guarantee not only the openness of the transactions and the accuracy of the weights and measures but also a genuine equality between the traders. Naturally, the artisan was free to sell a better product at a cheaper price than his neighbor. Though the price of wine and that of corn might be arrived at collectively by the traders at the market on a particular day, the prices charged by the pewter worker and the smith were less subject to comparison in the short term.

When it came to products involving more sophisticated workmanship, pricing was a more complicated matter. At the top of the scale was the goldsmith, who set his own prices and decided on the degree of risk he could take in the face of his rival's prices. He still had to reckon with the group that governed the work conditions even if it could not influence a customer's preference for Guillaume the haberdasher's belt buckles or Robin's pewter ewers. The statute prohibiting work in one's own home affected all trades: it was only by working in the dark—in the back of the shop or late into the night—that prices could be cut. The reason always advanced for this rule was that to carry out one's work in full view of the public was to guarantee its quality. But there was another, less openly admitted reason: it was possible in this way to keep an eye on what competitors were doing.

In both Venice and Lübeck, the same egalitarianism can be seen in the strict regulation of ship chartering. Once again, it was easier to control the poor cobbler or the baker, who did not relish the idea of a fine or a spell in prison, than the patricians who ruled over the town and the port. It was in vain that the small shopkeepers of Venice protested in 1356 about the de facto monopoly created by the Cornaro family and their allies in the supply of cotton, sugar, and salt from Cyprus. Federico Cornaro was then chief banker to the king of Cyprus, whom he received in his family *palazzo* on the Grand Canal. No one was prepared to bring them to heel. Free to set their own prices, the Cornaros continued to grow in wealth and fortune.

Marco Cornaro was to be elected doge in 1365, while a century later Caterina Cornaro was to marry the last king of Cyprus, James II of Lusignan. It was this same Caterina who, in 1489 would sell Cyprus to the Venetians. All this they were able to do at a time when most stallholders and market traders were forced to adapt to regulations tending to equalize prices.

This was certainly the intention when traders in Toulouse were forbidden from putting on display more than a certain amount of merchandise, or when, in Paris, any signs of wanting to open early or continue trading into the night were firmly quashed. There were special cases, however, as in 1316 when the provost of Paris made an exception for the "embroiderers and embroidresses," by having royal authority sanction a deceptive practice so as not to paralyze the progress of trade:

> There came to us the greater part of the men and women workers in the said trade who petitioned us, saying that, as in their proper trade it was decreed that no one in their aforesaid trade might open at night, and that it would have been a profitable thing if they could open since they would do good trade, we agreed to give them permission to work without thereby offending.
>
> Let all know that we, considering that this decision is to the common benefit of the people and the good people of the town of Paris and outside, have given and give them permission to work at night whenever they wish, doing good and loyal work.

So that no one should be ignorant of them, the municipality had prices announced throughout the town. Measures were taken to see that the town criers were not able to take unfair advantage of their prior knowledge of the arrival of merchandise or, since both types of information were announced by the same man, the death of a citizen. Just as the butcher of Sainte-Geneviève was not allowed to exceed his annual quota of animals for slaughter or the grain measurer could exercise his office only when it was his turn and then only once a day, so each town crier was allowed to announce only one death a day. It would not have done for a crier to benefit from a flu epidemic.

The Florentines placed more trust in the written word than in the hurried shouting of a town crier. The *Arte di Calimala* insisted that retailers of luxury cloth attach to each length of material a wooden tablet on which the gross price was legibly written. It was only by having the town crier call out ten different things at once—and as quickly as possible—that Charles VI's advisers were able to announce the reimposition of indirect taxation without the Parisians' noticing. They were to pay for this deception a few days later, though, when an attempt to impose the tax on the purchase of a bunch of watercress led to the insurrection known to history by the name of the Maillotins.

The fair was the organ for the proclamation of anticompetition regulations par excellence. Every fair began with the "presentation," a period of three to eight days during which goods were unpacked, exhibited, compared, and evaluated. No trading was done during this time; it was a time for looking only. In this way the quantities for sale were revealed. The laws of supply and demand came into play. Prices were established. Then—and only then—came the time for dealing: another three to eight days. A third phase was that of the settling and balancing of accounts and arranging of credit. A client would neither be taken by surprise nor obstructed. Information was freely available. Everything was there to be touched or weighed. One could go and ask what a colleague was offering and what was being asked for it.

The layout of the fairs made it possible to compare at a glance the quality of products that were similar because they came from the same sources. At the Lendit fairs, held in June on the plain between Paris and Saint-Denis, there was a "street" for the merchants from Louviers, as there were a Bernay, a Lisieux, and a Vire street. The merchants from Rouen sold their cloth in a cluster of four streets, known as the "Rouen market."

Subtle procedures began to appear, originated by the more developed sectors of those trades where selling at a loss was feared as unemployment was elsewhere. Thus the English Parliament in 1377 prohibited the goldsmiths of London from selling their products to anyone other than the gold merchants of the same town unless they could find a buyer prepared to pay three times the price normally paid by the merchants. In practice, this meant that small manufacturers were prevented from making a sale that they could easily have secured by cutting their profit margins. But no one objected if their sale had the effect of raising prices. The merchants were prepared to tolerate the artisans' dealings only when it suited their purposes.

To forbid direct advertising and rebuke, as inherently bad, anything done to attract the attention of the client is one thing. But, in fact, nothing prevented the merchant from doing what he could to attract the customer or show off the quality of a product. And no one could escape the obligation to inspire confidence through advertisement. Every possible means was acceptable, and all sorts of noneconomic associations were put to the use of indirect publicity.

All-important here, as a counterweight to the insolvent princes and their chaotic private business schemes, was the patronage of the nobility. A merchant who supplied the courts of princes and aristocratic households could thereby gain a reputation that would guarantee the probity of his dealings, the quality of his products, and the solidity of his credit. Fashion also played an important role. Seeing that Nicholas Bataille sold his tapestries to the uncles of Charles VI, to Louis of Anjou (the famous Apocalypse Tapestry) and to Philip of Burgundy, the Parisian customer knew from whom to order his baldachin or his chair-backs.

The nobility were not taken in, and in any case they took advantage of the publicity that they bestowed on their businessmen, for by improving the latter's position they received better service or, in other words, better credit terms. When, after a series of collapses of the great Florentine companies between 1343 and 1346, Pope Clement VI was forced to turn to the small Malabaila company in Asti, he did all he could to help his new banker expand. When the Malabailas took on the management of the funds of the papal taxes they were no longer a small company with only two branches in Bruges and London. Any way of drawing the attention of the economic world to the Asti company that had replaced the Florentines was to the good. The pope never missed an occasion to give proof of his esteem and confidence. He did more, involving it in the business affairs of princes; it was through the intermediary of the Malabailas that, from 1343, Clement VI made loans to the king of Castile, the duke of Brittany, and other smaller borrowers who, together, were to forge the new reputation of the company the length and breadth of Europe.

Keeping up appearances also depended on prestigious investments, investments that the superficial observer might be inclined to see as an unproductive diversion of public or family capital. There is no doubt that it was expensive to keep up appearances, and certain social classes—such as the Parisian bourgeoisie, eager for office and rank—were to invest significant sums in their houses and, before long, in their collections, thus removing capital from the economic marketplace. But the reverse was not true, and it was impossible to do good business without an imposing facade. Even if luxury was contained—and the elegance of the Florentine *palazzi* lay inside the courtyard and not outside facing the road—the solidity of the merchant presence in the city was an essential condition of confidence. Thus, in France, competition between the citizens of rival towns first led to the 24-meter-high vault of Laon Cathedral and then, successively, to the 30 meters of Soissons, the 37 meters of Chartres, the 43 meters of Amiens, and, finally, the 48 meters of the choir at Beauvais Cathedral. The latter, having overreached itself, was to collapse in 1284. Similarly, in the Hanseatic towns the proud facades of the merchant houses made a public statement of their owners' wealth without, however, giving too much away. Creditworthiness was shown in the height of the gables. Knowing that each partner was individually responsible for the company's future, investors felt reassured about their investments in the company by the visible signs of a fortune with sound foundations and strongly built walls, seeing it as a guarantee against the danger, ever present in their minds, of a bankruptcy without compensation. Before handing over any money, the investor, like the small saver, would want to know what this guarantee was worth.

However wasteful of time, energy, and capital it may have been in many cases, particularly within the circles of the French royal family, public office played a role in this show of uprightness, often increasing confidence and hence expansion. What better proof of reliability could there be for a merchant than having a seat on the town council? The municipal magistrates, whether the *échevin* in Paris, the *capitoul* in Toulouse, the prior in Florence, or the senator in Venice or Lübeck, were both in their own business and in that of their relatives, the best guarantors of those qualities—honesty, knowledge, and solvency—which make for good relations in the commercial or banking world. To gain the esteem of one's equals did not merely depend on chance. But it would prove sometimes to have been ill founded, and the system would then work in reverse. The fall of the great Florentine companies was to bring with it on two occasions, during the 1330s and the 1340s, the collapse of all those who had placed too much faith in the invulnerability of the recognized powers.

Family relations were all-important. The nobility expanded both vertically through society and geographically. When Johann Lange, a citizen of Nuremberg and associate of the Pirkheimers, married the daughter of a patrician household in Lübeck in the late fifteenth century, he found a new outlet for his enterprises, adding the Hansa routes as far as Danzig to the routes linking Nuremberg with Venice. These same family links were sometimes able to protect their members from the threats of economic risk. Just as a merchant was judged by his house and its gables, so was the network of information and substance provided by a good family, where direct links and connections by marriage complemented one another. Families might have the sons and nephews that were given to them, but they had the sons-in-law that they had earned.

More than in the ordinary judicial system, posts in public administration were particularly useful, being not only profitable but also good for publicity. While the businessman successfully acquired the contract to farm taxes or manage the mint, his closest relatives got involved in taxation in general. The banker levied the tax, but it was his nephew who fixed its rate. The great merchant families of the Parisian bourgeoisie were quick to see the advantage of having a relative in the Treasury or the Court of Aids that governed customs and excise.

A bishop's throne or cardinal's hat could also do a lot for a family's image. The appointments of Bartolo Bardi, bishop of Spoleto in 1320, Angelo Acciaiuoli, bishop of Florence in 1383 and cardinal in 1384, and Niccolò Guinigi, bishop of Lucca in 1394, provided useful publicity for the commercial and banking companies whose name they bore. For a generation it was an Acciaiuoli who was commonly known as "the cardinal of Florence." Jacques Coeur saw the advantages to be reaped and made his brother Jean archbishop of Bourges in 1447. The election of two members of the Medici family to the papacy—Leo X in 1513 and Clement VII in 1523—was to be the final expression of this kind of economic competition. In the necessary relationship of power and business, power was to become all-important. Son of a banker and father of a pope, Lorenzo the Magnificent exemplifies the change that had taken place in economic activity, which was no longer an end in itself.

SIX

Foreigners

*M*edieval people were apt to be xenophobic. Viewed with the greatest suspicion in a small town, the foreigner, or stranger, was almost equally suspect in a large city. Foreigners existed outside, and conspicuously apart from, the normal framework of local society and its organized groups.

Living on the Outside

The social group—already geographically defined and further sensitized by its jealously guarded privileges, more valuable when most restricted—defined itself with so many excluding clauses that it was not hard for someone to be an outsider. *Foreynes,* born in London but excluded from belonging to a craft, found themselves in the position of outsiders in their own town. A citizen of Nuremberg was *a fortiori* regarded more or less as a foreigner in the Hansa towns. A wine grower from Meudon would be aware of being an outsider when he delivered the wine from his vineyard to Paris. A baker from Bourg Saint-Marcel or from Corbeil was allowed to sell bread only three times a week—on Wednesdays and Saturdays at the covered market and on Sundays from a stall in Place Maubert—just as the *foreyne* in London was allowed to trade only in the district of Blancheappleton.

Living in these alien surroundings, foreigners were inclined to turn in on themselves, even when not required officially to live concentrated in one area; the many "Lombard Streets" found in European cities are sufficient evidence of this defensive attitude. Seeking as much a social group as commercial convenience, the Tuscans in Paris congregated beneath the walls of the churches of Saint-Merry, Saint-Jacques-de-la-Boucherie, and Saint-

109

Gervais, or in the cloisters of Sainte-Opportune and in the Calende on the Ile de la Cité. In 1296 we find fourteen Genoese merchants lodging with a certain Roger Boël who seems to have acted as a kind of professional landlord and permanent correspondent for the Genoese community, and even for a few Milanese.

The initiative to introduce new restrictions on trade sometimes came from the de facto group made up of foreigners who were eager not to mix any more than necessary with the locals. With the exception of Bruges, the Hanseatic League placed representatives in particular sections in each of its marketplaces. Whether in London, Bergen, or Novgorod, the merchant enjoyed a kind of extraterritorial status that both protected him and kept him at a distance. The pale was symbolic, since the merchant frequently crossed it as he went about the business of daily life. But it remained, nonetheless, a physical indication of an enclosure.

In the Hanseatic towns, such measures against the foreigner sometimes became more than merely symbolic. Subject to a "law of guests," the *Gästerecht*, the non-Hanseatic merchant was hedged about with restrictions. He might not travel into the hinterland. He was fortunate if his visit was not limited to a few weeks. After two or three weeks—or four at the most—he had to leave. He was forbidden to spend the winter in Cologne, Hamburg, or Brunswick. From the late thirteenth century, the Hanseatic merchants of Novgorod even cut off relations with the Russians altogether. Any association with them might in the long term have come to be seen as an admission that foreigners had some rights in business affairs. A century later the same interdict was issued in Bruges, this time against the Flemish merchants.

Increasingly, all over Europe, barriers were going up against the intruding foreigners—in other words, against foreign competition. They were not allowed to become citizens. Attempts were even made to prevent them from trying to bypass these restrictions by marriage with Hanseatic brides—something that the people of Nuremberg were, nevertheless, much inclined to do, like Johann Lange in Lübeck. They knew that, influential as they were in many markets, the locals could not do without them. In fact, the Hanseatic merchants proved that they could be reasonable in the face of their own protectionism. Those living in Bruges quickly found it convenient to take Flemish nationality so as not to be excluded from participating in business. The *Gästerecht* really interfered only with small-time foreign merchants, particularly the Prussians. The merchants from Holland and Nuremberg were able to adapt.

In this struggle against the integration of foreigners, the peak of absurdity was reached by the Livonian cities. Whereas Slav merchants had until the fourteenth century been received with the greatest tolerance, becoming firmly established in towns like Revel and Riga, now the gates were suddenly slammed in their faces. In 1399 the Slavs of Riga were excluded from all trade. Germans were even forbidden to learn the Slav language. These were pointless gestures perhaps, but barriers nevertheless.

Florence and Paris took the opposite course. On the banks of the Seine, from 1300, a company called the *Gaigne-Biens* was established by none other than the Florentine Guadagnabene family. The great merchants from Lucca in the fourteenth century soon ceased to be regarded as foreigners. Rapondi became Raponde, Burlamacchi became Bourlamet, and Cenami Céname. Spifame did not even have to change the spelling of his name. In just a couple of generations they had all become Parisian citizens, as good as any Jean Jouvenel from Troyes or Poilevilain from Rouen. The conditions were quite simple: "provided that he is deemed to be resident in Paris and to contribute to the dues, subventions, and business of the town." A few years later, Jacques Coeur became a member of the *Arte della Lana* in Florence.

It must be said that the newcomer could help pave the way to acceptance if he displayed his wealth by buying one or two properties giving onto the street. But it was not long before people forgot the humble origins—as sons or grandsons of laborers—of the respectable citizens of Paris mentioned in the early fifteenth-century tax rolls, the Johns of Bourg-la-Reine, the Johns of Saint-Leu, or the Simons of Rueil.

Foreigners were able to participate more easily in international trade and banking than in local business and retailing. English laws restricted Italian and Hanseatic businessmen to wholesale trading, to be carried on only in the larger marketplaces, that is, the ports. It was forbidden for them to conduct any trade inland. They adapted.

Restrictions were sometimes severe. The right to conduct "bakery business" in Saint-Germain-des-Prés was strictly reserved to those born in the Bourg Saint-Germain and those outsiders fortunate enough to have married a local girl. For even in a township at the very gates of the capital, anyone from outside its limits was still a foreigner. In Paris they were equally protectionist in the selling of haberdashery or of river fish. But the foreign cloth merchants, forbidden by a law of 1407 from retailing the cloth that they bought in the covered market, were quite free to sell the cloth that they had brought with them from Rouen, Brussels, or Lucca, while at the market they had no difficulty in buying cloth that they planned to export to Amiens, Tours, or Saint-Lô. The shop trade was, however, closed to them. The house on the street was not just an empty image. It was impossible to reach the town's clientele without having a strategically placed doorway beneath the high gables of a solid merchant house.

The Hanseatic League similarly restricted foreigners to import and export. Retailing was forbidden: not more than one sack at a time, said the rules for the wool trade governing the Hanseatic market at Bruges. That was not enough to build up a clientele. They were suspicious, too, of anyone who tried to build up a series of small enterprises. The merchants of Nuremberg, who might otherwise have acted as agents for all the artisanal and industrial production of middle Germany in the Hansa towns, found themselves banned from selling anything made anywhere except in Nuremberg itself.

The lesson was quickly learned that to have a foreign presence in a trading area was to risk the flight of capital. As energetically as the local businessmen, the rulers did everything they could to prevent merchants from coming in with their merchandise and leaving with their gold. A ban on monetary trading and the encouragement of exports meant that merchants were obliged to reinvest their profits. In reality, there were few states strong enough to control the draining off of money. Though many times reiterated in France, the ban on the export of currency was never strictly observed. Only the kingdom of England, which as an island was better able to control its frontiers, was successful. It was simply a matter of searching the merchants as they embarked to leave. Woe betide anyone carrying more than ten écus: anything above that was confiscated.

The problem sorted itself out of its own accord in the late Middle Ages, when the majority of payments in international business began to be made without resorting to hard currency, whether on account or by drawing bills of exchange—in other words, by the use of banking. The circulation of coins decreased, and there was no longer any question of allowing purchases on credit.

The presence of foreigners in the principal marketplaces was an essential factor in the diversification of taxation. In their desire to here attract and there restrict competition, the rulers treated foreigners according to the nature of their involvement in economic life. In London *foreynes* and aliens paid higher taxes than those paid by traders duly registered as Londoners. But this was turned around in the mid-fourteenth century when it came to dealing with the Hanseatic merchants, for the English wanted to discourage them from stopping at Bruges and coming no further. In Paris, the *forain*, whether from Clamart or Cologne, had to pay through the nose for his stall in the market. Furthermore, for all trade conducted by water he had to share his profits with the Parisian associate deemed essential by law but in reality of no benefit—the "French companion."

They were less sensitive in Italy where the system of taxation applied to business was already the object of negotiations and treaties. Thus, in 1204, the towns of Florence and Faenza agreed to a mutual system of preferential rates:

> The people of Florence and its surrounding districts who go to and stay in Faenza and its surrounding districts and who return from there shall be

safe and well in their persons and their possessions. They shall pay according to the custom of Faenza following the usage and custom of Faenza, and not more.

According to the said custom, 28 *deniers* were formerly levied per load and per bag, but for love of the commune of Florence, the rate will be reduced for the Florentines so that the people of Florence and its district will pay 12 Ravenna *deniers* per load.

Protectionism began to relax, becoming more moderate. But that did not mean that it was not carefully thought out. It did not occur to anyone—whether businessman or ruler—to treat the foreigner and the citizen, the outsider and the native, the traveler and the resident, in the same way.

Even the most open-minded individuals continued for a long time to see these merchants born and belonging elsewhere as rivals seeking to steal a share in the single mass of communal profit. The Italians in London and the Portuguese in Harfleur were the fortunate exceptions, able to enjoy a commercial relationship that benefited the country but was placed out of the reach of the locals. However insular he might be, the English wool merchant knew quite well that his wool would never reach Florence if Italian ships did not come to collect it. Such realism, however, was found chiefly among those rulers and entrepreneurs with broader intellectual horizons. The average citizen, the shopkeeper or the person in the street, could see only the wealth of the Lombards, for it was not the Florentine weavers whom they met on the banks of the Thames but rather the bankers, the international merchants, dealing in anything that was for sale, and, above all, in wool and cloth. And for the Parisian artisan, too, the words *rich* and *Lombard* were synonymous, whether it was the international merchant, whose glamorous lifestyle dazzled the small shopkeeper, or the small moneylender at whose counter a hard-up Parisian could pawn his miserable belongings. The social upheavals of the decades following 1380 and 1410 owed their violence as much to the hatred felt by debtors as to a true xenophobia.

The same contradiction could be seen at a lower level of society. Paris needed its immigrant bakers but kept them confined in a market limited equally in space and time.

Wars and political conflicts did much to stir up this xenophobia. The French who came to England during the intervals between fighting in the Hundred Years' War engaged the services of an English agent to assist them. The slightest hiccup in political relations meant, at least, instant expulsion for these merchants if not imprisonment and confiscation of goods. A disagreement over marine rights between England and Bruges—kindled by the Hanseatic merchants in Bruges—resulted, in 1351, in the immediate expulsion of the Hanseatic merchants then in England and the inevitable confiscation of their merchandise. Similarly, the alliance between Genoa and the League set up against France on the initiative of the Spanish led, in

1496, to the expulsion of the Genoese established in France. In such a climate it is easy to understand why Italians systematically gallicized their names in an attempt to seem less foreign. Henri Orlant, supplier of luxury spices in the Paris of Charles VI, was safer than Enrico Orlandi.

A few years later, xenophobia even caused an attack on the sacred word of the pope. The theologian Robert Ciboule did not hesitate, around 1449, to lay the blame for all the misfortunes of Charles VII's France at the door of foreign domination: "Great misery and punishment has come to this *kingdom* on account of its having been in subjection to people whose language we do not understand." This idea was to find echo in the words of Father Peresi, the great preacher of the end of days and the fires of damnation: "By his language we know a man's country of origin . . ." This was of course obvious to an Italian using *la lingua di sì*. But times had changed and Henri Orlant was well aware of it. His successors were careful not to refer to their Lombard origins.

Enjoying such obvious privileges, even if they had to pay for these privileges with services, credit, or taxation—something about which ordinary people were less well informed than the rulers—foreigners became less and less popular. The average Englishman detested the Italians, despite the price the latter had to pay for their privileges. All the Englishman saw was their favored situation in the marketplace. The English businessman was on more secure ground when he drew up his accounts: because they had their special "staple" on English soil, the Home Staple, by the mid-fourteenth century the Italians had captured more than half the exports of raw wool. Compelled to frequent the continental staple, the English merchants—the "staplers"—frequently protested at this situation but in vain: the Italians kept their position. Again, at the end of the fifteenth century, the English exporter was forced to calculate his losses when the same government of Edward IV put a halt to exports of raw wool in order to encourage the development of the local cloth industry, but exempted the exporting of wool by the Italians from any such restrictions.

Foreigners were rich by definition. If they were poor, they returned home or never left in the first place. In fact, this was an oversimplification, being true of the Lombard in Bruges, but not necessarily of all the Bretons in Paris. Importantly, it was but a step from such a view to the idea that such riches were ill gotten. What the foreigners got their hands on the local people had failed to earn. When the Englishman thought in this way about the Italians who came to London to acquire wool, he was not entirely wrong. From a merchant's point of view, any newcomer who took a share of the market was one too many. It was not so bad if the foreigner had come with merchandise or was staying just long enough to do a deal; everyone could see that this stimulated trade. But if he settled down or began to do well they began to complain. When the Parisian realized that the biggest fortunes in the Paris of 1300 belonged to the Italians living on the Rue des Lombards, Rue de la Buffetterie, or Rue de la Vieille Monnaie, he longed to go and set fire to these grand houses, the description of which, exaggerated by hearsay, fueled hatred and a desire for the settling of accounts.

And revenge was to be bloody. When, in 1332, the people of Skanör at the southernmost tip of Sweden woke up to the fact that for twenty years the Germans had been expanding and monopolizing business, there was a massacre. At the beginning of the next century the Teutonic merchants of Danzig campaigned to have the English expelled since the latter had brought their wives over, making it clear that they were intending to stay. But it was the Germans who were threatened in Novgorod in 1424; thirty-six of them were to perish in prison. Toward the end of the century, in 1494, Tsar Ivan III embraced the old tradition of hostility between the Russians and the Germans of Novgorod, having them deported to Moscow, a town where they had no wish or reason to be.

The usurer, whether Jewish or Lombard, was the object of every flare-up of xenophobia resulting from the anger of those in chronic debt. Even though they traded in many commodities—of which money was only one—the Jews were seen as the moneylenders par excellence; and the long-established tradition of their role did nothing to prevent them from being regarded as foreigners. The violence of the anti-Semitic movements that flared up all over the Holy Roman Empire at the time of the Black Death is well known. Throughout Germany, in Alsace or Avignon, this same hatred of the little man for the lender at interest lent color to the story—taken at face value by a credulous population—of deliberately contaminated wells. The resulting massacre of the Jews was seen as a way of exorcising a cataclysm straight from the Apocalypse.

The Lombards, too, were the object of the crowd's anger, as were the rich merchants and the small money changers. During the riots of 1382 and 1413–18, foreigners were chased through the streets of Paris. The wealthy houses into which the crowd broke their way had little to do with the small-time usurers so reviled by the poor. The looters were attacking rather those who too obviously manifested their newly acquired fortunes or positions. A standard of living that was hard to accept even in a native Parisian was unforgivable in a foreigner. It was impossible that it had been come by honestly.

In fact, fifty years earlier, the peasants had cheerfully massacred nobles with impeccable French origins. Social hatred will take on xenophobic overtones whenever it can. If Jews were not mentioned in the riots of 1413–18, it was simply because they had been banished from the kingdom since 1394.

Getting Established

Though welcomed one moment and regarded with suspicion the next, foreign merchants had, in fact, an important role in every marketplace. With the exception of the Jews, whose religion set them apart, it was not long before those outsiders who succeeded in becoming established started to behave differently from the foreigner who was just passing through. The more important merchants installed agents, associates, and "factors" in all their areas of operation. While not all enjoyed the same degree of autonomy or initiative, they maintained the essential links, both locally and further afield, of the network within which information, transactions, and financial regulation operated. All these things required an understanding of human nature, procedures, and products that would have been impossible for the old-style merchant who traveled with his goods. Now that the days were over when new sea routes were opening up, the temptation to put down roots was strong. Seeing this, the Hanseatic merchants entrusted their ships only to captains with wives and families and a part-share in the ship. It was important that they returned home.

Paradoxically, internal crises in the towns of Italy encouraged this colonization of the economic world. When, finding themselves siding with the wrong faction, Florentines or Genoese were banished, they were able, during their exile, to acquire a familiarity with other towns that led, sooner or later, to the establishment of branches of the business abroad. Very often, Florentines living in Paris or Avignon were among those who had temporarily been exiled from their home on the banks of the Arno. Nevertheless, they continued to represent the long-term interests of a town where in due course, as they very well knew, their position at home would be valued by the connections that they had established abroad.

In order to defend their common interests, the foreign merchants got together. If they were to obtain and preserve their privileges, concerted action and regulation of the competition were required. Survival in an environment that was always suspicious and sometimes actively hostile called for systems of mutual support that were as diverse as the needs of personal and professional life, ranging from prayers for the dead to arbitration in commercial law, and including assistance to orphans and the organization of a communal distribution service. Flemish merchants in Florence met together from the late fourteenth century in the Confraternity of Saint Barbara. The confraternities of the Catalan merchants had branches in Bruges. The phenomenon became so important that public authorities began to be alarmed, egged on by a church that was suspicious of any manifestation of popular piety not under its control. They had no objection to prayer and good works in themselves, but not within the framework of an interest group. In 1389, Richard II initiated an inquiry into the activities of confraternities in

England. Ten years later, Venice placed restrictions on their public ceremonies. In Florence, from 1419, all newly created confraternities had to be authorized by the Commune, the government of this city-state.

Signs of these confraternities could be seen within the town in the dedications of their chapels or the names of the streets. "Lombard Street" was a common name all over Western Europe. The Germans in Venice met together at the *Fondaco dei Tedeschi,* while in Harfleur there was a *Rue d'Espagne* and in Bergen a German Quay. The house of the Catalans in Cagliari was in *Via dels Mercaders.*

These national communities did not always define their position as precisely as the Hanseatic merchants, who would receive only "recognized" members into their midst. More often, the group was formed spontaneously, through a recognized mutual origin, language, and interest. Some organizations were immediately obvious, while others struggled. In Bruges, there was nothing in common between the six hundred Hanseatic merchants whose names were carefully recorded in 1457 and the few hundred Genoese or the twenty Florentines present there during the same period. The handful of Genoese spice merchants established in Paris at the end of the fourteenth century could hardly be said to have constituted a group, except insofar as they were linked by marriage. Nor could the merchants of Lucca fall into the category of a group, since, though they set up close links in order to divide up the available business, they knew how to pass themselves off as good Flemish merchants in Bruges or eminent Parisians in Paris, while adopting the *lingua di sì* of Avignon.

As soon as a group became organized and began to collect an income from the community, it acquired the means to present a distinctive collective personality. Voluntary donations, fines, or taxes, whether willingly or grudgingly accepted, became translated in the townscape into bell towers and high gables, giving the different national groups a physical presence. A church or a chapel where God or the saints venerated in the hometown or country could be worshiped; a hospice where travelers could stay, deposit their goods, hold meetings, and keep the communal coffers—all contributed to giving the "nation" a public face. This permanence gave it an advantage over the ephemeral manifestations of passing trade. The house of the Italians, in the Place de la Bourse, in Bruges, is a good example. The Genoese in Bruges attended services in a church dedicated to St. George, the Germans of Novgorod stayed and stored their goods in the courtyard of St. Olaf's church, while those residing in Venice had, in their *Fondaco dei Tedeschi,* a magnificent building on the Grand Canal, only a stone's throw from the Rialto Bridge. Symbolic of the profound unity and continuity of the Hanseatic League was the group of buildings in London known as the *Stalhof,* once again close to the bridge. This was the only example of an economic enclave that the

English were prepared to tolerate, the other merchants finding themselves forbidden to set up a national base of this kind.

Not surprisingly, people were crammed together in these mandatory warehouses. The Fugger company, in 1494, arranged to acquire a more spacious property for business, taking over the Venetian *fondaco* from the Carinthian merchants of Judenburg. As always, the best spots went to those who could look after themselves. The Fugger star was in the ascendant.

In this way the "nations" came about. This name was an echo, in the merchant world, of the grouping together of teachers and students in the universities, rather approximately, by their common origins. These nations already existed at the University of Bologna in the mid-twelfth century. They were officially designated in Paris in 1222. In both cases they were soon to become the most durable structures in the university establishments, acquiring their own administrative and financial systems. Groups were organized in Bologna representing Tuscany, Lombardy, France, Picardy, Burgundy, Poitou, Touraine, Normandy, Catalonia, Provence, Spain, Gascony, England, Hungary, Poland, and Germany. In the thirteenth century all these groups were arranged into two properly constituted nations: Cismontane and Ultramontane, or, in other words, Italians and non-Italians. In Paris the teachers and students of the Arts Faculty were divided into four nations: Normandy, Picardy, England—or sometimes Germany, depending on the accidents of political life—and France.

This was an approximate form of nationalism, where those from Scotland and Liège belonged to the same "English" or "German" nation, and Auvergne and Languedoc were placed in France but not Normandy or Picardy. But it was, above all, practical, reflecting linguistic needs and uncomplicated by useless definitions. Students who spoke the *langue d'oc* rarely came to Paris, favoring Montpellier or Toulouse, and the "French" nation kept to the boundaries of the old royal domain of the early thirteenth century. But it was nationalism for all that, reflecting the habit already current in all milieus of describing an individual by his origins. Among the nicknames found in Philip the Fair's capital that were derived from a person's place of origin were dozens of Langlois (the English) and Lallemant (the German), alongside many more called Le Breton, Le Normant, and Le Flamant (Flemish). An average Parisian might be known as Le Picart (from Picardy) or d'Amiens, which became Damiens. Origins were quickly forgotten, but the names lived on.

Thus it was easy for merchants to follow the example of the universities. They too felt, when abroad, that sense of community not immediately perceptible to someone who had never ventured far from home. Primarily it was a matter of defending their common interests, representing themselves before local authorities, and putting on a show of strength and unity in the face of competitors. Certain privileges could not withstand the assaults of local protectionism—or those of other national groups—unless a group stood together. The king of Aragon never missed a chance to remind his subjects of the importance of this defense, and it was he who guaranteed the representation of Barcelona's interests, entrusted overseas—and in Bruges—to "consuls" nominated by the town council. The consul in Syria even had the unenviable job of demanding that the Saracens return anything they might ever have seized from Catalan merchants.

Similarly, all over Europe there were attempts to suppress the frequent resurrection of the old law of reprisals, that disincentive to solidarity dreamed up by the locals whereby each foreigner was held responsible for the obligations of his compatriots. Maintaining individual responsibility was never an easy matter, since those merchants who stayed at home were always suspicious of the business partner who might well never return. Thus it was very much to the advantage of the nation to guarantee the obligations and contracts of each member: they would be less readily challenged. But the price could sometimes be high, as when all the goods of the Albertini and Strozzi companies in England were confiscated in 1375 in compensation for the 10,000 pounds that two Italian buyers had neglected to pay. Again, in the mid-fifteenth century, Jacques Coeur persuaded Charles VII to impose on all Spanish merchants in his kingdom the payment of an indemnity that was nothing other than the old right to reprisals or marque: "The collection made by the late Master Jean Mérichon, acting for the king, of certain taxes levied on the funds and merchandise of the Spanish for certain damages caused in Spain to Jacques Coeur . . ."

Jacques Coeur was reproached for having taken more than his fair share of what was explicitly designated "marques." But the agent charged with the job of evaluating the treasurer's goods was not unduly shocked by this generous usage of a law that every merchant knew led ultimately to deadlock. What did scandalize the king's men, once Coeur was toppled from his pinnacle, was that, by mixing up the claims, he had cleverly benefited from one imposed for damages caused before his arrival on the scene:

> The said Coeur was further charged with having demanded and unduly obtained several large sums of money in marques from the Genoese, from Provence and Catalonia, and specially of having added on the earlier claim of the Genoese, set up to recompense those harmed by the loss of the galley *Narbonne*, to the last claim made for those harmed on the galley *Saint-Denis* to the great prejudice and hurt of the said injured parties for whom the first and former claim had been made.
>
> For, by the adding and joining of the two Genoese claims, the payment to the first injured parties had been greatly delayed and diminished: whereas they ought to have been paid in six or eight years, they will not be paid for thirty, and they will not have many sous where they ought to have had every year pounds and écus.

The local authorities found it advantageous, in commercial dealings, to make use of of an authorized, well-known, and established agent. The Hanseatic merchants in London had an "English ancient" whose function was in all ways similar to that of a consul. When, in 1353, Edward III wanted to conduct negotiations on the economic position of foreigners in England, he called the representatives of the business world to appear before his council: seventy Englishmen, eight Italians, and four representatives of the Hanseatic League. In this way, they were able to discuss matters relating to customs or the rules of navigation. Thanks to its own internal structure, the nation became a collective reflection of its distant capital. Such a role, vital to the management of business, obviously depended on the foreignness of the foreigner.

The national group provided the necessary framework for all types of economic policing at the great international fairs, and particularly the Champagne fairs. With the increasing tendency in the fourteenth century for the great companies to stay put and develop branch offices abroad, the group's function in this area became less important. The merchant moved on but society remained in place. Even where the foreigner made no attempt to become assimilated—in Bruges, for example, and later in Antwerp—economic life during the fifteenth century no longer required these quasi-official representatives from distant markets. Portinari was present in Bruges, but anyone doing business with him had very little feeling of doing business with Florence. In Paris, where the fourteenth-century Lombard became a Parisian citizen in the fifteenth century, there was no longer the need for something like a Genoese consul when conducting business with Henri Orlant, whom no one would now confuse with Enrico Orlandi.

As long as there were common interests to be defended, the foreign colony had to maintain its internal laws, which provided the very conditions for its credibility and group cohesiveness. Thus, in commercial arbitration between nationals, the law and customs of their hometowns were kept. In fact, the king of France's judges were quite happy to have the Lombards do openly in Champagne what they would have done anyway without saying so: arbitrate on matters of commercial law. It suited them quite well in Antwerp to allow the Florentines to arrange their own matrimonial affairs. In 1390 local authorities came to the consul, Girolamo Frescobaldi, and four eminent members of his nation to ask them to explain the Florentine statutes pertaining to the possessions of a married woman.

On the other hand, it would not have done for a foreign legal system to be applied in the criminal court. Even the Hanseatic merchants, who applied their own legal system as successfully in London as in Bergen, could not extend it to crimes punishable by mutilation or death. The Germans—under the jurisdiction of their "English ancient," appointed by the king of England—could impose a fine on any of their fellow members who committed a crime, but the king of England could not permit them to hang each other in London. The Hanseatic merchants obtained this right, thanks only to the combined efects of the linguistic barrier and distance, in their Russian marketplace at Novgorod. With the exception of the Hanseatic merchants—and the merchants of Amiens, Nesle, and Corbie, thanks to a privilege of 1237—the *Carta mercatoria,* the merchants' charter of 1303, limited the judicial activities of foreign merchants to commercial arbitration; and even here they could only act as intermediary between the individual merchant and the king's officers, or, in some cases, as an unofficial advocate for foreigners in difficulty.

Assimilation

Nationality lost its meaning when the foreigner's ambition no longer was simply to become established but to assimilate. Here again, conditions varied, colonies were distributed unequally, and some local mileus were more welcoming than others. Although firmly closed to anyone not from a Hanseatic town, internally the Hanseatic League was very open to assimilation; it was common for a merchant to travel from one town to another. Provided that he did not go outside the League's domain, it was easy to carry on business in another town. Heinrich Castorp, born in Dortmund around 1420, set up in Lübeck in 1450. Five years later he was a citizen of that town. In 1462 he was a member of the town council. Eventually he would become burgomaster.

During the same period, by contrast, the election on 16 August 1464 of Christophe Paillart as a Parisian magistrate was annulled the very same day when the king's procurator noticed that Paillart had been born in Auxerre. And yet for twenty years this master of the audits had been a person of some stature in the town. The money changer Jean Le Riche was more fortunate in 1452: when accused of being a native of Bourg-la-Reine, he was able to produce witnesses to prove that his mother had traveled to Paris to give birth. There were even parishioners who could recall that the baby had been baptized at the Church of St. Paul.

During the years when Jean Juvénal des Ursins was archbishop of Reims and his brother William chancellor of France, nobody recalled that the man whom Paris could thank for having regained her economic privileges at the end of the previous century—their father Jean Jouvenel—would not have been eligible to be provost of these merchants whom he had revitalized, since he was born in Troyes. In actuality, Paris was quite liberal in such matters, but Christophe Paillart was foolish enough to take his ambitions where he should not have gone. Had the king's procurator been one of his friends, he might have kept silent.

Although the attitudes of merchants based abroad varied greatly, it was still possible to detect some quite characteristic national traditions. Thus it was that Florentine pride did not sit well with neglect of a merchant's origins. When he married Maria Bandini Baroncelli in 1469, Tommaso Portinari, like any good Florentine, was returning home to celebrate the major events of his private life. He came back again to serve in the municipal courts, finally returning to the fold for good in 1496, at the age of seventy, to die on the banks of the Arno. The small town of Lucca, a few leagues from Florence, left less of a mark on her children. Dino Rapondi, made a citizen of Paris in 1374, signed his name as Dyne Raponde, and we know that his compatriots and contemporaries Guidiccioni, Moriconi, and Burlamacchi became Guidechon, Moriçon, and Bourlamet. Grandson of a merchant from Lucca, Jean Spifame was in 1421 squire and captain of Conflans-Sainte-Honorine. As for the Genoese, they made themselves at home everywhere, merging into the local background within two or three generations. Henri Orlant was Genoese. His son Thomas, fortunately born in Paris, was a squire by 1435. During the same period Giovanni Sacchi was known to his clients, including the government of the regent Bedford, as the banker Jean Sac.

Paris did not have a monopoly on such cases of assimilation. The Genoese were equally happy to become citizens of Marseilles or Seville. When they left the Riviera, as the coast of Genoa was known, it was usually with the intention of staying away for good. Benedetto Zaccaria became one of the foremost members of society in Andalusía. In 1337 the admiral Emmanuele Pessagno received an estate and a pension from Alfonso IV as a reward for his permanent engagement, with his three galleys, in the service of Portugal. The Florentines returned home having made their fortunes; the Genoese who returned were those who had failed. On the fringes of the world of trade, where mercenaries hired out their professional talents as soldiers or navigators, the Genoese merchants were no less inclined to embark on long-term enterprises. Christopher Columbus was not the first. Philip the Fair's admiral was Benedetto Zaccaria. Genoese crossbowmen were to be found on every battlefield in the army of the French king during the fourteenth century. At La Rochelle, in 1372, Rainier Grimaldi led the fleet of Charles V, and Ambrogio Boccanegra—nephew of the doge Simone—that of the king of Castile.

Marriage was an important stage on the road to integration. His marriage to Michèle de Vitry gave Jean Jouvenel, son of a Troyes cloth merchant, his entree to everything that the Parisian upper classes counted as rich and influential. For the Nuremberg merchant Johann Lange, marriage to a daughter of a Lübeck patrician opened the doors of Lübeck society, which was the de facto government of the Hanseatic League in the Germanic towns. The Lucchesi, ever inclined to naturalize, embarked on a veritable flurry of marriages in Paris: Bartolomeo Spifame married Jacqueline de

Honfleur; Giovanni Spifame took as his bride the daughter of the humanist—and, more important, the king's secretary—Gontier Col; and Guglielmo
Cenami, or Céname, won the hand of the daughter of the great Parisian
lawyer Jean Langlois. Thus were the doors of society opened.

Naturalization in the strict sense of the word was less common. It
speeded up the process of integration by a good generation, but that could
be precisely the drawback. To acquire the privileges of natives without having
first proved one's credentials gave rise to suspicion. There are very few letters
patent for citizenship to be found in the registers of the French chancellery.
The English Parliament, which dealt with such matters, seems to have recorded equally few naturalizations. The king, on the other hand, could
grant foreigners a sort of citizenship, *denization,* the effects of which chiefly
pertained to taxes.

Foreigners were often content to rely on their business circles without
referring to the political authorities or making too much of a commitment
to the future. In London, as in Paris, Bristol, or Marseilles, it was often
enough for the foreign merchant to be made a member of the local community, a burgess or a citizen. He could in this way acquire privileges and,
above all, credit.

There was also public office. This was usually enough to ensure assimilation, providing de facto citizenship without making it irreversible. It opened
the way for the foreigner, without closing the door behind him. He was free
to stay, work, and set up in his new role. He could also return home,
retaining only the memory of a successful or unsuccessful deal. As financial
advisers to princes, these businessmen knew how to convert a function with
no specific title into the best of introductions into the financial world. In
documents relating to Philip the Fair, Biche and Mouche—Albizzo and
Musciatto Guidi de' Franzesi—were called variously "the king's knights" or
"treasurers." But the bookkeepers did not get bogged down in the formalities
of chancellery, writing simply "*Compte de* Biche" or "*Compte de* Mouche."
Everyone was familiar with what had always been their de facto position.
The Aragonese ambassadors, shrewd observers of the political scene and of
the real distribution of power, simply wrote in their dispatches "*Sire
Mouchet.*" As for their nephew, Tote Guy, "valet to the king" in official
documents and "collector for Flanders" to the bookkeepers, he was quite
simply, for the realists, "the merchant Monseigneur Enguerran de Marigny,"
a good description of the role played in Flanders and England by this
factotum who promoted—with the greatest discretion—the policies of the
pragmatic Marigny.

The same kind of situation arose in the England of Edward I, where
bankers and merchants could rise to the forefront of the business world
without taking on any form of citizenship. The Riccardi, bankers to Edward

I until their collapse in 1294, are referred to in documents simply as "merchants of Lucca." Their successors in the favor and credit of the last Plantagenets—the Ballardi from Lucca and the Bardi, Peruzzi, Frescobaldi, and other firms from Florence—sought nothing more than this dangerously privileged position. The only exception, in the time of Edward III, was Amerigo Frescobaldi who was Constable of Bordeaux.

Such was also the case of the counselor to Count Louis of Nevers in Flanders, the merchant Conte Gualterotti—he being no other than the factor of the Bardi family. We also know that, at the end of the fourteenth century, Dino Rapondi of Lucca was at once counselor, banker, and diplomatic agent for the duke of Burgundy, Philip the Bold, much as Mouche had been for Philip the Fair.

It was when he stopped being a merchant that the businessman became more truly assimilated. For as long as he juggled credit and kept the coins clinking he would remain what he had originally intended: a trader come to make money. Mouche might sit in the king's council with men like Louis d'Évreux and Gaucher de Châtillon, but he remained a Lombard to the last. Two or three generations later, such foreigners had demonstrated their desire for stability: they no longer exported their capital. They took their place in the social order and played at being local nobility. The grandson of a Lombard merchant, established in Paris, was now lord of an estate side by side with the grandson of a Parisian cloth merchant or of an advocate in *Parlement*.

They made their way more quickly in the towns, where high rates of immigration from surrounding regions made new faces and names a common occurrence. No one remarked on a foreign accent in Paris, Bruges, Antwerp, or London. But it was not until the opening of the routes to the Atlantic that it passed without comment in Rouen. The Parisian had seen everything: the peasant from Bourg-la-Reine, the banker from Lucca, the hosier from Troyes, the fish merchant from Dieppe, and the armorer from Solingen. They no longer wondered at the seneschal from Beaucaire with a southern accent come to settle his accounts, or asked why the Navarrais soldiers of Charles the Bad were Normans, or why the English soldiers of the Black Prince were Gascons. Rabelais poked fun at the Limousin accent of his schoolboy only in order to satirize a Latinizing pedant who wanted to "*ambuler jouxte la Séquene*" ("ambulate unto the noble Seine").

Reactions were less tolerant and assimilation slower for immigrants coming from a great distance and lacking go-betweens. The Slavs were as unwelcome in Danzig as the western Germans, and Lübeck rejected them while welcoming other Germans. Neither Paris nor London feared a wave of Florentines, and assimilating the Lucchesi caused no difficulties. The Parisians had no fear that they would replace the locals or that their own *langue d'oil* (French) would ever be ousted on the Place de Grève by the *lingua di sì* (Italian). But, in Danzig, up went the protective barriers.

SEVEN

Currency

The System

The system bestowed upon the West by Charlemagne and his son Louis the Pious was both long-lasting and coherent. The idea of minting pure gold had become a utopian dream, bimetallism an impossible luxury. The gold coin of the Roman Empire—its very name, *solidus,* indicating a reliability unaffected by time or place—was nothing but a memory in the minds of a few learned clerics. Even the *triens,* a third of a *solidus,* was becoming increasingly rare; they were hoarded, melted, or exported.

Charles minted a few coins for form's sake, asserting the claim of the Frankish kings to be heir to the Caesars with some *triens* issued in northern Italy and Tuscany. It was more a matter of exercising his sovereign right to mint in gold than of enhancing economic life by furnishing it with a means of exchange based on something other than the old practice of barter.

The West did not have enough gold to allow itself such a coinage, and the gold that was minted rapidly disappeared from use as money. The emperor Louis the Pious was to be the last, around 820, to mint a *triens,* which was apparently never seen in circulation. The only gold coins encountered were the odd Byzantine hyperper or the occasional Arab coins from Spain or Sicily—otherwise nothing.

So it was not with gold that payments were made, but with good silver *deniers.* Louis the Pious had laid down strict instructions in about 825 that 240 of these coins should be struck for one pound in weight (equal to some 490 modern grams) of silver. Thus a *denier* weighed approximately two grams.

The first devaluation, in 865, was the work of Charles the Bald. The *denier* became lighter, and for a pound of silver 264 coins were minted.

125

Nevertheless, the habit of saying that a "pound" (*livre*) was the equivalent of 240 *deniers* continued. Thus was born the monetary "pound," no longer anything to do with the pound weight. It is this same pound that we encounter at the time of St. Louis when the royal mints of the kingdom of France struck the *denier tournois*—it was minted at Tours—at a rate of 217 coins to the mark, or 434 coins to a pound weight, and of an alloy that was 3¾ pure silver. This *denier* was nevertheless fitted into a system where twelve *deniers* made one sou and twenty sous a "pound."

Everyone knew the *denier tournois*, at least in northern France. But there were as many different sorts of *denier* as there were mints, and these had multiplied as the unifying authority of the Carolingian king collapsed, continuing into the centuries known as the feudal period when old political frameworks broke up into smaller units. In the French kingdom, for example, only the money changers were able to deal with the different *deniers* from Paris, Toulouse, Melgueil, Provins, and the other towns where mints had been established. The Champagne fairs made the Provins *denier* so popular that the Italian cities were not embarrassed to mint their own *provinois*, which were not forgeries in our sense of the word but rather a coinage aligned in weight and name with the Champagne coin. The common people would generally make do with the local equivalents. It was well known in Paris that five *tournois* were worth four *parisis*.

Even if this was a coherent system, its foundations were shaky. There was a shortage of silver, with only a few mines and these generally poorly exploited. The monometallism established by the Carolingians was the lesser evil: during a shortage of the means of payment—something that was never resolved—it was inspired by realism.

For two or three centuries, it seemed that this system might go hand in hand with expansion. Exploitation of the mines started up again with a renewed vigor born of need. From 960 onward the deposits in the Harz Mountains, near Goslar, yielded both copper and silver in abundance. Mines that had been closed in Carolingian times were reopened, and new techniques, such as the use of mills to drive the drainage pumps and winches, made up for some of the profitability that had been lost with the end of the old system of slavery. In the Alps, Vosges, and Jura, the mining of silver proceeded at the same rate as that of copper and lead. New deposits were discovered at the same time, both in the eastern Alps and in Saxony.

But none of this was enough to sustain a return to a monetary economy stimulated, since the beginning of the second millennium, by the upturn in population and most obviously represented by the figure of the urban merchant. Open-cast silver mining gave small yields, and the hoarding of gold coins continued to discourage the expansion in monetary circulation. Silver was used to make table vessels, chalices, and reliquaries for the nobility and the churches, causing severe shortages for the mints. It can be said fairly that investing in a work of art was a normal way of hoarding silver. Another less obvious form of hoarding was the burying of coins, the discovery of which—usually by accident—provides such a wealth of interest for the modern numismatist. It was always possible, in case of need, to melt down crucifixes and chalices, goblets or decorative buckles. But so long as such objects were kept for a rainy day the precious metal could not circulate in the form of coins.

An economy with expanding objectives and horizons but with no sign of a systematic means of payment spelled inflation. At the time of Louis the Pious, around 820, the *denier* weighed two grams of pure silver. Around 1000, the *denier* of the early Capetians weighed one and a half grams and was still made of pure silver. But already the less scrupulous nobles were prepared to issue false coins with a silver content that was smaller but detectable only to the professional money changer. The currency war was beginning, which for centuries was to consist of trying to lure away one's neighbor's precious metals by offering a better rate. One could then make good one's losses by cheating on the alloy. Long before the English businessman Thomas Gresham formulated a law on the matter during the sixteenth century, it was well known that "bad money drives out good."

A century and a half later, at the peak of the Champagne fairs, the king of France's *denier* was made of an alloy containing only half silver. The obvious weight of the piece—even so, now only 1.27 grams—failed to conceal the fact that it now contained barely 0.64 grams of pure silver. At the low point of this system, around 1230–50, the *denier tournois* contained only 0.35 grams of pure silver. Inflation had nibbled away 83 percent of the Carolingian *denier*. It was clear to all: the silver coin had turned black.

Thus we can imagine the sackloads of metal brought to the great fairs when debts were being paid and trading in luxury goods conducted on a European scale. When rents began to be paid in cash—money that no landowner would now dream of going and spending on the spot—the peasant's rent might take the form of a bag of minted coins. It cost the countess of Champagne three quintals of black coins—a good cartload—to buy the neutrality of Philip Augustus in the face of an uprising in the towns. One can imagine the weight in metal for a cargo of wool, a load of spices, a delivery of amber, or a Byzantine ivory triptych.

As the activity of the thirteenth century began to falter, but before anyone could anticipate the social and economic crises to come, the West began to feel the need for monetary "multiples" that would not be simply a great pile of black coins on the weighing scales. But it was easy at the time to confuse these two expressions of insufficiency: monometallism (that is, all silver) and the single denomination (the *denier* and nothing but the *denier*). We need to examine what might have led to the renunciation of these two fundamentals of a monetary system so well suited to the period of its creation in about 800 and so dramatically ill suited to the needs of the early thirteenth century.

The West first attacked the single denomination, and this was a wise decision. Weighing, carrying, estimating, and counting so much debased metal was wasteful. Carting lead or paying the huge sums now used in major trade in vast piles of inferior metal seemed ridiculous. The great reform of the thirteenth century, and by far the best, was the "heavy coin," or *gros*. It represented a return to the time of Charlemagne.

Venice set the example with its *matapan* of 1203. Florence followed cautiously with a *soldo*, in other words something not seen for four centuries: a real coin worth one unit, twelve *deniers* to one *soldo*. They failed to recall that the Roman *solidus* had been of pure gold. The new coin was a silver coin, but it was a "heavy coin."

During the same period, theoreticians began to wonder about the relationship between gold and silver. In a monetary system based solely on silver, gold had, like any other merchandise, a commercial rate. It was well known that one weight of gold was equivalent to roughly twelve times its weight in silver. This was the monetary ratio of the bimetallism of antiquity—the gold coin, the *solidus*, was worth twelve silver coins, twelve *denarii*—which was why a sou worth twelve *deniers* emerged as the monetary unit and standard, regardless of the pure silver content of the *denier*. There were, of course, also those who pointed out that twelve was a sacred number. There were twelve apostles, but there were also twelve months in the year. Twelve is one of the arithmetical expressions of the natural order of things. So twelve was adopted by those who concluded in the 1250s that a gold coinage was not necessarily a privilege just of the Byzantine emperors or the caliphs.

St. Louis, in turn, decided to mint a new heavy coin of silver. This was the *gros tournois* of 1266, worth twelve *deniers tournois*. After so many hundreds of years in which the *sou tournois* had been a money of account—a theoretical multiple of the coins in actual use—now at last it had become reality. Thirteen years later, Edward III followed his example and gave England the groat. The rest of Europe followed suit, minting "heavy" silver coins. Bohemia, for example, began to use the *groschen* in 1296.

These coins were naturally of pure silver, while the *denier* continued to become less and less pure. Thus there was no attempt to retain the simple arithmetical relationship between the sou and the *denier*. From the thirteenth century the *gros tournois*—always struck at a rate of 58 coins for a mark (a weight of c. 8 ounces) of pure silver—began to be taken as equivalent to 15 *deniers*. The *gros* was no longer the *sou*. With its sou of 12 *deniers* and *livre* of 20 sous, this monetary system was to remain the ideal scale, to which the very different coins in actual circulation and daily use for payment would refer at all times, and at a rate determined by the circumstances of the money market.

The same reasons that gave rise to the heavy silver coins were to lead to gold coins. From the black coins, 70 or 75 percent lead, to the pure silver coin, it had been necessary to increase the weight of the coin in order to achieve the ratio of 1:12, that of the sou to the *denier*. St. Louis's minters struck 220 *deniers tournois* from an alloy mark, but only 58 *gros* from a mark of pure silver. Twelve coins of 1.11 grams of black metal were worth one coin of 4.22 grams. Moving to gold—or rather, returning to gold—meant once again multiplying by twelve, but without any increase in weight. At last it would be possible to settle accounts in the world of international trade without being loaded down with sacks or cartloads of coins.

Florence and Genoa took the initiative in 1252. The trade of both towns was equally shared between the eastern Mediterranean and continental Europe. The two precious metals were, as a result, equally balanced—and in abundance—in the Italian markets.

The Florentine florin and the Genoese *genovino* were immediately and enthusiastically received throughout Europe. With the patron saint of Florence, St. John the Baptist, on one side and the fleur-de-lis on the other, the florin was soon to symbolize the budding prosperity of Florence as well as stability in monetary standards. Before long the West was not content only to pay in florins; it started to count in florins. During this period, Venice, after a long hesitation, finally followed Genoa's example, striking a gold *ducat* (from the Latin *dux* or "doge") in 1284.

England and France did not wish to be seen as lagging behind, not so much for economic reasons, one must admit, as for the principle of the thing. Gold coins retained their symbolic value as an affirmation of sovereignty. It had been in this spirit that in the sixth century King Thierry, eldest of the sons of Clovis, had dared to place his own effigy on the gold sous minted in his kingdom. In the thirteenth century, neither the Capetians nor the Plantagenets were prepared to relinquish the trappings of an imperial past to the Italian city-states. Moreover, it was tempting to take advantage of the collapse of the Germanic Holy Roman Empire, by then in no shape to rise to the bait. Frederick II, weakened and excommunicated, died in 1250. Between the death in 1254, after a reign of only four years, of Conrad IV and the election of Rudolf of Habsburg in 1273, the Empire got bogged down in the Great Interregnum, relieving the neighboring kings of an annoying rival. As for Charles of Anjou, in whose Sicilian kingdom Byzantine and Arab gold coins were still circulating, he did not hesitate to mint his *augustale*, where the imperial effigy alone is a profession of political faith.

Henry III was the first to take the plunge. In 1257 he made a tentative step toward a gold coin but did not follow it through. England was not to have a proper gold coin until 1344.

St. Louis followed in 1266 with a "gold *denier* of one écu," of the same weight as the *gros tournois*. The very name of this new coin shows the extent to which people were accustomed to think that there was no coin but the *denier,* and that all coins were therefore *deniers. Denier* (from the Latin *denarius*) simply means "coin," and people long continued to refer to "gold *deniers*"—a meaningless expression—and *deniers* with this or that head on them.

This gold coin had to have a rate: the écu would be worth ten *sous tournois.* In other words, the value of gold was set at ten times that of silver. At this price it seemed that the royal mints would have a job to find gold to mint: it all disappeared. It is even possible that clandestine melting-down caused the few coins that were put into circulation by the royal mints to vanish. The very small number of surviving coins has led historians to conclude that the size of this minting must have been fairly insignificant. Nevertheless, the first step had been taken. The Capetian monarchy had shown that it was not only the Byzantine emperors or the Italian towns with their constant references to membership in the Holy Roman Empire who could produce gold coins. But Louis IX was not satisfied with mere gestures.

The idea took root, which had been the intention. In 1270 Philip III the Bold followed with a "queen *denier,*" opening the way to a series of gold coins that persisted until the last *louis* of the Third Republic.

Two important decrees, of 1263 and 1266, laid the foundations in France for a new monetary system, though one that made more sense politically than economically. The product of a century-long Aristotelian debate on the role of the state in defining the foundations of all social relationships, reform was based on the implicit principle that the rate of exchange should not be uncertain. The ruler should have a right to a monopoly over the issue of and profit from minting the coinage, which was prescribed in the public interest. This right included that of "renewing," or revaluating the currency (*renovatio* or *mutatio monetae*) if the "common profit" demanded it. In practice, this provision, which was advanced by jurists every time the king wanted to intervene in the daily life of his subjects, was soon to acquire a technical meaning: the currency had to be "renewed" if the commercial rate of the precious metal deviated from the face value of the coin to the extent that there was a risk of speculation and the loss of gold or silver to other regions where the valuation was different.

To "renew" meant to correct. The common people were mistaken when they believed that the prince converted his currency in order to make gains on the direct profit he derived from a new minting. In fact, speculation was not uncommon in well-informed business circles, and there are occasional cases where the interests of the speculators determined a particular decision made by the prince. But such changes came about for the most part when a crisis, caused by a shortage of the coinage, came to a head. Much more frequently than people imagined at the time, even informed merchants who were ever inclined to credit their colleagues with illicit profits, the prince changed the rate because he had no other choice, because the money market required it, and because he had to supply the *res publica* with the means of payment.

The reform carried out by St. Louis was inspired by principles taken from Aristotle and Thomas Aquinas as well as from Roman law. The royal coinage had a privilege over and above all others: the king's money had an obligatory rate throughout the kingdom, while that of the barons and churchmen applied only to their own territories. This meant that in a kingdom that had been greatly extended by the conquests of Philip Augustus and in the succeeding years, the king's coinage was—or ought to have been—the only one. The barons were forbidden to mint any coins but those sanctified by custom, the effect of which was to oblige these mints—belonging to dukes, counts, bishops, and abbots—to strike only old-style *deniers,* coins that were soon to be used only for change.

These regulations were accompanied by practical politics. The Capetian kings started to buy up anything that resembled a seigneurial mint. As early as the beginning of the fourteenth century the royal coinage in France had to a great extent ousted the others. The increasing power of the principalities at the time of the Hundred Years' War, however, was to have an adverse effect on St. Louis's legislation. Now Burgundy, Flanders, Brittany, and a few others—not to mention Lancastrian Aquitaine—began to mint all those different gold and silver coins which the king had reserved for himself. By this time there was no longer a variety, as there had still been in the twelfth century, of different *deniers* such as the *deniers tolzas* or *deniers provinois.* Now it was the turn of the Breton "gold knight," the Flemish gold *riddre,* the Burgundian *philippus,* and the écu from Guyenne.

For all that, bimetallism finally became established in Europe. Hungary achieved it in 1308 and Bohemia in 1325. Gold was minted in Lübeck in 1340. Poland and Sweden alone had to wait until the sixteenth century.

This new diversity made a money of account more necessary than ever. While trading at a distance involved, despite the existence in theory of official monopolies, all kinds of currencies in the settling of accounts, the need for a standard of reference was obvious. Often a currency that was familiar and, more important, known for its stability was taken as a reference point. This was the case with the Florentine florin. Even more frequently, and usually for local transactions, people stuck to the old system of the pound (*livre*) and the sou, based on a *denier* that had ceased to be the main coin but still had a place through its old connection with the other deniers. The *livre parisis* was worth twenty *sous parisis* but, more significantly for the merchant, was worth twenty-five *sous tournois.*

The pressing need for a money of account that referred to an actual coin made it necessary to be specific: a pound or a sou "of the good small Paris type" or "of the old *tournois* type." Thus people were more familiar with pounds and sous than with *deniers,* whether real, current, or obsolete. The pope in Avignon even continued, at the beginning of the Great Schism, to issue "Chamber" florins so as not to deprive the accounting system of the Apostolic Chamber—the financial wing of the papacy—of its real monetary support. The pope's treasurer had in fact been paying for a long time in "current florins" of the papal state of the comtat Venaissin, in "queen"s florins" of Provence, in French "crown écus" and even in "Aragonese florins." But no one would have dared, in the 1380s, to continue to count in "Chamber" florins if this type of coin was not still being issued. All in all, it mattered little whether a payment was made in one or another of the currencies available in the payer's purse.

Money Changers and the Market

The smallest of payments, therefore, required, in addition to a modest knowledge of arithmetic, a familiarity with the coins in circulation—something that the small shopkeeper or innkeeper could not hope to attain. If you wanted a drink, it was wise to start by putting a recognizable coin down on the table. A soldier from Bedford quartered in Paris in the spring of 1424 experienced at first hand the disadvantages of having the wrong kind of money.

With two companions, the Englishman Sander Russel had eaten and drunk his fill at the sign of the *Écu de Bretagne,* a tavern in Place Baudoyer, behind the *Maison aux Piliers (House of the Columns)* that was then the town hall. The "lady of the hostelry" asked for three or four Paris sous. The Englishmen took out a gold écu, assured her that it was worth twenty-six Paris sous and asked for change. The hostess maintained that the écu was worth at most twenty-four sous. Refusing to pay at such a rate, Russel proposed simply going and changing his coin "in town." Seeing that the Englishman was going to leave with his écu, the woman said that she would keep the coin while waiting for Russel to return with a suitable currency. Russel clearly had nothing but this one coin that could be changed without loss, so offered as security a Rhine florin, a very inferior coin, for which the Englishman knew quite well the money changer would give him a poor rate of exchange. It would take Russel an hour to change his écu and the woman was certainly not going to accept, as a pledge for the wine he had consumed, a Rhenish florin that might be a fake. She refused. The soldier got angry: "By the devil, we could quite well have gone out or left this place! And yet we are quite willing to pay our share!"

By now furious, the Englishman smashed two empty glasses—*deux woires wis*—against the wall. A sergeant who happened to be there tried to calm him down. Heated words were exchanged, and Russel remarked that it was easy enough to understand, hearing their language, "what kind of people they were." The sergeant accused the three of them of being thieves. Daggers were drawn and the sergeant collapsed down the stairs, stabbed to death. In the struggle, he had lost his belt with his purse. "Small change in *doubles* and the odd piece of silver" were picked up in the tavern. History does not relate whether the innkeeper's wife took the opportunity to recoup her losses.

Let us put ourselves for a moment in her place. She would at least have recognized the crown écu of 1420 (66 coins to one mark-weight, 22 sous 6 *deniers tournois* at the time of issue) and the crown écu of 1419 (64 to the mark, 30 sous), not forgetting the écu of 1411 (64 to the mark, 22 sous 6 *deniers*) and the pre-1411 one (61⅓ to the mark, 22 sous 6 *deniers*). She was perfectly entitled to hesitate in the face of so many different coins that continued to circulate despite the decrees published to reinforce the royal directives. All these écus had on one side the arms of France with three fleur-de-lis surmounted by a crown, while on the other side was a cross in a quatrefoil. All had, in any case, been depreciated by Bedford in 1423 and replaced by the *salut* (salutation), which was at least fairly easy to recognize with its depiction of the angel greeting Mary behind the two shields of France and England.

The soldier and the innkeeper could not agree on the rate of exchange of the écu. Other similarly humble people were increasingly having to seek out the money changer, whether to change a coin or to have it verified or valued.

The requirements of the merchant, the businessman, and, indeed, the financier were of another order. In his report of his management for 1362, the bookkeeper for the papal treasury notes that he has received 15,654 florins, 1,397 leopards, 299 écus, 103 sheep, 5 royals, and 60 pounds 6 sous 2 *deniers* in silver. And that was not the half of it:

> Of the florins there are 4,223 Chamber florins, 3,869 Sentence florins, 7,438 heavy florins, 16 ducats, 5 Genoese florins, 31 Aragonese florins, 7 French florins, 59 florins of a lesser weight, 6 Cambrai florins.
>
> Of the écus there are 271 old écus of good weight, 1 English écu, 1 Bavarian écu, 2 old écus not of good weight, 17 counterfeit old écus, 8 Philip écus.

Let us move forward a century. In the years 1476–80 the response of the faithful of Burgundy to the offer of an indulgence filled the boxes placed in fifty-five churches for that purpose—from Groningue to Mâcon—with some eighteen thousand gold coins of seventy different types. The papal representatives found more than thirty different varieties in the collecting boxes of Antwerp, Lille, and Auxonne alone. The 128 coins dropped into the box of the small town of Semur-en-Auxois were of eight different species. Out of 61 gold coins deposited in Haarlem twelve varieties could be counted. There were coins thought to be obsolete, like the *klinkaert* écu from Flanders, dating from 1426. And there were coins from lands as far away as Bavaria, Aragon, and Venice.

Ten years later, when the States General of the *langue d'oc* region sought to deal with this monetary anarchy, they found they had as many as twenty-seven different gold coins and twenty-five silver. The Utrecht florin was encountered in Montpellier, as was the Venetian ducat, the Foix écu "with two cows," the *riddre* from Flanders, the Milanese double *denier,* and the Berne *car.* Still in circulation too, after so many years, was the Jacques Coeur *gros.*

Both the accountant and the merchant would soon have become confused if it had not been for the money changer, the man who could recognize the different coins, weigh them, and evaluate them. Fortunately, he was to be found in the center of every town. In Florence the *Arte del Cambio* (the guild of the money changers) was, after the most important merchants' guild, the *Arte di Calimala,* the second of the "Major Arts," coming before that of the importers of silk and silk fabric—the *Arte di Por Santa Maria*—and that of *la Lana* (wool). The money changers had established themselves in the Mercato Vecchio (Old Market) by the church of Or San Michele, among the trading groups that lined the main thoroughfare between the Duomo (cathedral) and the Palazzo della Signoria. Their Venetian counterparts were to be found on the Rialto Bridge. In Paris, as early as the beginning of the twelfth century, the money changers had taken over the Grand Pont, the only, and therefore vital, bridge over the Seine until the fourteenth century, linking the right bank of the Seine, where business was conducted, with the Ile de la Cité and the left bank, where the center of government and the colleges were found. Later the money changers shared the bridge with the goldsmiths, but it was always known to the Parisians as the *Pont au Change.*

Out of 503 rich Parisians taxed in 1423, we find 43 money changers. Of the twenty taxpayers paying the highest sum of tax, ten are money changers. From the time of the reestablishment of the municipality in 1412 to the takeover of the town hall by the king in the 1450s, we see that no fewer than four provosts of the merchants and nineteen magistrates had started out in the trade of money changer.

The diversity of coinage in circulation was, of course, related to the diversity of mints. This variety owed everything to the international regulations that allowed purses and carts of money to travel long distances. But it depended also, to a large extent, on the trade in minted metal. From the early days of bimetallism, speculators in the West noticed that the relationship of gold to silver in Alexandria, one of the principal ports in the East, favored those who were exporting silver to Egypt and importing gold into Western Europe.

This balance of trade with the East was certainly advantageous, and protected Italy from dangerous exports of currency. Florence, Venice, and Genoa had enough merchandise to send to Alexandria in Egypt, Trebizond across the Black Sea, or Kaffa in the Crimea. Trade was unlikely to be unilateral. Short-term speculation was also practiced: the Florentine money changer Lippo di Fede del Sega amassed no less than 2,300 silver florins between June 1317 and March 1318, putting them back into circulation a few months later after a slight rise in the rate of exchange. In fact, Lippo di Fede was speculating on a relatively low rate, and resold his coins to the mint when it was temporarily short of silver. This was speculation, but it did not involve any export of currency.

It even happened, in case of need, that the Italian money market came to the aid of its colonial markets. The Grand Council of Venice, for example, tried on 29 July 1353 to remedy the shortage of coins felt in several regions of Venetian Romania. A plan was formulated to mint new coins, of somewhat inferior quality despite being called *tournois*, and leave to the local officials the task of putting them into circulation as fast as possible:

> That, for the good and benefit of the Commune and our territories of Korone and Methone [in Messenia], Negrepont [Euboea], and Crete, it shall be ordered that there be minted here "*tournois*" made up of 8 ounces of copper and 1 ounce of silver, giving 80 *tournois* to the mark.
>
> And let the greatest possible quantity of these coins be sent to the above mentioned lands, with instructions to the rectors to spend them for suitable expenses, and to do everything possible to put them into circulation.
>
> And let these coins be valued at 3 *deniers* for each *tournois*. As for size and imprint, let them be as the Signoria sees fit.

France did not have the same capacity for trade with the East. This did not prevent her making efforts to buy gold for minting coins. The system was thus open to the worst kind of speculation, which takes advantage of a disequilibrium and thereby makes matters worse. From the end of the thirteenth century, ships started to leave Montpellier loaded with sacks of silver coins. This movement, which the royal decrees were powerless to stop, caused a shortage of silver and consequently of available small change in everyday life:

> To all the dukes, counts, barons and judges living in our kingdom. . . . We desire them to keep and hold firmly to our decrees issued on the subject of the coinage, and to oversee strictly that no coins foreign to our kingdom circulate without an exchange rate, nor should they be taken or given in payment in your lands and justices. You should have the ports and roads

of your lands and justices well guarded so that no one can carry or have carried silver or silver alloy or forbidden coins out of our kingdom.

It was an impossible situation. The government was forced to devalue the money of account, or in other words raise the rate of exchange of silver coins. Instability aggravated the shortage. The money changers found themselves increasingly in demand. After all, they were at one and the same time advisers and speculators, capable of influencing the king and informing their clientele. Informed by their long experience, they were able to note down in their account books, day by day, the rates of the coins in difficulty. The king of France's mint was to pay dearly for this premature introduction of bimetallism, but it was to give the money changers a privileged role in society.

The money changer could not, unaided, evaluate every type of coin in all its aspects. Certainly, with the aid of his scales he could determine whether or not those using the coins had clipped the coin, the legal description of which was well known to him. He could refuse it if its real weight had fallen below the legal margin of doubt—the "remedy" or "tolerance"—generally provided by the monetary statutes in order to take account of the technical imperfections of the minting process. Thus the market would refuse a coin made smaller by those who attempted to remove some of the precious metal with a pocket knife. But there still remained some uncertainty about the coin itself: there was no method, no practice, apart from melting down the coin, for finding out the exact content of the metal. Even the least expert eye could distinguish between "black coins"—of two-twelfths or three-twelfths of pure silver—from "good coins," made of a metal that looked like silver. But there was no expert who could measure the content of the *gros* of 11 *deniers* 12 *grains* instead of the 12 "*deniers* of alloy" that signified pure silver. Nor could anyone calculate the quality of the 24-carat écu, the 23-carat "sheep," or the "crowns" of 23⅛ carats. The money changer therefore kept a register of the different coins and their characteristics, as defined by the regulations governing the issue. He would carefully record the differences that distinguished one mint from another or one minting from the next: a tiny symbol, a dot, a cross, or an asterisk.

To avoid falling prey to deception, he also had to become expert in the fluctuations in the price of precious metal and hence of the commercial rate of coins. Naturally these rates varied from day to day and from market to market, depending on the demand in the marketplace for this or that means of payment. A difference in the rate, however minute, between Pisa and Genoa or between Barcelona and Montpellier was enough to spark off speculation. What could upset the economy of a city could do the same for a kingdom.

Obtaining up-to-date information about the state of the money market was not the only concern of this pen-pushing businessman. The price of the florin was as important to anyone wishing to manage a business as the price of wool or salt, or that of forward exchange. In order to speculate, just as to fight against speculation, the businessman had to understand price mechanisms and fluctuations in the short term. Whoever was best informed was obviously the winner.

Monetary protectionism meant continuous imposition of restrictions on the circulation of currency. It was believed that this would prevent the export of the precious metal as well as speculation. Thus there followed a succession of regulations, particularly in France after the return to bimetallism. It is easy to understand why the privileges granted at the fairs, exempting some merchants from such regulations, were so important. Certainly, the fairs provided a very real opportunity for the speculative export of currency. But the risk of this happening was less than the advantage gained from such opportunities for conducting trade. The citizens of Lyons let Louis XI know their views on the matter when, in 1466, he was thinking of allowing the fairs in Geneva to compete with those in Lyons:

> If it is said that on the occasion of the Lyons fairs a large amount of gold and silver is lost to the kingdom, which did not happen before the said fairs, and this to the prejudice of the king, the answer is clear, for the truth is the opposite. Before the said fairs, in fact, many people of this kingdom passed the said metal out of the country. . . .
>
> It is true that, by means of the said fairs, we do not let out of the kingdom any gold and silver, if it is not the gold or silver of other foreign countries, in the form of coins which, by means of the said fairs and their freedoms, have a rate of exchange and are accepted in payment in this kingdom during the said fairs for their fair price.

It is important to remember that the fair cleaned the market. It policed the circulation of money. The money exported was chiefly in foreign coinage, allowed in for the duration of the fair. Without this process, these foreign coins would remain unduly within the kingdom. It was true that it could be a profitless operation, but the people of Lyons constantly stressed the ultimately positive aspects of the balance sheet:

> Even if a part leaves the kingdom, much remains. And also, by means of the said fairs some people bring to the fairs large quantities of metal and silver coins from the Germanies and elsewhere outside the kingdom and which is worked in the king's mint in Lyons.

The temporary relaxation of the ban on visiting the Geneva fairs finally brought supplies to the mint. The argument rested, of course, on something not mentioned by the merchants of Lyons: the balance of trade. The fair brought in the precious metal if it managed to export more than it imported, taking account of noncash compensations and payments. A fair with flow in only one direction, such as that held in 1313 at Écouis by the king's counselor Enguerran de Marigny, was a disaster: the Flemish merchants brought their cloth and bought nothing.

There was no misunderstanding, either among the prince's counselors or among the merchants: regulations were one thing, the money market quite another. If foreign coins had remained abroad and French coins in France, the money changers would not have been making their fortunes on the Grand Pont. The same would have been true if officially depreciated coins had not been seen in circulation after a "renewal." Here, again, the role of the money changer was essential to the running of the money market: he gave the old coin its new value.

Mutatio Monetae

Changing the coinage means modifying the relationship of precious metal to the money of account. In the bimetallic system that grew up in the West, it also meant the modification of the relationship of gold to silver. This adjusted the legal rate of exchange of coins to the new balance of the market, even where that balance was still fragile. The mints could not find metal to mint if they bought too cheaply, while at a time of inflation the rates rose. When the rate was too high, on the other hand, the prince could find as much metal as he wanted, but the market would reject an overvalued coin. Thus *mutatio* was a corrective device by means of which the rulers tried to stick to economic reality. It was not an arbitrary whim of a prince and his "evil counselors" looking for instant profits. Besides, there were many cases of *mutatio* without new issues of coins, and it was only in cases where new coins were issued that the operation made a profit for the mint.

There were three ways of revaluating the currency. Whichever was employed, it always involved changing the quantity of pure metal that corresponded to the standard unit of currency, or—and it amounted to the same thing—of changing the price of the minted metal.

The first method was to give to the coins already in circulation a new legal rate, conforming more closely with the money market. This was the method chosen by the future Charles V when lieutenant of the kingdom for his father John the Good, who was a prisoner after his defeat at Poitiers:

> The gold *denier* with the lamb (*à l'agnel*), which has been and is still made, shall henceforward be taken for 30 *sous tournois* for one coin and not more.
> The silver *deniers* that had and still have a value of 8 *deniers tournois* each shall henceforward be taken and given in payment for 3 *deniers tournois* and not more.

At the time of its issue, four years before, the "sheep"—or "lamb"—*denier* was worth 25 *sous tournois* in money of account. By now making it 30 sous, Charles had devalued the *livre tournois* by 20 percent in two years. He was neither the author nor the master of this devaluation. He was reacting to the market so as not to ruin an economy already suffering from high taxation resulting from war and defeat. Devaluation was even more severe with silver: the "silver" coin, as the *châtel fleurdelisé* (castle and fleur-de-lis) was known—although it looked pretty black with only 25 percent silver—was still worth 8 *deniers* when issued on 13 September. In relation to silver, the *livre* had thus fallen by 62 percent. The result was confusion as far as the small coins were concerned, particularly those which were so necessary in the daily life of soldiers. When the time came to pay the king of England the ransom for the king defeated at Poitiers, the French currency was to fall in relation to gold as well.

The second method was more complicated. Here the inadequate coins were replaced by other more suitable ones. This reminting had one immediate advantage: it allowed the prince—or the town—to receive the small profit due from the minting, known as the *seigneuriage*, which, with the cost of manufacture, combined to form the difference between the cost of buying the metal by the mint and the selling price that was the legal rate of the coin issued. The new minting also had the advantage of influencing public opinion, since the content of a person's purse now looked different. But the new coins could be measured by the money changer only if he applied a test, albeit a relatively simple one. When the same coin passed from a value of 25 to 30 sous, the rate of inflation and change was apparent to even the dullest of brains. When a new coin was issued, although no one had any illusions about what was happening, it was more difficult to calculate its value.

Naturally the new coin would at least differ from the preceding one in weight or legal value, or, most commonly, both. When the design on the coin changed, the difference was quite clear, as when Philip VI brought out successively a shield, a lion, a pavilion, a crown, an angel, and a chair. A quick glance at one of these coins was sufficient to tell them apart. It was impossible to confuse them, even without a set of scales to tell you that the heavy "angel" of 1341 was minted at a rate of 33 to the mark (7.42 grams) while the "shields" were issued at a rate of 54 to the mark (4.53 grams).

Things were less clear when, in 1311, the last Capetians issued a "lamb" (*agnel*) of 58⅓ to the mark equal to 20 sous, another "lamb" in 1313 of 59⅙ worth 15 sous, and in 1322 a "lamb" of 59⅙ worth 20 sous. Ordinary people saw all these coins as simple "sheep"—so named after the image they bore of the Paschal Lamb—ignoring differences like the inversion of the design. They were unlikely to understand the degree of the king's revaluation of the *livre tournois* with a coin whose legal rate of exchange went down in 1313 by 25 percent after it was made 1.4 percent lighter: ⅚ of a coin more from each mark of gold, or 0.059 grams of gold less in each coin. Nor would they have noticed that this increased by 31.6 percent the weight of gold to which the money of account corresponded. Faced with such changes in a coin that nevertheless continued to look the same, even the most well-informed gave up, leaving the money changer to rule supreme.

And he was in an even stronger position if the prince opted for the third possibility, the one condemned by morality: a change in the quality of the metal. The coin would keep the same design, the same name, and the same weight but it would contain a little less precious metal. Such changes were relatively rare in the case of gold coins, which continued to represent an affirmation of sovereignty: a prince would hesitate before lowering the value of pure 24-carat gold when it was something of a political symbol. It was quite common, on the other hand, to change the metal of silver coins. These changed little in appearance, since it was not advisable to increase the cost of making coins of low value. Huge numbers of sous, *gros,* and *deniers* were produced, all looking more or less the same from one minting to the next, but containing anything from $2/12$ to pure silver.

This was deception. Even if there was nothing clandestine about the minting, it left a sense of ambiguity. During the fourteenth century the Italian jurist Bartolo, a master of Roman law, defined the limits of public morality in the area of money:

> *Mutatio* is legitimate when the intrinsic goodness of the coin changes, while its form and material remain pure, and then one can say that it is a different coin all together.
>
> Similarly, when the intrinsic goodness of the coin does not vary but its value does vary so that the florin is worth more or less than it was before.

Change that affected the "material" only was alarming, because it upset one of the fundamental beliefs of society and threatened the public order. Here was the state putting its stamp on something suspect while the public authorities soothed the doubters. Bishop Nicole Oresme, counselor to Charles V and translator of Aristotle, referred to the "public good:"

> Renewal by alteration to the metal is certainly a forgery worse than altering the weight, because it is much more learned and less obvious. It can thus harm more and be even more injurious to the community.

Scarcity of coinage was thus a political drama in which the actions of the prince or the town had a less than innocent role. But such "renewals" were the prince's response, not that of the businessmen. He who issued the coins decided on a renewal in order to avoid an impasse. The businessmen, by contrast, would initially be taken by surprise. Like everyone else in the thirteenth and often even into the fourteenth century, they had to submit to these changes, sometimes understanding the reasons, always criticizing them. But before long they were looking for a long-term solution to these revaluations that were so frequent and so contradictory. They were eager to lessen the effects of the instability and insecurity of money that were causing them at least as much of a problem as their difficulties with actual payment. The great question was no longer "how shall I pay?" but "how much do I owe?"

EIGHT

Payment

*T*hat instability was bad for trade was something felt by everyone from the humblest peddler to the businessman well versed in monetary mechanisms. In fact, all too often the effects of a crisis became one with the causes, and the paralysis resulting from a lack of currency was hard to distinguish from that deriving from the uncertainties that accompany any change, even if the latter claims to be a remedy for the insufficiency. But there was also belief in the miracle cure that could breathe life back into the currency: "Thus, trade, which is dead or slack, would be entirely recovered by means of the black coinage and the extensive issue that will be made of them."

This was the advice given to Philip the Fair by the money changers of Tours, Troyes, Orleans, and Poitiers: salvation would come with the multiplication of coinage, even if it was base silver. Quantity, not quality, was the answer. During this period, others less competent than these money changers even recommended a return to the old heavy coin.

Instability

Ordinary people were ignorant of the workings of the monetary system. They saw the changes in the coinage made by the prince not as a reaction to fluctuations in the economic climate but as an expression of his will. They believed that the prince made changes in the currency for the profit he might derive; to benefit the landowners, in the rare cases where the money of account was strengthened; or to ruin the nobility or the clergy, in the more frequent cases where money was devalued. It went without saying that any change would benefit the speculator. In any case, the high cost of living that resulted from the devaluation was always his fault. Everybody had a story to tell about the real culprits, the "bad counselors." We read in the anonymous *Parisian Journal* (*Journal d'un bourgeois de Paris*) how in 1427 "because they bore the arms of France, the small gold 'sheep' were set at a rate of 12 Paris sous, when formerly they had been worth 10 sous." It continues:

> The day after the decree had been made, it was impossible to obtain bread or wine or any necessity of life with French *doubles*. The money changers would not give out either *deniers* or *oboles* for them. Yet the common people had no money but that, which was worth nothing.
>
> Seeing that their loss was great, some people cursed Fate in public and in secret, saying what they thought about the rulers.
>
> Many threw their money into the river over the tops of the money changers' stalls because they could get nothing from them: for eight or ten Paris sous they could not have got, at most, more than four or five silver coins.
>
> In the week that the changes to the currency were proclaimed, there was thrown into the river, from sheer despair, more than fifty florins or their value in other coins.

This gives us a good picture of the reactions and irrational behavior that greeted the "cry"—the announcement at every crossroad of a new decree—of a revaluation. Demonstations of discontent were more likely than a calm adjustment to the new rates of exchange. But what the writer of the *Journal* indicates most clearly is something incalculable in mathematical terms: the loss of confidence. In the darkest moment of the monetary crisis during the regency of the duke of Bedford, the "raising" of the "sheep" from ten to twelve sous represented a devaluation of 20 percent in relation to the money of account. This did not justify the 80 percent fall of the black coinage. Despite its name, the "silver piece" was only $5/12$ pure silver, but it was issued with a value of 5 *deniers*. To get four or five—that is, some two sous—for eight or ten *doubles*, was no more reasonable than saying that a person could not pay with those same *doubles*. The truth was that people were suspicious, and also angry, in the face of this frightening diversity of coins that allowed the market to dictate the rules. Even with coins of intrinsically equal value, there were some that were bought—or accepted, which amounts to the same thing—and some that were rejected. We are back to the story of the Englishman Sander Russel. The fate of each coin lay ultimately in the hands of the dealer and the client; the market depended on mutual agreement, and we can see how the attitude to the coin in the town counted for at least as much as its weight on the scales or its metallic content estimated by biting the coin.

Confronted by this monetary instability, the businessman was faced with the problem of how best to conduct his business—how to pay for purchases for future delivery, how to pay back loans, how to pay rent.

Devaluation harmed the creditor and hence the capitalist. An increase in the value of money was, on the other hand, disastrous for the debtor, the consumer, and the tenant. The first lowered the value of property and discouraged investment; the second caused social upheaval. It is well known how, from the thirteenth century, the fixing of rents due from the peasants for their land in pounds, sous, and *deniers* led quite simply to the ruin of the landed nobility.

The shrewd merchant was, of course, able to adapt to these monetary changes. This was generally what the prince feared and prohibited in advance, for anything that sought to alleviate insecurity nullified the effects of the monetary policy. If economic operators were going to sabotage the whole thing, there was obviously no point in changing the money without at the same time remedying the problems that had made the action necessary in the first place. The response of the business world can be summed up in the one principle: insist that the agreement be drawn up in a standard unit of currency that will keep its intrinsic value despite the passage of time and the surprises that time can bring.

For those who understood the monetary system, the simplest method was to stipulate payment in weight of precious metal. Instead of counting in ducats or crowns, one counted in marks and ounces of pure gold and silver. If the weight and material of one species were known, then it was possible to find its equivalent in another coinage.

The financial administrators of the Plantagenet Henry II proceeded along these lines as early as the twelfth century when paying the taxes collected from the shires, counting in a fictitious coinage made of pure metal and known as "silver coin." In this way the royal treasury protected itself from surprises. When paying his dues, the sheriff would naturally do so with the coins in circulation, but he paid more of them as their value fell. While the Henry II *denier*—much more valuable, it should be stressed, than the *tournois* of his contemporary Louis VII—consisted of 94 percent pure silver, it cost the sheriff of Yorkshire 389 pounds in current coins to pay what he owed for a tax farm fixed at 365 pounds in "silver coin."

During the following century, the Neapolitan treasury of Charles I of Anjou kept its accounts in ounces of silver. The governments of Charles VI and Henry V did the same at the peak of the monetary crisis of 1417–22, when the coinage went from 29 to the ounce to 120 in 1419, 408 in 1421, briefly touching 1,440. Without doubt the worst coin of the entire Middle Ages, this *florette* contained a quarter of a twelfth of pure silver although set at the unbelievable rate of 20 *tournois deniers*. It is clear that by now the Paris mint was unable to get hold of the metal needed for its mintings. Thus the tax established by letters patent of 24 March 1421 over what was to become Lancastrian France was officially qualified with the words "marks of silver ordered to be collected and raised." The intention of the royal government was to "mint and make a good coinage for the profit of all." Each town was taxed a certain weight in silver: in Troyes, for example, 500 marks, the equivalent of 122,375 kilograms. In Paris, the overall tax of which is unknown, every taxable citizen had to pay between 2 ounces and 50 marks, the most frequent sum being 4 ounces, which is to say half a mark.

The business world rarely made this kind of stipulation. The royal treasury was prepared to accept payments in metal or in kind. In other words, sometimes the tax collector was paid in silver plate or obsolete coins as well as in coins currently in circulation. If he was not a money changer himself, the tax collector could sort all this out with their help. But the merchant had no use for the metal fragments received daily in payment for a piece of cloth or as repayment of a loan. The chief reaction of businessmen to the uncertainty in regulation was not to pile up heaps of silver coins but, like the simple shopkeeper, simply to begin to count in real specie.

The public powers naturally opposed this with firmness, if not always with success. In 1330, when Philip VI was trying to regularize the circulation of money affected by the first financial measures linked to the Hundred Years' War, a decree reminded people that agreements should only be drawn up in money of account:

> Malicious people have attempted to corrupt our decrees in every way in several manners, and especially in trading, in contracts and in lending, in gold *deniers* and in *gros tournois,* to the damage of ourselves and of our people, which much displeases us.
>
> We forbid anyone to be so foolhardy as to trade, make deals, or lend in gold *deniers* or in *gros tournois* but only in sous and pounds or the coinage that we are using at the moment.

In fact, everybody fixed the price of goods and calculated credit and debt in *gros* or écus, and particularly in florins. Such payments required, however, the assistance of a well-informed money changer, and matters became complicated when the payer took from his purse as many varieties of coins as were then in circulation. The business world thus saw itself rapidly forced to practice feats of calculation that were to lead to new accounting systems, based on actual coins and, more particularly, on the least erratic coinage, that in gold. One way or another, it was always a matter of endowing a gold piece with subspecies that it had never possessed, and borrowing names and relations from the old official currency ultimately based on the silver coinage of Carolingian times.

Whereas the entire official system was based on the *denier,* or, in other words, on the memory of the silver piece, the system that was most secure rested on a gold coin, taken as a point of reference because of its repute and preserved as such despite the changes in the gold coinage itself.

The safest reference point in the eyes of all was the Florentine florin. It was little wonder that with a variety of marketplaces, business circles invented accounting systems linked to the florin, with subspecies determined in relation to the local silver coinage and gold florin at the precise moment when the new usage had become established. In Florence itself, where the 29-sou florin had long been known, a "florin sou" was invented, invariably counted as 1/29 of a florin. When the lack of silver took the florin to 65 sous in current money, the florin sou found itself revalued from 12 to 27 *deniers*. The business world was thus able to shelter itself from crises in the currency.

The florin was also adopted on the other side of the Alps. From the mid-fourteenth century in Forez and in the Lyonnais, and later in Burgundy, contracts specified florins, with subspecies inspired by the local coinage. One florin was worth 15 *sous estevenants* in Comté, and 12 florin *gros*—still referred to as "light *gros*"—in Forez.

Elsewhere, similar systems caught on, with theoretical subspecies, based on gold coins or the local coinage. Thus in Languedoc the merchants and notaries adopted, around 1420, a system of *gros*-écu with an écu *gros* that was to remain 1/18 of an écu, this relationship being determined by the rate of the two real coins in the years around 1410, when the "crown" écu was worth 30 sous and the *gros* 20 *deniers,* or, in other words, eighteen times less. But the écu *gros* was not, and never would be, real.

The Genoese Grand Council went so far as to institutionalize the businessman's suspicion of the system inherited from the Carolingians. On 21 June 1447, it made payment in gold obligatory for all commercial exchanges—banking operations—and for the settling of all business with foreigners. The late fourtenth century was a period of relative stability for the Genoese. Still fresh in their minds was the gold ducat, worth 25 sous, and a *gros* of very good quality—23/24 pure silver—worth 2 sous. Half a century later, they took this as the basis for their new system. From 1451, shortly after the ducat had reached a rate of 44 sous, they counted in "good coin," that is, according to a system based on the ducat.

With the ducat worth 44 sous, in that same year of 1451 the pound naturally remained at 20 sous. The relationship was preserved. The "pound (*lira*) in good coin" was then worth 20/44 of a ducat, whatever the ducat might be worth. Subspecies were created: the sou in good coin was long to be in common usage, with an initial value of 1/44 of a ducat. As for the pound, which kept its former value, it was this coin that was described as "current money." It remained at 20 sous, and was always closely linked to silver insofar as its real value was concerned. At the end of the century, the ducat was worth 64 sous in current money, the latter, like much of Europe, suffering very much from the general shortage of silver. Over fifty years, current money had lost 45 percent of its value against "good money." But business did not suffer.

Wherever we look, countries were beginning to link their accounting systems to a more real currency. At the heart of these monetary upheavals, accounts and contracts that had remained faithful to the old ways also began to make concessions to realism. We find references to pounds in "strong money," old *tournois,* and even—with the date, of course—to the actual currency in circulation: "the money that circulates in our time."

The more adventurous thought up ways of pegging prices, or even including cancellation clauses, as in the following case of a weaver from Toulouse who intended to pay his rent by weaving cloth to the value of six *livres tournois.* It was 1421, the peak of the monetary crisis. The pound was collapsing. There was no sign that inflation would slow down. It was therefore reckoned that work done in payment of rent should not be worth less than six pounds of the old currency. In this way the property owner felt protected from the drawbacks of leasing in times of inflation. But the tenant also felt protected against the possibility of a return to a strong currency. Now, even if this happened, there was no chance that he might be asked to do more work, and he would pay his rent in silver at the rate of the old money:

> It has been decided that, during the period of weakness of the current coinage, the nobleman Guilhem Pagèze will give to Bernard Capelle what is necessary for his trade, that is to say, thread for his cloth.
>
> And the said Bernard will make a measure of cloth for the price that was customary and that the other weavers were accustomed to receive in the time of the old money, up to a sum of six *livres tournois* of the said old money.
>
> It has been agreed that, if the money should become stronger and return to the state of the year 1414, Bernard will no longer be obliged to make the said cloth for the said Pagèze, but only to pay the said sum of pounds at the times agreed.

A Substitute for Money

All this attempted, more or less successfully, to offset the effects of the instability resulting from the periodic shortage of metal for the mints, made worse by the hoarding of coins that was one symptom of the market's reaction to a rise in the exchange rate. It did nothing to solve the shortage itself. On the margins of the European economy, bartering, in which monetary standards were expressed in kind, was still common. In Novgorod they still counted in "leather money." Here the standard unit of currency was a sable skin. Forbidden, in their dealings with the Russians, to engage in transactions worth more than a thousand marks, merchants from the West thus managed partly to get around such prohibitions or limitations. But bartering was carried on in the West, too, and "leather money" was in constant use as late as the fifteenth century in Barcelona as in Venice, in Ragusa as in Bruges, where sable skins were exchanged for spices or coral and simple squirrel skins for oil or wine. Seemingly paradoxical—but in no way unusual—is the account of Durand Carol of Barcelona, who in 1445 paid a "price" of twenty-two dozen black lambskins for seventeen sable skins.

The first reaction to scarcity was, of course, the hunt for new supplies of metal. Everyplace where silver had ever been mined saw renewed activity in the late Middle Ages. Veins that had been thought to be almost exhausted were again worked, their profitability being assured by the rise in prices, particularly of silver. Some speculators went further, not only extending mining activities but also leasing the right to mint coins. One such speculator was Jacques Coeur, who revived the lead and silver mines in the Lyonnais, particularly at Pampailly. In Bohemia, as in Hungary, production increased.

At the same time, new routes to the gold of the Sudan were sought. Marco Polo's routes had followed silk and spices. Even if Western Christendom now and then expressed its desire to renew its links with the hypothetical Christian kingdom of "Prester John"—in an Ethiopia more imaginary than real—and even if there had been no delay in getting to Tunis, Ceuta, or Sijilmasa at the crossroads of the great caravan routes of Africa, Western travelers of the fourteenth century, less and less attracted by exploration to the East, were now looking specifically for direct access to the land of gold. The great traveler Ibn Battuta forged these routes when he left Marrakech in 1352 for his long journey around Africa that took him to Timbuktu, Gao in Mali, and to Agadez. He explored the Ahaggar Massif in the Sahara and then crossed the desert a second time to reach Sijilmasa and, finally, Fez where he carefully recorded his recollections, not without a certain amount of embroidering.

Ibn Battuta fed the imaginations of generations of travelers, but he did not find a quick route to the gold of the Sudan. Western businessmen were not satisfied to know that gold existed in plenty among the populations visited by the great caravans. What they wanted was to get their hands on the gold, in large quantities and at the lowest price. It occurred to them to explore the sea routes, by traveling around the coast of Africa. Europe's discovery of the Canary Islands, Madeira, Cape Blanc, and Cape Verde was due to the explorations of the Genoese, the Normans, and the Spanish. In 1445 Dinas Diaz discovered the mouth of the Senegal. Ca da Mosto traveled up the same river ten years later, before exploring Gambia.

Although the name Rio de Oro (river of gold) aroused their hopes, Europeans gained more sugar and grain from this adventure than gold. The salvation of the European monetary market was eventually to come from a most unexpected quarter: America.

While the hunt went on for silver in the ground and gold across the sea, it was vital to find some kind of substitute for money, the value of which had continued to decline as a result of economic growth. Crises within this same economy had affected the most important aspect of any currency: its reliability. Alongside a system of barter—a necessarily limited framework—other nonmonetary methods of payment began to flourish.

The primary method that did not rely on metal was accounting. The practice of transferring funds created a type of bank money by which the volume of business could ignore the supply and circulation of coins. Money changers and "banking" merchants accepted deposits, which made it easy for them to make transfers of credit from one client to another. Precious metals were now used only to settle any differences, according to adjustments of varying degrees of complexity. Gold and silver coins were used chiefly in more humble spheres of economic life, at the shopkeeper's stall or for wages. The solder's wages were paid in coins, which ended up, like the wages of the mason or the valet, in the hands of the innkeeper. An embroidered girdle would be paid for with a few coins, as would a wine barrel or pewter jug.

Credit settlements were the rule between the wholesaler and the retailer, but even so the payment would eventually be made in cash, as was inevitable given the nature of the transaction: it is hard to see how else the wholesaler could balance his accounts when selling sheets or salt to a retailer.

Matters did not really change until the advent of banking proper, that is, trading merchandise for credit or bills of exchange. Today's lender could be a borrower tomorrow. Borrowing on credit was not necessarily the action of a poor man, and one could quite readily deposit money with a banker and then ask him for credit for a medium- or long-term venture at a later date. Although there could be no transfer between accounts of the moneylender and the poor man come to pawn his rags for three sous, it was easy enough for a Genoese banker who could draw a bill of exchange on his colleague in Bruges and pay in Genoa a bill drawn by a colleague in London.

The practice became more widespread when a number of fellow citizens found that they each had a page opened in their name at the same bank for deposits that they made in cash and that they could dispose of as they saw fit. It was by drawing on his "column" in the *Casa di San Giorgio,* and on the interest he acquired from the deposits recorded in that column, that the Genoese merchant was able to pay for goods and services. Once again, the technical backwardness of the rest of Europe in comparison to the business world of Tuscany, Lombardy, Genoa, and Venice was made painfully clear by economic reality. Thanks to this nonmonetary method of payment, the Italians were to suffer less than their foreign counterparts from the shortage of metal for coinage. Financial transfers were common practice for the Medici in Florence and the *San Giorgio* in Genoa, and they offered the best remedy for the problems smothering business. The Genoese merchant did not have to worry about making sure his interest was paid when it fell due. Instead he had it transferred to his column in the *San Giorgio* account books. With a simple bill of exchange, or even by word of mouth, he could use it later to make payments.

Even better, he could reckon on his savings maturing. The Genoese notified clients when interests would fall due. Thus classified by date, the *lira di paghe* was a genuine form of bank money, and was instantly appreciated for its convenience. While the whole of Genoese society was buying up shares in *San Giorgio*, the *lira di paghe* was used to make all kinds of payments, be it a simple purchase or a complex business deal involving commercial or banking speculation.

Underpinning this bank money was always the initial deposit in cash. Fiduciary money was derived from the circulation of debts in trade and from the drawing of bills of exchange. It was only later on, in the mid-fifteenth century, that Italian business circles realized that they could quite simply pay bills of exchange in writing. During a period of three years and nine months, 160,000 lire passed through the hands of the Genoese Giovanni Piccamiglio, of which only 12,000 lire was in cash.

Proper endorsement, whereby goods or a letter of credit could circulate simply with the addition of instructions at the bottom or back of the document, made a timid appearance in the early fifteenth century, for example, in some deals between Tuscans in Valencia and Barcelona. By the middle of the century, it had become common practice in both Florence and Genoa. The rest of Europe, while aware of the Italian practice, did not try to follow suit until the sixteenth century.

Nevertheless, fiduciary money remained limited in its scope by the circumstances that gave it its name—"faith" money. Although it was known throughout Europe, it was of real concern only to a narrow band of society, those businessmen who knew one another as well as the worth of their credit. This hurdle was not overcome until modern times, when the bank note, guaranteed by the state, replaced the old system based on personal relations.

NINE

Capital

*T*here were those who wanted to do more than confine themselves to local trading in small shops, where the products of international trade were merely redistributed, or in the town markets that sold produce from the surrounding countryside or pewter jugs made by local craftsmen. But to expand they needed sources of capital other than the modest sums earned by the shopkeeper or artisan. On the eve of the economic crises of the fourteenth century, the only large fortunes were still those of the landed aristocracy, whether of recent or more ancient creation; and they were richer in land and the increasingly devalued income from it than in ready money available for economic enterprises. It was becoming increasingly difficult for the individual entrepreneur to organize fleets of ships or the movement of cargoes, to take advantage of credit available on long-term sales, or to reinvest any profits. As for financing an industrial enterprise, from the buying of raw materials in often distant markets to the marketing of the finished products, it was out of the question. This was a period when it was necessary to operate within economic horizons that included the buying of wool in England or of alum in Asia Minor along with the selling in Alexandria of luxury cloths finished in Florence, or the supplying of silk from China and furs from Russia to the cosmopolitan clientele in the courts of princes or the papal curia.

To finance the equipping of a ship in Lübeck or Genoa, to install cranes in Bruges or Barcelona, to oversee the operation of the dyeing works in Ypres or Florence—no cloth merchant or money changer could hope to manage such activities on his own. Even the most modest equipment, such as a watermill—for grinding wheat or fulling cloth—would have represented a crushing expense for someone who might need to use it only three times a year.

And then there were the attached risks, only too evident in the case of a ship that could sink or run aground. In fact, risk lurked beneath the surface of all economic ventures: circumstances could change, demand might fall, and debtors were unreliable. This element of risk made it natural for the investor to enter into joint ventures that facilitated diversification: far better to own twelve shares in twelve boats than to own outright a single boat that might take its cargo of hopes to the bottom of the sea.

Capital and Work

It all started with the merchant ready to invest his own capital—labor, skills, and cash—but at the same time eager to expand his business by calling on the capital of others. He would get a response from another merchant in a similar position—someone who could not be everywhere at once but who did not, for all that, intend to deprive himself of chances to diversify his investments and opportunities to make money. Interest might also come from the smaller businessman, who could not expand in proportion to his profits. He was materially unable to reinvest his profit, however modest, in his own enterprise, limited as it was by the ill-balanced relationship of profit to growth and reinvestment. The baker had spare capital, for he could not anticipate a growth in consumption of bread in his neighborhood, and so too the smith, for he could hardly increase the technical capacity of his forge by 5 percent each year.

As for the financial products of the tertiary sector, they too called for reinvestment outside their own domains. The jurist sometimes earned more than he spent. The canon could not use the income from his prebend, or stipend, to purchase a bishopric. The financier did not intend to tie up all his money in loans to princes even if it was to this that he owed his original climb to wealth. They all looked outside their own spheres of activity for speculative ventures and securities. They wanted a form of reinvestment that would not use up their time and that would provide them with a simple cash return in exchange for their calculated risk.

The first idea to emerge was to pool resources for one particular venture. This is what the owner of a delivery of merchandise was doing when he entrusted the job of transporting and selling it to others. The only risk involved for "active" merchants—the ones who traveled and worked—was to their persons. Short of being assassinated on the road, nothing would happen to them. Their share of the profits were correspondingly small: they were paid for their time and effort, and perhaps for their skill. They were not so much partners as errand boys, or carriers. They would have been salaried employees were it not for the fact that their earnings depended on their success. If they had been rewarded according to conditions fixed in advance, they would not have a share in the profits. The most they could expect as reward for a successfully concluded piece of business was a more favorable deal the next time. If they were sons or nephews of the owner of the goods, they could hope to be made a partner or even an heir. If they were mere employees, they would secretly hope for a raise. If they were themselves merchants, they had nothing to hope from this deal but the knowledge that others would do the same for them at a future date.

No one could travel in every direction at once, and the merchant was well aware, when he conveyed not only his own fish but also that of a colleague to the inland towns, that he was thus saving himself the cost of transporting the next load of fish when it would be the turn of his colleague. For the Venetian who could not spend his time at sea, a compatriot off to Egypt was an opportunity to be seized. The Hanseatic merchants soon became masters in the art of using brothers, nephews, and neighbors: those traveling to Novgorod would carry more business than they could have financed themselves. People began to be more systematic in their methods. The four Mulich brothers, established in the late fifteenth century in Lübeck, Nuremberg, and Frankfurt, were very successful in saving time and money spent in wasteful traveling by commissioning each other. Similarly, the Hanseatic *Sendeve* (commission) was able to provide a counterbalance to individual enterprise. Here it was more a matter of saving precious time than money. The commission confined itself to acting as a contractor for commerce.

Another step was taken toward a form of capitalism when two merchants, one inclined to manage the business and the other more interested in increasing the value of a sum of money, combined their skills in an operation, agreeing to share the profits. In this system of *commenda,* both took risks: one might lose his money, the other his work. The "active" merchant had no guaranteed recompense, as he would have had from a "commission" where an agent was paid a fixed sum for performing certain services. It was up to him to see that there was a profit. This was clearly a type of partnership, and it was usual to have a notary draw up a contract to that effect.

This arrangement would not have made sense if the "active" partner, or merchant, had not contributed real skills and a readiness to take risks. He brought to this association his knowledge of the market, clients, and middlemen, his judgment as to quality and price, and his ability to assess the best itineraries and return cargoes. In return he received a share—often a quarter and sometimes, in the fifteenth century, a third—of a profit that resulted partly from his own abilities and not just from the quality of the merchandise entrusted to him. The type of contract favored by the Hanseatic merchants generally awarded half of the profits to the seagoing merchant. This generous arrangement probably reflected the greater dangers faced by navigators from Lübeck or Riga on the stormy Baltic compared to those met by Mediterranean sailors from Venice or Barcelona.

The *commenda* appeared in many different guises depending on the economic milieu, now favoring short-term, scattered operations, now joint operations and long-lasting frameworks. Since the fourteenth century, the Venetian contracts of *colleganza* show clearly the Venetian inclination to individual enterprise—encouraged by the permanent involvement of the republic in the structure of economic life—and their suspicion of any kind of joint operation. Each investor spread his capital, and entered into contracts, with the largest number of partners possible. Operations were kept simple: one contract for one voyage or one deal. Venetian trade thus presented a network of contracts, where the merchant who stayed at home reckoned up the journeys he had financed while the merchant who traveled to London or Alexandria could count as many silent partners as he had separate loads in his hold. It made little difference whether the merchant traveled or stayed at home. Either way, the one who returned had to give a full account of each operation without any compensation other than his own personal profit or loss on each contract.

The same rudimentary capitalism governed business in France and England. Even the most dynamic entrepreneurs were able to carry out their plans without having to enter into the arcane world of credit proper—something that they postponed for as long as possible. Eventually, after the Hundred Years' War, we see how the merchants of Rouen increased the number of their "bottomry loans," a type of contract whereby the ship was mortgaged in order to raise the money needed to provide the necessities for its voyage. These contracts did not link the capital lent with any particular share in a cargo but, without creating a formal partnership, nevertheless played an important role in maritime insurance. The loan was not reimbursed until the ship arrived, when the business deal, generally involving a sea journey, would be concluded by the sale of merchandise that had belonged to nobody but the "active" merchant.

More often, from the fourteenth century onward, genuine partners began to share the contributions, risks, and profits. The so-called sleeping, or silent, partner was sometimes a very active businessman, but one whose activities were in another area, or who chose not to become involved in a particular business simply because he had other things to do. Thus we see contracts of *commenda* bringing together fishermen and fishmongers, merchants and mariners, farmers and butchers. Many such contracts were designed to make the best use of a particular piece of equipment, a workshop, or a trade. On the basis of half of his future profits, a Toulouse innkeeper took out a loan for one year of a hundred *tournois* pounds, converting them immediately into a few barrels of wine to sell at once. Similarly, a burgess let out his wagon, on the understanding that he would get it back after a year, together with three quarters of the profits made by the wagoner. So, too, a money changer invested a few wooden beams in a half-shares contract with a carpenter.

This type of contract became one of the typical investments of the small saver, and a common means of development for small businesses. We see how, in Barcelona, whoever wanted to increase savings lent them to an artisan or merchant whose business thus received a small injection of money without having to incur the burden of paying a fixed rate of interest regardless of the enterprise's outcome. Thus notaries, courtiers, artisans, or merchants—anyone—might invest their money medium-term in the business of a cloth merchant, a veil weaver, or a coral importer.

Sea trade allowed the "active" merchant a freedom that a land-based enterprise could never have offered. It involved the risks associated with the long-distance reinvestment of profits as well as the choice, at the destination port, of a return cargo, often a decisive factor in profitability. The outward cargo was known in advance. Only the person accompanying the ship could decide what was to be brought back. The contracts were careful to place limits on this freedom, but it was not enough to prevent disputes: the merchant who had done no more than fund the enterprise would sometimes criticize his partner for missing a good opportunity. The Catalan Anthoni Berga, who put up the money for a dispatch of twenty jars of honey to the East in 1432, was of this opinion. Expecting to receive a return cargo of pepper and *baladi* ginger, he was dismayed to find that the seagoing merchant, Johan de Vilasecha, had brought back *maqui* ginger. The Barcelona market was already awash with *maqui* ginger, and the price was collapsing as a consequence. Berga refused a straight division of the profits, feeling that they were too small through the fault of his partner's poor judgment.

In this embryonic capitalism, every type of financial participation could be found, from sea and land contracts of *commenda* relating to a single operation or sea journey to the many different kinds of investment that could be dreamed up by the ingenuity of the business world. Some were truly examples of joint ventures, while others were simply investments, distinguishable from interest-bearing loans only by the nature of the financial product: a variable income was amply justified by the possible risk. Naturally the time frame allowed for a *commenda* in large-scale business ventures was the time needed for a journey, to travel to and from the East or back and forth across the North Sea. The investment *commenda*, on the other hand, could have a time span of any length, but one that was fixed in advance. It was usually for a period of one year, during which time the active partner had sole control.

The Genoese were to combine these two forms of *commenda*—each of which paid back investments and work with a distribution of profits—in an unusual synthesis. This was the "society of the sea," an organization that drove the world of business further down the road toward a more specifically capitalistic structure. During the fifteenth century, contracts were extended over longer periods, although financial participation was proffered for a fixed time span but for a variable and sometimes unlimited number of operations. The more important merchants took on so many of such contracts to finance their dealings in Asia Minor, the Bosphorus, and the Crimea—or Bruges and London for that matter—that Genoa, and even Marseilles, where the Genoese example was always present, saw a great increase in the concentration of capital. Without giving investors the responsibility that would have made them members of a Tuscan-style *compagnia*, a much more advanced type of capitalism was emerging than that encouraged by the individualism of the Venetian republic. It was this concentration of capital that offered new possibilities for business, which would never have arisen if each operation had remained confined within the financial and technical constraints imposed by the limited activities of the single operator.

It is important to stress that there was nothing systematic about this association of capital and work in the *commenda* system. There are many examples of contracts where the active partner contributed his active involvement in the enterprise and was, for this contribution, remunerated in the same way as the other investors. The itinerant merchant would transport not only his silent partner's cargo but also his own. The artisan who agreed to rent out the use of his workshop might at the same time use it to store his own materials and serve his own clients. And the merchant who, in essence, contributed nothing more than his skills was often a young man richer in hopes than real experience.

The Partnership

The joint partnership was a different matter. Here the active merchant was a participant in a joint enterprise in which the capital invested by all partners had no aim other than that of promoting the growth of business. The active partner in a *commenda* contract had risked his life and his reputation but the capital of others. Here the managing partner was also risking his own financial future. Although still a merchant like any other, he was drawing additional capital into his own enterprises.

Two or three merchants would form a partnership for an objective that, though often determined, was rarely limited. This did not exclude them from becoming similarly involved in other such enterprises. A businessman on a relatively modest scale like Francesco di Marco Datini in the late fourteenth century had gone into partnership with Lotto Ricci for "Florentine goods," with Tuccio Lambertucci in the running of three shops selling hose and cloth, with Toro di Berto and shortly afterward with Gherardo Guidalotti to trade in salt on the middle Rhône, and with Tommaso di ser

Nastagio for trade in practically everything in Avignon and on the lower Rhône. The Great Schism—when there were two papacies, one in Rome and one in Avignon—and the likelihood of an Angevin and papal expedition into southern Italy presented an opportunity for Datini to go into partnership with a Milanese manufacturer to produce two hundred basinets, the metal helmets that, fortunately for suppliers, needed to be replaced when they were dented. Finally, after he had returned to Prato, he joined up with the Milanese Basciano da Pescina in a successful business, trading in a wide variety of goods between Lombardy and Provence, while also dealing in the English wool needed for the Tuscan textile industry.

Such partnerships never involved more than a small number of participants, and they tended to be bound as much by family ties as by contracts. The Hanseatic merchants often made use of these family connections in order to ensure that businesses were jointly owned, and that no one person could take them entirely into his own hands. Thus trading was often able to continue between Lübeck and Bergen even after the death of the person who had set up the arrangement. We have the example, at the end of the fourteenth century, of Hildebrand, Sievert, and Cesar Veckinchusen, three brothers, originally probably from Revel in Livonia on the Baltic, who agreed to share out the markets of northern Europe. Hildebrand is known to have been successively at Bruges, Dortmund, Riga, and Lübeck before setting up permanently in Bruges. Sievert moved from Revel to Cologne before settling in Lübeck. Cesar seems to have remained all this time in Revel. At one time or another, one or another of them was active in Frankfurt, Mainz, Danzig, and Novgorod. Their partner Peter Karbow ran things in Venice. They successfully kept up a high level of trading during the first twenty years of the fifteenth century, despite difficulties caused by a rashness that might have been called daring had it not eventually ruined the three brothers.

Such partnerships were not characterized only by the small number of people involved. They were usually also set up for a fixed period of time. The need was still felt to combine financial capacity and work ability in any business operation or trading enterprise. A quarter of the partnerships set up in Toulouse between 1400 and 1450 were for a period of less than a year, and one-third for a year. One in ten, at most, was established with the intention of doing business over a period of five years.

Profits were normally shared in proportion to the amount of capital invested. The problem was giving a capital value to that essential contribution, the activity or work of this or that person. In Genoa, the "society of the sea" granted the active merchant one-half of the profits in exchange for his contribution of one-third of the capital. Only his share of the capital was affected in the event of loss. This was a system not so different from that of the *commenda*. In this way the active merchant might lose the capital he had invested but would still earn something. Similar arrangements can be found in the Hanseatic towns, although the active merchant's payment rarely exceeded the pro rata payment for his capital investment. Here, however, the activity was reciprocal, and a silent partner in one venture set up with his brothers might be an active member of another venture with the same people. Even if the legal contract of the partnership restricted it in terms of both time and trade, in spirit it was already becoming a proper company in which someone who one day works for others benefits on another day from the others' work.

Thus the partnership was the ideal framework for technically complementary activities. It was impossible for one person, in any one particular area, to deal with everything and be everywhere at once. But there were common interests. The shopkeeper who sold in the town worked closely with the tradesman who traveled to the regional markets. The innkeeper made common cause with the wine buyer who inspected the vineyards. The large entrepreneur needed contacts in the local markets. Someone operating on a European scale preferred to deal with local traders in each marketplace who were able to take advantage of local privileges and contacts. In order to take over a tax-farming operation, the capital of the larger merchant was vital, but it was only the man on the spot who could levy the tax on jugs of wine served retail, on vegetables sold in the covered market by local growers, or on the bales of cloth that were carried through the city gates by horses or men.

Because it was necessary to divide the risks and to consolidate capital, and because it was beneficial to share responsibility for collection, the right to levy taxes was generally leased out to partnerships. On more than one occasion, however, the king of France was forced to issue an order limiting the number of *"compagnons,"* based on the proceeds: " No [tax] farmer may take more than one companion for the collection if it is not more than 300 to 500 pounds; above 500 pounds up to 1,000, two companions; and above 1,000 pounds, three companions."

If we are to judge by the number of court cases brought in Paris, these rules were not well received. Nor did they conceal the diversity of relationships between the principal tax-farmer, whose name the tax-farm often bore, and his companions who were often simply silent partners, although they sometimes might be more actively involved. There were also multiple farms, where two tax-farmers shared one contract, each levying taxes on one product or alternatively on a quarter of the total. Sometimes a tax-farmer might even operate the levy for one part of the year, handing it over to someone else and turning to another activity, fiscal or commercial, for the rest of the year.

The Hanseatic merchants often made use of partnerships in order to interest a ship's captain in a possible trading deal. Both shipowner and merchant, the captain was rarely the employee of the merchant who entrusted his goods to him to transport across the Baltic or the North Sea. At the same time he seldom owned his ship outright, possessing perhaps only a quarter or an eighth share. On one trip, he would transport both goods entrusted to him by his partners and merchandise that he had acquired independently and that he would sell for his own account. Often the owner had the same share in the capital, represented by the ship, as in the investment that was the cargo—a perfect illustration of the division of profit and risk.

The Tuscan, on the other hand, had found other methods of financing business. Developments in banking had removed the impediments experienced by the businessman wishing to expand. The great merchants, who were also the great bankers, received enough cash deposits to make it unnecessary for them to look outside their own business for the capital needed to finance a variety of trading activities that—although differing in time span, place, and objective—remained always, but not exclusively, complementary. The partnership was to remain the ideal arrangement for small businesses. Tuscan merchants were to develop more evolved structures for larger enterprises.

These new developments in Tuscan business, after 1350, led to a distinction between the three functions apparent since the beginning of shop trade: finance, management, and wage labor. True capitalism was to be born of this distinction. It would make it necessary to keep books and render accounts, leading to modern techniques of analytical and systematic accounting.

We see the beginnings of such a system with Francesco di Marco Datini, who, as principal partner in nine multipurpose partnerships in various parts of Europe, in fact headed a "group" partnership, the unity of which depended on a single capitalist's ensuring a coherent commercial policy and on each partnership's being complementary to all the others. Datini's two main partnerships were based in his hometown of Prato. One dealt in making woolen cloth and the other in long-distance trade. The activities of the latter were extended, and even diversified, by partnerships established over the years in Florence, Pisa, Genoa, Avignon, Barcelona, Majorca, Valencia, and, lastly, Ibiza, not to mention the secondary companies, more or less specialized offshoots, such as the salt trade on the Rhône. Together they formed an economic group with no legal basis other than the responsibility taken equally for each and every one of these enterprises by one man, Francesco Datini.

The partners, sometimes former agents, were, moreover, allowed only limited freedom of maneuver. When Datini was setting up a partnership in

Avignon with Boninsegna di Matteo and Tieri di Benci, he immediately put a considerable portion of the financial reserves out of the reach of any initiatives his partners might want to take:

> In the name of God, Amen.
>
> Account book of the merchandise and rents that I, Francesco di Marco Datini of Prato, assign in Avignon to Boninsegna di Matteo of Florence and Tieri di Benci of Florence on this day 1st December 1382. . . .
>
> The said merchandise and rents amounting in all to 3,866 gold florins, on which sum we agreed, I Francesco and Boninsegna and Tieri. And it should follow as below:
>
> We, Boninsegna and Tieri, agreed with the said Francesco that of the aforesaid sum, which belongs entirely to Francesco di Marco, the said Francesco must leave the sum of 3,000 florins of 24 sous each in their care, either in merchandise or in rents.
>
> The remainder, that is, 866 florins, will be deposited by us in his account, at the beginning of the year in cash, in *deniers,* so that we have under our care the sum of 3,000 florins.
>
> The said Francesco is content and wishes that Boninsegna and Tieri may trade in the way they see fit with the said merchandise entered in this account book, and with any other merchandise which may seem to them useful to trade in and profitable for the benefit of the said Francesco.

So these were agents with a real interest in the business, and given real scope for initiative. But it was always for Datini's profit, and the capital invested in cash remained at his disposal.

The advantage of this arrangement is obvious: the volume of business increased, while the risks remained limited on account of the division. Datini understood very well that none of his partners was in a position to claim a significant share in the running of the business. With only five or ten thousand florins of capital at his disposal, a partner in Avignon or Valencia could scarcely pronounce on general policy on a European scale. Francesco di Marco, on the other hand, free to develop trade with Barcelona or to cut back on the flow toward Avignon, remained the sole master in charge.

Taking their inspiration from the *commenda* or the "society of the sea" (sea loan), others developed the idea of establishing limited partnerships that drew widely on available capital without involving the operator in any of the responsibilities. Legalized in Florence in 1408, "limited liability" made it possible to attract investments from small and often timid savers who never risked more than a small portion of their funds in a single investment. These associations of creditors with equal and transferable shares—nothing prevented an investor from participating in several of them—encouraged the concentration of capital without requiring any diversification of talent. Thus, in the case of banking, business did not call for the presence of partners in the four corners of the globe; correspondents were sufficient.

The limited partnership seemed at first to offer little more than another opportunity for depositing money, but with one essential difference: the partners took a share of the profits rather than a fixed interest rate for their investment. This was attractive to both the entrepreneur and the investor. The former got his capital, which he had to pay back only if he made a profit. The latter saw a speculative investment capable of appreciation at the cost of a limited risk.

The fact that shares were transferable represented enormous progress: since a partner could withdraw when he wanted with his share of the profit, he rarely insisted on a prompt auditing of accounts. Generally he was satisfied that they were always in order. A person hesitating to invest in the medium term could be reassured, knowing that he could get his money back when he wished. For the businessman with plans for the future, this permanent redistribution of capital opened the way for medium-term enterprises. It was obviously advantageous to be able to take initiatives and launch enterprises, with or without taking the time for a voyage, of a duration of six or twelve months. But this was conditional on one thing: it was vital that credit and confidence be preserved so that the share offered for transfer might seem attractive to other investors in the marketplace. As in depositing money, the limited partnership relied on the good reputation of the concern.

The Genoese made good use of the financial flexibility of the limited partnership, forming themselves into "carat" companies. Just as pure gold consists of twenty-four equal carats, so the company was divided into twenty-four equal shares. In practice, there was nothing to prevent the "carats" being further subdivided, and a Genoese who invested his savings in a hundred different businesses was only too happy to buy a quarter of a carat: 1/96 of a ship or an enterprise. Thus, in the mid-fifteenth century, we find a socially diversified capitalism, with shares on offer in companies set up for trade in alum from Asia Minor, coral from Tunisia, or mercury from Spain.

With such a variety of possibilities for investment, those with spare capital could choose where to place it, spread the risks, and indulge in speculation on the likely monetary rewards. The carat companies, set up for a specific purpose, were very frequently linked to the exploitation of a monopoly or a privilege. There was the Khios *magona,* the *Magona del Ferro* (the Iron Ore Cartel) for Elba. In Genoa, there were so many state creditors that they eventually regrouped as the *Casa di San Giorgio.* It was up to the individual to know whether it was the right moment to buy a quarter of a carat in a company importing fruit from the kingdom of Granada, or whether it would be better to invest in a new tax-farm leased out to *San Giorgio.*

Similar systems began to develop, for the same reasons, north of the Alps. Whether an entrepreneur or an investor, the businessman remained in control of trade or of the uses to which his capital was put. French and Germans alike began to divide ownership of ships into shares. The large

Hanseatic howker often belonged to thirty-two or sixty-four partners. From the twelfth century onward the Toulouse mills were the property of *pariers,* owning joint shares in one or more mills. From the 1370s, mill companies were divided into eighths—*uchaux*—and each *parier* owned a half, a third, or several eighths. The twelve mills in Bazacle represented 89 eighths in 1367 and 96 in 1478.

The *pariers* were still no more than a group of individuals jointly taking advantage of a feudal concession, more part of a shared lordship than of a an emergent capitalism. It was because the *uchau* was, from the very start, transferable that enterprises formed on this basis did not need to go into periodic liquidation, unlike merchants' partnerships that were formed for a single piece of trading and then dissolved. *Pariers* came and went, but the mill remained. A market in *uchaux* emerged. Shares were given a value that took into account the possible profits resulting from political, military, or economic circumstances. If a mill burned down, resulting in the collapse of the company's *uchaux,* another mill would prosper, grinding everyone's grain while the unfortunate owners attempted to finance their rebuilding. There was even a correlation, easily understood in relation to foodstuffs, between demographic developments and variations in the rate of the mill *uchaux.*

This kind of capitalism embraced every kind of distribution, whether geographical or social. Those involved in the Genoese *magona* in Khios, where the Phocaea alum destined for the West was collected, were so con- scious of their public image that nearly all of them adopted the name Giustiniani after the dominant family in the cartel. How better to illustrate that these masters of global trade were an oligarchy, which also tells us that these capitalists were few in number and that shares in the cartel were confined to a small circle. Hardly more accessible were the companies formed by those burgers of Lübeck who combined their capital to exploit the salt marshes of Lüneburg. The situation in Allevard, in Dauphiné, was quite different since shares in the iron mines were often owned by the miners themselves. And it was normal for the artisans of Nuremberg and Cologne to invest in their neighbors' businesses. Here it was no longer a matter of influence, but of attitude.

Money tended to move toward the more open investments, and hence those that were geographically remote from the large urban centers. Thus the capital invested in Bosnian mines was in the hands of German, Italian, and even Greek financiers.

The same need to pool capital induced Castilian sheep farmers, as early as the fourteenth century, to join together in a national association, the *Mesta.* All those with capital to invest in the wool industry, from the great lords to those monasteries richest in grazing land, foremost of which was the Escorial, owned their flocks jointly and managed them collectively right up to the final stages of sale on the international market. It was as important to choose the right moment and place for moving the sheep to or from the mountains as to ensure the proper regulation of a market in which, as we know, the merino wool from Castile had begun to pose a threat to the wool traditionally produced from English sheep. The latter, though superior in quality because of its longer fibers, was becoming too expensive for many wool industries. This consolidation of business through the *Mesta* led, not surprisingly, to the emergence of commercial centers, be it the autumn fairs at Medina del Campo or Riaza where the seasonal transport of sheep to Andalusia was arranged, or the winter fairs where, in the south and particularly in Villanueva de la Serena, buying and selling were finalized.

Here again can be glimpsed the premises of a capitalism emerging, above all, from the pooling of capital and separation of the three functions of finance, management, and operations. The *Mesta* consisted of great landowners, managers of the herds, specialized merchants, and, of course, shepherds.

The Company

While such forms of partnership became increasingly common throughout Europe, in Tuscany businessmen had long preferred a more complex and fruitful structure: the *compagnia*. Since the beginning of the fourteenth century, major financial capitals of the Western world such as Siena and then Florence were dealing increasingly in concentrations of capital that were not only larger but also more permanent and at the same time more flexible, available for use in a wide variety of enterprises.

Investment very soon became a very separate activity from trading or banking. Salaried agents rose to the rank of "governors," that is, directors of the company branches that were being established all over the world as a result of expansion. There even appeared in the more advanced companies a very new figure—the "minister" or, as we would say, the salaried general manager. In this role emerged those talented employees of the Medici company Giovanni Benci and Francesco Sassetti.

The foundation of the company was the family. There were very few companies where nominal capital, as opposed to the assets deposited by investors and used for the day-to-day operations of the business, was not effectively controlled by one or two families, often united by judicious marriages. Despite the restructuring that resulted approximately every four years in the moving around of the junior partners, this family base ensured continuity in business, in name, and in brand quality. As we have seen, public confidence played an essential role.

Given the wide age range of its members, the company became an inexhaustible human breeding ground, making the family name much more than merely a name over the door. Shortly before its collapse, of the fifteen branches constituting the powerful Florentine Peruzzi company in 1335, six were run by a partner or, in London, by the son of a partner. Of these, three—in Bruges, Naples, and Paris—were members of the Peruzzi family: the son, nephew, and cousin of the principal partner, Giotto di Arnoldo de' Peruzzi, who had given his name to the company.

The managers of the big companies made use of these family connections, finding it advantageous to promote this visible unity of a community of interests. Around 1465, while the Florentine Pigello di Folco Portinari was running the Milanese branch of the Medici company where he was succeeded by his own brother Accerrito, his two sons Folco di Pigello and Benedetto di Pigello were in Bruges with another of his brothers, the great Tommaso di Folco Portinari, who had just taken over from his cousin Bernardo di Giovanni Portinari. Their young cousin Folco di Adoardo Portinari was also in Bruges, soon to be joined by his elder brother Giovanni. Their younger brother, Alessandro di Adoardo, was soon to be posted to the London branch.

In Germany during this same period, the members of the Fugger family were sharing the responsibilities of the family business. The eldest, Ulrich, ran the business in Augsburg, forming close links with the emperor, Frederick III. Andreas and Johann spent some time in Venice. Peter and Georg followed each other in Nuremberg. In Rome as the secretary to the papal chancellery, Marcus was able to help his brothers in a variety of ways. One daughter married a Meuting, a member of the family's chief rivals in the marketplaces of middle Germany. As for Jacob, the most famous of the Fuggers at the end of the fifteenth century, he first took minor orders and was content to spend some time as a canon. But he was released back into the secular world in 1478, and it was to Venice he went to assist his brothers and learn the business.

As in a limited partnership, the partners of a company shared risks, profits, and losses. But an innovative idea had emerged in the company, that of collective liability, strongly underpinned by the prohibition of membership in more than one concern. In a limited partnership the whole point was to diversify investments into a variety of businesses, thus balancing the risks. The company, by contrast, wished to maintain its exclusivity. It was still possible to invest money with a neighbor or elsewhere under different legal terms, but it was possible to belong to only one *compagnia.*

It was a system that generally worked well. If the Peruzzi liquidated their company in 1335 with a 15 percent loss on their capital, previous liquidations had, since 1300, assured on average an annual dividend of 15 to 20 percent. From 1322 to 1329, the dividend paid out by the Alberti company was between 9 and 16 percent. Whether because of greater daring

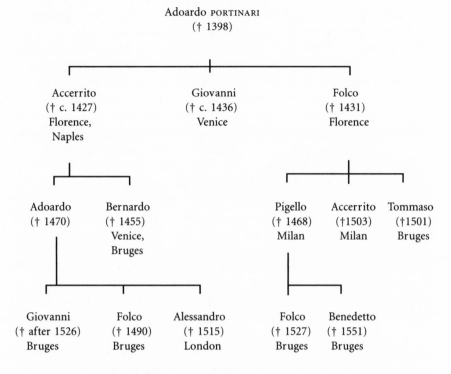

Adoardo PORTINARI
(† 1398)

Accerrito
(† c. 1427)
Florence,
Naples

Giovanni
(† c. 1436)
Venice

Folco
(† 1431)
Florence

Adoardo
(† 1470)

Bernardo
(† 1455)
Venice,
Bruges

Pigello
(† 1468)
Milan

Accerrito
(†1503)
Milan

Tommaso
(†1501)
Bruges

Giovanni
(† after 1526)
Bruges

Folco
(† 1490)
Bruges

Alessandro
(† 1515)
London

Folco
(† 1527)
Bruges

Benedetto
(† 1551)
Bruges

or skill, Rosso di Ubertino degli Strozzi was able to give his partners, between 1330 and 1340, an annual dividend of from three to ten times the capital invested. During the fifteenth century, the Medici gave their partners equally generous returns if we discount the collapse of the Bruges branch. Between 1430 and 1450 the Geneva branch yielded 30 percent, and after this date more than 60 percent.

The practice of depositing capital was not for the Tuscan companies just one of a variety of activities; it was an essential constituent of the system. By accepting deposits and remunerating them without merging them with the nominal capital put up by the partners, the company increased its liquid assets. It did not, for all that, increase the number of people who had the right to intervene in the running of affairs. The depositor did not have any inside knowledge. He received no statements of account except perhaps his own. As one of a number of creditors he had the right to check up on his investment and receive the interest due, but not to know the source of the money with which he was paid. And this interest was determined solely by the relationship of supply and demand in the local credit market. The volume of business did not come into it, nor yet market trends. In fifteenth-century Italy, the companies paid between 8 and 15 percent a year. When credit became easy to obtain, the rates in interest fell. In Lübeck, for example, between 1280 and 1310, interest rates fell from 10 percent to 5 percent.

There were advantages in such a system: a guaranteed interest for the depositor, available capital without a sharing of power for the partners. But it did not protect companies that incautiously extended their working capital beyond their real capacity. At the first crisis of confidence, at the first whisper of impending or long-range problems, depositors withdrew their money. Companies that had placed this money in overly ambitious enterprises were quite unable to pay it back. The closing accounts of the Bardi company showed assets of 1,266,775 pounds, of which the nominal capital accounted for less than 100,000 pounds. To borrow twelve times that amount in order to develop the business was to put it at the mercy of any crisis of confidence.

The very worst examples were those of 1342 and 1346 when depositors en masse withdrew the money they had invested with the Peruzzi and the Bardi. Although things were not always so dramatic, the obligation of the companies to pay out interest due to depositors, whatever the state of the business's finances and even when it was in deficit, put them in difficulties as soon as shortage of cash on the market raised interest rates to the average levels in commerce and banking. There were few enterprises and periods in which profits exceeded 12 percent. Not everyone could be a Medici, and not everyone was served by a Sassetti. Taking on investments at 10 or 12 percent meant undertaking to exceed that rate in profit.

The risks were so serious that economic operators came up with two forms of protection. One, dear to the small entrepreneur, was the carat company, previously described, which encouraged a multiplicity of small investors. In this case they attracted the same small savings that might have gone to the great companies in the form of investments, but did not have to guarantee the interest, while the carats were only remunerated at the rate of profits realized. The other protection against massive withdrawals was the fixed-period deposit. Here, of course, savers were quick to sense the cautious motives inspiring such a system and became suspicious.

The chief danger, however, stemmed from the enormous size of companies whose branches jointly conducted business with the attendant risks. The system of subsidiary firms, first used by the Tuscans in the 1370s, was above all a response to the interdependence so dangerous to invested capital. It tended also to develop local initiative, the only way of dealing with the paralyzing slowness of communications. The obvious place to react to events and opportunities was on the spot. The rational capitalism of the great decentralized companies, which emerged during the fifteenth century as the ideal structure for seizing control of business on a European scale, thus tended to distribute capital among several firms with identical interests, allowing each manager to best act on opportunities and take risks, for profit or loss, according to a global policy represented by the collective name of the parent company. From the time of Giovanni di Bicci, the real founder of the banking company at the end of the fourteenth century, this was the policy followed by the Medici. Business was distributed by dividing the capital.

Decentralization was no more than a fiction as far as capital was concerned. The family, or families, that managed the parent firm was understood to be the chief partner in the subsidiary firms. This was more obvious with regard to management: a junior partner, often chosen from the younger members of the main family and remunerated by a share in the profits, was, in the branch, better placed than the Florentine head office to make immediate decisions about people and business. The important thing, however, was always the division of risk. When the Bruges and London branches of the Medici went bankrupt in 1480, overburdened by the weight of their loans to the government of Mary of Burgundy, the rest of the Medici empire viewed the collapse of Tommaso Portinari, who was too closely associated with Charles the Bold, and his brutal liquidation by Lorenzo the Magnificent as if it were of no concern to them. In the Bruges debacle, everyone naturally lost what he had invested. But in Florence, as in Venice, Pisa, Rome, or Milan, or in Geneva, London, or Avignon, the company of Lorenzo the Magnificent did not lose a single florin. The loss in Bruges was an isolated event, having no repercussions on the capacity for investment or the credit of any other members of the company.

Despite the autonomy that made up for the slowness of communications, the system of subsidiary firms was also a unifying factor during the fourteenth century, providing a global perspective on the European business scene, the ability to adapt different pursuits to a fluctuating economic climate, and the mutual supply of information thanks to a network that extended the length and breadth of the economic world. The company kept what was most important to its credit, both political and financial: the unity of the brand name as represented by the name of the company. Even if the Medici in Geneva were independent as far as capital was concerned, it was to the Medici that the Geneva businessman went—knowing that, despite the different names, he was dealing with the Medici—when referred, in the years between 1430 and 1450, to Giovanni Benci, then Ruggieri della Casa, and finally to his former assistant, Francesco Sassetti, who, as we know, would go far in the company. Between the Peruzzi and the Acciaiuoli of the fourteenth century and the Medici in the fifteenth, the public saw nothing wrong in the passage from the branch office to the subsidiary firm. All they knew was that they were going "to the Medici" (see Map 6).

The general policy pursued by Sassetti when the greater Medici began to play at being princes rather than merchants was, in particular, to retain the prerogative of creating subsidiary firms whose presence on the spot depended on a global appreciation of the needs and circumstances of the economic world, not simply on a specific view of the local situation. Since capital was the concern of a well-managed company, it was not only a problem, in 1452, of knowing whether or not a subsidiary firm of the Medici company was needed in Milan where Francesco Sforza was establishing his newly won power, but also of judging whether Milan was really the best place to exploit available capital to create a new firm.

The first of the great Medici, Giovanni di Averardo de' Medici, known as Giovanni di Bicci (d. 1429), began to diversify within Italy at first. Starting with the small banking business that he entered in 1382, when it already had four branches—in Florence, Venice, Genoa, and Rome—one partnership followed another. Giovanni di Bicci was young and so he was sent to manage the business in Rome. Ten years later he bought up the share of the principal partner, his cousin Vieri di Cambio de' Medici. He went into partnership with a small group including one of the Bardi, moved his head office to Florence, developed his subsidiary firms in Venice and Rome and then one in Naples. In 1402 and 1408, he created two industrial companies for the manufacture of woolen cloth.

His sons Cosimo di Giovanni (1389–1464, known as the *Pater Patriae*) and Lorenzo di Giovanni (1395–1440, the first of the Lorenzos) at first continued their father's business, still in partnership with the Bardi. In 1426 they opened a branch in Geneva, a town whose fairs were then at their peak. The council in Basel offered them the opportunity to open a temporary office in that town in 1435. In 1436 they set up a limited partnership in Ancona. That same year, so as to avoid having to convey everything to Flanders by the intermediary of the Bardi and the Borromei, they set up their Bruges branch, entrusting the running of it to Bernardo Portinari.

By 1441 the Medici had, besides their strongholds in Florence—the original company and three manufacturing firms, one for silk and two for wool—five commercial and banking subsidiaries in Rome, Venice, Ancona, Bruges, and Geneva. To this they added in 1442 the Pisa branch, and in 1446 one in London—originally simply an offshoot of the Bruges branch—and one in Avignon, the latter supervising affairs in Marseilles, Montpellier, and Toulouse. The company's map was completed in 1452 with the creation of a branch in Milan and in 1464 with the transferral of the Geneva subsidiary firm to Lyons. At the same time there was a Medici presence in the northern markets, and we find them in Lübeck from 1413.

The distribution of business can be seen clearly from an examination of the balance sheets. Of the 75,000 florins in profit made in 1451 by the

Map 6. The Medici Company c.1450

whole of the "group," the bank in Florence accounts for 13,000 florins (17 percent) and the three industrial firms, also in Florence, 18,600 florins (25 percent). Thus hometown business accounted for 42 percent of the total. As for the nominal capital, three-quarters of it was in the hands of three Medici family members, Piero di Cosimo and Giovanni di Cosimo, sons of the *Pater Patriae,* and Pierfrancesco di Lorenzo, their cousin. Piero di Cosimo was at this date the father of a two-year-old child, Lorenzo, who was to become *Il Magnifico.*

With the exception of Pisa, where the Medici held only a third of the capital, they held the majority share in all the subsidiaries. In Avignon and Geneva they owned as much as 87.5 percent, the remaining share being in the hands of Francesco Sassetti.

Expansion continued in the time of Cosimo. With the improvement in relations between Florence and Francesco Sforza, the Milan branch became an essential piece in a game that was henceforward to be more political than strictly economic. Bad management by Accerrito Portinari, brother of Pigello who had so successfully run affairs in Milan, was to make liquidation inevitable. Tommaso, the third son of Folco Portinari, the former director of the Medici bank in Florence, was not much more fortunate in Bruges where, as we have seen, the credit that he was obliged to offer to the duke Charles the Bold drove him into liquidation shortly after the duke's political fall. But Cosimo's company, and later that of Lorenzo the Magnificent, compensated for these setbacks. Under the shrewd management of Francesco Sassetti, recalled to Florence from Geneva in 1458, the company was able to set up in countries where new developments were beginning to reshape the map of the economic world. The Medici were to be found at the fairs at Antwerp and Berg op Zoom. They had agents as far away as Lübeck and Barcelona.

They seized every opportunity, and it came as no surprise when the pope turned to them in 1462 for financial help, leasing them the farm on the alum trade recently started up in papal territory at Tolfa. This discovery had been something of a godsend, coming as it did at a time when the Turkish advance in Asia Minor had recently put a stop to the centuries-old trade in alum from Phocaea.

The success of the Medici was exceptional, but they were not alone in the European market. Founded in 1380 by Joseph Hompys, the *Grosse Ravensburger Handelsgesellschaft* quickly established firms all over Europe. Naturally appearing first in the Germanic countries, subsidiaries were established in Cologne, Nuremberg, and Vienna. Subsequently firms were set up in Berne, Geneva, and also Pest. In Flanders there were branches in Bruges and Antwerp, while Italy had them in Genoa and Milan, and France had one in Lyons. The company was represented in Spain in Barcelona, Valencia, and Saragossa. Thus the partners were able to reach all corners of Europe, without having to operate through the Italians. In the following century the Fugger family was to follow this example. But the Germans were tactful: they did not go so far as to open a branch in Florence (see Map 7).

Thus, at the end of the Middle Ages the fortunes of the merchants took off in a way that would have been hard to imagine at the time of the Champagne fairs. The capital invested by Cosimo de' Medici and his brother Lorenzo, and later by his nephew Pierfrancesco, rose from 180,000 florins in 1429 to 235,000 florins in 1440 when Lorenzo died. Around 1460, at the peak of the *Pater Patriae*'s career, the sum was 400,000 florins.

But the business world was beginning to look outside this sphere. It was no longer a matter of diversifying their investments, as the great merchants of the early fifteenth century—the contemporaries of Datini or of Giovanni di Bicci—had done. Now the contemporaries of Cosimo began to assume the mentality of landowners who needed finances to maintain their social standing, or even of shareholders living off their company's income.

These newly wealthy businessmen, together with those enriched in public service—though in reality these were often one and the same, or at least of the same family—began to buy their own premises in the center of town, and of a grandeur fitting to show off their success. This concern for a style of life on a par with their influence began to manifest itself in a series of economically unproductive investments. The Venetian and Florentine *palazzo* and the Parisian *hôtel* represented capital that had been diverted from business. Aspiring to an aristocratic life, with all it involved in terms of servants and grand edifices, the businessmen devoted themselves to this new type of investment, just at a time when the old feudal world, now collapsing with the fall in income from the land, was turning its back on it. They bought land, estates, and lordships.

This land was not bought as a source of income, but rather as a secure investment intended to balance the speculative ventures made in banking and commerce and as a political affirmation of their arrival in the ranks of the great and powerful. In those countries where the old nobility kept its rank and attraction, wealth was nothing without land. So we see the burgess of Rouen or Lyons begin to use the name of the seigneury purchased by his father in place of the patronymic with its odor of fish or moneylending. The Venetians who had grown rich through their trade with the East bought up estates on the mainland. The Florentines built villas in the surrounding Tuscan countryside. As for the Parisians, they competed in the luxury of their town houses and discovered the charms of property in the country.

This did not mean that they were not looking for security. The diversification of investments ensured a regular income—from houses and estates, from town houses, and even government bonds when Florence and Genoa

Map 7. The Grand Society of Ravensburg c.1450

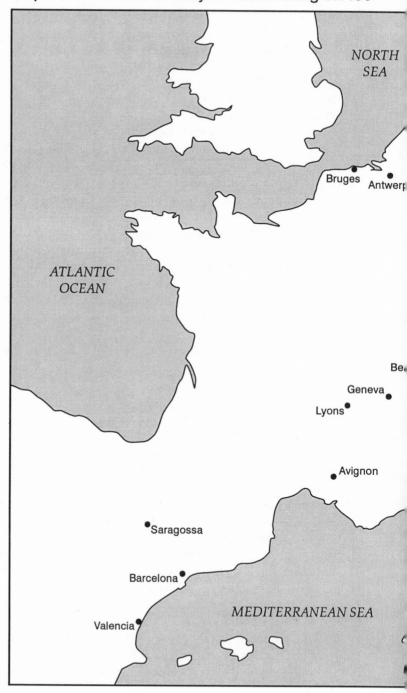

NORTH SEA

ATLANTIC OCEAN

Bruges
Antwerp

Be.

Geneva
Lyons

Avignon

Saragossa

Barcelona

Valencia

MEDITERRANEAN SEA

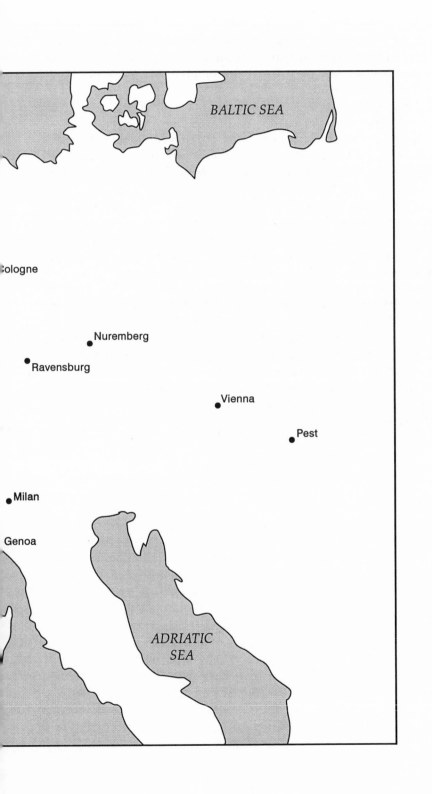

made public debt the basis of their economic policy or when Venice made it the foundation of its fiscal system. At the peak of his career, Cosimo de' Medici had half his fortune—apart from property—in *luoghi del Monte,* that is, bonds in the public debt of the republic.

To look at these figures, it would seem that only a small part of the merchants' fortunes were invested in commerce. One Andrea Barbarigo, an important man in Venice during the 1460s, placed no more than 10 percent of his available capital in enterprises that were genuinely commercial; yet these enterprises had led to the glory of La Serenissima. We should not be tempted to think that this was merely an oversight. Barbarigo wrote to his son about his motives in his will: trade does not bring in profits. If we realize that in Florence the state *luoghi* yielded a guaranteed 5 percent and even 15 percent if one knew the best time to buy—in times of economic crisis—then it is easy to understand why the great commercial powers began to collapse, crushed beneath the weight of rent and palaces.

Nor should we ignore the role played, regardless of the political regime, by investment in power, the costly lure of public office that enhanced a man's standing and rank outside the world of trade. In France, and particularly in Paris, where all the great merchant families bought aristocratic titles, they rushed to serve the king, seeking appointments in finance or the law, in the aristocracy in fact. Everywhere the route to fame passed by way of municipal service, and it cost as much to be a counselor in Lübeck as it did to be a *capitoul* in Toulouse or a *priore delle arti* in Florence. The power that came from trade and banking tended to express itself in a municipal post and a political role, both of which diverted and consumed energy and capital.

TEN

Business

ew merchants could survive by trading in a single item. The varying needs of different economic regions led to the organization of diversified trade. The lands to the north lacked sunshine and wanted wine. The wine-producing countries were generally short of grain. Wool came from England, Spain, Languedoc, or Provence, while alum came from the East or from Italy, and the dyes—woad, indigo, saffron, cochineal, khermes, and *roccella* or *orseille*—from a variety of places. Although this situation encouraged reciprocal trade among marketplaces and rotating cargoes, it did not necessarily mean that every single merchant diversified.

Universal Trading

Reinvestment of profits provided the first stimulus for universality. Until the development of the money market in the fourteenth century, businessmen had only two alternatives: to ensure the recovery of their earnings or to use their profits to buy goods for the return journey. The first meant leaving the capital idle—for as long as six months in the case of long-distance trade—so the choice was obvious.

The introduction of bills of exchange—of banking and the movement of capital—did little to change the basic problem. While it was easy enough to bring money home, nobody was prepared to pay high rates for freight and risk returning without a cargo. Although such voyages were tolerated in certain kinds of trade such as that of salt, where convoys would sometimes return home empty from the Baltic, the business world was nevertheless unanimous in regarding them as a last resort. Once again it was a matter of financial sterility: what was to be gained from leaving capital and ships idle just because there was nothing to be bought for the moment in the Russian or Baltic ports?

Even when a single product was enough to generate a flow of trade, collective ingenuity generally managed to create an inverse flow of some other product. The monolithic single-product trade currents did not lend themselves, either in time or in space, to such reciprocal arrangements, although that would clearly have been to everyone's benefit. The fleets carrying wine did not arrive in London just at the time that the sheep had been sheared. The salt ships reached the Baltic well before the main fishing season, even though fish were not available until the end of this period. By contrast, it was also possible to see the same ships that transported the alum required by the Western textile industry from Khios to Genoa returning to the East with products as different as wool cloth from Genoa and Florence—usually Flemish cloth finished in Italy—Italian or German gold work, even fruit from the Riviera, or oil from Apulia taken on at the port of Barletta.

Although vital to the West, a product like alum, from Asia Minor, was heavy and relatively cheap. Thus it was expensive to transport, costing some 16 percent of the buying price of the alum itself. Although partially remedied by the large variety of goods exported to Constantinople and the Black Sea, the imbalance in the flow of trade was further complicated by a financial imbalance. Profits from the sales made in the East could be only partially reinvested in the purchase of alum, the production and price of which was controlled by Genoa. Thus it was essential to find a complementary cargo in the East that was not only not heavy but also costly. The answer was spices, particularly pepper, although the major center for the latter was Alexandria rather than Constantinople. Similarly expensive but light to carry were the exotic dyes. Although Western dyes were perfectly adequate for everyday life and nobody would have dreamed of replacing woad with its Oriental equivalents, nevertheless, the costly purple and indigo were highly prized. And last, there was silk. Its high price—ten to twelve times that of pepper, weight for weight—reduced the cost of the transport to something like 0.5 percent.

The Genoese shippers balanced out their journeys in the following way: on the way to the East they carried moderately heavy merchandise of good value; on the return to Genoa they carried heavy goods of low cost, rounding out the cargo with light but costly goods.

From the thirteenth century, this attempt to balance weight and price led to return cargoes that themselves engendered regional redistribution. Flemish cloth was exchanged in Italy for products from the Orient, which were then resold by Bruges to London, Lübeck, Cologne, and Paris. It was traded at the Champagne fairs or in Paris for French or Burgundian wine destined for non-wine-producing regions on the North Sea and the Baltic.

In Russia it was exchanged for the wood needed by the naval shipyards on the Channel and the Atlantic, for honey produced in the West, or for highly prized furs. During a period when the climate was becoming cooler, these costly furs became a very precise and subtle expression of social position among the upper classes. The flow of trade to the West brought ermine for the dignitaries at the papal court, sable for the Parisian magistrates, and squirrel for the Hamburg merchants. In exchange, cargoes of the violet woolen cloth produced in Brussels, marbled brown cloth from Saint-Omer, vermilion cloth from Arras, and purple striped cloth from Ghent traveled to the markets of Bergen and Novgorod.

And it was not only Flemish cloth. Exported from Bordeaux and La Rochelle, wines from Guyenne and Aunis were exchanged for wool and cloth from England, fabrics from the rural weavers of Normandy, dried fish from the Channel and the North Sea, and cereals from the Paris basin and the Polish plains. The wine convoys did not depart empty from either London or Bruges. When, in the fifteenth century, the English first attempted to export the products of their expanding cloth industry, they knew that they could be sure of return cargoes of wine from Gascony, iron from Spain, and dyes from the East.

More subtle, however, were the diversified trade currents that arose from a deliberate decision to exploit an economic opening. It was not just a question of simple linear exchanges, depending on the resources available at either end of a trade route. Increasingly taking advantage of bargains and the local economic climate by diversifying their activities and seizing opportunities, merchants no longer set out to sell one product and bring back a second. Rather, they went to see who was selling and what was being bought. They were not afraid to unload only part of their cargo or to take on a complementary cargo that they could unload profitably in a local market. They might seize on unforeseen possibilities or temporarily advantageous prices, selling when they had not originally intended to sell and returning home with some unexpected cargo, taking the client or the competitor by surprise. Their success depended on their luck in the ports of call.

This was a very different kind of business from the direct trade in alum from Khios or salt from Bourgneuf. In a trading region such as the North Sea or the Mediterranean, or even just the Iberian coast of the small inshore trader, it is possible to trace the beginning of multidirectional trading, ever on the lookout for profit. Many Italian merchants made their living this way, taking on cloth or wine in Naples and oil or cotton at Bari or Barletta. From Naples they took salted meat to Catalonia, and to Venice they brought Sicilian sugar. In Tunisia they took on coral, which they resold in Marseilles or Genoa. Should the opportunity arise, they dealt in Provençal salt. They would take advantage of the arrival of a load of spices in Alexandria, or of a good price for gold thread in Constantinople. From ports on the Crimea such as Kaffa to those on the Sea of Azov such as Tana they bought, depending on what arrived, silver from the Caucasus, boxwood, and Tartar, Circassian, or Georgian slaves. They financed all this by the provision of grain and weapons, thanks to which those marketplaces threatened by the advancing Turks were able to survive well into the fifteenth century. At Trebizond, where the routes across central Asia converged on the south side of the Black Sea, they might find silk newly arrived with a caravan, or fish from the latest sea harvest. Here, too, they could find copper or silver at a good price. All this would be sold along the return route—the slaves in Barcelona, the gold thread in Pisa.

The Hanseatic merchants, too, were on the lookout for a good deal in the course of their voyages: wood and furs from Prussia or Russia; leather from Scandinavia; metals from Norway; fish from the Baltic; grain from Pomerania; tin from Cornwall; sea salt from Brittany or from the salt pans of Lüneburg; Gascon wine bought in Bruges and London; goods from the Orient, and woolen cloth brought from all over the West and sold in the markets of Bruges and Antwerp.

Anything was worth buying as long as it was salable. Any business was good business. It was not long before those in search of extra profits in the ports of call extended their activities to the money market—to banking—and to industrial production. Besides, to diversify one's business did not simply mean multiplying opportunities. It was also the simplest response to the risks involved in speculation. For anyone dealing in spices in Alexandria and alum in Bruges, a weaving workshop in Florence represented security.

Diversity, born of necessity in the important maritime trade, was soon to affect all aspects of commercial trading, even those having little or nothing to do with the sea. During the 1480s, on his frequent journeys between Augsburg and Venice, Jacob Fugger became aware of the possibilities offered by the mineral wealth of the Tyrol. His family had dealt in cloth and spices for twenty years; now he added metal, particularly copper and silver, and goods manufactured by the new German metal industry.

This diversity even survived the introduction of bills of exchange that reduced, without making entirely redundant, the economic need to reinvest profits. As always, it was up to the merchant to make a decision on the spot: those who were well informed on relevant matters might make a deal at a profit or on credit one day; another day they might use that profit or credit for a particular purchase of goods available at an advantageous price on the local market or fetching a high price in a more distant market.

It is here that a gap opens up that would lead to the gulf between the world of the entrepreneur and that of the shopkeeper. Small traders were condemned by economic restrictions to their particular specialization, and this was reinforced by corporatism. Confined within the system of organized guilds, they had neither the means nor the desire to break free. The cutler remained a seller of knives, but the haberdasher began to sell English alabasters and Byzantine ivories. While some drapers remained confined to their stalls, selling pieces of cloth for doublets to their regular customers, others financed the purchase of wool by an industry they had established before exporting its products to the four corners of the world. On one side of the divide stood a man like Jacques Coeur; on the other was a small shopkeeper like the one tricked by Master Pathelin in the fifteenth-century play.

Even to those who would never reach the heights of a Fugger or a Medici, the major markets for the collection and distribution of goods on a regional scale could offer the possibility of participating in this diversity, bringing international trade within their grasp. Those merchants who were most firmly established were able to take control of the redistribution of objects that were as varied as demand itself. Thus the richer merchant classes of Bruges—and later, at the end of the fifteenth century, of Antwerp when this port in Brabant overtook Bruges—were able to benefit from this redistribution, embracing the whole of northwestern Europe, of everything carried across the North Sea by those seagoing merchants trading between the Mediterranean East, on one side, and the Russian and Scandinavian Baltic, on the other. The merchant of Bruges or Antwerp was an experienced trader to whom any notion of specialization was foreign. Financially and technically he was able to undertake the sale and, above all, the re-export of whatever arrived in the port. This universalism led to increasing numbers of specialist brokers who established themselves in the larger ports and who were able to judge and advise on any type of merchandise. No longer dealing with the practicalities of trade, such businessmen had become coordinators and financiers.

To a lesser degree, all ports offered similar opportunities. Rouen, for example, was the port of entry for maritime trade, opening the way to the towns and regions along the Seine and its tributaries. In the mid-fifteenth century a certain Jean Baudouin was supplying central France and particularly Paris with wheat and oats, herrings, cod, and salmon, and even Spanish figs. When in Paris, he took the opportunity to buy wine that would be sold in the inns of Normandy. Guillaume du Bois similarly supplied sugar and ginger, wool and wine, oil, paper, and cloth from the Netherlands and Normandy to the French interior. His compatriot Cardin Pelletier, who had a quick eye for exotic goods being unloaded on the quayside at Rouen, kept Paris supplied with sugar, cotton, alum, paper, figs, grapes, and almonds.

During the same period, the Toulouse money changer Jean Amic, son of a draper and son-in-law of a spice merchant, was trading between Languedoc and Catalonia in everything that appeared on the market in Toulouse,

Montpellier, and Barcelona: cloth from Languedoc, Normandy, or England; woad from Lauraguais; wood from Aragon; and wax, saffron, copper and steel, silver vessels, horses, and even wine.

The Hanseatic merchants were no less eclectic in their dealings across the Baltic. In Riga, Revel, Bergen, and Novgorod they extracted products from the hinterland with as much energy as they put into bringing goods from London or Bruges. It was important to make trade balance in the Baltic markets, for the Hanseatic merchants were deeply suspicious of paper payments and exchanges. The return cargo outweighed any other considerations, but the extent of the market exploited in both directions was such that their concern to fill the ships discouraged any kind of specialization.

Although much more restricted, the large markets of the capital cities and courts offered a diversity that the traders saw as an opportunity, insofar as they could free themselves from the constraints imposed by the guilds. An important merchant might be a member of the guild of spice merchants, fur traders, or mercers, since he had originally come from one of these trades and, given the legal structures of urban life, he had to belong to some kind of organization. Nevertheless, he would attempt to win over customers in many other areas. When the statutes intended to limit competition prevented him from having a monopoly over any one market, he would instead establish himself as the single supplier of everything for his particular clients. Although often listed as money changers or drapers on the registers, the "Lombards" in the Paris of Charles VI, and those Frenchmen who followed after them, did their best to impose their services on both princes and citizens, in the manner of the Florentine—and later the Lucchesi—companies in Avignon that served the papal court and the cardinals. Among the goods they had to offer were precious plate, gold work, luxury woolen cloth, and furs; whether luxury goods or horses and manuscripts, for them it was all one.

This is precisely what Jacques Coeur was doing in the 1440s when, though misleadingly described as "treasurer," he kept a kind of luxury bazaar that supplied the court of Charles VII. After his arrest, the public prosecutor Jean Dauvet, entrusted with the job of seizing and managing the ousted treasurer's estate, discovered an astonishing collection of exotic items. Among the hundred vital things needed to clothe, feed, and amuse a court were found "two chests full of ostrich feathers," eventually sold in Geneva. Nor should we forget the lioness that Jacques Coeur kept in Lyons and that the king had brought to Paris: it had cost 25 écus in payment to the wagoner and 12 livres, 12 sous, and 6 *deniers* to Jacques de la Layne, "who has always tended the said lioness" and who, in exchange for this sum, agreed to "convey her and tend her until she is handed over in the aforementioned town of Paris into the hands of the guard of the king's lions, and this to include four lengths of waxed cloth with which the cage of the said lioness has been covered."

The distance between the shop and international trade was great. Some would always stick to the narrow specialization of the producer who retailed his own product in one of the regional supply trades that depended on local resources. The wine grower from Suresnes and the forester from Villiers-Cotterêts, coming to Paris to sell their harvest, would take nothing back with them, apart from the odd souvenir. The English wool trade, although on a different scale, was organized along similarly specialized lines: the "woolmen" directed wool to the ports, while "staplers" sold it at the continental staples. Payment was received in the form of bills of exchange. The stapler had to worry about other things than buying wine, and the woolman would not sell Gascon wine, bought in Bruges, in the English countryside where he found his wool. Trade in products unrelated to wool was left to others, to the "merchant adventurers" who were exploring all the ports of northwestern Europe.

For the most part, French, English, and German merchants adapted well to a degree of specialization forced on them by the small amounts of capital available for investment in their businesses. Even in Italy, the majority of merchants was not inclined to juggle simultaneously with furs and spices. Inventories drawn up after a merchant's death show, in all countries, a remarkably homogeneous collection of goods in the storeroom. On the other hand, cloth merchants who stuck to cloth, or goldsmiths who confined themselves to working gold and silver, were unlikely to turn down the chance of a deal suited to their level or reach, should one present itself, however foreign it might be to their profession. Thus we see merchants moving tentatively into money changing or taking on a lease for tax-farming. None of this greatly enlarged their horizons, however. The butcher was likely to be the local tax-farmer as long as the tax did not involve butchers.

The great Italian companies, defined at least as much by their universalism as by their capitalist structure, were light-years away from the small world of the shopkeeper. Francesco di Marco Datini was a member of the Florentine *Arte di Calimala* as well as the *Arte di Por Santa Maria* that already was representing the silk merchants. Although he had no branch in the Paris market, only a correspondent, he was, around 1400, selling silks and velvets from Lucca, fine silk and cottons from Perugia, embroideries and jewels bought in various places, weapons from Toledo, leather from Cordova, and paintings from Siena and Florence. In Paris he bought Limoges enamels as well as painted cloth from Flanders, used to make into curtains, bed canopies, or even wall coverings. In Bruges, Datini sold scarlet cloth, red logwood, and raw cotton. Into Avignon he imported Milanese weapons and Tuscan haberdashery. He notes, too, that he was dealing in Languedoc salt in Orange and Carpentras.

A few years later, the Venetian Andrea Barbarigo traded in woolen goods from Florence or Malines, spices from India, Syrian cotton, gold thread from Byzantium, leather goods from Italy, tin and pewter from England, and even slaves bought in Tana on the south shore of the Sea of Azov.

As for the Medici, with their eleven companies established throughout Europe, they also dealt in raw wool, fine cloth, and silk as well as alum, scarlet cloth, oil, spices, tapestries, and works of art. In Florence and Rome they were officially bankers.

It was not only in Florence and Rome that they performed the role of banker, though Florence had always been the most important since the time when Giovanni di Bicci de' Medici had first received on deposit money entrusted to him by the papal legate to Romagna, Cardinal Baldassare Cossa, who had extorted it from Pope Gregory XII. Cossa constantly reminded the pope of the weakness of a papal state incapable of financing its own defense. This money, hastily withdrawn in 1409, at the time of the opening of the council of Pisa, was to be used to overthrow Gregory XII and give the church a third pope. Less than a year later, Cossa was pope. The father of the Medici bank had played his cards well.

But his successors were no less interested in taking on leases for monopolies, such as rights to the industrial and commercial exploitation of the famous Tolfa alum mines. The Medici were also to become known as industrialists in Tuscany.

As we have seen, before the arrival on the scene of the Fugger family in the late fifteenth century, the Germanic world had only one Italian-style company: the *Grosse Ravensburger Handelsgesellschaft,* founded in 1380 in Ravensburg (see Map 7, p. 172–73). A number of Hanseatic families and merchants from Nuremberg formed companies with multiple interests. Families like the Castorps, the Lumbergs, and the Veckinchusens were able to take advantage of their presence in the marketplaces of the North Sea and the Baltic to profit from the natural diversity of medium-distance sea voyages. A number of Nuremberg businessmen even acquired citizenship in Lübeck, thus breaking away from the restrictions imposed by the xenophobic Hanseatic League and gaining a share of the new opportunities.

There was perhaps only one Frenchman who emulated the Italians: Jacques Coeur. He attempted, in the mid-fifteenth century, to make his own way without the almost inevitable involvement of the Genoese, the Venetians, or the Florentines as intermediaries in order to gain access to the markets of the eastern Mediterranean. Drawn to the resources of Asia just at the moment when Turkish advances were prompting the Italians to explore other horizons, he attempted to exploit the opening to the Mediterranean, to which end he outfitted a merchant fleet of four galleys sailing out of Montpellier. He traded with Egypt and Syria, Cyprus and Rhodes, and

Barcelona—but not, it should be noted, with Seville or Cádiz. Spurred on by the very nature of his functions as chief supplier to the king and the court, he turned to his advantage everything that came his way along the trading routes so well traveled by the Italians. He exported cloth and canvas. He imported spices. His ambitions extended to land-based trade, and he coveted Scottish wool and Tuscan silk, wheat and wine, weapons and horses, metals and salt. There was nothing particularly unusual about this: Jacques Coeur was simply doing in 1450 what the Gallerani family had done in 1300 and the Datini company a century later.

He turned to manufacturing as well, buying papermills and taking over the silver mines in the Lyonnais and the salt pans of Languedoc. Financial speculation went hand in hand with this diversification of activity that would one day lead to a genuine form of integration. Jacques Coeur speculated on the exchange rates and took on the farming of the mints. He traded in letters of marque, exploiting his influence as only a counselor close to the king could do. He even provided credit to ransom prisoners of war.

Nevertheless, the structure of Coeur's business affairs differed very little from that of other French entrepreneurs. The antithesis of Italian capitalism, the business affairs of Charles VII's treasurer remained in the hands of the essentially solitary master of what was basically a one-man show. As long as he was able to exploit his advantageous position as confidant to the king, this was a strength. Before too long, it proved to be his weakness.

The Development of Industry

More than a form of diversification, industry was the technical complement to trade. If we exclude minor urban artisanal manufacture—the work of the cutler or the tailor—all industries depended on three factors: raw materials, capital, and labor. The latter was, of course, closely related to wages, which were a matter of financing.

In fact, it was very unusual to find any kind of large-scale production that could rely entirely on the local supply of raw materials. Even the English cloth industry of the fifteenth century, using the best wool in the world, could not manage without alum, Spanish cochineal, or oriental khermes. Normally installed near water—the one thing that could not be moved—and close to a plentiful supply of those heavy goods difficult to transport, like wood or coal, the metal industry rarely found its ore on the spot. Although well provided with water, forests and—thanks to the Verneuil seams—iron, the Norman metal industry depended as much on Spanish iron as locally mined ore. The brass-pin industry, which developed in the late fifteenth century, was entirely dependent on imports of copper and zinc. As for the metal industry in Nuremberg, it would have been nothing without copper from Saxony, Bohemia, and Hungary.

The most important industry of the Middle Ages, textiles, was never able to free itself from the need to import. The Flemish weavers used English wool, those in Tuscany English or Spanish wool. The dyers of Ghent and Florence used woad or saffron provided by the merchant. The silk factories of Lucca were even more dependent on the raw silk bought in the ports of the Black Sea. In other words, trade and industry were technically interdependent, reflecting both the manufacturer's need for supplies and the importer's need for demand.

If things had gone no further, there would have been no more than cooperation. But whenever production exceeds local needs, a new intervention by trade is called for. This time it was a question of selling. It was not a problem for the baker: the man was in the bakery, his wife at the market stall. But exporting iron spades and swords from the Ruhr to Paris, or the violet cloth of Malines to Barcelona, was more than just a matter of offering the product to the customer.

For the merchant, whether he was involved with the raw materials or the finished product, it was all a matter of timing. Wool had to be bought three months before it was processed. Cloth was sold six months—or six years—after it was produced. The merchant, meanwhile, had to finance the operation. Neither the weaver, the fuller, nor the shearer was in a position to advance any capital. It would have been far beyond the financial capacity of these highly specialized workers to find such sums, and unimaginable to find an impoverished fuller buying cloth for fulling and then reselling it. Not one of these artisans had the means to finance the whole process, or to take on the investment for the six months that were needed to see the cloth through the twenty-five or twenty-six workshops involved in the chain of manufacture.

The simplest solution was also the most logical. Accustomed to financing medium- or long-term deals and normally paying himself both for his work and for the money invested, the merchant found himself naturally inclined to play the financier. The textile industry was, furthermore, completely straightforward, each procedure part of an orderly sequence. Supplier but not seller of the raw materials, and exporter of the worked cloth, the merchant had no difficulty engaging artisans to do the different types of work. Since they were paid on the spot, it was soon apparent that they were reduced merely to selling their labor, paid by the day for the more humble type of work, or by the piece, as were the following shearers from Lyons, who managed to retain a semblance of autonomy:

> The shearing of cloth is paid for each length of scarlet cloth at a rate of three sous four *deniers,* and for each length of Rouen cloth at one sou and eight *deniers* and for Bourges cloth at two *deniers* and for a length of Lan-

guedoc cloth at eight *deniers tournois,* and a length of other cloths of lesser value five *deniers,* and for other cloths the same.

What had originally been a matter of making a financial advance in a purely commercial deal was transformed, during the thirteenth century in Flanders and the fourteenth century elsewhere, into the merchant's taking complete control of the economic organization of production. When, in the fifteenth century, the merchants of Nuremberg advanced money to the Thuringian smelters on their future deliveries of copper bars, we are seeing an elementary form of speculation in which the merchant buys a harvest before it is reaped. This is still buying on credit. But things changed when, from the thirteenth century onward, merchants of Ypres or Douai decided in advance on the quantities and colors of the cloth that they had ordered from the artisans, providing them with the necessary materials: the merchant had become a businessman.

Quite independently, the same process was taking place in another context, when the auction of leases for exploitation of industrial monopolies called upon significant masses of capital of the sort that only the big financiers were in a position to provide or collect. Such a man was Tidemann Limberg, well known for his dealings in wool and wheat, who, in 1359, acquired the rights to the English lead, silver, and copper mines at Alston Moor. The right to exploit the alum mines of Tolfa was granted, in 1462, to the great bankers who had contacts with the Roman Curia. From 1465, production and export of alum were to be closely linked.

Such takeovers of production did not go unchallenged. In a position to be both employer and banker, masters in town and in the markets, the new manufacturers made the law. The artisans began to feel the noose tightening. Recounting the wrongs committed by the patrician Jean Boinebroke, who had recently died in 1286, an inhabitant of Douai, Riché de Monstreuil, vividly describes a bleak dilemma—whether to work for Boinebroke or to have no work at all:

> Riché de Monstreuil, a sworn witness, said that Alice Houvastre, wife of Piéron Houvastre, said to him on several occasions:
> —I have taken wool to Master Jean, where I have suffered great losses!
> And the witness would say to her:
> —Since you lose there, why do you take it?
> And she would say:
> —I had no choice. I cannot be paid any other way if I do not take the wool.

According to the conditions set by Jean Boinebroke, artisans would not be paid for work already done unless they continued to work for him. In other words, they lost all independence. There was no longer even a question of discussing salary. Another witness describes the situation so far as the workers were concerned: "The witness said that he spent three days working on many of his lengths of cloth. And when the time came to be paid, he [Jean Boinebroke] would count only two days."

The subjection of the wage earner was increased by the fact that he or she was also the master's tenant. In order to recoup the salary he paid out, Boinebroke obliged a cloth dresser to live in one of his houses, at the same time doubling the rent. The victim had to agree; it was either that or unemployment:

> I dressed thirty good pieces of cloth for him, for each of which I should have had nine *sous parisis,* and I only received seven.
> And I rented a small house from him, situated at Four des Eaux, for six *livres parisis.* And it suited me very well.
> When I had earned [the price for the dressing of thirty pieces of cloth], he put me out of the house and into one with a rent of eleven *livres,* against my will. And I suffered greatly because of this and sustained much loss.

There were others who received even worse treatment, like Robert Perruce, forced by Boinebroke to move house: he too moved from paying a rent of six *livres* to one of eleven. The manufacturer had promised him enough work to enable him to pay such a rent, but he did not keep his promise: "Sir Jean made him leave this house and go to Wes to a house costing eleven *livres.* And he was supposed to send him work to earn money. And Sir Jean did not send them sufficient for it to be worth what he owed."

The rent would be hard to find. The tenant had become a debtor, at the mercy of the employer.

The Supremacy of Trade

It was hardly surprising that in the textile industry, the most important industry of the Middle Ages, there was a need for someone who could organize the work and coordinate industrial production. Others were ready to take on the job of management, especially among the ranks of the skilled artisans and thus deriving strength from a social position not easily disputed by other trades. In the thirteenth century the Flemish weavers, backed against the merchants by the dyers and fullers, were more than willing to claim the role of production manager. This was a period when industrial workers were enjoying exceptionally favorable circumstances. The next century saw a very different situation, when the Florentine workers rose up—particularly in the famous *Ciompi* episode of 1378—against the economic dictatorship of the "Major Arts" of the *Calimala* and the *Lana.* The thirteenth-century weavers of Ghent had free access to English wool available at the continental staple; there was no need for a merchant to go to Bruges or Saint-Omer for wool, and, because it was close at hand, it was possible to buy small quantities requiring only a small investment of time and money. Similarly, in Bruges it was possible to find customers from all over the world. The people of Flanders were well known for their reluctance to travel; it was easy for the artisan to imagine that the international market of Bruges was sufficient, particularly as the trading importance of the Champagne fairs declined, to ensure a steady flow of production.

During the 1270s, the Parisian weavers suffered from similar illusions. They, too, saw that they had a market close at hand. Everything could be bought and sold in Paris. The truth was that the conflict between the weavers and the drapers was just one of many in the long history of disputes between different trades. Weavers and dyers also clashed, as did, later, the two fur guilds. Because they paid a tax for the right to exercise their trade—the *hauban*—one group was exempted from all kinds of restrictions. Merchant goldsmiths and artisan goldsmiths in London also had their differences.

Such conflicts profited no one. On the contrary, there were generally three losers. In the short run, the artisan had to give way, forced to recognize his failure as a manager. In the longer term, such disputes led to rigidity, preventing adaptations that might have saved the trade. In Ghent, as in Paris, the collapse of the cloth industry was due in part to the fact that the merchants' domination was poorly supported by the guilds. The third loser was the merchant, who would have to look elsewhere for new opportunities. Not all would find them.

The weaver who saw himself as master of his affairs because he had wool on the quayside and a customer at his door was underestimating several things. First, there was the cumulative effect of professional pride: as responsibility descended down the manufacturing scale, so did the claims made for the product, and the dyer would start to speak in the same terms as the weaver. Second, the weaver underestimated the amount of capital he would need: the client was not a customer at the market stall, and he rarely paid in cash. Finally, he failed to understand the complexity of the skills required to be a successful businessman.

For it was the merchant, better than any other, who understood the market, and even the trends in fashion, at any given moment. It was merchandising that drove the production, during the fourteenth century, of lighter fabric demanded by the new taste for close-fitting clothes. Men finally turned away from the ample long robe, except on those occasions where the wearing of such formal garments—as in the law courts, for example—continues to be required to this day. It was now the period of the front-buttoned pourpoint, the *gipon* laced down one side, and the tightly fitting jerkin. Women began to wear the tight *cote* and laced *corset*, the *surcote*, which emphasized the shoulders and hips, and the *cote hardie*, buttoned from top to bottom. Customers no longer wanted the thick woolen cloth that conformed to regulations laid down by authorities in the thirteenth century and that had been more suited to the fashion for ample draperies.

Similarly, the world of trade was able to control the introduction of vivid colors. It was well known that such dyes lacked fastness, but as fashions began to change more rapidly, the cut or the setting of a sleeve changed so frequently that the chief quality of a piece of wool ceased to lie, as formerly, in its durability.

The merchant also had a better understanding than the artisan of the competition. Wool was rivaled by fur, the vogue for which, with an ever-increasing range of skins and colors, was expanding. And silk, which could provide the sought-after lighter material, was becoming more common as production started up in the West—in Tuscany and Lombardy, and later in Touraine with the efforts of Louis XI.

In addition to skills as a negotiator, the businessman could offer manage-rial abilities. He was better qualified than the artisan to analyze the costs of production. From the beginning of the fourteenth century, the directors of the Del Bene company, one of the most active members of the *Arte della Lana,* put to use the same methods, in their management of the industry, that had permitted their colleagues in the *Arte di Calimala* to measure the returns from their commercial enterprises. A few years later, the great Flemish drapers were in a position to assess the effects of a rise in salaries, particularly after the fall in population resulting from the Black Death, on the costs of traditional fulling. This consisted of treading the wool with the feet and was considered by many to be the only method that did not damage the fibers. The organized guilds of the cloth towns attempted to defend the quality of their product by hedging the industry around with technical regulations. The merchant circles, by contrast, presented themselves as cham-pions of technical innovation in the name of economy. For the former, the fulling mill was an infernal machine that broke the fibers; for the latter it represented a way to increase productivity and hence to cut manufacturing costs. Only thus could the merchants establish themselves in a market where the play of competition was unrelenting.

Industrial entrepreneurs, preoccupied with the need, as merchants and financiers, to break down the traditional rigidity of the professional bodies, could not effectively bring about change except by physically moving away from the urban centers where corporative strength was greatest. This move was to make the fortune of those small towns without any traditional industry and also of the countryside.

This kind of development was particularly marked in the textile industry. A new figure emerged: the "manufacturer," the person who was simultane-ously creator of the economic structure, supervisor of technical processes, employer of waged producers, and master—with all the attached risks—of commercial production. During the fifteenth century, the English cloth makers even went so far as to provide the rural weaver, in addition to wool and orders, with a loom and other necessary equipment. But even the most humble guild did not escape increasing control by the merchant. In a medium-size town like Toulouse, comb makers, dice makers, and cauldron makers were both financed and managed by those who had access to a clientele.

Commercial contacts were an advantage. Another was the possession of financial means. As the means of production became more complex, so those who manufactured the product began to find themselves relegated to the position of mere wage earners. Even if the tendency was to become established in small towns and the countryside, the great companies effectively absorbed the small urban workshops. We can see how in fourteenth-century Tuscany purely industrial companies existed within collectively owned groups. Francesco Datini was thus chief partner in a cloth company in Prato, just as in Florence, in the fifteenth century, the Medici were to own two subsidiaries manufacturing cloth and one branch for silk.

This takeover of production by the merchants extended, furthermore, to areas of activity that were entirely foreign to the owner's business interests. Even in London, we find a rich fish merchant in 1325 owning a brewery, while a haberdasher of 1456 had no objection to being included as a member of two "companies," that of the haberdashers because that was his own trade and that of the pewterers because he had thought it a good investment to buy up the chief workshop making dishes and ewers for middle-class tables. Extraordinary combinations were to be found, often as a result of physical proximity; a London ropery, for example, belonged in 1399 to the local spice merchants. All this proves only one thing: the versatility of the businessman. No matter where profit could be made, it was always good.

Only the Italian companies went so far as to create an integrated industry, of the sort that the Flemish cloth makers, though not slow in taking over those workshops that supplied their trade, had only groped toward with their "factories." The smaller of these Italian companies were content merely to facilitate production, using intermediaries for the export of the product. The great companies, on the other hand, heirs to a long tradition of complementarity in the exploitation of different markets, were organized on a scale suited to their economic horizons, with well-established vertical links. Here again it was the Medici who perfected the system. Having obtained alum since 1465 through their banking branch in Rome, which also awarded contracts for the mines in Tolfa, the Medici branches in Bruges and London were able to supply wool to the Florentine cloth industry, which then supplied the nine commercial branches distributing its products to the entire world.

Small enterprises, such as those formed at shop level, quickly collapsed in the face of this high concentration of capital and effective coordination of initiatives. The artisans, who produced in small quantities, found themselves unable to react to fluctuations in the market. Above all, they were in no position to resist the political pressure of the big commercial producers. Pressure from the merchant goldsmiths of London resulted in a law, in 1377, that prevented ordinary artisans from marketing their own products: the producer would henceforth have to go through the merchant. The Hanseatic merchants of Bergen were similarly successful in preventing artisans from trading, though the latter had formerly sold the products manufactured in their workshops on the market stall.

Even when artisans were not relegated by statute to the workshop, it became increasingly difficult in practice for them to appear in the market. In Charles VI's Paris, the important French and Italian businessmen effectively took over the sale of gold and silver goods to princes and prelates. Working a precious metal that did not belong to them—customers supplied the gold at the same time that they placed their orders—and setting sapphires and rubies supplied by their clients, the goldsmiths were reduced to mere workers who were paid piece rates. And what was true for gilded and bejeweled crowns and ornamental table decorations (such as the *nef*) was equally so for tapestries and embroideries sold to princes. A document relating to such a sale makes it seem as if this Parisian merchant was also the maker of the goods:

> Let it be known by all that I, Colin Bataille, merchant dwelling in Paris, agree and confess to have had and received from Josset de Halle, treasurer of Monseigneur the Duke of Burgundy, the sum of two and a half gold francs for the bedspread of six squares covered with serge for the bedchamber of Monseigneur the Count of Nevers, with which aforementioned sum of two and a half francs I express myself satisfied and fully paid by the said treasurer and all others. Witness to this my seal, placed on this receipt on the 12th day of January in the year 1396.

This same Nicolas Bataille is also the man often thought to be the creator of the famous Apocalypse tapestries, sold to the duke of Anjou twenty years before: even historians have been deceived in this case.

From the fourteenth century, the onetime merchant began to figure as a businessman and prime mover of industrial change. The entrepreneurs in the inland towns were the first to take the initiative, perhaps because their commercial enterprises did not correspond to the cycles of navigation. The complex and recurring time frame of their affairs lent itself to the longer view required in manufacturing. It was in Florence, or perhaps Milan, that we first find industry emerging as the main activity of the merchant, equal in importance to trade. The arrival on the scene of the major Genoese merchants in cloth and silk, together with the metal industry of the rural Apennine workshops, did not make itself felt until the fifteenth century. Merchants from Rouen similarly came only late to the cloth and metal industry of Upper Normandy. Access to the sea had long been the most essential commercial requirement. Those who did not have such facilities looked elsewhere.

Paradoxically, it was during this same period that Florentine interest in industry was beginning to flag. Absorbed in banking and dazzled by a commercial empire that was opening up new maritime horizons to them, they left it to others to exploit newly expanding industries like metalwork, glass, and paper. Lombards and Germans were to dominate in these astonishingly open markets. Jacob Fugger built his fortune on the exploitation of the copper and silver mines of the Tyrol.

During the last two centuries of the Middle Ages, industrial development in Europe would owe much to the interest shown by the world of trade in the financing and control of manufacturing. The social structures of this world, unlike that of the artisan, provided a favorable milieu for initiative, development, and innovation. While artisans began to stagnate in the constrained and compartmentalized world of corporate protectionism, merchants retained their freedom to branch out in all directions. The Florentine could join more than one *arte*, the Londoner several "companies." A merchant who achieved a certain financial status and geographical penetration could sell anything and participate in everything.

They intervened everywhere. The Flemish cloth merchants clearly noticed which way the wind was blowing when they began, in the thirteenth century, to encourage and finance a rural industry that refused to be held back by the guild statutes of the large cloth towns. They were the ones to produce new qualities, new colors, and new types of cloth. They introduced new procedures, starting with the fulling mill and the spinning wheel. To these hardheaded realists, the advantages of increased productivity greatly outweighed the risk of defects caused by the machines.

These were the businessmen who discovered the profitability of the "factories" where work was done for rural wages, out of the reach of the social movements existing in the great industrial centers. The political demands of the Ghent guilds go a long way toward explaining the success of the village workshops financed by the "manufacturers"—in reality, rich merchants from Ghent and elsewhere. Both at home and outside, markets began to feel the effects on prices. Much more than the artisan who measured prices logically by the extent or duration of his labor, it was the merchant who understood these prices, facing daily, as he did, problems of sales and slump.

Thus industry became part of a market economy on the scale of the world of trade. The opening of maritime relations with England led to new developments in the Florentine textile trade and contributed to the decline of the great Flemish industries in Ypres, Douai, and Ghent. Edward III's ban on wool exports stimulated the cloth industries—based on Spanish, Italian, or Provençal wool—of Languedoc, Tuscany, and even Normandy. Brabant, effectively neutral in the conflict between France and England, owed the expansion of the textile industries in Malines and Brussels to new political developments.

Contrary phenomena were no less noticeable. Changes in the industrial map had their effect on the market. Because it was controlled by the wool merchants, the development of the cloth industry in England—still an industry associated with small towns and villages—led to a kind of commercial Malthusianism. Around 1350 some thirty-five thousand sacks of raw wool were being exported each year; a century later, on the eve of the ban on exports, barely five thousand. By contrast, the decline of the Flemish industry and the arrival of emigrant workers from Flanders resulted in the blossoming of a quality textile industry in Holland in the second half of the fourteenth and in the fifteenth century. This led producers to secure their own supplies of wool as well as to export finished cloth. This was to make a significant contribution to the growth of trade between Holland and other countries, which included salt from Brittany, wine from Gascony, and wheat from Prussia and Poland. Once again, the world of business had proved its oneness.

ELEVEN

Credit in the Marketplace

*L*end to one another without expecting anything in return." When, in his Gospel (Luke 6:35), St. Luke recorded the very general remark made by Christ—"Love ye your enemies, and do good"—he never imagined that he might be laying down a scriptural, and therefore indisputable, basis for one of the most serious obstacles ever imposed on economic development. In reality, neither the theologians who wrote about the evils of interest nor members of the Church councils who more than once condemned it—particularly firmly in 1215 in one of the canons of the fourth Lateran Council—were taken in by a text clearly not referring to the remuneration of investment. The Old Testament has even less to say about economics, reminding us only that one should not behave with a compatriot (Exod. 22:25) or a relative (Lev. 25:36-37) as would a usurer with a client. Indeed, the Scriptures were explicit: "Unto a stranger thou mayest lend upon usury; but unto thy brother thou shalt not lend upon usury" (Deut. 23:20). The Psalms praise God's generosity and the prophet Ezekiel condemns usurers, but none of this seemed to imply that economic relations should be paralyzed. But the principle of any scholastic debate was to take as its premise the "authorities," and there was no authority to rival such an apparently explicit line from the Gospels.

Theory and Practice

The forbidding of usury—as lending at interest was called, regardless of the rate—was thus based on firm authority. As economic life increasingly demanded a greater precision in decisions made about commercial procedures, attitudes toward usury became more clearly defined, derived from

something more than a mere gloss of the Gospels: the reasons were philosophical, theological, and, indeed, moral. St. Luke's words merely gave added
weight to a formulation whose strength lay in its conciseness. *Mutuum date,
nihil inde sperantes* (Lend hoping for nothing again; Luke 6:35) had all the
qualities of the proposition laid down at the beginning of the *disputatio* in
the universities. Nothing more was needed to establish a rule.

At the same time, the medieval world was strongly marked by the
theological principles of work and profit. Work was one of the punishments
for original sin and, indeed, the one that struck home with the most force,
for the merchants and artisans of the Middle Ages would have been unlikely
to mistake the drudgery of their daily lives for the earthly paradise. Man
was condemned to earn his bread by the sweat of his brow, as woman was
condemned to bring forth her offspring in pain. Thus any profit not involving labor seemed wicked, the essence of *turpe lucrum* (filthy lucre), and an
attempt to deceive God.

In men's eyes it was theft. The great theologian Peter Lombard's *Sentences*
of c.1150, a work that was long one of the basic texts of scholastic teaching,
placed usury among the list of sins related to theft. A little later, the legate
Robert de Courçon, who in 1215 gave the newly founded University of Paris
its first statutes, proposed the establishment of a council with the task of
eradicating usury from the Christian world.

The philosophers did not stop there. One of the teachings of Aristotle
that had come down to the Middle Ages stated that money in itself is
something sterile. It can produce wealth only through the effect of work,
and not through that of time. Time belongs to God and money created by
time is, strictly speaking, stolen from God. To appropriate for oneself the
fruits of time is to commit the sin of pride and smacks of original sin.
Thomas Aquinas, following Aristotle, arrived at the same conclusion as the
scholars of canon law interpreting Genesis.

In condemning profit as a product of time, the Aristotelians were at
one with the moralists who saw interest as a product of idleness. Why should
ten sous make twelve simply through the passage of time? Where would
the two sous of interest come from? In the mid-thirteenth century, Thomas
Aquinas put it very simply in his *Summa Theologica:*

> To accept usury for the loan of money is in itself unjust: because this is
> selling what does not exist and must obviously give rise to inequality, which
> is contrary to justice.

The Church too, though by a different route, was moving toward a
rejection of any kind of dealing in credit. It had been noted in ancient times,
as in Athens, that falling into debt led to a loss of liberty. However slight,
and apparently in conflict with the acceptance of slavery, social considerations
played a not insignificant role in the condemnation of usury. The medieval

businessman was, as a result, forced to invent ingenious ways of getting around society's objections.

One thing quickly became apparent: the number of those who could immediately and directly reinvest their profits in the expansion of their own business was very small. It would have been naive to imagine that a cloth merchant could buy and sell ever increasing amounts of cloth, as everyone was well aware. A smith would be very unlikely to progress from one forge to two as a result of successive profits. Although a baker could build a second oven, he would not automatically reach this stage as the result of a linear progression over a period of twenty years. A number of merchants were persuaded to seek to reinvest elsewhere by a variety of factors: place, availability of labor, saturation of clientele in a market open to competition, and the inability of the majority of trades to expand. Reinvestment presupposed a money market.

It was essential to justify profits not legitimized by any kind of work, but without which money would lie idle. That this was unproductive was apparent even to the least observant. From the thirteenth century, theologians of this period of economic growth, often themselves sons of the merchant classes or close to them, agreed to define the cases where profits from lending were not sinful in the eyes of God. At the same time, canon law modified its strictures, attacking excessive usury rather than the practice itself, and settling for a moral judgment whereby lenders at interest were allowed a place in Heaven on the twofold condition that they make partial restitution in the form of a legacy to the Church and a period of repentance in the heavenly waiting room called Purgatory.

As the rules were relaxed, flying in the face of divine will, there were some, like St. Bernardino of Siena, who ventured down this path only with the greatest caution. Other, more practically minded people, conscious of the absurdity of a paralysis that would benefit no one, particularly not the poor, soon began to tolerate the practice of usury. Antonio di ser Niccolò Pierozzi, son of a Florentine notary who entered the order of St. Dominic in 1405 and became archbishop of Florence in 1445, was inclined, as a result of both his origins and the demands of his ministry, to pay particular attention to economic realities. Moralist, theologian, and historian, St. Antonino, as he was known, could not ignore a subject so central to the daily lives of his flock in this world but so problematic for their salvation: profit. Thus we find him in the forefront of those jurists and moderate theologians whose theoretical writings were able to procure for the businessman not so much the means of working, but rather a way to enable him to be at peace with his conscience while working.

The first "exception," and the one that embraced all the others, being both general and yet at the same time solidly realistic, concerned loss or damage suffered by the lender as a result of delay in the repayment of money. Even if the interval before repayment was intended to be very short, the essential point was that elapsed time could be taken as a delay. So the *damnum emergens* (compensation for damages) could justify interest for a year on a sum lent without interest for a week.

Sometimes it was a matter of how the words were interpreted. The *stipendium laboris,* the salary for work or fair wage, justified interest insofar as it was, in this case, not interest at all: the lender had put himself out, accumulating expenses and charges. In other words, work had been performed. Things were not entirely clear-cut, because profit was understood to apply to the period immediately following the work. The profit was legitimate, but such a solution could not go very far.

By contrast, other, more ingenious theorists, attempting to free themselves piecemeal from restrictions that could not be tackled outright, came up with a notion openly borrowed from the world of business: the *lucrum cessans.* "Profit that ceases" (or, in modern terms, "opportunity cost") is what the lender might legitimately have earned if he had disposed of his money elsewhere. Obviously, it was necessary to go along with the pretense that the lender had parted with his money only with the aim of obliging a friend. It is the borrower who was considered to be taking the initiative in the deal. The lender who responded favorably—and free of charge—was obviously depriving himself of other advantageous and legitimate investments, *Lucrum cessans* was, in other words, monetary compensation for the obliging friend who was putting himself out. A difficult argument to advance where the remuneration of bank deposits was concerned, it was one of a whole series of justifications that gradually eroded the Church's blanket condemnation of lending at interest.

One thing was certain: damages for delayed repayment, profit from work involved in the act of lending, and compensation for deprivation of capital were three examples demonstrating that usury was not necessarily a bad thing in itself. This view supported those people who condemned excessive profits without denying the principle of lending at interest.

Some theologians even went so far as to consider the risks involved in investment. *Periculum sortis*—the dangers of chance—was the risk taken in lending to someone embarking on a hazardous business venture. And which enterprises are without risk? The lender shared the risk, particularly if sea voyages were involved. Thus he found himself entitled to a share in the profits. Many theologians were, however, inclined to disregard this effect of Fortune: the case was justified only if the creditor lost his credit—in other words, if he was the owner of part of the cargo, which placed the entire operation outside the sphere of lending at interest. The dangers of chance stood up as an argument only where misfortune made the debtor insolvent.

But in such a case it was hard to see how he could pay the interest. Thus, usury could not ultimately be justified by risk except in a situation where the debtor was in no position to pay.

Similarly, the daring justification of *ratio incertitudinis*—the uncertainty for the creditor who puts money into a business of dubious legality—was usually rejected. It is a common view that no one should be able to profit from illegal activities. On the other hand, no one would pay in advance—for a cargo not yet arrived, animals not yet weaned, or unharvested grain—unless there was an advantage in doing so. It was well known that selling in advance above the "fair price" was not entirely aboveboard. However, prices could change over a period of time, as St. Antonino of Florence was prepared to admit. But he was almost the only one to do so. Experts in canon law were fiercely hostile. Why, they asked, not have oneself paid, in that case, for the possible risk of cancellation of contract?

Such was the theory. Echoing the edict of the fourth Lateran Council, the provincial council of Trier, in 1227, banned all interest-bearing deposits. The universal council of Lyons, in 1274, refused a Christian burial to those usurers who did not make amends before their deaths for the "wrong" done to borrowers by charging them interest.

Necessity forced the pace of the introduction of the practice. It was clearly understood in Italian business circles that the availability of credit on a large scale was necessary for economic growth and equilibrium. Businessmen were skilled at keeping theologians and specialists in canon law well away from the management of business. Scholars and theoreticians had no desire to paralyze society; and, in any case, they were themselves borrowers by necessity, when they were not lenders by opportunity. Rulers borrowed ceaselessly, and no one was deceived when, instead of paying interest in ready money, they remunerated such loans with privileges and commercial advantages. A necessary condition for obtaining business at court was to allow credit, if not to make explicit loans.

Hard-up princes had always made use of pledges in lieu of payment, sometimes even turning to the usurer. During the period of his wild schemes at the start of the Hundred Years' War, Edward III pledged, along with his gold crown and precious stones, the 45,000 florins lent to him by the archbishop of Trier. Around 1320, Edward I, count of Bar, pledged his silver plate to the Lombards. His grandson, Duke Robert, did the same in the 1380s, pledging not only his own silverware and jewels but also those lent to him by his close relatives. In a similar arrangement, his son-in-law, Enguerran de Coucy, almost lost the most precious items of the collection—those which Robert de Bar had been in no hurry to redeem and which the Lombards were now on the point of selling.

The princes, ever ready to legislate on the subject of usury, were careful not to forbid it altogether. Attempting to moderate the practice and limit its excesses, which could seriously affect the social and economic order, but having no desire to paralyze the economic lives of their subjects, rulers like Louis VII and St. Louis were content to fix an annual maximum rate for the Jewish usurers of 33.5 percent, leaving no one to doubt that this would also be the tolerated ceiling for Christian usurers.

At the height of their splendor, the Avignon popes rewarded their Italian bankers by allowing them an effective monopoly over supplies of cloth of gold or ermine, pearls or Beaune wine. As the Schism began to run into difficulties, Benedict XIII was only too glad to be able to raise credit—against which he pledged the revenues of the Apostolic Chamber—from the Lucca and Asti bankers established in Avignon. His rival in Rome, Innocent VII, on the other hand, had to offer as security to his bankers—and in particular to Giovanni di Bicci de' Medici—his "precious miter" and his palace at Civita Castellana. The documents do not beat about the bush, never saying "a miter" when they can add "our lord's precious miter." There is no doubt they are referring to the papal tiara. For a period of four years, as the bankers passed the loan from one to another, the tiara changed hands. When the last person to have it in his possession, the Florentine Antonio di Giovanni Roberti, finally returned it to Gregory XII in April 1409, it cost the pope 12,000 florins to redeem, a sum that he borrowed by means of new guarantees.

At the same time, the government of Charles VI found that the only way it could raise money to finance the enterprises of the duke of Orleans was by pledging the royal crown. It was necessary to impose a supplementary tax on salt, in June 1407, in order to buy back the crown. A few years later things were even worse: the crown was dismembered, and its fleurons divided among bankers from Lucca and Genoa, princes, and even the citizens of Paris. The duchess of Alençon, who received one of the larger fleurons as a pledge for 15,000 francs, was quick to pass on the loan and get rid of the pledge.

The documents are clear enough. Clement VII's treasurer, a bishop, felt no compunction in mentioning in his accounts, often several times on each page, sums paid in interest for loans: *pro interesse, pro lucro et interesse, pro dampno et interesse*. At other times the loan is simply described as *mutuum cum usuris* or *mutuum sub usura*. Such expressions were avoided when the lender was a prince or a cardinal, but not if it were an Avignon moneylender. An important banker in the Avignon market who presented himself publicly as the obliging intermediary for an anonymous usurer did not fool many people.

Encouraged by the mendicant orders, the ordinary citizens of Metz fell into the habit of stating coldly in their wills that such business had nothing to do with either the pope or some cardinal, legate, or bishop. Around 1295, we even find a case of a notorious usurer being buried in the cloister of the Dominican monastery. There is evidence of some connivance by the executors of his will, who were none other than the Dominican prior and the father superior of the Franciscan monastery. The bishop demanded that the pope do something about this affair, which was rapidly taking on the appearance of a scandal: the body was dug up, things were rectified by compensating the victims, and then the usurer's body was returned to the cloister.

Though so daring when faced with the storms of the North Sea, the Hanseatic merchants rapidly grew suspicious of credit. Cautious in the thirteenth century, they were entirely hostile to it by the fifteenth. The reasons advanced were inspired by a purely economic ethic: credit was a form of adventurism. It facilitated risky ventures. It created price instability: one person would buy at too high a price because he could not pay with ready money; another would sell at a loss in order to get rid of an excessive debt. The Hanseatic merchants, orderly and cautious by nature, had been shaken by some spectacular bankruptcies. The wealthy merchant Hildebrand Veckinchusen had been arrested for debt in 1422. The only Lübeck merchant who ventured into banking proper, Godeman van Buren, was bankrupted in 1472.

On the shores of the North Sea and the Baltic, it was believed that credit created colossi with feet of clay. The fall of the Bardi a century earlier in Florence had been a warning: the Hanseatic merchants began to mistrust growth based on easy money. While the Italians attempted to do something about the feet of clay, the Hanseatic League preferred to avoid the colossus altogether.

But there was another reason for this hostility, which had nothing to do with morality: Hanseatic merchants were jealous of the advantage gained by their rivals from their use of credit as a means of financing. Xenophobic as ever, the Hanseatic merchants correctly realized that to tolerate credit would be to benefit the Lombard bankers whose system of lending on future profits the Germans had first seen in play in Champagne and later in Bruges and London.

Despite some marginal limitations, credit appeared to be on the increase up to the fourteenth century. There were exceptions: the statutes of the Novgorod market banned it as early as 1295, but Novgorod was a market where they still used barter. The scale of values and prices often had little to do with money: they counted in sable skins. And Novgorod was always deeply suspicious of anything new. Things were different in Cologne or Lübeck: here they lent and borrowed, bought and sold, on credit. Even local government was prepared to use loans. Such things were carried on discreetly but without embarrassment.

Suddenly, in the middle of the fifteenth century, everything changed. The Hanseatic businessmen—those in the foreign marketplace ahead of those under the rule of the Diet of Lübeck—woke up to the rapid foreign takeover of the money market in their own economic territory. A certain Baglioni, early in the century, had managed to establish himself by taking a wife in Lübeck, creating a banking network with branches as far apart as Basel, Florence, and Danzig. An agent of the Medici followed, while German businessmen from Regensburg and Nuremberg began to appear. In the face of this concentration of credit, the Hanseatic League was in danger of experiencing that same colonization which it had itself imposed, through its control of commercial trade, on its foreign markets.

In 1399, it was the turn of Riga and Revel to ban the use of credit in any dealings with the Russians. Two years later, the Diet of Lübeck prohibited, for the first time, the use of credit in Flanders. The Hanseatic merchants in Bruges, with their knowledge of the market beyond the world of the League, protested this as madness and succeeded in having the measure withdrawn. This did not prevent Riga from insisting that goods bought in Flanders should be paid for in cash. In fact, the Revel and Riga trade with Bruges quickly turned to barter: wax and furs for cloth and spices. The next time, in 1417, the explicit ban on the use of credit in trade with Flanders was successfully upheld. The Hanseatic branch in London even contemplated, in 1462, extending the ban to the purchase of cloth in England.

There remained the petty loans, the short-term loans of everyday life. It was always possible to lay one's hands on a couple of marks, to be paid back in a month, in Lübeck or Hamburg. But the ban on credit operations contained the germ of the Hanseatic League's demise. It was easy for the Dutch and especially the English—who openly practiced all forms of credit, from lending at interest to the futures market in the most diverse types of goods—to occupy the position that had been rejected by the great German ports.

The World of Credit

Despite the debate being waged within the Church, merchants thus learned very early how to get around the canonic ban, counting on the experts in canon law to find a justification for practices born of necessity. From the very start, therefore, economic expansion was accompanied by credit, the diversity of its forms responding to the evolution of its functions. But this growing complexity was also a reflection of the development in technical expertise. Credit had emerged as both the basis of business and a business in its own right.

Economic development meant that it was possible to obtain money at a favorable rate. In the thirteenth century, credit was advanced at a rate of

75 percent in Austria. In Venice, where money was in abundant supply, the rate was 5 percent. Though they might complain in Austria, it made no difference to business. Certainly nobody in Venice objected to the 5 percent, which was simply a payment for a service like any other.

The most common form of credit was that on sales. In wholesale trade between professional traders, just as in retail sales between clients and suppliers, payment in cash was and continued to be the exception rather than the rule. Nobody expected the prince to pay immediately for his wine or his jewels, or the burger for his bread or his logs. Cash would have been the rule at the tavern, had it not been for the regulars. The traveler would take out his purse, as would the burger, for a purchase in a district where he was not known. Otherwise, what the locals owed was noted down in the shopkeeper's book or notched on a tally stick—a stick of wood split or cut (*taillé*) in two—or just stored in memory. The popular plays of the time—the *Farce de maître Pathelin* (written about 1464) and some others—give a humorous reflection of a problem all too familiar to the audience, even if they had not personally experienced such an unscrupulous lawyer: "I need some money, Master Peter / for the cloth I lent (*prêter*) you!" The cloth merchant can scarcely believe his eyes: the lawyer who a moment ago had come into his shop to buy six lengths of cloth is now in his bed, when it is time to pay, saying that he is very ill, and has been for a long time:

> By God, I do not understand
> How this accident befell him,
> For he came today
> And we bargained together
> Or so it seemed,
> I cannot understand it!

It had seemed quite normal to measure out the cloth on his counter and let the lawyer go away with it. That the lawyer had made a purchase without having the price on him was perfectly usual. Even without contemplating credit over a long period, it was up to the tradesman to come to his client to get his money. The merchant uses the words "sell" and "lend" (*prêter*) interchangeably. To lend six lengths of cloth that the client makes into a garment is certainly selling, given that cash payment does not happen. The cloth has gone. In his exasperation with a client who is now pretending to be ill, the merchant does not give up:

> What kind of nonsense
> Is this! Now, quickly! I shall
> Be paid, in gold or in coins,
> For my cloth that you have taken!

The unfortunate cloth merchant knew—or thought he knew—what kind of man the lawyer Master Pierre Pathelin was: an important man and a neighbor. It was not until the industrial era that the anonymity of urban society led to a more universal use of cash. By the twentieth century it became normal to pay even the doctor or the dressmaker immediately, whereas in the previous century they would have sent out their monthly or annual account. Today the credit card is breaking down this anonymity with its bank guarantee, and restoring cash to its original role as a small payment needing no documentation.

Credit did not mean delayed payment in every case. A buyer who settled accounts on delivery was in reality obtaining credit. Delayed delivery, on the other hand, could represent a kind of financing by the buyer. A butcher might buy animals on the hoof when still too young for delivery. A cloth merchant paid the artisan for the cloth that the latter would weave or dye. The butcher profited by paying a lower price; this was profit at a risk, however, for he lost everything if the cattle died. The chief advantage, nevertheless, went to the seller. The farmer could increase the size of his herd or flock more than would have been possible with only his own capital. The weaver could pay for the purchase of wool and the salary of his journeymen. Everyone understood that this kind of credit—often extended for terms of six months or a year, the payments sometimes made in installments—was a necessary condition for expansion, rarely equating changes in rate with usury. Selling on credit was quite normal in some markets, and it would not have been possible to compare rates.

Buying on credit meant taking a risk, but it also meant having first choice; only a fool would pass up such an opportunity. And it would be an ill-advised seller who waited for a cash sale in a market where prices might fall once needs were satisfied by credit sales.

Those who understood the process were not deceived: to sell on credit was to make a loan. Whether in the form of a deed drawn up by a lawyer or a simple acknowledgment signed by the debtor, an agreement that puts a loan in writing often mixes the two notions of credit and loan. This is clear in the case of an English merchant stapler who delivered some bags of raw wool to two merchants of Leyden for the price of a hundred pounds sterling payable on a fixed date in Antwerp. The agreement does not say that he had sold them the wool on credit: he had "paid for wool for them." The deed in question concerns not the sale made by the Englishman to the Dutch merchants but the loan resulting from the purchase by the Englishman, from his English suppliers, of wool eventually destined for the Dutch merchants. He had paid in their stead. No one could accuse such a deal of involving usury.

A legal arrangement of this sort reveals clearly the sophisticated nature of the financial organization of the continental staple for English wool. Interest was disguised in the notion of credit. More frequently it was concealed by the difference in the rates of exchange, a difference facilitated and justified by a time lag frequently aggravated by distance. The rates of monetary conversion could easily change from one day to the next.

The calculation was so precisely made that this interest, concealed with such skill, was established *a priori*. The only thing that remained to be established was the duration of the agreement. Thus the terms of payment regulated the market, in a subtle interplay of factors that maintained a very real price stability. Depending on the interest agreed on by the parties, wool sold at the staple would be paid for at the next fair in Antwerp, Bruges, or Berg op Zoom. They simply had to choose among eleven or twelve well-established dates on the annual trading calendar. These periodic meetings of merchants explain how it was possible to postpone the settling of deals. The staplers' agents simply had to go around the fairs to collect the payments.

It was with a similar combination of rights to a loan and a land rent that Jacob Fugger, like the Genoese who were reimbursed for loans to the public debt by rights over the iron from the island of Elba or the alum of Phocaea, gained control over the copper and silver produced in the mines of the Tyrol and Hungary. When Fugger advanced eight Rhine florins to the Habsburg emperor, in exchange receiving a year later a mark—280 grams—of refined silver that he sold for nine florins, he was both making a loan at a rate of 12.5 percent—speculating, without much risk, on a medium-term rise in the price of silver, a metal that was well known to be insufficiently available for the needs of the economy of the West—and effectively taking control of silver supplies to the European market.

The deal could be even more advantageous in those cases where the businessman succeeded, as the Fuggers sometimes did, in delaying that share of investment of least interest to the borrower. Instead of advancing eight florins to the Habsburg count of the Tyrol, the latter being responsible for financing the extraction of ore at the rate of some five florins to the producer, some years Jacob Fugger so arranged things that he immediately paid the count only the three florins he was left with, agreeing to pay the producer on delivery, that is, a year later. The five florins owed to the producer were thus immediately recouped when the ore was resold. Although the Habsburg government was not deceived, and was prepared to agree to such a deal only on condition that the loan was extended to two years, the future banker to Charles V still earned an annual interest of 17 percent, a rate justified by the extended period of uncertainty over the price of silver at the time of resale.

Credit relating to unpaid accounts soon came to represent, under these conditions, an important percentage of registered assets—between one- and two-thirds. When Italian companies carried out their periodic audits, we notice that the value of the loans is always considerably greater than that of the cash in hand and, sometimes, of the stock.

Familiarity with credit led to a market in loans. One person might be glad to transfer a loan, or to reduce the number of loans held. Another might wish to diversify investments by the acquisition of commercial stock different from that connected with his own business. Thus, from the 1250s in Italy, and during the fourteenth century in France and England, the notion of the futures contract begins to make an appearance.

In Metz, where merchants seem to have been reluctant to accept deferred payment for goods supplied to princes, money changers often took the place of the purchaser, rewarding themselves with a share of the profits. Of the 3,695 francs owed by the duke of Bar to the Metz bankers Aubert Augustaire and Pierre de Tournai, 1,513 francs corresponded to goods supplied directly by them—wine, wheat, spices, horses, plate, and jewels—and 636 francs to payments made by the bankers to other merchants.

In effect, such a contract meant advance payment, and naturally justified an adjustment in price. In such transactions, each person gained in proportion to the dates of payment, the latter sometimes being offset by variations in risk. When purchasing a ripening harvest, three winter months were less attractive than three months in spring when the sun was already stronger. The sections in the Italian manuals on the equivalence of payment dates—that is, the average due date of several bills of different maturities—reflect the growing complexity of this trade involving both regulation and speculation.

At the same time, the "amicable loan"—which had nothing to do with friendship—flourished. The word simply meant—and no one was fooled—that the lender expected nothing in return. Such a loan was in the spirit of the Gospels. Of course, this was no way to finance the breeding of a flock of sheep for wool or to pay for the year's supply of wine. The amicable loan was used particularly by the lower classes. Artisans and shopkeepers, master craftsmen, and apprentices might lend their peers the two sous they needed, more likely for eight days than for twelve months. This type of loan did not involve any banking activity.

One thing should be made clear: for small sums, or very short-term loans, even the greatest in the land followed the example of the more modest borrowers. When a prince or a cardinal lent, *amicabiliter,* five florins to the king or the pope, or when a simple cleric of the Apostolic Chamber lent ten sous to the papal treasury, it simply meant that a passing dignitary took it upon himself that day to advance five florins or ten sous for a small payment from the coffers. It made no difference to income.

"Amicable" meant free of interest. But, in reality, nobody could obtain credit at this rate, even for a day. But these small loans found a whole range of devices for charging interest that could scarcely be admitted and were concealed in ever more ingenious ways in the receipts. We occasionally get a glimpse of them in the account books. The most common practice, against which the preachers, who saw perfectly well what was going on, fulminated in vain, was to get someone borrowing five écus to sign for six. Depending on the period of repayment, this could add up to a fair amount of usury. More complicated, and requiring the drawing up of a legal deed despite the cost and time involved, was the loan agreed on "amicably" for a very short period, with a "fine"—an indemnity—being stipulated should repayment not be made within the period agreed on.

In a simpler version, the interest was qualified as a "gift": there was nothing to prevent a person from giving a present of money to someone who had done him a service. If the parties trusted each other, the gift might be made at the time of the repayment. Otherwise, it would be made at the time of the loan, which was the same as asking for more than the actual loan. Having lent 500 florins to Pope Clement VII on 15 July 1381, his subdeacon Jean de Bar on 12 December received from the treasury 500 florins in repayment and 15 florins as a gift. This relatively modest rate—7.4 percent—is explicable when we recall that Jean de Bar was an important figure in the Curia, with close personal ties to the pope. Similarly, when Clement VII borrowed 20,000 francs from Enguerran de Coucy in 1384, the Apostolic Chamber arranged for it to be repaid over fifteen months from the revenue of various papal collections, but had 6,000 francs paid immediately to de Coucy "for the 20,000 francs that the pope owed him." In such cases, the lenders seem not to have been concerned about their interest, or to have had no other choice: Clement VII and Coucy were hand in glove.

Things were rather different for Corrado dal Ponte, a merchant from Asti, from whom the same papal treasury borrowed 5,000 Aragon florins in 1391. Clement VII's credit was no longer what it had been ten years before, when all the might of the Angevins had stood behind his banner and he was still seen as capable of resolving the Schism by "extralegal methods," in other words, by force. Corrado dal Ponte arranged to be paid immediately 162 florins of current usage and 11 *deniers*—equal to some 181 Aragon florins—"for his interest and his expenses." In other words, he would be receiving 5,000 florins as payment for a loan that had been brought down to 4,819 florins.

The amicable loan was practiced between acquaintances. Although it was not necessarily precluded, the requirement of a pledge was generally avoided. This formality was, on the other hand, essential when seeking the services of a professional usurer who lent out a few sous in exchange for a pledge of a widow's old clothes or the dented pots and pans of a hard-up artisan. He kept a shop suited to his business, a kind of bric-a-brac shop where the sorry scraps of the poor lay in heaps. People would hurry by with fear or disdain, depending on the degree of their need.

Not all pledges were alike, and it was easier to sneer at a pledge for ten sous than one for ten thousand pounds. The Cologne banker who accepted as pledges the crowns of Edward III and Queen Philippa of Hainaut, the one who received Innocent VII's papal tiara, and the one who got hold of a fleuron from Charles VI's crown do not appear to have been anything more than successful merchants who considered it just another business deal. At certain levels of credit, leaving a valuable pledge or committing a future revenue amounted to the same thing. To hand over one's tiara or to promise the forthcoming tithe were not signs of suspicion but rather of good practice. Credit is never forthcoming without some kind of a guarantee, and any precious possession is better than nothing, when waiting for repayment. For the banker to princes or pontiffs, lending against a pledge was just one of the many relationships formed with a well-known and favored clientele. Not a few important merchants in Paris—Frenchmen as well as Lombards—would be astonished when a furious mob attacked and pillaged their houses, accusing them of usury. At times of popular unrest, the frustrations of the chronic debtor were more than once directed against a neighbor's creditor.

The true usurer, whom one approached without recommendation or negotiation at times of extreme need, lived on the margins of society. This was a profession handed down from father to son, or taken on for want of something better. Jews played a vital role here, since they were able to ignore the ban of the Christian Church. They were known already in the earlier Middle Ages as pawnbrokers in the majority of towns in the West. As time went by, they continued to perform the same function in those countries that did not expel them or that offered them refuge and a place in which to operate, as the Comtat Venaissin, for example, offered to the Jews expelled from France in 1394. But, it should be stressed, usury was not the only activity in which Jews were involved. Although they often ended up by specializing in pawnbroking, they were also small shopkeepers, artisans, or peddlers. After all, they had to sell the unredeemed items when loans were not repaid. The usurer thus returned to being a shopkeeper, and his premises became a secondhand shop.

At the risk of disapproval from respectable merchant society, Christians also took part in this modest lending, entering into competition with the Jews. The Church turned a blind eye, leaving these dubious Christians to wrestle with their consciences. Even the most hard-line doctors of the Church knew perfectly well that usury was necessary in a world where the poorest members of society had no other means of meeting the unexpected, be it illness, lack of work, or a delay in the payment of wages. Sentences for heresy, sorcery, blasphemy, sacrilege, adultery, or violence against the clergy are well documented, but there are no instances of a usurer receiving a sentence that would have prevented him from pursuing his profession. The court might annul a disputed agreement because it was tainted with usury, and might fine the offender, but then he was free to begin again. This did not stop the Italian Franciscan Luigi Peresi from thundering from the pulpit against the Auvergnat usurers, somewhat naively deploring the halfhearted measures taken against them:

> If the pope or the king of France ordered the usurers on pain of death to give up their trade, and women to give up their horned headdresses [*cornes*], they would be quick enough to obey!

What was most feared was not the interest to be paid but the hardship that resulted from interest that could not be paid. Although there was little the lender could do about it, the situation could rapidly become critical. The rich cloth merchant of Douai, Jean Boinebroke, held sway over a little empire of debtors, all dependent on him for their employment. Illness or death quickly brought about the ruin of a family. One woman dyer found herself entirely at his mercy when he confiscated her woad and, to add insult to injury, ridiculed her:

> Agnès la Patinière, daughter of Druon le Patinier, wife of Jean du Hoc, said under oath with the agreement of her husband that, when her father died, his lordship Jean Boinebroke had a proclamation made concerning Marion, wife of Druon le Patinier, for a debt that she owed him.
>
> And he stopped during this period a delivery of woad, and Lord Jean took this load of woad for his own convenience, the load being worth twenty *livres parisis* more than what was owing.
>
> Jeanne aux Clés said under oath that a good twenty-six years ago, Agnès la Patinière had some woad all ready to put in the vat, which woad was taken by Sir Jean for the debt owed to him by Marion. She does not know what the debt was, but she saw the woad being measured out. She was four years old, and heard Agnès asking Sir Jean for twenty *livres parisis* for the extra for the purchase of this woad. And Sir Jean said, "Good woman, I have no idea what I owe you, but I shall remember you in my will!"

Prominent among those usurers who operated on the margins of the Church but did not feel themselves entirely excluded from it were the Italians. These were the "Lombards," modest Piedmontese business-men—very different from the great Tuscan or Genoese merchants—from Asti or Chieri. While not attempting to rival the Florentines—those from Asti did not reach Avignon until the late fourteenth century, as a result of the Great Schism which kept those loyal to the pope in Rome and out of business circles for a time—they came with the intention of carving a small niche for themselves. Although apparently without contacts, a family from

Asti, the Royers, successfully established pawnshops in several towns north of the Alps, coming to ressemble a proper banking company through a mixture of pragmatism and concrete skills. Others, like the merchants of Cahors, and, more generally, those professional moneylenders popularly known as "*Cahorsins*," attempted to compete with both the Jews and the Lombards. From the end of the thirteenth century, both princes and towns granted them the right to keep pawnshops, in exchange for a fair rent together with some rather vague moral exhortations. In Flanders, for example, they were enjoined to lend without usury. This probably did not exclude remuneration for money lent—otherwise what would the lenders live on?—but only the excessive rates that we think of as typifying the modern definition of usury.

Companies like that of the *Grands Cahorsins* or the Paon company then successfully set up in Bruges. But, just as the Jewish moneylender could scarcely fail to be a shopkeeper as well, so the Lombards and *Cahorsins* who formed into companies rapidly began to assume other functions, which we would now call banking. Since moneylenders had strong coffers in which to store their customers' pledges, the public felt confident about entrusting them with their cash deposits as well. A more general trade in money and credit began to take place: the era of banking was at hand.

To read the interest rates mentioned in court cases, one might easily imagine that fabulous profits were made. For the borrower sometimes found it convenient to go to the judge and complain of usury rather than to pay back a debt with interest. The judge had no choice but to condemn the usurer. The agreement would be declared illegal and the borrower absolved of any debt. This trick often rebounded on the borrower, however, since he might, at a later date, be forced to seek credit elsewhere and on harsher terms. And the cost of usury was limitless. A rate of two *deniers* per pound per week—equaling 43.33 percent a year—passed for relatively normal. For a very short-term loan, or one without significant guarantees, a rate of 20 percent a week surprised no one. When the pope in Avignon was forced, at the time of the Great Schism, to go to the most sordid usurers in the market, it cost him on average between 28 and 36 percent a year.

But we should not draw the wrong conclusions; the usurer's real profit was meager. The poor fellow who pawned his motheaten gown for three sous at an interest rate of two *deniers* to the pound per week knew full well that he would never return to redeem his garment and that, in fact, he had sold for three sous something that the ragman might not have wanted. The usurer knew it too, wondering whether he could find a buyer prepared to pay four sous for the gown. In the case of pearls and rubies, the risk was that he might make a mistake in valuation of the pledge—not all usurers were experts in precious stones. And then there was the risk that circumstances might change: to have a coffer full of precious stones was one thing, but to be sure that they would be in demand on the date when the unredeemed pledge became the property of the pawnbroker was another. In the case of secondhand clothes, the risk of being let down by circumstances was just as great: a warm winter will not make the fortune of someone with a shop full of old coats and ragged covers.

It seems, then, that pledges were most conveniently used in the case of medium-size loans. A citizen who pledged a silver ewer or a belt against a loan to meet a pressing bill or an unexpected expense would be likely to want, eventually, to redeem his property. This was someone who would pay the high rates of interest demanded by the usurer.

The fertile minds of those holding or seeking capital did not fail to find other legal formulae to assure themselves of the remuneration necessary to obtain credit. One procedure that stretched canon law to its extreme limits was that of "sale for repurchase" or *remere*. Here, someone looking for credit and owning some property sells the latter—be it land, house, or movables—while reserving for himself the right to repurchase it after a certain period. The lender, who is buying something that he knows he will eventually have to return, gains through this maneuver a sum of interest more or less cleverly disguised in an overestimation of the worth of the property—hence the obligation of repurchase—without in fact getting paid the price declared at the start. This is another version of the old technique of recording a sum larger than the sum actually lent. But, in this case, there is in addition a pledge, some profitable part of the estate of the noble or bourgeois borrower. In such an arrangement, it was possible to have a loan that exceeded in value anything that the borrower could normally offer as a pledge in the way of furniture, plate, or clothes.

Involving inherited estates as pledges for loans meant that a certain number of transfers of property took place, resulting in the constantly changing situation of the world of the landed gentry. Just as an old lady might leave her *surcote* with the Lombard moneylender, so many nobles of the time were forced to hand over their land to their middle-class creditor, finding themselves temporarily without sufficient funds to take advantage of the delay in the repurchase clause.

Experts in canon law did not know what to think about this system of *remere*. If the buyer was receiving profits from a piece of land purchased in this manner, then clearly interest was involved. The entire business was thus illegitimate, unless the profits were to be deducted from the value of the loan, in other words, from the debt. Just as the difference between the usurer who took in old clothes as pledges in exchange for three sous and the banker who took rubies or pearls in exchange for a thousand pounds was more one of status than of nature, so too was that between someone who borrowed on the strength of a pledge of some object and someone who sold in order to repurchase, or *remere*. In one instance the debtor went to the usurer, in the other to the businessman.

There were other, more complex procedures, only possible in an environment, such as Genoa, where it was possible to juggle one's money between public and private loans. It can be seen as a kind of installment purchase: a person goes to a lawyer to sell something, then to another to draw up a deed that conveys to the seller, in exchange for payment, legal rights to the profits of the thing he has sold. There still remains a visit to a third lawyer to draw up a third deed, annulling the sale. In this transaction the pseudo-seller has had the benefit of the sale price for the entire period between the sale and its annulment. And in the complexities created through the involvement of the three lawyers, each ignorant of the other or pretending to be so, the pseudo-buyer keeps for himself the rent paid for a piece of property of which he has never had the use either by right or in practice, and that looks remarkably like interest.

In the end these were all complex inventions designed so that available money could profitably slip into the hands of whoever needed it for living or work. Everyone took part to some extent in this game, in which credit was given in exchange for remuneration that was justified to a greater or a lesser extent. The amicable loan, the pledge, the repurchase agreement, and all the other procedures dreamed up to deceive a Church that balked at them, yet let them pass, were still a long way from proper banking.

Deposits and Transfers

True banking came a step closer when businessmen began professionally to accept deposits of capital unconnected with their own estates or their company capital. Even before 1200 in Italy, and a little later in Metz and Bruges, and despite the unambiguous condemnation by the Council of Trier in 1227, money changers were taking deposits. They were the obvious choice because, in the first place, their job handling and changing coins meant that they generally had strong coffers banded with iron; second, their competence silenced any arguments about the nature and quality of the coins deposited. Kept in case of hard times, the deposit was, for the client, originally simply a reserve. In a will drawn up in 1295, the widow of a citizen of Metz bequeaths to her daughter the silver that the money changers Geoffroi Jallée and his brother Androwat "keep at their table." Again, in the years 1366–69, it occurred neither to the money changers Collard de Marke and Guillaume Ruyelle nor to their clientele—nearly four hundred citizens and businessmen of Bruges—that such deposits should grow with the passage of time. The client did not have the feeling that he was investing his money, even less that it could yield a profit. He was simply putting it somewhere safe.

We notice, however, how certain entries in the money changer's account book were making it possible to settle accounts between different clients through simple compensation. Thus were born transfers, based entirely on the public's confidence in the money changer's daily account book. The chronological order typical of a day book made fraudulent interpolations impossible, as did the fact that the entries were written in such a way as to leave no blanks on the pages. In addition, statutes regulating the money changers' keeping of the books, in many Italian towns, stipulate that only roman figures—believed to be more secure—might be used.

So far the financial techniques involved were of a modest scale. If people had begun to use the word *bank*, it was because the money changer's stall was called, in Italian, *banco*—a counter, bench, or board. The stalls where deposits were made or transferred through account books were called *banchi di mercato*, the counters where trading was done. The principal market of this kind took place in Venice, at the Rialto Bridge, where the *banchi di scritta*, the writing desks, were located. By the end of the fifteenth century, the Rialto market would be the largest market for money deposits in Europe. In Barcelona a *Taula de cambi* began to play a public role: since 1401 it had become an annex of the town treasury. In Bruges, activity was concentrated in the square known as *de la Bourse* because the Van de Beurse family had placed its coat of arms on the facade of one of the patrician houses. The name was taken up in Antwerp where, in the fifteenth century, the money changers' meeting place was called the "Bourse."

The astute Florentines began to distinguish between the *banchi minuti*, the small banks of the money changers who dealt in cash, took deposits, bought precious metals, and on occasion sold smaller pieces of jewelery or plate, and the *banchi grossi*, the "big banks," or commercial and banking enterprises run by the large companies. A growth in confidence was helping to lay the foundations of the economic practice of depositing: it was becoming acceptable for the money changer, in exchange for the service he rendered by offering the security of his coffers, to engage in his own business with the money for which he was accountable. Marke and Ruyelle, in Bruges, kept only half or even a third of the sums deposited in ready cash. The remainder was used to finance commercial dealings. The money changer was turning into a merchant.

On the other hand, the "banker," in the strict sense of the word, was not the only person whose coffers and competence inspired confidence. Plenty of merchants looked after deposits, as did those innkeepers who acted as both advisers and guarantors for merchants in transit. For someone constantly on the road, it must have been a great convenience to be able to leave the profits of a deal or a season with a local agent who was also the landlord of the inn at which he stayed during each trip.

But there was nothing here to nourish other types of trade. Money on deposit is not working. Whether money changer or innkeeper, whoever holds a deposit and makes use of it becomes a borrower. To use a deposit without declaring it was frowned on. To lend deposited money to a third person was doubly bad, and few money changers ventured to do it. Occasionally they might get involved in the settlement of some local debts in a transaction that could be counted as an amicable loan. Some Flemish money changers tried this in Bruges, with the blessing of the count, who was also their feudal lord. It was the count himself who was their principal borrower.

For the money changer to become a banker in the broader and more modern sense of the word, he had to become involved in dealings other than simply changing currency at different rates of exchange. "Manual" changing was at that time part of a larger business enterprise in which society or the great merchant pulled the strings. The Italians in Bruges thus dealt in *deniers* just as they dealt in cloth, spices, or furs. The holders of the *loges,* or stalls, on the Pont au Change in Paris were known to be able to trade in all kinds of goods: the relatively narrow horizons of the manual money changer were obviously not those of someone like Jacques Coeur who, mistakenly speculating on the recovery of the Parisian market, held for a while—and in vain—the lease of a money changer's *loge.*

In Florence, as in Venice or Genoa, the spice trade seemed to the great merchants to hold out the largest rewards. Here could be found all the diverse functions of a modern bank. This was not the case, however, for the small money changers who were content to earn little more than a salary for services rendered in keeping someone's money and returning it when requested. Nevertheless, in the smaller markets and even in Toulouse, money changers attempted to respond to demand and, rather clumsily, to trade in a variety of commodities.

For the movement of money collected through taxes, the state felt the need for a more dynamic system than the simple recording of entries and withdrawals used in the royal treasuries of Paris or Winchester, or in the papal treasuries of Rome or Avignon. In 1356, Venice made its first attempt to create a state bank that could perform the gigantic task of reconciling Venetian tax revenues from customs and tolls with the state bonds resulting from the systematic dependence on public borrowing. A new attempt to bring order to the republic's financial affairs in 1374 was similarly unsuccessful. Other failures, in particular that of Heinrich Castorp's municipal bank established in Lübeck in 1461 and bankrupted ten years later, underlined the difficulties involved in bringing state finances within a single system. The taxpayers were suspicious.

The only success of this kind was the *Casa di San Giorgio.* Before its foundation in 1407, creditors of the Commune of Genoa had been grouped into associations formed to exploit the income from land or taxes, given in pledge; these leases were known as *compere*. In this way Genoa discounted its revenues by passing on to others the task of management and the expenses that went with it. One *compera* might levy for the creditors the tax on imports of wine. Another, for other creditors, had, since 1346, exploited the Khios market that dealt in alum from the mines of Phocaea. Each creditor received the interest from his share, or *luogo* (Italian for "place"), in the concern. In the fourteenth century the interest on a *compera* stood at some 5 percent; in the fifteenth century the *San Giorgio paghe* (interest payments) yielded only 4 percent or, after 1463, even 3 percent.

The system of *compere* had, however, two disadvantages for the state: first, discounting was done at a significant loss, the revenue paid as interest on the *compere* greatly exceeding the state debts thus paid off; second, the doge's government was unable to gain any kind of overall view of its own financial system. The state revenue and public debt were only very approximately under its control. Thus a unified body, the *Casa di San Giorgio,* was created, being a fusion—both active and passive—of the *compere* in force at that time.

This "House of St. George" brought together all the creditors of the Commune in order to exploit, in their name, all those revenues assigned to payment of the public debt. In practice, it was a deposit bank of infinitely greater efficiency than the money changer's counter. *San Giorgio* opened up "columns" in its account books in the name of anyone wanting to invest. To make a deposit meant henceforth buying a line, or a *luogo*, in a column. Just as the Genoese, in the fourteenth century, had begun to buy shares, or "carats," in this or that *compera*, so, in the fifteenth century, they began to buy *luoghi* in San Giorgio. In a short time there grew from this practice a simple form of capitalism, within reach of many people. From the great merchant to the humble artisan, all were to have their columns.

The nature of lending became blurred. The risk run justified the profit made by the creditors in a *compera*. No one now questioned the morality of the *paghe,* the interest paid according to the amount of *luoghi* owned, or the revenue from goods allocated to the *Casa*. Buying *luoghi* became the most common, and indeed the best, form of investment. But it was something that could last only as long as the Genoese economic empire continued to grow.

Since *San Giorgio* paid interest only after a period of several months, the *paghe* registered and inscribed on the normal maturity dates in the depositors' column began to resemble nothing so much as credit. The Genoese found it convenient to regard this credit as negotiable. The *lire di paga* were those sums that were registered, discounted, and quoted at a price relating to the length of time before payment was likely. They were eventually to become a form of paper money, the value of which varied but could not be forecast. People paid in *lire di paga* according to the day's rate.

The habit grew up of concluding commercial transactions by means of a simple transfer of *luoghi* or *paghe* from one column to another. Whether written or oral, the order to transfer was carried out immediately. Instead of demanding payment of interest and at the same time settling accounts in cash, the Genoese got accustomed to leaving their *paghe* in the columns of the *San Giorgio*, keeping them there as available capital easily accessible through transfer.

Since the fourteenth century, in the largest Italian markets, private agreements had been sufficient to carry out this kind of business. Before 1350 in Florence—and around 1370 in Pisa—a banker could transfer a sum from one account to another simply on the sight of a signed note. However, the two parties had to hold accounts with the same banker. By opening its books to the whole of Genoese society, the *San Giorgio* freed the system. By the fifteenth century, a spoken order was considered valid, provided that it was given in the marketplace and in the presence of witnesses. The Venetians would move in the same direction.

Thus, between 1350 and 1450, there began to emerge a banking system with obvious advantages. Developing from the management of different currencies through "manual" money changers or businessmen who had extended the diversified activities of their house or company to money changing, this system could offer both the security of a deposit that could be recovered at any time and the convenience of transfers between clients of the same depository. The disadvantage was that the deposited money did not grow in value from day to day, the saver obtaining remuneration for his deposited money with *San Giorgio* only on the uncertain terms pertaining to the sharing of profits. The other main disadvantage—and here Genoa is the only exception—was that it did not allow deposits to be linked to true investments since credit and future transactions were restricted to the local sphere. Deposits were useful, but they did not lead to financing or revenue on a scale with the businessman's horizons.

TWELVE

Toward Modern Banking

*T*he practice of usury or amicable loans could not, any more than that of deposits or written transfers, provide the economy with the financial means needed to supply the credit so vital to economic life. The existing systems were sufficient for the everyday needs of the citizen, but not for the businessman confronted by market opportunities. Thus, not surprisingly, businessmen created a new system: the drawing of bills of exchange, or *tratte*, which was to pave the way to modern banking.

Bills of Exchange

The exchange involved here is not essentially different from what we have already encountered at the money changer's stall: the exchange of one kind of money for another. The diversity of species at the beginning and end of the transaction—in both time and space—was to remain an essential condition for the smooth operation of drawing. Equally important were the methods for disguising the payment of interest beneath the differences in rates of exchange, something the nonspecialist found hard to grasp. But this exchange was no longer simply manual. The money changer, as we know, gave out coins in exchange for others received, everything passing from hand to hand. The client gave florins and received écus. The essence of the matter lay in the act of changing; everything was immediate. There were no delays and no written documents, apart from the record of accounts that the money changer was entitled to make and that was vital for him to keep if he looked after deposits in a variety of coinages and hoped to make any kind of a profit. The drawn bill of exchange could not, of its nature, be immediate. For the florins that he received, the dealer, called the *cambiste*, drew a bill of exchange in another market, where another *cambiste* would supply the "taker" of the bill—that is the "giver" of the florins—or his agent with écus.

It is not immediately apparent how a money changer handling gold and silver coins at his counter on the Rialto could debit one of his colleagues who worked in Paris at the Pont au Change. The *cambiste* who drew a bill of exchange was first and foremost a merchant, a dealer with a far-reaching clientele who consequently had accumulated credits and debits in other marketplaces. It became increasingly easy to transfer money as business partnerships developed and commercial companies acquired new contacts through their branches in different marketplaces. For the florins it had received, the Florentine office of the Bardi had no difficulty in finding someone to take écus in Bruges—the Bardi branch office. There was no need even to have an account with the paying *cambiste:* if the payment he made in this way in order to execute an exchange exceeded what he owed to the agent, the payer would simply credit him with a temporary balance.

Merchants had originally invented the drawing system in order to facilitate long-distance payments and thus avoid the transport of cash. One merchant might be reluctant to carry precious metal, always at risk of theft or loss. Another might have no desire to dispatch a sack of coins, or even a wagonload of sacks, to settle his accounts abroad. In this context, the four parties necessary to the transaction came into play. The one who wanted to make a payment from a distance was the "taker" of the bill. He gave the coins in exchange for a bill of exchange. He might be a successful businessman or a small trader owning only ten *livres*. No questions were asked of the person bringing money.

It was a different matter for the person drawing the bill of exchange, the "drawer." Nobody would give him gold in exchange for promises without confidence in his reputation, his creditworthiness, the volume of his business, and its track record. The drawer was often an important merchant. As time went by, the principal drawers were increasingly the great companies.

It was not lack of confidence that typically prevented a small merchant from drawing bills of exchange: it was quite possible to be a mere shopkeeper and have a reputation for honesty. It was more a matter of his poverty of contacts. Anyone involved in business on a European scale could be sure of finding credit in London, Barcelona, or Alexandria; this was not the case for the spice merchant in Castelnaudary. Bills drawn by small operators continued to be confined to family and local circles. In his own quarter of Paris, a Norman would be able to draw a bill of exchange on his brother back home in Rouen or to pay another for his cousin in Évreux. The drawer was defined by his credit and his contacts.

The third party to the operation was the "drawee," or agent of the drawer. He was located in another town, but had a similar function to the drawer. When the operation was reversed or continued on to a third party, he would be the drawer, unless the balance was settled through shipment of merchandise. If the taker drew a bill of exchange in order to pay in another market, the drawer's agent would often accept it in order to pay what he himself owed in the market of origin. The two loans did not necessarily cancel out each other; the overall movement of credit maintained the balance.

As for the "beneficiary," he resembled the taker, to the extent that sometimes the two were confused. The essential difference lay in place, not persons.

These businessmen knew enough about accounting to realize from the earliest stages that the operation resulted in credit. From the moment that the bill of exchange—whether a contract or a letter, as we shall see—arrived in Bruges from Genoa, or in Barcelona from London, the drawer found himself in possession of money paid by the taker. He did no more, for the moment, than deliver a piece of paper of no intrinsic value: a sort of obligation that would cost him nothing until its due date for payment. Thus he was a debtor for a sum that he would not really pay back until the day when the agent on whom he had just drawn the bill would demand a reciprocal service.

The same thing applied when the drawing was intended to pay a commercial debt of the drawee to the drawer. The latter could feel that he had been paid, by the taker, for what the drawee had received in merchandise. But he was paid immediately, whereas the merchandise might not yet have arrived, or payment by the recipient of the goods would have arrived only at a later date. In this case, the drawer was not borrowing but rather indirectly anticipating his credit. However it was used, the bill of exchange greatly facilitated payment by extending what even the most unsophisticated could recognize as credit.

Whereas, for many, the bill of exchange seemed no more than a convenient means to transfer funds while avoiding the physical transport of coins, others immediately recognized its true value in the improved possibilities of credit that it offered. It was this credit that—from an economic, if not religious, point of view—justified the rewards gained by the taker through fluctuations in the exchange rates. The taker had invested in the exchange and would get his money back only at a later stage; thus it was right that he should be compensated.

This was very different from the kind of profit that the manual money changer or the pawnbroker received from his loans. In the drawing of bills of exchange and their traffic, it all rested on the trade in goods and the credit it engendered, on commercial activity and the flow of trade, and on

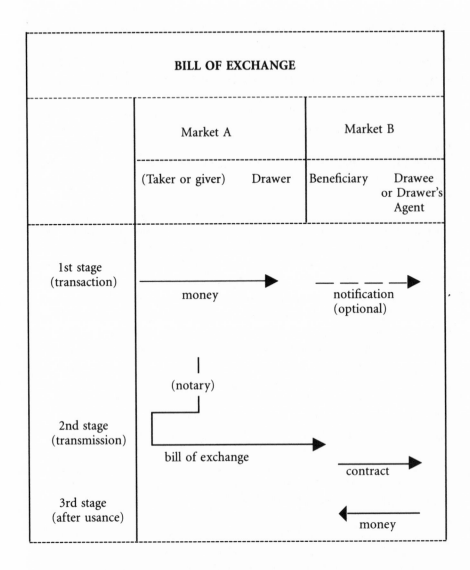

terms of maturity. The modern bank, born of this long-distance trafficking in futures, was the offspring of trade and its ramifications. Thus it was that, initially, banking centers grew up in the commercial marketplaces where trade in goods made available a variety of loans. Bills of exchange were drawn only in markets where money was available, and money was never to be found on its own. Bills of exchange followed, or accompanied, wool or alum, cloth or silk, iron or wine, becoming part of the play of commerce and a form of investment.

Commercial reinvestment was a simple matter in itself, held back only by material constraints. It was necessary to find something to buy in Bergen or Constantinople with the profits from the sales made there, or to find something to ship there in order to buy. Further considerations related to transport costs and time spent at sea. Why make a profit in only one direction? Financial investment in the journey had, hitherto, to produce results and, if possible, a profit on both the outward and the return trip. The bill of exchange was exempt from such constraints and could also liberate major commerce from them. A three-sided operation was easy, allowing someone to pay in one place for what was owed in another, since analogous settlements between the parties would restore the balance. It became possible to obtain money in the marketplace where it was needed, rather than where one had credit but no use for it. It became a matter of course to finance a purchase in Trebizond or Kaffa by means of a bill of exchange drawn on Bruges or the Champagne fairs, and this new flexibility enabled businessmen to detach export from import: it was no longer necessary to import English alabasters to France because one sold French wine to the English. The reuse of the ship became a matter for its owner, that of money a matter for the merchant. It was no longer necessary to think only in terms of immediate return journeys.

From this time forward, the business world could pursue a deliberate, rather than contingent, European policy. The great Florentine companies, who in the fourteenth century took over the movement of funds linked to papal taxation, accumulated money received from the English clergy by the papal collector in London and used it to buy wool there. This way they avoided having first to transport the wool needed by the Florentines to Avignon, where little credit drawn on London was available. When the Alberti *antichi* transferred the sums received by their agents in Torun or Cracow from collectors in Poland to the Avignon Curia, they did not have to worry whether or not there was something they needed to buy in those cities.

Even if it was obviously a form of credit, the bill of exchange was also a payment, and a very flexible one, in terms of both time and space. It was also the least onerous method: we have only to think of the cost involved in organizing the transport of currency at a time when travel was fraught with risk. The risk of a banker going bankrupt was slight compared with the flight of an armed escort. In France, England, or Germany, until the mid-fifteenth century, the business world continued to regard bills of exchange as the chief method for the settlement of payments. It was only later, toward the end of the century, that they realized—as the Italians had done three hundred years before—that there was no longer a need to make use of payments in order to trade in credit. The bank began to move away from commerce.

Nevertheless, it remained closely linked to it. It was the commercial balances that, from market to market, determined the price of money; and it would be an unwise banker who ignored them. For this reason, bankers often chose to create a chain of exchange: Bruges on Barcelona and Barcelona on Florence, rather than making a direct exchange from Bruges on Florence. The currency of Aragon was little esteemed and fetched a low price in Bruges, where they had no use for it, whereas Florentine florins were much sought after and fetched a high price. And the *cambiste*—who was, first and foremost, a merchant—knew that, in the Barcelona market, credits were accumulated by the Italians of Bruges who sold more there than they bought. An exchange from Barcelona on Florence was thus an opportunity to be seized. The same thing happened, at the end of the fifteenth century, when bills of exchange from Bruges and particularly Antwerp destined for the Italian markets were routed via Geneva.

And so a new type of banker was born, much more the international businessman than the simple money changer whose activities were restricted to the town in which he plied his trade. We have seen how the term *money changer* had been extended from signifying someone who swapped coins to include any professional dealing in small finances, those who took deposits, and even pawnbrokers. In the fifteenth century, the word *changer* was used to designate dealers in bills drawn on the great financial markets, even if the more restricted markets—of which Paris was now one—continued to use the same name for those money changers who were principally financiers and depositaries. In Bruges, Antwerp, London, Barcelona, Genoa, and Florence, the functions of money changer and *cambiste* became increasingly linked. There was no longer any profession involving money or banking that did not greatly expand its activities to this area of trading in bonds with fixed maturities abroad. Such transactions continued to be described as "exchange" because, among other things, they involved the exchange of one currency for another.

Bankers made their profits from this ambiguity. We have seen what a Tuscan company could gain by intervening simultaneously in English wool and the movement of funds to the Avignon papacy. A century later, the Medici were to be both "depositaries of the Apostolic Chamber"—in other words, bankers to the pope—and tax-farmers, holding the lease for the management and commercial development throughout Europe of alum from the papal mines at Tolfa. Similarly, the money earned by the English staplers from wool sold on the Continent, then transferred by continental haberdashers to agents in London, was used by haberdashers in Calais and elsewhere who had bought luxury goods in Flanders. The sale of the latter to an English clientele supplied the staplers with cash that would be used to purchase new cargoes of wool. Thus, as in so many other places, commerce supported the trade in money to its own benefit.

And there were further benefits to be had. With money being turned around so quickly, it was rarely counted in cash. In a world suffering from a severe shortage of available metal, hence a shortage in means of payment, businessmen were quick to understand the immediate advantages of a system that organized the settlement of accounts without reference to hard cash. The bill of exchange helped the medieval economy survive through a period of expansion, the circulation of credit supplementing the money supply.

Furthermore, banking meant that a trader could offer a better deal. It was easier to do business if one could offer to lend money or facilitate the financing of a deal. The loans made by the Florentines to Edward III were the price they had to pay to gain fiscal privileges for their wool trade. During the same period, the German Tidemann Limberg, a businessman from Dortmund established in London, was able to purchase, in exchange for a loan advanced to the same Edward III, the concession for the Cornish zinc mines. In the same way, other Germans from Cologne and Dortmund bought licenses for the export of wool and even the lease of the customs farmed out by the English exchequer. In the fifteenth century, a monopoly over the papal alum was the Medici's reward for the granting of loans. Their position in Bruges, in the important alum market in northwest Europe, depended on the credit advanced, not without some risk, by the director of their Bruges office, Tommaso Portinari, to Charles the Bold and Marie of Burgundy. None of these figures—Bardi, Limberg, or Portinari—would have doubted for an instant that the bank was anything but a single component of a complex political and economic system.

Some bankers gave up trading in goods altogether. From the 1300s, the Gianfigliazzi—active between 1283 and 1325—specialized in loans in Provence and the Dauphiné. Similarly, the Florentine Jacopo Scaglia de' Tiffi was first and foremost banker to the count of Burgundy, Othon IV, later becoming adviser to his widow, Mahaut d'Artois. But, at the same time, the Guidi family—Biche, Mouche, Tote, and Vanne—were as busy dealing in royal revenues as in lending out money, in taxes at the Champagne fairs as in the policy of trade relations with the cloth towns of Flanders. They pursued the latter policy on behalf of Enguerran de Marigny, who was eager to see a rapid expansion of his fairs in Écouis in Normandy. At a later date, the Florentine and Lucchesi bankers to the Avignon popes were still essentially merchants; and it was as suppliers to the papal court that they repaid themselves for the amicable loans they advanced to the pope and his cardinals.

However limited, in the fifteenth century this evolution toward the separation of banking from merchandising certainly benefited from the protection afforded—thanks to rights of "protest" and re-exchange—in a banking activity that was quite distinct from the credit available in other markets. In fact, the caution of these daring early bankers was enough to facilitate such protection and to restrain the powers of the bank. The businessman knew that trade in goods, with the real credit that it engendered and deposited in a clearly defined marketplace, was the best way to counterbalance the boom in lending rates that, had it remained purely speculative, would have introduced chaos into a market already hard to control. They were daring, but they were not mad.

The dangers that lay in wait for the incautious were illustrated by the collapse in 1335 of the banking enterprise of Hermann Klendenot. And yet this Klendenot was a serious and well-regarded man, who sat on the council and took risks only when backed by a solid base of respectable capital. Amid the euphoria of the recent years of expansion, he had created a system of finance separated from commerce. He had anticipated everything except the harmful effects of expansion itself: thanks to the general prosperity, available money had the effect of lowering interest rates. Klendenot saw the revenue from his investments collapse. Clients became anxious. The banker had to break into his capital. He was ruined. The news spread quickly, convincing more than one person of the need for caution.

A few years later, it was the turn of the Bardi and Peruzzi firms to collapse. They had opted for the opposite course, and the ideas of businessmen on the subject now received a jolt. The only conclusion they could draw was that it was wise to be wary of princes. Nevertheless, with regard to the structure and strategy of individual economic enterprises, it was a fact that one seemed to succeed where another failed. The risk of bankruptcy became another justification put forward for the charging of interest for money, regardless of where that money might be invested.

The great fairs bestowed a cyclical character on commercial trade. Taking note, the *cambistes* were quick to draw the necessary conclusions. Because merchants were bound to be there on certain days of the year, financial settlements tended to be transacted at the fairs. Since the maturity dates were predictable, it could be said that the payments were, by common agreement, "domiciled" at the fair of Saint-Ayoul at Provins, at the Whitsun fair in Antwerp, or the All Hallows fair at Berg op Zoom. For someone wishing to conceal interest charged for the duration of an exchange, it would have been extremely convenient to have available such a range of maturities justified by the customs of commerce.

The fairs had been the periodic meeting places first of regional commerce and then of long-distance trade. Developments in transport, particularly the advent of sea transport for heavy goods, left them without their raison d'être. There was nothing to stop a person from buying raw wool or wine in bulk at the fairs—in the fifteenth century, wine was still sold in mid-June at the Lendit fair—but there were better markets, often closer to the centers of production. English wool was bought in London or at the staple on the Continent, Spanish wool at Medina del Campo, Gascon wine at Bordeaux or Bruges, Burgundy wines in Paris. Some of the fairs disappeared, including the majority of the Parisian fairs, made redundant by the permanence of the commercial market in the capital during the fourteenth century. Others appeared, prospering through their specialties: wool in the fourteenth century at the fair at Medina del Campo, silks and spices in the fifteenth century at Lyons. It should be noted that these luxury goods engendered a volume of financial transactions on a scale suited to the establishment of banking facilities in these places.

Most fairs managed to continue in existence through the increasingly organized market in maturities: money at term was quoted, depending on where the payment was expected to be made, just as people quoted standing crops or returning cargoes. Some fairs maintained a certain balance between their commercial and financial functions. That of Boston, in England, was careful not to neglect its wool and cloth. Berg op Zoom retained its role in the distribution of English cloth. The Frankfurt fairs remained the largest European market for German products such as canvas, tools, weapons, wine, and herring. Leipzig attracted furs from Poland and Russia. And the fairs in Geneva kept control over a transalpine trade with its wealth of products from Italy and northwestern Europe.

Others upset this balance by turning to the "exchange fair": here the settling and payment of bills of exchange was enough to bring together people and negotiable assets. Thus it was that the financial role of the Champagne fairs delayed their decline, expected since 1300, for another quarter of a century. Similarly, in the fifteenth century, it encouraged the survival of the Lyons fairs, despite competition from Geneva and the ports of Languedoc. It provided an added facility, eagerly sought by businessmen when they attended or sent their agents to a fair: information about the world. Financial speculation, as carried out by the *cambiste*, here took on its true role in "business." In a legitimate open market, it found its rationale.

From Contract to Letter of Credit

When a bond was contracted in one place and settled in another, the exchange was sealed with a contract. Medieval people went to a notary or *tabellio* for everything imaginable, be it to hire an ox or take on an apprentice. Little wonder, then, that they also asked the notary to draw up this document. When the bill of exchange first appeared, in the 1200s, it took the material form of a contract drawn up in the presence of a notary and witnesses. The rediscovery of Roman law during the previous century suggested that it was necessary to write out all the details in order to be sure that the deed was secured, clarified, and executed. The complex structure imposed on the document by legal formulae—even if quite simple for those who understood what it was about—weighed it down with a procession of clauses, seen at the time by those who used such a document as the best defense against that most feared of all possibilities—invalidity. So instead they waived exceptions, established guarantees, and invoked a battery of spiritual and temporal penalties. Above all, to make sure that the point was correctly made, they said the same thing three times over. Chancelleries were familiar with the procedure. "We have given, released, and granted," says one. "We instruct, order, and command," runs another. That was how it was done, and to do otherwise would have been most unwise.

The contract of exchange thus wrapped up in a long-winded document the essential point of a recognition, an obligation, an order to pay. The final beneficiary was rarely named and played no role at this stage in the proceedings. The drawer owed the taker the money that the latter had just given him and agreed to have it returned to whoever was nominated to collect it. The result was that the beneficiary had no rights in this most fundamental arrangement. Consequently there was no action that he could take either against the drawer's agent if he did not pay or against the drawer if he had drawn a bill of exchange too rashly. The only creditor was the taker: if the bill of exchange was not paid, he was the loser. Businessmen saw this as an opportunity to transform exchange deals into a means of credit: the time lapse before payment was not the time needed to make the transfer but, it was becoming clear, a period of loan.

Thus, on 26 January 1308, according to our method of counting the years from 1 January, Vanne Guy—brother of Biche and Mouche and at the time a partner of the Tolomei—summoned a Sienese lawyer, who happened as if by accident to be in town, to his home in Bordeaux. Vanne Guy had to pay a thousand florins at the Champagne fairs:

> In the name of our Lord, Amen. The year of the birth of our Lord, one thousand three hundred and seven, fifth proclamation, the twenty-sixth day of the month of January, in the second year of the pontficate of our lord the pope Clement V,
>
> In the presence of myself, notary, and the undermentioned witnesses, Raniero Griffi, citizen and merchant of Siena, partner in the company of the Gallerani of Siena, in his name and in the name of all the partners of the said company, for the exchange and the price of a thousand gold florins which he has confessed and recognized to have, in his name and in the name of the said partners and company, had and received from Vanne Guy, his countryman and merchant from Siena, partner in the Tolomei company of Siena, paying and counting in his name and in the name of the said partners,
>
> has promised and agreed to the said Vanne, receiving and stipulating in his name and in the name of the said partners, to give and pay to the said Vanne and to his partners and to each of them for all or to their representative or proxy appointed for this reason, at the Lagny fairs currently

being held at Lagny, as just payment, two thousand one hundred and twenty-five *livres* in small *deniers tournois* of which *tournois* one old silver *gros tournois* is worth forty *deniers* or thereabouts.

Although deemed to be necessary, the heavy precision of the lawyer's text is overwhelming. Everything is duplicated, and more than once. With anything less the lawyer would not have given his guarantee. And it should be remembered that he was paid by the length of the deed. If they were to do without it, merchants would need to create their own laws, their own arbitration processes, and their own jurisdictions, reaching a consensus about the language of business agreements for use in such contracts. They became increasingly unwilling to pay for a lawyer or for the parchment in order to renounce, as here the Gallerani partner is doing, twenty methods of breaking the obligation, when to try even one of them would certainly have been to exclude from the market any businessman daring to risk it. Our lawyer of 1308, however, is forced to err on the side of prudence. Anyway, that is what he was there for:

> The said Raniero renounces the exception of the sum had and not counted, the exception of the abovementioned confession, recognition, promise, convention, obligation, and exchange not really made, the exception of things not done as it is said,
> and the benefice of new constitutions, of the decrees of the divine Hadrian, the privilege of the cross, the privilege of jurisdiction of each party, all assemblies of judges and places, and all other exceptions.

Vanne Guy, who here puts himself down as Sienese since he was at the time a partner of the Tolomei, is doing no more than exchanging through this deed—twice the length of these quotations and taking up the whole of a skin of parchment—one thousand florins payable at one of the Champagne fairs in small *tournois*. At a rate—clearly not disputed and hence well known by the merchants—of 2 *livres*, 2 sous and 6 *deniers* to the florin, that makes a sum of 2,125 *livres*. But what mattered to the anonymous drawee—whose identity is not a matter of importance to Vanne Guy, since it was easy enough to find the Gallerani representative at Lagny—was the rate of the *tournois*: these were the small *tournois* quoted at 40 *deniers* for an old *gros*. It was to be hoped that a change of the royal coinage would not, as a result, mean fewer coins or a reduction in their silver content.

The Genoese and Venetians would draw up contracts of this sort throughout the fourteenth century. The French and the Spanish proceeded in this way until the end of the fifteenth century. Despite the cost, the practice had its advantages. The contract remained in the lawyer's records and was canceled only when he had sight of the receipt of payment. In other words, the parties were protected against possible loss by the copy (*grosse*) of the lawyer's record, issued to the taker in exchange for his florins. He would not have handed over good money merely for a piece of paper that might get lost. Now there was a record, with a definite date, in the safe hands of a witness of repute since he was invested with sovereign authority.

In Tuscany, however, these methods seemed unnecessarily cumbersome, and the Tuscans decided to risk simplifying their procedures. Since at least as early as the 1200s, it had been essential that the drawer did not delay in informing the agent on whom he had just drawn an exchange. The presentation of the contract by the addressee—the taker himself or his own agent—would not then come as a surprise. The "letter of notification" had no obligatory format or legal value. It was this document, nevertheless, that triggered the financial mechanism of payment: on receiving this notification, the drawee could integrate the payment of this bond, coming from elsewhere, into his own book of bills received and paid. The term "letter of payment" became common.

People began to realize that it was possible to give the letter of notification to the taker at the same time as the copy (*grosse*) of the contract. After all, it was in the taker's interests to send this letter, and as quickly as possible. The term "letter of payment" was turning into a bond. Even if the parties were not sufficiently close to justify mutual trust, it began to seem sufficient merely to send the letter. The taker kept the contract in case of a dispute. If the drawee paid on sight of the letter, the lawyer's deed had simply served as extra security. People began to speak of a "letter of exchange."

This development became possible only with a significant rise in the merchant's level of education. The drawer had to sign his letter. His agents would have to be able, at the very least, to recognize and identify his signature. This simplification of procedures could be imagined only in a world crisscrossed by couriers, a world where the merchant was used to pen and ink.

The advantages quickly became apparent to those who often made use of bills of exchange. From the time when the contract began to be used simply as an extra guarantee, it seemed that the lawyer's records were sufficient on their own, without a need for a written contract. The lawyer's minutes were jottings recorded, with copious use of abbreviations, in the lawyer's registers. Although they were rough notes, the minutes were nevertheless the original records and, as such, inspired faith. There seemed little point now in drawing up a *grosse* as well, or in paying for a long-drawn-out, formulaic version of the same thing, of use only in case of dispute. There would be plenty of time to ask for a written *grosse* should things come to court.

The thirty lines of a solemn deed were replaced by the three lines of a simple letter. It cost no more than the price of the parchment or, later, paper. Even better, since the letter cost very little, it was possible to enjoy the luxury of sending two or three copies, duly numbered, by different porters and, perhaps, by different routes. Thus the transaction became more secure. Soon people began to save on the minutes as well, that is to say, on the cost of a lawyer. The important thing was for the exchange to be described with precision, in the language of the businessman. By the fifteenth century, there remained only the financial data, devoid of formulae:

> In the name of God. 26 April 1465.
> Pay by this first letter of exchange within 75 days, made to Piero de' Medici and company, 1564 ducats, that is 1574 *philippes* for the value paid to us, and put it, by you, in your account. Christ keep you.
>
> > Niccolò Manelli and Giovanni Chanigliani and company,
> > in Valencia.
>
> *On the reverse:*
> To Giovanni Salviati and Pietro da Rabatta and company,
> > in Bruges.
> > First.

The letter of exchange had been made possible by the expansion of business networks and, in particular, branch offices. Once again it was Siena and Piacenza that first experimented with the new system, as early as 1225. Florence was to substitute the letter of exchange for the contract a little later; the first documented date is 1291, but the first step may well have been taken around the middle of the century. Genoa followed, though the contract continued to be used for a long time there, the caution of the Genoese stemming from their long association with the risks of sea trade. They could not afford to risk everything at once.

Since it was the Italians who dominated the banking market in Bruges, people there quickly became accustomed, from the first third of the fourteenth century, to this letter of exchange. It greatly simplified operations and, when it came to it, ruffled very few feathers in a marketplace in which lawyers and Roman law were simply extras introduced from the social world.

Venice adopted the letter of exchange only after 1350. The fact that both law and tradition in La Serenissima effectively prevented the creation of multinational companies would limit much of what the Venetians could have established based on long-distance trust.

France, England, and Germany began to use the letter of exchange only in the fifteenth century, and even then with great hesitation. Letters were sent, but people continued to make contracts, that is, when they did not prefer to send wagonloads of gold and silver. In the 1390s, there were still plenty of papal collectors who knew of no other method. The collector in Toulouse, Sicard de Bourguerol, like Pons de Cros in Puy, dispatched 80 and 84 percent of their remittances to the treasury in Avignon in this way. During the same period, by contrast, papal revenues in Castile were arriving

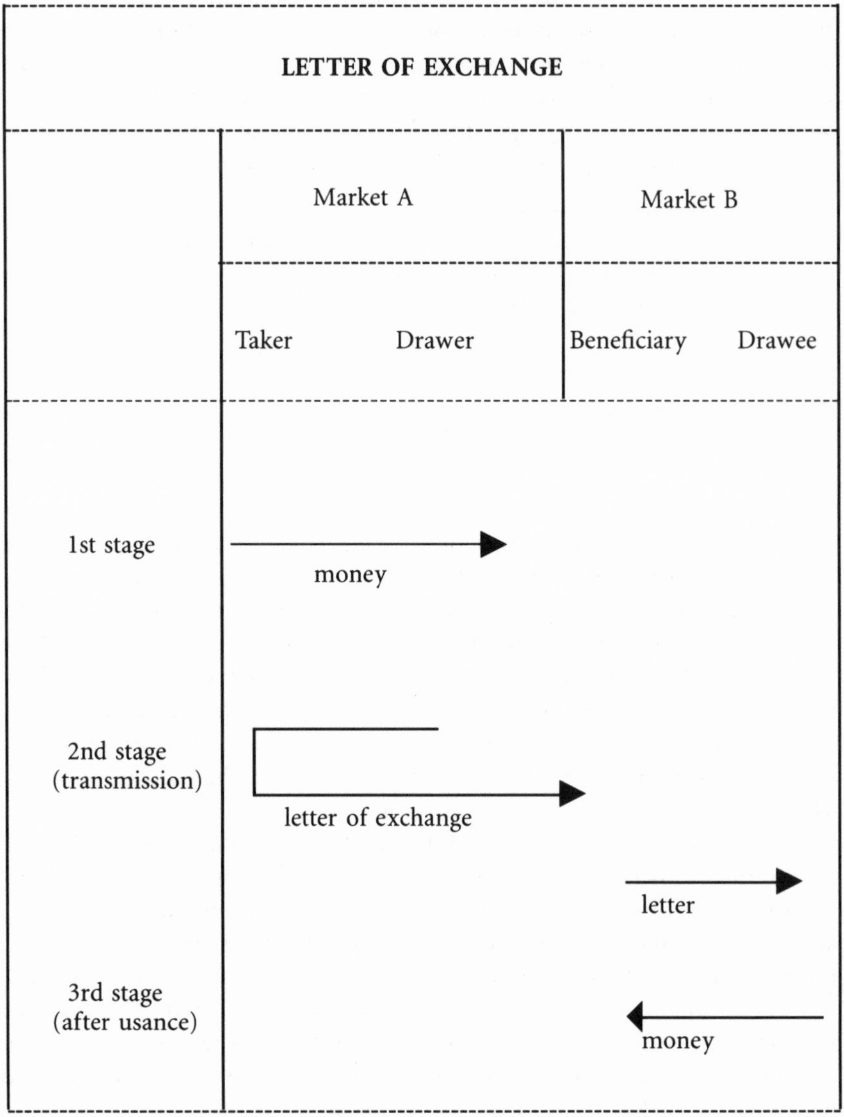

LETTER OF EXCHANGE

	Market A		Market B	
	Taker	Drawer	Beneficiary	Drawee

1st stage

→ money

2nd stage
(transmission)

⌐→ letter of exchange

→ letter

3rd stage
(after usance)

← money

as bills of exchange from Seville. The difference is easily explained: distance influenced the choice of method.

But it was not only distance. Vicko von Goldensen, a Hamburg merchant, sent bags of gold and silver to Bruges to pay for his purchases.

By this time, the Italians had long since stopped using a notary, even to record a "minute" in the "writs." The Tuscan bankers carried on business by signing letters of exchange—and nothing else. Elsewhere, even when a merchant dared omit the contract stage, the constricted commercial network acted as a brake on the new banking practices. Merchants from Toulouse would draw on the fairs at Pézenas and Montagnac, or on Barcelona, or even on the Geneva fairs. If they could overcome their suspicion of credit, the Hanseatic merchants would draw on Bruges. The letter of exchange made banking easier. Nevertheless, it should be remembered that a merchant could draw only on a marketplace where his signature was known.

Any delay in payment, in effect, resulted in credit. From a theological point of view, indeed, this was the chief drawback of interest: it resulted from the passage of time. Whether in the form of a contract or a simple letter, the bill of exchange was payable on a precise date: on a feast day or at a fair. We have seen the array of dates offered by the annual cycle of fairs such as those in Champagne or Flanders. Very soon, however, it seems to have become desirable to stipulate clearly a delay in payment that owed nothing to the time needed for dispatch. To draw a bill in Genoa payable in Provins on the day of the Saint-Ayoul fair had little meaning if it was not known when the letter would arrive. Whether a month preceded the feast day, or a week, would make quite a difference for the bill. The result, first appearing in the fourteenth century, was a letter of exchange payable at a fixed time—the usance—determined in each market by custom and running from the date of arrival of the letter or, more precisely, from its presentation to the drawer's agent, that is, the person who would have to pay it. On presenting the letter, the beneficiary would be paid within ten days in Venice for a bill coming from Florence, in thirty days in Barcelona for one from Bruges. For a bill of exchange from Italy drawn on London, the usance was to be three months.

The primary reason for the usance was the convenience of the agent, giving him time to find the money either in his business or by negotiating with others. It was also, for the two parties in the place of origin, a period of assured credit. It would have been hard to understand, otherwise, why usance was fixed in proportion to distance—with the journey time obviously being over and above that—and not to the sum in question. Finding a hundred écus to honor a debt was no different, whether the order to pay came from Florence or Montpellier. Usance—a justification and a regulator of interest concealed within the rates of exchange—thus quickly became one of the options available to businessmen from the moment they no longer had to pay for bales of cloth at Lagny but instead could obtain medium-term credit in Genoa or Barcelona, which then could be used for speculation and investment.

Fictitious Exchange and Trade

When presented with a letter of exchange, the drawee had two possible responses. He could accept it—and pay it at usance—or he could refuse it. The statutes of Genoa gave him twenty-four hours to let his choice be known. In fact, the choice was easy; for anyone who knew how to read, it was clear enough.

The only creditor was the taker. There was nothing to be done about someone who refused to pay a bill from Genoa in London. The taker's agent, or drawee, could easily claim that the situation in London was not what the taker in Genoa had believed, and that he did not have the money available. The beneficiary, who had been waiting for money in London, could protest and call on witnesses, but he could not argue about the terms.

He would do better to call a lawyer and have a statement of refusal—a "protest"—drawn up. Some people made life more complicated for themselves by drawing a letter of exchange in the reverse direction: the disappointed beneficiary drew on the drawer in favor of the taker—a procedure of no use to anyone. A simpler response was to return the disputed bill with the protest. The drawer, clearly embarrassed, would repay it to the theoretically aggrieved taker. To insist on payment meant a delay and a lot of lost time. If one wanted a loan, it meant a long period of credit—the time for two journeys. If a verbal agreement had been made at the outset and a market destination chosen according to the period of time desired, a disputed exchange from Florence on London could give a guaranteed six months of credit; the role played by chance was reduced to short-term fluctuations in the money market.

Sixteenth-century documents make it clear that usance should not be paid, and references to the "agreement of *ricorsa*"—return or re-exchange—are not found in documents until after 1550. In the fifteenth century, the "re-exchange" of a bill would have appeared accidental. In reality, from the fourteenth century, bills were returned so frequently that this practice cannot be accounted for simply by defaulting drawers. Someone drawing so often on agents apparently so reluctant to pay would never have kept his clientele. This is clear from Genoese documents, after 1450, that make a point of mentioning unusual protests. The others passed without comment. At the end of the fifteenth century, whatever the actual destination of such letters of protest, Tuscan custom was to speak of "London exchanges."

But, for shorter periods of credit, these "London exchanges" were drawn on Geneva or Barcelona.

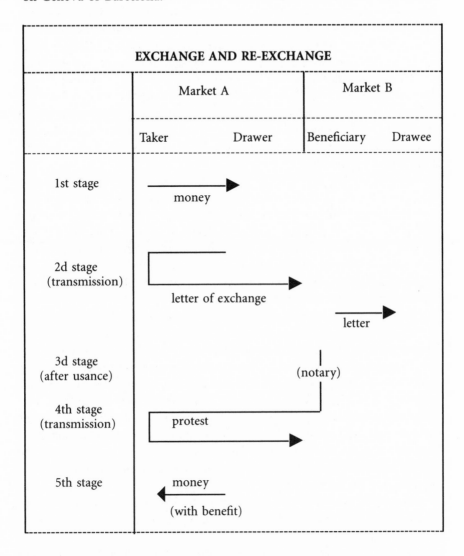

A new usage grew up in the fifteenth century that was to simplify the calculation of the rates of exchange and virtually guarantee the taker's profit. Instead of each market reckoning its own rate of exchange for foreign currencies, the business world gradually came to an agreement whereby certain markets set a fixed rate of exchange. This meant that other markets had to calculate the rate of one local unit according to a varying number of foreign currencies. Italy set the rate for Bruges: if the florin or the ducat in Florence or Venice were already worth a certain number of Flemish *gros,* then the same, in reverse, would apply in Bruges. Venice set the rate for Florence, the exchange rate being expressed as a certain number of Florentine sous to the ducat. At the same time, it became customary for Geneva to set the rate for Genoa, with the écu worth a certain number of Genoese sous.

This might have been nothing more than a matter of monetary vanity, but, in fact, national pride was considered less important than the need to reduce the risks of exchange. A tacit agreement supported a currency's exchange rate, fixed by brokers according to supply and demand and at the highest level in the market that set the rate. For it was the most important market that set the rate.

Even if the bill of exchange was paid—which did not exclude credit, since it was often combined with payment at a distance—the operation was not necessarily concluded with payment in some reliable currency: many businessmen were satisfied simply to have their account credited. But whether or not the payment was made in cash, it was the reciprocal rate of the two stipulated currencies that ensured the creditor's interest. Since the rate was different in the two currencies, the return to the money of origin doubled the interest of the re-exchange.

Despite the disapproval of the Church, "London exchanges" were transacted without even sending a letter of exchange. A Florentine drawer would note down in his books that he owed ten florins payable to Venice in heavy lire. Two weeks later, he would repay his creditor the eleven florins resulting from the re-exchange. A purely notional exchange, relying on the guaranteed difference in the rates between Florence and Venice—where the rate was fixed—this "dry exchange" no longer had anything to do with any kind of commercial trading. And yet it was trade that had made this kind of operation possible. Because the commercial balance of the two towns had formerly been tipped in favor of the great Adriatic port, it had become the custom for Venice to fix the rate for Florence. As everyone knew, the exchange rate was highest in the market that fixed the rate. This was taken into account in the calculations preceding an exchange, and even more so in the case of a re-exchange.

Whatever the advantages of the system for this or that individual, the rates of exchange depended on the financial market. They were particularly sensitive to fluctuations in the balance of exchanges and payments from market to market: a permanent deficit normally made money expensive. But it was known that ultimately the interest rate—the price of money—depended on the quantity of money available for investment. Any rise in the interest rate that increased rates in those principal markets which set the rate caused rates in the unfixed market to lower correspondingly.

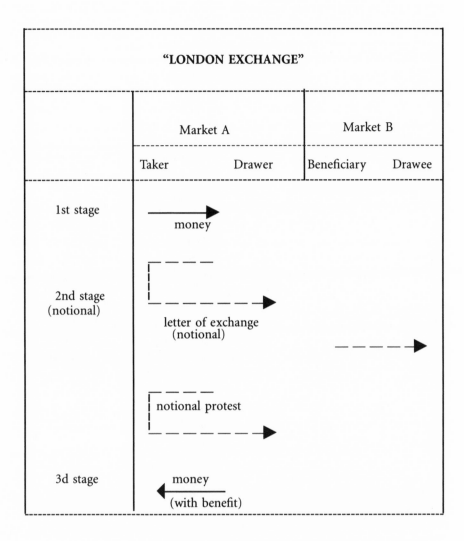

A change in the currency obviously had an immediate effect on exchange rates. Whether it was done for reasons related to the financial market or as a result of internal politics, a devaluation might benefit some people while strengthening the currency would favor others. From the fourteenth century, and as an immediate consequence of the return to bimetallism in a troubled Europe, such monetary change became yet another element to be reckoned with when wrestling with the complexities of rates of exchange and the relationship of gold to silver. Historians have described this period as one of "monetary war," because monetary changes could have the effect of paralyzing the enemy or—by bringing about an exodus of money—harming a neighbor. Although contemporaries often overestimated the frequency and extent of the changes, the rates of exchange in the big markets like Bruges or Genoa also suffered from the effects of the speculative activities of businessmen in quest of profit.

It was not all profit for the *cambiste*. He had his expenses. Exchanges were not always profitable. Around 1450, the Genoese earned overall between 8 and 10 percent annually on "London exchanges." More irregular in his means and ambitions, the *cambiste* in Toulouse made between 3 and 17 percent, but this was in large part thanks to exchanges the interest on which was not entirely commercial. A known and relatively risk-free profit could be made in the important marketplaces. In the less frequented markets, profit was more speculative, and they were used only occasionally by the professional. Thus, it is clear that profits from exchange activities could vary greatly. It was easier, and cheaper, to draw an exchange on Bruges in Florence than on Paris in Le Puy. The papal collectors for the pope in Avignon knew all about this, since they had to transfer their takings to Avignon without making use of the important urban markets of London and Bruges. Unwilling to pay the excessive rates demanded by a money changer or spice merchant from Rennes, Clermont, or Lodève, who would be most unlikely to have an agent or financial counterpart in Avignon, many collectors preferred to take to the road themselves, or send someone with a bag of gold tied to his saddle.

For the letter of exchange to play its full role as an instrument for payment and credit, capable of remedying the shortage of money in medieval Europe, it needed only to be capable of endorsement. It appears that a number of *cambistes* in the fifteenth century came up with this idea that was to greatly facilitate the circulation of bills. In each case it seems to have been regarded as an exceptional procedure, in response to a particular set of circumstances and not to be repeated. No one understood at the time that this was the way forward for banking. All they saw was the immediate convenience of an ad hoc arrangement.

Thus the first endorsed bills were creatures of circumstance. A bill of exchange for 617 francs was drawn in 1410 from Montpellier on Barcelona in favor of Gherardo Cattani of Lucca. Instead of being paid himself, Gherardo endorsed it at the bottom in favor of a fellow countryman. Things became more complicated when the new beneficiary himself attempted to endorse the bill—literally, on the *dorsum* or back:

> In the name of God. 5 February 1410.
>   Pay by this first letter, 16 days after sight, to Gherardo Cattani four hundred and eighty-three *livres*, twelve sous and five *deniers*, that is, £483.

12s. 5d. of Barcelona, for 617 francs 7 sous 8 *deniers* now had by us at 15s. 8d. to the franc. Make good payment and place in the account of Bartolino di Niccolò Bartolini of Paris. Christ keep you. Pay 16 days after sight.

I, Gherardo Cattani, am content that with the abovementioned *deniers* you do the will of Jacopo Accentanti.

Antonio di Neve, of Montpellier. Greetings.

[*On the reverse:*]
I, Jacopo Accettanti, am content that you give for me the said *deniers* to Andrea de' Pazzi and company.

Address:
Francesco di Marco da Prato, in Barcelona.

We do not know why the Florentine Pazzi did not cash the sum written out in words and figures—a precaution that has continued to this day—in the letter of exchange from Montpellier. The endorsement in his favor was crossed out, and Accettanti wrote right after it: "canceled." Then he took his payment. Not for a second did he or Cattani show any awareness of breaking new ground. Cattani simply found it convenient to transfer his credit, and Accettanti was quite ready to do the same.

The pope's Florentine banker who, in 1430, drew an exchange in Rome on Barcelona also saw the convenience in such an arrangement. The drawer was the confessor of Alfonso V of Aragon; the drawee or drawer's agent was the king himself, which is to say his treasurer, who was to pay to the Barcelona branch of the Pazzi company. This was already an unusual bill of exchange, a bond of a cleric who had needed money in Rome, undoubtedly for his master the king, and who is repaying a banker in Barcelona for what he borrowed in Rome. It becomes even more extraordinary when one of the Pazzi partners in Aragon, Francesco Tosinghi, "endorses" the bill in favor, apparently, of the Pazzi's manager in Valencia, where the king happened to be at the time. Was this a real suspension of credit, what the Italians called a *girata* (a "turn-around" or endorsement). It would seem rather that it was a simple acquisition. The beneficiary had no intention of pursuing the king. None of this indicates that they had seen how an endorsement might in future extend the function of the bill of exchange as fiduciary money.

Things were rather different when a well-known London stapler, John Feld, sent some wool to Calais. On 31 October 1447 his agent Lowes Lyneham sold some of it for £247 to a merchant from Bergen, Peter Laurenson. The latter hands over two "letters of payment," one for £124 payable at Whitsun 1448 and the other for £123 payable on the following Michaelmas day. In June 1451 there was still £67 outstanding from the second letter. Tired of trying to get his money, Lyneham passed the letter to a third person, the haberdasher John Petyt. Petyt agreed to return it to Lyneham or to Feld himself if the whole sum was not paid before 1454. In the event, he used it to pay some merchants from Flanders for various goods, the latter merchants ending up as holders of a bond against Peter Laurenson.

Petyt had given Lyneham a guarantee: a bond on the staple of £80. Seeing no sign of his £67, Feld tried unsuccessfully to recover his letter and then insisted that the payment be made. Petyt objected that he had done all that he could, having brought a case against Laurenson in the court in Bergen.

The matter would have been of little importance had it not been for the letter still in circulation and the two bonds traveling in opposite directions. Originally, there had been no bill of exchange, but only a recognition of debt and a guarantee. This did not stop Petyt from using his letter as a means of payment, discounting a sum that he could not himself collect. Of course, the whole process was ruled by the fact that the haberdasher Petyt was, or was thought to be, in a position to make a debtor in Bergen pay up. Here again, in this discounting of a bill, as in the Barcelona endorsement, it was momentary convenience that prompted an ad hoc solution. Two bills are exchanged to avoid a journey. There is a material convenience, but it is in no way a simplification of the procedures. In London, too, they were still far from the monetary flexibility that would come about as a result of endorsement. The idea was not perfected until the sixteenth century, and once again it was the Florentines who got there first.

Even in fifteenth-century Tuscany, they were a long way from the modern bank. As in their accounting methods, everything was in place, but nothing was, as yet, exploited. The essentials were there: a combination of credit and payment; stimulation of business beyond the volume of monetary circulation; an appreciation of how profit and loss relate to distance in economic space and the fixed dates on which loans mature. Constrained by religious objections to the lending of money at interest, the businessman had found, and was beginning to master, the financial techniques and stratagems that would get around these objections. Banking was born of commerce, as much of its needs as of its opportunities. Over the course of three centuries it had evolved its own functions. It had also traced an entirely new financial map for Europe.

THIRTEEN

The Risks of Business

*T*here is rarely profit without risk. It is this same risk, *damnum emergens* or compensation for damages, that theologians eager to unlock the mechanisms of investment recognized as early as the thirteenth century as one of the few justifications for monetary remuneration. Just as farmers, say, are threatened by cold and disease, it was also inherent in commerce, which was threatened by both loss and slump and yet always ready to seize the quick profit at the price of risky operations. From the moment they started to expand, medieval businessmen took a speculative risk. Shipwreck was not the only peril of business.

The Risks

The first risk connected with large-scale trading was, nevertheless, that of loss at sea. There were storms that threatened, delayed, or diverted ships. There was the enemy fleet in time of war and pirates at any time. In fact, land routes were no more secure: wagons were broken by rutted roads, horses gave up in midstream, the woods were riddled with bandits, while a veritable horde of brigands was wont to attack any merchant foolhardy enough to risk crossing the Tuscan Apennines. But the risk of the chosen route is in proportion to the capital expended on it. More is lost if a ship is captured by Barbary pirates than if a packhorse falls into a ravine. Even if the sea routes attracted only heavy goods of little value while luxury items were more often transported by land, the volume of investment in shipping continued to grow with the great fleets from Genoa and the Hanseatic League, with their convoys of wine, salt, or alum, sailing in convoy for mutual protection, but as a result laying themselves open to natural risks and contingencies. The Hanseatic League was forcefully reminded of this when, in 1449, their entire fleet, together with some ships from the Netherlands that had joined them, fell into the hands of the English. One hundred and eight ships were lost in one fell swoop, together with their entire cargo of salt—salt that the fisheries on the Baltic would wait for in vain.

It was not long before the transporters agreed to make financial risks the responsibility of the chartering merchants. The former risked their lives, the latter their money. On balance, the merchants seem to have preferred the risk to any increase in the transport costs. In the majority of ports, it became normal indeed to add an astonishing clause to a contract: the charterer was to pay any ransom demanded should the captain or the crew be captured. The Hanseatic regulations went even further: if any sailor in the hour of danger had made a vow to undertake a pilgrimage, the merchant was to pay the costs of his journey. It is not hard to understand how such stipulations came to be made. When a ship is in danger of sinking, how much is due to the bad weather and how much to the ineptitude of the captain? Was the route chosen the best one? Could the danger have been anticipated? Was the danger so great as to merit a dying vow?

Equally common in the practice of commerce is the risk that comes from fluctuations in the exchange rate. Glut or scarcity of a commodity, varying quality or desirability of a product—all these are elements in the fickleness of a market that the speculator tries to anticipate if not actually to manipulate. A vital factor here was time: time lost on the road, time wasted waiting for a caravan, a protected convoy, or a favorable wind. As the days passed, often in vain, merchandise rarely gained in value; it might well lose value. Even if there were enough clients to go around at the journey's end, the first comer made the best sales. The last might well be left with no clients or nothing more to sell.

These risks also depended for a large part on social and economic structures, which reflect attitudes particular to each country and city. They were slight when a communal organization guaranteed a measure of security. The Venetian convoys, for example, were expensive, but they were escorted, and the reputation of La Serenissima was at stake when it came to the matter of the security of the state's sea trade. They were similarly minimal when the authorities deliberately put a curb on more daring enterprises. Thus, in 1403 the Hanseatic Diet forbade the majority of ships from sailing between St. Martin's Day and the feast of the Chair of St. Peter at Antioch, that is, between 11 November and 22 February. A few exceptions, made in particular for the large Prussian ships well suited to confront the winter storms, meant that this official calendar was not in practice rigorously enforced. Nevertheless, it was able to prevent the loss of many ships that might otherwise have ventured out in unfavorable weather in an attempt to prevent others from profiting from a particular merchandise.

The enforcing of such restrictions meant, of course, that opportunities were missed. When the Hanseatic fleet arrived in Bourgneuf to collect a cargo of salt in 1485, they discovered that there was no salt. Since no one dared risk going elsewhere to take on another cargo, they were ordered to return home, despite the obvious economic madness of such a decision—better an empty ship than a change of plan. By contrast, the risks were all too real whenever individual initiative triumphed over the economic and technical circumstances. In Genoa, a trader could do as he wished, but so could his competitors. He who dares wins—or loses. It was in such a context that the various forms of insurance began to be proposed.

In addition to the natural risks, speculation adds those calculated risks which balance possible losses against increased profits. Used to the challenge of unprotected sea voyages, the Genoese rarely hesitated to take up other equally dangerous journeys. Entrepreneurs less familiar with the risks of sea trade had another view of what is reasonable in business. Chiefly involved in trading by land, the Florentines had been badly burned by the collapse of the banks that had sanctioned, in the 1340s, huge amounts of credit to the princes. They had thus grown wary of excessive risks, incorporating this cautiousness into a governing rule. "Trade less," wrote Giovanni di Paolo Morelli, "but more safely." There could be no stronger condemnation of hazardous speculation.

And yet, what trade does not require an element of calculation? Underlying all contracts is the expectation, or at least the hope, of a profit to be made. Allowing payment on credit obliged the merchant to take account of the possible rise or fall in prices. Who would be so naive as to pay ten sous today for what would be worth only eight tomorrow, particularly if the goods cannot, in any case, be delivered until the day after that. When Veckinchusen, in 1420, thought that the price of French salt would rise, he hastened to place an order. A speculator but no adventurer, Veckinchusen had simply tried—and failed—to take advantage of a good deal.

The most common kind of speculation was the act of buying, stocking a warehouse, and canvassing for markets. The most typical was the bank, with its interaction of fluctuating debits and credits, its moving scale of interest rates at home, and its rates of exchange set from one market for another. Whatever the cost when mistakes were made, the only significant profits seen in medieval business came from dealing in money. In fifteenth-century Florence, profits from the local distributive trades averaged over the years about 8 percent of the invested capital. Major international commerce, with its ability to offer long-distance trade and the secondary industries that it engendered, was able to guarantee a better return of some 12 percent. But these activities—which were due for the most part to the *Arte di Calimala,* the Guild of Cloth Finishers—had to be funded by capital from outside investors, who had to be given a share in the profits. By the time the partners had recovered their contribution of 7 or 8 percent, and other investors had been paid back at a rate of 6 to 10 percent (depending on the lending rate on the market where the price of money depended on its availability or shortage at any given moment), the entrepreneur from the *Calimala* guild was left with a mere 2 to 5 percent profit a year.

To look at these figures, it would seem that the profits made in banking were unequaled. In the case of a simple transfer of funds by contract or bill of exchange where the operation presented no risks—no hard cash changing hands—and where the drawer of the bill of exchange got paid for a transaction and could enjoy the use of the money for several weeks, the profit to the bankers was on the order of 8 to 10 percent. In the case of the very limited risk of lending money to solvent citizens, the net profit could be as much as 15 percent. If the risk was greater—in the case of a foreign borrower or a dangerous enterprise—an annual profit of 30 to 35 percent compensated for any possible losses.

The banker was already taking a risk with the ordinary merchant. The banker to princes had to go further. He speculated on the expectation not of direct remuneration from the loans advanced but rather of what might well be a valuable—though in reality an uncertain—commercial advantage. In addition to the interest on the loan, a banker could hope to receive the net product of increased trade, which would become all the more profitable as the conditions became more advantageous. To lend at 10 percent and to see a relaxation of restrictions and taxes would be all profit if the businessman did not find himself caught within the vicious circle of a financial tie with someone stronger than himself. The advantage was real enough, but the banker knew that he would lose everything if he refused to allow further credit—and he could lose everything on this loan.

Speculation is always tempting. More than by interest, risk was compensated by privileges. Concessions and franchises were obtained by granting credit without necessarily expecting repayment. In this way the king of Sicily financed his monopoly on wheat exports, while the king of England bought free access to his island's wool. Similarly, the pope, by farming out the Tolfa alum trade, made his bankers pay a high price for the monopoly of supplying the industrial markets of Western Europe.

The businessmen of Augsburg were doing something very similar when, taking advantage of the prince's rights over the silver and copper deposits, they made credit available to him, receiving in return free, and carefully measured, access to production from the mines. When, in 1456, the Meuting family lent 35,000 Rhine florins to Count Sigismond of the Tyrol, it was with the guarantee of an allocation from the silver mines. Whether individually or through the intermediary of their municipal government, the citizens of

Augsburg advanced many loans to emperors and princes between the thirteenth and fifteenth centuries, which were repaid to a greater or lesser extent
by privileged access to the mining industry.

But it was just this practice that led to the collapse in 1300 of the
Riccardi company of Lucca, overwhelmed by the loans that it had granted
in both France and England in order to establish its position. Half a century
later, the Peruzzi company had given Edward III credit of 500,000 florins
and Robert of Anjou, king of Naples, 100,000. The Bardi went even further,
advancing 900,000 to the English king and 100,000 to Robert. During the
same period—the 1340s, which were to see the collapse of those apparently
impregnable fortresses, the great Florentine companies—a merchant of far
more modest standing in comparison with the Bardi or Peruzzi, Tidemann
Limberg of Dortmund, was able to lend Edward III £14,000 sterling. When
it came to repayment he was no luckier than, in the following century,
Hildebrand Veckinchusen who had lent 3,000 crowns to the emperor of
Luxemburg, Sigismond.

They had witnessed the bankruptcies of the 1300s and the 1340s. But
history was to repeat itself. The Mannini company of Florence had, in 1395,
advanced in Paris the money needed for the forthcoming marriage of the
king of England, Richard II, to Isabella, daughter of Charles VI. With Richard
II overthrown and the rapprochement with France now a vain dream, the
Mannini were ruined. The Lancastrian monarch, Henry IV, was not prepared
to pay off debts contracted by someone he had just ousted in order to
seal a policy of which he disapproved. The Mannini were bankrupted. A
compatriot, Deo Ambrogi, was nevertheless prepared to take on their loan,
thus acquiring at a low price what might be an advantageous position in
England if the alliance with France was revived. Ambrogi was risking everything on a marriage between the widow of Richard II and Richard's usurper,
Henry. He was to waste both his time and his money. When, in 1420, Henry
V of Lancaster married Catherine of France, another daughter of Charles
VI, the banker was no longer alive to remind him of the Mannini loan.

Naturally, some princes were more reliable than others, but the business
world rarely had a choice in such matters. The most they could do was to
hope for future favors, or possibly even reimbursement, or otherwise put
it down to profit and loss. The citizens of Nuremberg followed this course
in 1437, when they were obliged to lend 2,000 guilders to Emperor Sigismond—though, in fact, he had asked for 4,000. The council carefully set
aside the recognizance of debt sealed with the royal seal. But the town
treasurer, a realist, entered the sum in his accounts as "given" to the emperor.
On the assumption that they would never see their 2,000 guilders again, it
simplified his account books.

Tax-farming and similar leases were equally risky, but this did not stop big and small speculators alike from eagerly competing for them. The system was simple: the prince or town auctioned the right to collect a particular tax or toll, the yield of which was unknown. The successful bidder paid—for one or several years—the price of his bid, after which any taxes he levied went to him alone. He might farm a tax on the passage of goods, on wholesale sales, on retail, or consumption. In France this was called the *aide*, in Italy the *gabella*. There were taxes to be farmed on the activities of the mints, mines, or salt pans. In 1346, Tidemann Limberg obtained the lease to farm the Cornish zinc mines. In 1466, the Medici offered two florins per *cantaro*—50–80 kilograms—of alum extracted at Tolfa. During the same period, Tommaso Portinari outbid the Arnolfini of Lucca, obtaining for himself and for the Medici the right to farm the *tonlieu* at Gravelines, in other words, the tax on coastal traffic between Calais and the Netherlands. This was a daring move, since speculation on Anglo-Burgundian relations, at a time when the future Charles the Bold was beginning to take over power from the aging Philip the Good, appeared extremely risky.

Speculation is simple even if the considerations involved are complex. If the market was favorable, the tax-farmer kept the entirety of the difference between what he had levied and what he had to pay for the lease of the farm. In reality, the prince and the town were better able than the farmer to protect themselves from accidents of circumstance. If the excitement of the auction or the competitiveness of the bidders pushed the price of a lease too high, it meant certain ruin for the taker. If there was a slump, a collapse in indirect taxation would follow. The summer might be wet and the salt pans cost more to keep going than they earned. At the same time, finance officers did everything they could to limit the excessive profits that a tax-farmer could make at the end of a prosperous year or in a suddenly expanding market. In France, someone who paid a hundred *livres* for the lease of a collection that turned out to be particularly profitable might lose his lease at the end of three months if some other candidate, unsuccessful at the first auction, offered to *tiercer*—to pay an extra third—thus taking over from the first farmer. The latter would have taken all the risks at a time when the profitability of the farm was not entirely clear; now he might have it taken away from him if the gain began to exceed a third of the price he had paid. Economic growth was thus of little benefit to anyone but the king. Similarly the Apostolic Chamber, in leasing the alum rights to the Medici, stipulated that, whatever happened, the pope should receive two florins per *cantaro*, and that an extra third should be added if the price of alum exceeded three florins.

At the end of the century, Jacob Fugger was repaid for his loans to the Habsburgs with rights to the production of silver from the Tyrolean mines—a more secure guarantee since it was less dependent on political circumstances.

When he financed Maximilian's wars against Venice, Fugger was unlikely to run the risk of seeing the seams of silver-bearing copper dry up.

Such tax-farming leases were, then, limited speculations in which the risk was all too real and the profits limited. In reality, there was nothing in common between the Medici bidding for the papal alum, or Jacques Coeur acquiring the farm of salt pans in Languedoc, and the butcher of Rouen who acquired the right to farm the tax on butchers' stalls for twenty francs. The big businessman could speculate on the commercial advantages that might be gained from leasing exploitation rights that would give him at least a local monopoly. He put in the highest bid in order to cut out others, control an integrated trade, and set up his own economic empire. When Augustin Ysbarre and his sixteen partners paid half a million *livres tournois* for the right to farm the exploitation of the seven mints that supplied the entire coinage for Burgundian France, they, like Biche and Mouche a century earlier, had their eye on controlling the movement of money and the market in precious metals in the kingdom. The butcher, by contrast, was looking for no more than a bit of profit on the side, an occasional investment: he speculated on medium-term profit, not on his entire economic standing.

The right to farm the toll on the high road through the Bussy gate in Paris was awarded, in 1450, for seven *livres* to a man who was placing all his hopes on a recovery of overland trade. If lucky, he might have made, at best, a profit of three or four *livres*. As it turned out, things went badly, and the following year no one was prepared to take over the farm for more than four *livres*. The most important of the farms offered by the Parisian administration was that of the tax on *pied fourché* (cloven-footed), that is, on bringing game into town, which could cost between three and six thousand *livres*—depending on the year—to acquire. But even this offered each of the four or five businessmen who grouped together to bid for it a net profit of barely two or three hundred *livres*. Tax-farmers were always threatened by a possible deficit, as four prosperous Parisians found to their cost in 1462. These solid citizens, well-known innkeepers like Robert Turgis—landlord of the *Pinecone*, patronized by the poet François Villon—or respected wine merchants on the Place de Grève, had thought they were on to a good thing when they successfully acquired a group of farming rights on the sale of both wholesale and retail wine; they were wrong. These often quite modest speculative ventures sometimes led to a court case followed by financial ruin.

Though still quite limited, real profits started to show only after the passage of time, when good years could balance bad and risky farms could be offset by the relative security of other enterprises. Like all gamblers, unlucky speculators had to wait for their luck to change. The modest farmer of the taxes due from the five Parisian leather guilds—harness makers, tanners, dressers, stitchers, and purse makers—petitioned French treasury officials in 1493: "That it might be their pleasure, in order to compensate him for the said losses, to lease to him the said farm of the five guilds for the following four years." They had learned the lesson that there could be no real profit except in the long term and then only for those with the means to spread their investments. Though a good deal for those whose fortune was already made, speculation on the setting of taxes could be a bitter disappointment for those who expected too much from a farm and started afresh ten times over in the hope of recovering their losses; speculation could only widen the gulf between those who succeeded and those who failed.

Other risks, however, resulted from the structural weaknesses of business. The dangers of overspecialization had been realized early on. Bankers understood this well and did their best to avoid overloading the banking side of their enterprises. The collapse of the Buonsignori company in Siena in 1298, no less than the bankruptcies in Lübeck in the fifteenth century, had demonstrated the ephemeral nature of credit. The 1300s saw the sorry effects of fierce competition that simultaneously carried off the Riccardi, Mozzi, Franzesi, Frescobaldi, and Scali companies.

Most important, it was from this time forward that the risks facing the businessman encumbered with open-access deposits became apparent. In 1318, from assets of 1,266,775 pounds, the nominal capital of the Bardi company was only 100,000 pounds, less than a twelfth. Many companies tried to limit their vulnerability by accepting only restricted-access deposits, but the depositor was not blind and placed a price on his trust: a deposit that was not returnable on demand was remunerated with a higher rate of interest. Thus the banker paid for his peace of mind by a marked reduction in profit margins that were, as we know, already slim.

This vulnerability put the banker at the mercy of rumors, uninformed predictions, and the speculator's expectations. Bad news could turn into panic in no time at all. Everyone rushed to be first to be paid while there was still money in the coffers. And yet, of course, a company took deposits only in order to increase its investments. There would have been no point in serving interest on money kept in cash.

So no one was in a position to reimburse depositors if they all presented themselves at the same moment. In 1342, there was panic at the doors of the Florentine bankers in Naples when the news arrived of Florence's rapprochement with Ludwig of Bavaria and thus of her move away from the Angevin camp with Naples at its head. There followed a rapid succession of bankruptcies. The Dell'Antella, Buonaccorsi, Cocchi, Perondoli, Corsini, and Castellani banks all closed their doors. The following year, the same nervousness seized Florence when news came of Edward III's defeat in Flanders. The Peruzzi had invested too much in Flanders for them not to be losers. In turn, the Peruzzi's failure brought the Acciaiuoli down with them. Three years later, in 1346, the aftershock reached the strongest fortress in the world of banking: the Bardi stopped all payments.

And yet, despite the cost in terms of depositors, even the most secure businessman could not avoid committing his money to loans. There were plenty of Parisian bankers, involved in some way in the business affairs of a faction, party, or prince, who would be ruined as a result of the successive political reversals during the difficult years of the civil war. They lost their loans on the assassination of Louis of Orleans, as they were victims in 1413 of the Armagnac reaction against the financial pillars of a Burgundian power brought into disrepute by its Cabochien allies. The turmoil created by a Burgundian return in 1418 destroyed them utterly. It also spelled ruin for those in the Armagnac faction who had prevaricated, along with those businessmen who had halfheartedly sided with a "peace faction" after having reluctantly supported the Armagnac side.

In this alternating pattern of banishment, violence, and even massacre, the ruin of a second wave of businessmen did not further the fortunes of the first to be ruined. Political misfortune was all the more likely to turn to mercantile catastrophe when business was so clearly linked to the exercise of power. The Pazzi conspiracy of 1478, directed against the policies of the Medici rulers in Florence, undermined the standing of their financial enterprise even though it had by that time ceased to be the foundation of the Medici's power. When Charles VIII's arrival on the scene led to the collapse in 1494 of Cosimo de' Medici, Lorenzo the Magnificent's incompetent successor, it meant also the final collapse of a company that was already fragile—badly managed by Giovanni Tornabuoni, who had failed to see the direction events were taking, and further weakened by the excessive spending of a young man who had become a cardinal at the age of thirteen, the future Leo X, Giovanni de' Medici. When, in 1547, a member of the Medici family became queen of France, the bank whose name she bore had long since ceased to exist, not because it was no longer of use to the future grand dukes of Tuscany but because it had failed. A banker was not a prince and could not always stage a return from exile.

From Caution to Sterility

For all that, it was necessary to live amid such perils. Nobody forgot that risks justified profit. But it was always possible to limit the effects.

The first cautionary measure was to have access to precise and speedy information. It was essential for the speculator to know the future plans of well-placed people. It was necessary to be able to see war or peace coming, to know what would sell, how one's partners' credit stood. An informant on the spot could be of inestimable value. A confidential note from the

Florentine lawyer Ser Lapo Mazzei to the agent Luca del Sera of November 1407 warns:

Cristofano:

> He is in difficulties. According to the rumors and the opinion of others, he is in debt in Florence and elsewhere. I do not think that his eight hundred florins are worth up to a thousand, for he has no credit.

Timely precautions were not, however, a substitute for structural arrangements. Several types of capitalism were in existence only as precautions against an excessive concentration of risks. The grouping of companies under a collective name, such as Datini set up around 1390, was nothing more than independence inspired by caution. The autonomy of capital in its branches had no other purpose, in the great fifteenth-century companies, than to protect the collective against the risks lying in wait in each and every market and enterprise.

More simply, every businessman had long known that the only way to balance good investments against bad ones was through diversification—of horizons, merchandise, and activities. By taking on a variety of enterprises in varied and often quite modest operations, businessmen from Venice, Lübeck, or Toulouse had begun early on to practice a form of elementary, but generally effective, self-insurance.

The measures quietly introduced in the 1300s by the Florentine companies and, at the end of the century, by those of Lucca, who were equally concerned that competition between compatriots should not turn to the disadvantage of all, can also be seen as a type of precaution against risk. Dividing up risks was one thing; but it was important not to aggravate them by being divided among themselves. As became clear from the first great failures, excessive profits from solitary speculation were always short-lived.

During this same time, business circles began to discover the advantages of secure investments in which a small return was balanced by a smaller risk. The short-term view of adding to profits—or losses—through a series of unrelated operations now seemed outmoded. Eventually, proper long-term investment plans were constructed, naturally little more than an empirical reaction to a succession of opportunities, but leading, nevertheless, to the creation of an estate expected to last several generations.

Merchants began to look toward the rural economy, hitherto regarded only as a supplier or a client. Well before being seized by the desire to play the landowner, they could see that land represented something solid that was lacking in their carefully constructed world of speculative activities and perishable goods. The climate could, of course, be unreliable and harvests could be bad, but this was nothing compared to the variability of fashion or changes in the market resulting from war or peace. It was precisely because business yielded relatively high returns that the merchant could allow himself the reassurance of a part investment, with low returns but guaranteed in the long term. Capital in the form of land had not disappeared.

From the thirteenth century, the middle classes began to put money into purchases of land: generally small holdings or manors from which, like any landowner, they received an income expressed in the picturesque, colorful, but no longer strictly accurate style of the old accounts as follows:

> *Item* 60 capons in rent per year, each capon valued at 8 *deniers parisis*, or 40 sous.
>
> *Item* 40 hens in rent per year, each hen being valued at 6 *deniers parisis*, or 20 sous.
>
> *Item* Christmas loaves, about fifty per year, each loaf valued at 4 *deniers parisis*, or 16 sous 8 *deniers*.
>
> *Item* Christmas round loaves in exchange for forest grazing rights, estimated to be worth per year 5 sous.
>
> *Item* sales and forfeitures, valued per year at 10 sous.
>
> *Item* 850 eggs in rent per year, each hundred valued at 14 *deniers parisis*, or 9 sous 11 *deniers*.
>
> *Item* a goose each year in rent on Saint-Rémi's day, for the price of 12 *deniers parisis*.
>
> *Item* half a pound of almonds per year at a price of 4 *deniers parisis*.

Not for a long time had landowners levied the half hens and half pairs of gloves owed on some feudal estates. Nor were they content any longer to receive fifty loaves on Christmas day and nothing for the rest of the year. In the early fourteenth century, when citizens of Reims already owned a quarter of the land—and often the best land—in the surrounding countryside, it was paid for in silver, in a handful of coins, which, by their small number, would be the ruin of a social class whose power was too exclusively based on ownership of land. These low rents favored purchases: land was sold cheap as, in the late thirteenth and early fourteenth centuries, the income from land gradually dried up. Valuations generally retained a capital value equal to ten years of revenue. Though not expecting more than a secondary profit, the merchant could not resist purchasing a few parcels of land.

By the fifteenth century, having by now gotten hold of considerable portions of land in the form of farms, tenures, villeins' fiefs, vavasories, plots of land given over to wheat, patches of pasture, and rows of vines, the businessman perceived the need to consolidate this piecemeal collection and even to buy whole estates. He introduced innovations into the rural economy, including speculative agriculture, in which the harvest might be risked, but never the land itself. Furthermore, he was able to initiate procedures tried and tested elsewhere into the management of these landed estates.

Regional resources permitting, businessmen were not reluctant to integrate their rural activities into the network of their urban trade. For someone speculating in the short term on wool from sheep on the hoof belonging to others, there was nothing odd about investing another portion of his capital, in the medium term, in sheep rearing. The Languedoc *gazaille* contract offered, with its equivalent of a loan guaranteed by livestock, an investment as attractive as one in a bank but better protected. Because of the importance of woolen cloth in both regional and international trade, the business world everywhere had a great interest in sheep rearing, which led to research into investments and the control of supplies. Such were the activities of the English woolmen and, in Tuscany, the capitalists of the *Calimala* and wool guilds. Integration and security developed hand in hand.

Such investments were still primarily concerned with economic matters. Although mortal, a sheep was less ephemeral than the rate of exchange. If disease did not strike down the herd, a sheep could serve as interest. Things were rather different when the businessman, in search of a secure home, decided to manifest his wealth and splendor in stone on the outskirts of his hometown. There is no doubt that such displays were in large part a normal expression of bourgeois vanity. The days of communal rivalry were over, when towns had been prepared to pay huge sums in order to ensure that the vaults of their cathedral rose higher than those of their neighbors. The fourteenth century saw the arrival of personal ostentation and the beginning of the great merchant dynasties. Taking the form of town houses at first, then grand country houses, the passion for building seized a social class that hitherto had spent all its money on goods. The sums spent on appearances, represented by decor and collections of painting, furniture, and other objects, soared, as the following description attests:

> The door of the *hôtel* was carved with wonderful artistry. In the court-yard were peacocks and other decorative birds.
>
> The first room was enriched with various paintings and instructive texts, attached to and hanging from the walls. Another room was full of all sorts of instruments, harps, organs, hurdy-gurdys, citterns, psalteries and others, all of which the said Master Jacques knew how to play. Another room was furnished with chessboards, tables, and other types of games, in great number.
>
> *Item* a beautiful chapel, where there were desks on which to lay books of wonderful manufacture, which could be drawn up to various seats, far or near, to the right and the left.
>
> *Item* a study where the walls were covered with precious stones and sweet-smelling spices.
>
> *Item* a chamber in which were furs of a variety of kinds.
>
> *Item* several other rooms equipped with beds, tables ingeniously carved and adorned with rich covers and tapestries of gold thread.
>
> *Item* in another chamber was a large number of crossbows, some painted with beautiful figures. There, too, were standards, banners, pennons, hand bows, pikes, faussarts, bucklers, axes, guisarmes, chain-mail of iron and lead,

pavises, targes, shields, cannons and other devices, with every kind of armor. And, briefly, there were all things necessary to war.

Item there was a window made with wonderful skill, through which one could put a head made of sheets of metal through which one could look and converse with those people outside. . . .

Item at the very top of the building was a square room with windows on every side in order to look out over the whole of the town. When it was used for dining, wines and meats were brought up by means of a pulley, because it would have been too high to carry them up.

And above the pinnacles of the *hôtel* were beautiful gilded statues.

This description, from the time of Charles VI, is of the residence of an important Parisian citizen, clerk of the accounts Jacques Duché, heir of an already wealthy merchant family. Duché was by now an eminent figure, distancing himself from the mercantile activities of his family. Nevertheless, this *hôtel* on the Rue des Prouvaires was exceptional, causing much talk, including this description in which Guillebert of Metz exalts the splendors of the 1400s in order to contrast them with the harshness of the following decades. We should not imagine that every Parisian merchant around 1400 had this number of weapons—sufficient to withstand a siege—nor would he have given concerts using his collection of instruments. Master Jacques Duché's *hôtel* represented, nevertheless, an ideal that caused the passerby to stop and dream and corresponded well to a certain model of middle-class investment.

Bourgeois opulence was always in part self-advertisement, even when local customs reserved the sight and knowledge of such riches for the initiates. The *popolo minuto* saw only the austere facades of the Italian *palazzi* from the street; the world of business prided itself on being allowed to penetrate inside. These investments in stone, tapestry, frescoes or rubies, though unproductive, nevertheless represented an essential part of insurance against misfortune.

This can be seen clearly when the craftsman had to value a particular jewel of exquisite workmanship: the only thing that counted was what could be measured and what could be melted down: pearls, precious stones, gold. In the inventory of the crowns and hair ornaments brought from Italy by Valentina Visconti on the occasion of her marriage to Louis of Orleans, the estimated value amounted to scarcely 5 percent of the cost of fabrication, often by famous goldsmiths. At this price the jewels were, like the merchant's stock or coffer, a reserve, used to raise cash in difficult times and restored when prosperity returned. Even if the gold was not melted down every year, the loss—compensated, on another level, by changes in fashion—was generally less than losses incurred through erosion in the value of money. A crown of gold and rubies for a prince, a ewer of incised silver for a great merchant, or a chaplet for a child all represented secure investments, giving pleasure rather than paying interest, but always available in case of need.

When the fashion for building in stone and decorative opulence coincided with the race for public office and power, as was the case in Parisian society after 1450, expenses on appearances triumphed over the search for security. Even if such expenditure provided employment in particular trades, from the embroiderer to the mason, the result was to direct capital away from economic investment.

Another form of protection from the risks of speculation, which began to take on increasing importance in the fifteenth century, was *rente*. For two or three centuries, landed estates, both in town and in the country, had already taken an extra portion from property that yielded only a moderate return by charging an extra perpetual rent, a sum payable at the outset. This way it was possible to get twenty *livres* straightaway. This rent had to be paid twice a year, in perpetuity. The landowner thus found himself tied down to a mortgage. The *rentier*, on the other hand, did very well in the long term. It was even more profitable for someone who, at a later date, redeemed a *rente* due to be repaid. Of course, the sum was quoted at the rate of the cost of the money, but it represented excellent security.

In hard times, when the owner of land or a mortgaged house could no longer pay the *rente* since he had long since stopped drawing any profit from the borrowed money, the property had to be put up for sale. The person best placed to make a purchase at low price was, of course, the *rentier*. Originally *rente* had been an investment without much breadth and without risk. It became a stepping-stone in amassing estates for those—important townsmen, advocates and notaries, magistrates and tax officials, businessmen—who had available both capital with which to buy and the influence that went with holding *rentes*.

State revenue bonds did not give the same results though they normally offered similar advantages insofar as security was concerned. Bonds in the municipal credit banks of the Italian towns, like the various *Monti de' Paschi* and the *Casa di San Giorgio*, represented safe investments yielding a limited return. Speculation in this area was necessarily limited to buying low and selling high. The swings were small and rarely risky, since rates were quoted according to the date of maturity. But investors got back their investment and the system could sometimes be convenient, as in Genoa, for the movement of funds within the confines of the city.

For a long time the mounting debt in the towns had been one of the principal causes of social tension. The patricians in charge of municipal government thoughtlessly encouraged public borrowing, approving good rates and making repayment possible by widening the tax burden. Thus the poorest taxpayer was paying for the income of the rich. When sovereign power became involved, as in France at the time of St. Louis and Philip the Fair, this debt gave royal officials the excuse they were looking for to interfere in municipal affairs. The king was able to make decisions about how the tax burden should be distributed, suppressing the more extreme speculation, and taking permanent control of the function of municipal institutions. Most important, the officials of the accounts and the bailiffs and seneschals organized a radical financial shake-up that was often called a "consolidation" of the debt. Nevertheless, and despite the king's admonitions, the victims of this consolidation, involving the repayment of capital without interest—"usury"—even though it was due, knew exactly what they were doing when they went out and bought more bonds on a town grossly in debt. Such was the case in Noyen:

> In that the town would be too hard pressed to pay such a large sum, they petition our lord the king that he allow them to lower the interest rates.
>
> And for those who wish to receive payment for their life bonds, that the interest be deducted from their sum, since they will have received more than the capital.
>
> And it seems to the auditors of the accounts that these people bought very riskily what they have bought since the ban issued by our lord the king, that is, ten years ago.

There was a collapse of confidence. More bonds had been sold than the town could pay for. The time of expansion—the thirteenth century, when merchant aristocracies had not found it unreasonable to assume a continuation of such growth—was over. It was time to confine oneself to what was possible. Just as war and the costs of fortification and garrisoning led to a more precise method of accounting in municipal expenditure, so the economic crises and the resultant aftershocks felt in prices, salaries, and monetary rates led to greater caution in the anticipation of revenue. From the fourteenth century, bonds became a safe investment for nervous citizens and clerics and, for businessmen concerned with securing a portion of easily available money, a very convenient complementary investment.

Whether it went for prestige spending or cautious investments, all this was deducted from the global mass of capital available for investment. This was all too apparent when, in the fifteenth century, a Parisian marketplace was wiped off the map. The more important activities were now connected with those trades catering to a modest middle-class opulence—the mercers even took over one of the galleries at the Palais—and trades involving building, food, and service. Parisians were acquisitive, like the rich money changer Jean Taranne, beheaded in 1418 by the head executioner, the sinister Capeluche. Taranne owned two town houses, a *hôtel* in Saint-Germain-des-Prés, and three estates, at Chaillot, Vanves, and Saint-Cloud, that provided him with all the trappings of a lord, not to mention an excellent wine for his cellar—Chaillot was a much-prized wine—and wood for the winter.

Richard Le Pelletier, an important citizen of Rouen, represents another type of person and another kind of economic sterility. He invested widely all over the Normandy countryside, his descendants eventually joining the ranks of the nobility. In twenty years, from 1450 to 1471, he bought up no less than thirty-nine *rentes* on landed property and thirty-seven fiefs of varying importance.

Although more interested in investing in real business deals where returns were based to a larger extent on speculation, even Jacques Coeur found a certain reassurance in land and stone: as well as his palace in Bourges, there were houses and châteaux with their estates in Berry, not to mention profitable properties and vineyards in Burgundy.

And he was not the only one. Tidemann Limberg bought fiefs in eight counties of southern England, previously held by the Benedictine priory of Wilmington in Sussex from the king. In Lübeck, Heinrich Castorp took over the mortgages of some forty houses. In Metz, the nephews of the great banker Philippe Le Gronnais—creditor until his death in 1314 to the duke and all the aristocracy of Lorraine—were, as early as the 1340s, able to live on their revenues and landed property. They never returned to trade.

The careful risk-taking of the Florentine businessmen shows us the extent of the desire to insure against risk, and the caution that would lead to immobility. The director of the Medici company, Francesco di Tommaso Sassetti, himself invested, between 1462 and 1466, only 68.6 percent of his available funds in the company that he managed, whether as nominal capital or as deposits. Furthermore, he divided these investments among four branches of the company. By contrast, he had used 11.6 percent to buy property in Florence and the surrounding countryside. Purchases of furniture, books, and plate accounted for 19.8 percent. One florin out of three had gone into unproductive investments. Nevertheless, two out of three florins were invested in the Medici firm—something that in 1489–90 the ruined Sassetti, after his desperate attempt to rescue the Lyons branch, was to rue to his dying day.

In Venice, where regulations imposed by the state on business activities limited risk, we see the guardians of the young children of Andrea Barbarigo investing some 10 percent of their inheritance in economic enterprises. The rest went to buy a house on the Grand Canal, estates on the mainland near Verona and Treviso—as well as a property in Crete, bought by Andrea—and bonds in the public debt.

The most extreme example was that of Cosimo de' Medici, "the Great." In 1460, at the peak of his company's fortunes, half his personal fortune was invested in *luoghi* in the *Monte*, in other words, in state loans. And the lord of Florence speculated only in a small way, buying at the right time when there was a crisis.

The slowing down was obvious. As they grew rich, businessmen began to put down roots. Let the ambitious merchant take risks, it was not something for persons of rank. Long before snobbery required the descendant of a merchant to keep quiet about the origins of the family fortune in trade, success brought about a *rentier* mentality. Few bourgeois families now continued to play a role in economic life for more than three generations. Of course, some families would have disappeared from the ranks of society had they hesitated in the face of the cost of marriage and keeping up appearances. But this was not what was happening here: the great families once prominent in business were still present in the town two centuries later, only now they had changed occupation. The Braques, Barbous, Barbettes, Bourdons, and Genciens who had made their fortunes, and are recorded as being among the most highly taxed people in the Paris of 1300, have disappeared from the tax rolls in the years 1420–35. Some were in the Parliament, in the Audit Office, the Court of Aids, comfortably supported by landed revenue and guaranteed pledges. Still in the rolls is one obscure Barbette, the cloth merchant Jean Marcel, last of an illustrious line of cloth merchants and money changers. But he and his family had long since made their exit from center stage.

Toward Insurance.

It was possible to limit the risks of business by pulling out, dividing, or piling up one's capital. It was also possible to attack head-on the material risks that were, above all, derived from the insecurity of land and sea routes. Larger ships—nefs—were proving better able to withstand storms, ensuring a better return on capital by reducing or eliminating the dead season and by transporting cargoes that were more important and hence more easily diversified. By transporting coral at the same time as grain, or amber with wood, the risks of selling at a loss were lessened. Slump, whether general or local, the result of time passing or competition in the marketplace, rarely hit both pepper and cotton at the same time. The increase in tonnage also favored the division of shares in ships and cargoes, another effective means of minimizing risks. A Hanseatic ship lost at sea in 1345 had been chartered by twenty-six merchants; another, in 1430, by thirty-nine. In 1468, following a shipwreck, sixty-two merchants were found to have an interest. The number of merchants bearing a loss continued to increase, but each one held only a very small share in the enterprise, which represented an equally small part of his total business.

Better designed to deal with natural adversity, the merchant ship was also better defended against human predators. The Hanseatic League provided escorts for its salt fleet. Jacques Coeur supplied his merchant galleys with strong artillery. Venice dispatched its armed convoys of state ships in all directions. No one in Venice thought about the technicalities of financial insurance: better to rely on the merchant's astuteness in choosing, in accordance with his knowledge of the prevailing risks, between the cumbersome state convoy and private ships, which were less expensive but also less secure.

Financial insurance answered another need: that of spreading the risks without any diminution of initiative. It was important to be able to do what one wanted at the moment one wanted to, without having to bear sole responsibility for all the risks. This coincidence of individualism and speculation was to lead to the birth of modern insurance in those spheres of business where daring was tempered with a mistrust of excessive risks. In Genoa and Florence, a cautious start was made in introducing the procedures of marketing and banking. A form of insurance—at first more a state of mind—developed from these beginnings. Italy was to adopt it very quickly, with the one exception of Venice, which had its own form of insurance. As with the majority of the intellectual techniques that emerged from the Italian melting pot, the rest of Europe adopted them only more slowly, and not until the sixteenth century.

A relatively simple step in this direction occurred with the involvement, in the thirteenth century, of a third party, who had not had any part in the commercial operation at its inception. He made his own very speculative profit from his role in supporting the first merchant. A simulated sale was sufficient to transfer responsibility, along with the property. Thus we find the Genoese Benedetto Zaccaria selling, in 1298, to his compatriots Enrico Suppa and Baliano Grilli 650 *cantari* of alum—more than thirty tons—that a ship was getting ready to transport from Aigues-Mortes to Bruges by way of the direct sea route that until recently had filled the Italians with alarm. Zaccaria agreed from the moment of signing to buy back the alum in question as soon as it arrived in Bruges. The price of the repurchase was agreed to in advance: naturally it would be higher than the price of the sale. The difference between the two prices would be what it cost Zaccaria to limit his risks: between Aigues-Mortes and Bruges he was risking nothing other than his boat. During this period, exchange transactions were becoming more sophisticated. Selling alum in Aigues-Mortes did not yield the money for repurchase in Bruges. In Bruges, Suppa and Grilli thus lent Zaccaria the sum needed for him to buy back the cargo from them. The loan was effected by a bill of exchange, payable in Genoa.

In other words, the two Genoese received no payment in Bruges, where, on this occasion, they had no reason to go. In the first stage, they paid the price of the alum. At the end of the transaction, following the time needed for the voyage and the exchange, they were paid in Genoa, with a profit.

In the meantime, Zaccaria had sold his alum in Bruges and financed his return cargo with the price he received.

It was a complex operation, involving both insurance and credit. Zaccaria had risked only his ship. For several months he had had the benefit of the price of a cargo of alum that he had sold for ready money and bought back on credit in order to sell it again for cash. As for Suppa and Grilli, they had earned 26 percent, more than twice the simple lending rate, in a credit operation without risk.

A century and a half later, the Genoese still used this method, regarding it as a useful way of supplying credit for maritime ventures. Elsewhere, insurance in the full sense of the word was not usually sought in a market where risk seemed as normal a part of the long sea voyages to the Atlantic or the North Sea as was trade with the East. It had so low a priority that, at a time when roads were so unsafe, no one could imagine insuring land-based commerce. It was, of course, unlikely that the fifty or sixty wagons that formed veritable caravans of copper traveling between the Tyrol and Venice would all overturn at once, losing an entire cargo—equivalent in mass to that in a single ship. The Zaccaria-style fictitious sale insured the cargoes at sea because it financed them. Despite bandits in the Alps and Apennines, the wagons traveling up and down the continental routes did not call for such financing. It was the massive scale of maritime trade that gave rise to insurance.

Outside Italy, different methods emerged for limiting the risks of commercial investment. Many of the loans pledged against merchandise—known as bottomry loans—were a happy combination, as in the Genoese system, of the opening of an account and the transfer of risk. If the cargo disappeared, the pledge vanished; there would be no reimbursement. As ever, it was necessary to justify the difference between the money earned and the money paid back. Although complicated, the Genoese system had the advantage of simplicity at the end of the transaction: the merchant dealing with the transport—Zaccaria in the example given here—had merely to opt for repurchase or to abandon his claim. The secured loan favored by the French and English put the lender-insurer in a delicate legal position before the courts—that of usurer.

The most skillful operators in the end were the Florentines, who preferred to view insurance simply as a specific risk transaction, but one extended to the most diverse risks and essentially different from the financing of commerce. In Florence, it was not a matter of selling and repurchasing but of recouping, through insurance, the value of a transaction that had concluded unsuccessfully, because of either a lost cargo or an unlucky piece of speculation. This type of insurance—known as *alla fiorentina* although it originated at the same time in Pisa—was nothing other than insurance as we know it today, premium insurance. From 1320 onward, the commercial operator or banker is found to pay a premium, before embarking on a business deal, equivalent to the difference found in the Genoese system between the selling price and the cost of repurchase. The premium was the reward for the person taking the risk for him. No credit is involved here; it is purely and simply a surety.

> On 7 September, in favor of Baldo Ridolfi and associates, we insured for one hundred gold florins the wool transported from Peniscola to Porto Pisano in the ship of Guilhem Sale, of Catalonia. And for the said hundred florins we received in cash three gold florins, and we insured against all risks, as it appears in the deed drawn up by Gherardo di Ormanno, signed with our hand.
> The said ship arrived safe and sound in Porto Pisano and unloaded in October 1384, and we are discharged of the insurance.

> On 10 September, in favor of Ambrogio di Bino Bini, we insured for two hundred gold Milan ducats the cloth transported from Porto Pisano to Palermo in the ship of Bartolomeo Vitale. And for the said two hundred ducats we received eight ducats, and charged the debt to the account of Ambrogio, page 174, and no deed was drawn up by the hand of any person.
> Arrived safe and sound in Palermo.

For the businessman who got himself insured, the advantages were obvious. The Florentine system did not require the same movement of money as that of the clumsy Genoese system, nor the dubious use of the secured loan. The price of the insured deal was not estimated in the fluctuating money rates except in the case of a loss. Usually the business went no further than the payment of the premium—3 or 4 percent for a crossing in the western Mediterranean. Procedure could be simplified, which in turn generated a greater use of insurance. Thus it is that the simple *schedula*, drawn up by a specialized broker and signed by the insurer, begins to make its appearance in Florence after 1380.

Revealing of the attitude of Tuscans in the fourteenth and fifteenth centuries, the use of premium insurance favored the concentration of trade and capital so necessary for the operation of great companies. Thinking always in terms of large-scale maritime trade, the Genoese increased the shares in their ships and cargoes, multiplying beneficiaries even at the risk of complicating the structure of the business. By taking out insurance, Florentines found security for the most diverse transactions without diminishing the influence of their company through a division of property. As for the insurer, himself a merchant at other times and in other businesses, he took on a calculated risk by insuring several operations at once. This was effectively forbidden in the Genoese system, which was too financially demanding for the insurer who had to immobilize his capital while waiting for the repurchase. The speculative aspect of the insurer's investment lay in the fact that not all risks were indemnified. On the other hand, it was easy enough to divide up this risk: several financiers could combine in insuring a single operation.

For reasons that were easy to understand, the premium varied with the business and the dangers involved, as with the operator and the moment. It was raised for small trade in small ships that were difficult to protect. War or peace, winter or summer—everything had to be taken into account in a variable market in order to fix the cost of the risk assumed by the insurer. In 1460, it cost some 36 percent of the insured value to guarantee a ship for a year, though no one could know what would happen in the intervening twelve months. For a single voyage, when it was easier to perceive what might transpire at a distance of two weeks or three months, it cost—*alla fiorentina*—1.5 percent from Genoa to Marseilles, 5 to 7 percent from Genoa to England, and 10 percent from Genoa to Flanders. Merchants paid for the time, but also for the uncertainty. They would always have to pay more to insure salt, which dissolved if the ship sank, than for barrels that would float.

The greatest losses were those sustained in sea trade, and it was here that the most systematic use of insurance was made. The premium system, because it cost little and left the insured capital free, and also because it allowed for the insurance of an indefinite amount of capital, eventually came to cover all kinds of risk. A tax-farmer with a lease on the consumption of salt could also think of insuring himself against the possibility of an epidemic. Genoese businessmen, impressed by the Florentine method, began to insure themselves against the death of figures like the king of Aragon, the pope, or Cardinal Fieschi, whose demise might have an adverse effect on their enterprises by upsetting the politics of the market. Here the risk is obscured. Security has quite simply become an item in the calculation of costs.

FOURTEEN

Accounting

*A*t the start of trade, there was addition and subtraction. There was money in the cash box and merchandise in the shop; they were there only at one particular stage in a succession of simple operations. Knowing what was coming in and what was going out, what one could sell and what one could pay—such were the rudiments of commercial management. Even so, needs began to differentiate on the basis of whether the merchant, artisan, or shopkeeper managed his own business, cash, and shop or was in charge of an appointed agent responsible to him. The need for an account book was hardly felt by the baker who, each evening, counted up the sous and *deniers* received for selling bread rolls at eight sous a dozen. Of course, bookkeeping would have given him the means to check his accounts, but for whom? against whom? If eight sous were missing from the cash box, whose fault could it be? The cutler knew exactly when he had sold his last knife and whether or not he needed to buy more blades from Germany or Normandy. The cloth merchant could see how much cloth he had left, and the spice-merchant did not need an account book to notice that the sack of pepper was getting low.

Understanding Business

As business developed and responsibilities were differentiated, bookkeeping provided the manager with a means of justifying his actions and the owner with a way to keep a permanent check on affairs. If stock increased and was distributed among several shops, no one would think of trying to manage the restocking just by looking at the shelves. As for the cash box, they would not leave it to guesswork to figure out who had paid and who had been paid. When a businessman felt the need to employ a clerk to look after his cash, it was no longer enough simply to know what was in the till at the end of each day.

By the time business had grown to this size, the contents of the cash box and the stacking shelves were no longer enough to provide a complete picture. Even public accounting, as carried out by the royal treasuries—which, above all, had to keep a record of sums received and paid for the day when the collector or treasurer would be called to account for them—also had to keep reminders of what should have been or was due to be received, unpaid bills, and maturing loans. A government did not decide upon war or peace according to the state of finances in the exchequer. Similarly, a simple "day book" listing receipts and expenses was insufficient to record forecasts of production or supply, recovery of loans, reinvestment of profits, tying up of capital, and speculation in the market.

Two developments in particular, credit and capitalism, called for a precise understanding of the complex dynamics of business. Long-term credit by its nature implies maturities that could run beyond the date for rendering accounts. In the short term, ten sous lent and noted down in expenses were compensated by ten sous repaid the next day and recorded in the receipts. Since it would be impossible to say whether the sum actually lent consisted of those identical ten sous, the matter of interest did not complicate the final accounts. And the borrower's receipt was enough to jog the creditor's memory. It was another matter with regard to a six-month credit period when accounts were rendered three times a year. Even annual accounts were upset by medium-term loans if they were recorded shortly before the books were balanced. It was clear that no account book could help the financier manage his affairs if the money he lent before Christmas and recovered at Easter was reckoned one time as deficit and the next as profit.

Under the different systems that resulted from the practice of making deposits and forming partnerships, early capitalism imposed a new obligation on entrepreneurs: the head of a business also had to render his accounts. It was not enough simply to take on deposits or partners; later he would have to justify decisions taken, demonstrate profit and loss, and distribute the profits.

But it was also for his own benefit that he had to develop a method for analyzing the economic climate. Investments required by the credit market could not be chosen at random, any more than those prompted by observation of the clientele's purchases and tastes. When the cloth and spice merchants had to restock, they were guided by the rates of turnover in violet Malines cloth or the blue-brown cloth of Saint-Omer, or of pepper or soap.

Nor were the prices of goods set at random. Too high and sales would be poor: the merchant was not alone in the market, and he knew it. If he set the price too low, he sold at a loss and would be ruined. To establish prices in a rational way, it was necessary to take into consideration factors as diverse as the real price of a credit purchase, the salary of a worker or wagoner, depreciation of a tool, or warehouse overhead. It comes as no surprise that the need for analytical accounting first made itself felt in the cloth industry, the first economic arena to have a complex financial structure that followed on the heels of its sophisticated production techniques.

Thus the concern of the most progressive businessmen—and, once again, the first to get there were the Tuscans and Genoese—was, throughout the thirteenth and fourteenth centuries in which modern accounting originated, to rationalize the management of business by integrating its elements into an authentic system with permanent controls. It soon became clear that such a rigorous integration would require all values in coin and in kind to be incorporated into a range of known and arithmetically practical units. A money of account was needed, be it theoretical, like the pound (*livre* or *lira*), or actual, like the florin.

Convenience in accounting was given precedence over clarity in the monetary system. Profits from exchange and re-exchange—in other words, bank profits—were earned at the cost of stability. To achieve these profits, the business world had no hesitation in abandoning the traditional and unstable money of account based on the silver coin and its multiples—often very different from the heavy coins in circulation—preferring a money of account based on the gold coin and its imaginary subspecies.

Account books, then, needed to handle currency conversion, and the majority of entries were the result of a complex operation. Devaluations or revaluations that occurred in the course of a bookkeeping period did nothing to simplify calculations. It would be fair to conclude that Italy's relative financial stability favored the birth of the new analytical accounting, whereas instability in France was largely responsible for discouraging Parisian businessmen from following Italian practice despite the fact that they had close dealings with Italians on a daily basis.

Figures

The starting point was the inventory. The elements fell into place of their own accord as the accountants—in other words, the managers who knew that one day they would be answerable to their partners—developed their methods. This juxtaposition of parallel books, which was to lay the foundations of the double-entry system, was born of need and experience, not of theory. The same tendency occurred not only in Florence, Siena, Lucca, and other Tuscan towns, but also in Genoa. It was a Genoese, Luca Paciolo da

San Sepolcro—and a Franciscan, of all things—who produced the first guide to the accounts of a merchant estate. An instant success and for many years used by the business world, this manual described the structures and processes of modern accounting.

Meanwhile, Europe had become familiar with Italian practices, adapting them to a greater or lesser extent to their own needs. It was, nevertheless, a slow process, as much through suspicion as through a lack of urgency. At the end of the fifteenth century, there were many examples throughout the West of account books kept by businessmen and their employees. As yet there was no system, outside the Italian companies, that could give a permanent account of the economic situation of an enterprise.

Every bit as much as correspondence, bookkeeping became part of the normal activities of a merchant. Whether the head of the firm or an employee taken on for a time to keep the books, the accountant was not exactly a professional bookkeeper. The accounting profession would be born at a later date, with regard to both taxes and merchandise. For the time being, account books were gradually becoming a customary tool of commercial work, greatly encouraged, in the fourteenth century, by the fall in the price of paper, which now was within the reach of all. The effect of the relatively low cost of paper on the rapid expansion of bookkeeping in local government is well known. The merchant, who might have thought twice before using expensive parchment, was prepared to pay the cost of paper if it meant keeping track of his affairs.

Changes in legal attitudes went hand in hand with this new habit. The notary whose signed minutes had tended to replace the deeds drawn up and sealed in the chancelleries now found himself being bypassed as people turned increasingly to private contracts. As the middle classes became more educated, businessmen were increasingly willing to accept a simple paper signed by a colleague, a letter, or a record in an account book as a legally binding document. The development of the bill of exchange as a credit instrument was yet another result of this promotion of the private signature—in itself significant of a level of civilization in which an authentic merchant culture could take shape.

This represented another argument in favor of accounting. Since it was clearly in no one's interest to waste time and money on procedure, it was often agreed that a legal value should be placed on the note of a debt written in the creditor's book by the debtor himself. The pontifical treasury went so far as to ratify the authenticity of its accounting by noting, in the margin of the expenses column, the names of two or three witnesses: payment thus became indisputable, and the treasury saved itself the trouble of sending several thousand receipts. Both officers and merchants with accounts in the papal treasury knew how to turn this very simple form of proof to their own account. Each kept a strict eye on the other to make sure that their own payments were carefully noted as received, with the date, in the treasury accounts. Some people, nevertheless, insisted on a receipt and were quite capable of turning up one fine day to record a number of earlier payments that shortage of time had prevented them from having entered at the time of payment; the various dates of the original transactions were included in the record. Examples of such "adjustments" are clear evidence of the interest that partners in the treasury had in seeing that their loans, or the balance owing, were put down in writing. An entry in the treasurer's book was at least as sure as a sealed receipt.

Despite advances in the art of accounting, along with an awareness of the drawbacks, the merchant used—as did the financial officer for his public accounts—roman numerals in his calculations. European mathematicians had long ago begun to understand the advantages of the arabic system (originating, in fact, in Persia) with its nonrepeating numbers and, thanks to its zero, a value determined by a number's position. The number 2,378 was infinitely more convenient than MMCCCLXXVIII. Scientists in Spain were using the new numbers well before the year 1000. Gerbert of Aurillac, even before becoming Pope Sylvester II in 990, and still only a teacher at the episcopal school in Reims, was already timidly beginning to use them, inscribing them on a set of counters. But merchants long remained suspicious of these arabic figures, seeing them as too easy to falsify.

By the 1250s, however, Italian businessmen were already familiar with the new numerals, though they were still very different from those we know today. The French, Spanish, Germans, and English adopted them in the fifteenth century. They all used them because they were convenient, but they treated them with suspicion. Realizing the advantages of performing arithmetical operations using a system of place value, they used these arabic numerals for rough calculations and in the margins of account books, but for a long time this was the only place they were to be found. They were used solely for the quick arithmetical checks that an individual might want to make for himself.

The merchant was quite happy to use arabic numerals—or to "sign by the abacus" as the Italians put it— for anything that could be verified: the year, the page numbers in an account book, or an arithmetical recapitulation. He would not use them for the day's date, more difficult to be sure of than the year, and absolutely not for anything that might constitute an obligation.

There were at least two reasons for this reluctance, both of a practical nature. First, there was the problem of the shapes of the arabic numerals. These were not yet definitively fixed, either in form or, particularly, in orientation. Perhaps because counters marked with a figure in the center played an important role in the diffusion of arabic numerals, it seems that they could be written whichever way up the writer preferred. An impression of uncertainty surrounded the figures, very different from the immutable shapes of the roman numerals, which in any case—since they were letters—consisted of familiar shapes. An entry in arabic numerals was thought to be easily falsified. A simple pen stroke could completely alter it, or so it was thought for a long time to come.

The second reason was equally realistic: they could manage very well with roman numerals. Roman numerals adapted very well to the use of the abacus, or rather, to the squares on the carpet or checked cloth (whence our word *exchequer*) on which the counters were moved around. The medieval person, whether merchant or tax collector, counted slowly but accurately and saw no reason to go any faster. Monitored by the twentieth-century historian armed with a computer, we find that fifteenth-century accountants very rarely made mistakes, except for frequent—but easily detectable—errors in copying.

The medieval merchant thus did not see the advantages of arabic numerals or place value that were to be of such benefit to the astronomers of the period for their calculations of large numbers, decimals, and complicated operations involving fractions. For the merchant doing his own books, all this was for scholars—a change in habits, a new fashion, and one in which he saw little point.

Partners and the Ledger

The idea of noting down debit and credit is very old. As would be expected, it first appears in the management of large estates. An individual lending ten sous to his brother-in-law might remember it, but not the baker who was paid for his bread at the end of the month or the tax-farmer of a lordly estate who levied and received rents of all kinds and maturities. It became all the more necessary to create a "third-party account" when the enterprise's relations with third parties—creditors and debtors—took on greater importance, along with the irregularity typical of the increasingly sophisticated financial dealings. The money changer at his bench could give *tournois* in exchange for sterling or écus for florins without any need to note down who received what. The cloth merchant, on the other hand, could not manage in this way, buying, as he did, wool on the hoof, wool on credit to be delivered on the return of a ship, and financing the work of the weavers and dyers without ever seeing the cloth that he would ultimately sell to other cloth merchants. The latter, uninvolved in production, would pay him on a date fixed according to custom and circumstance. Even more complicated were the dealings of the *cambiste* who drew bills on the Champagne or Flanders fairs, paid those drawn at Bruges or London, and settled with Genoa or Venice, and all this at different rates of exchange. Neither the cloth merchant nor the *cambiste,* who could not, in any case, have known all their commercial or banking partners, would have managed without keeping a strict account of credit and debt.

For the baker the tally stick was enough. This stick of wood, split down its length, was still being used in some parts of rural France in the early twentieth century. The baker—the creditor—would keep one half of the piece of wood while the customer—the debtor—would take the other. With each purchase, the two pieces were brought together and a notch was marked. When the client came to settle his debt, the notches were removed with the slice of a knife and the process started again. Although lacking in subtlety, the system had certain advantages: it was simple, quick, and, most important, it did not involve knowing how to write. Even a well-run exchequer like that of the king of England was still using this system in the twelfth century for its regular loans.

Anyone managing an estate was well advised to compile, once and for all, a list of his permanent debtors. Then all he had to do was look it over on the due dates and make sure it was kept up-to-date. The "memorials" of the royal exchequers kept lists of this kind: vassals owing military duties, peasants owing days of work or of carting, and tenants who owed taxes or rent for their pieces of land.

Towns did the same, prompted by the endemic debt of the thirteenth century to draw up a list of their creditors in order to estimate both the size of the public debt and the extent to which the municipal government could extend its borrowing. The accounts of the town of Calais go back to 1262. A "Book of Debt" was scrupulously maintained in Hamburg, Lübeck, Riga, Stralsund, and in the majority of the Hanseatic ports from the last quarter of the thirteenth century.

Since the town's creditors were generally the richer citizens, the community's debt was the personal debt of those who governed the town. Such a list was thus important to businessmen since it put an official stamp on their loans.

These lists of maturing payments and rents were to give rise, in the thirteenth and fourteenth centuries, to the *censier,* a census or detailed inventory. In the fifteenth century, a notary was involved, making it a binding legal document, the "terrier" or register of landed property. A businessman from Lyons with aspirations to nobility had the following document drawn up for his country estate:

> Jean Estévenin, of Lozanne, is acknowledged to hold the goods and possessions listed below:
>   First, half of the land formerly belonging to the late Pierre Estévenin, his father, situated at Lozanne at the place known as Peylapuel. . . , under annual and perpetual service and law of an eighth of a measure of wheat,

half a measure of oats, an eighth of half a hen, half a lamp of oil, Chazay measure, one *obole* and a twelfth of a *denier tournois*.

Needless to say, the landowner is very unlikely to have received any of these dues as defined. A whole hen once every sixteen years and a complete *tournois* every twelve years might have been more practical. Money in lieu of dues in kind may have been equally acceptable.

The tax collector had a similar approach. He knew it was pointless to go from door to door expecting each person's dues at the first request. It was not always easy to find the sum, and the tax collector would have to come back more than once. The tax roll, compiled on the basis of the previous tax roll and produced with a note of the sums due this time, was thus little more than a reminder. More important was a second document, written out at the time of the attempt to levy the tax. Usually the tax collector would note in the margin of each document the words "paid," "paid so much," or "nothing."

Those in charge of collecting the tallage, or tax, in Paris between 1421 and 1438 were more devious. They left the record established by a first list, known as the *recette* or receipt, unchanged, entering onto it, despite its name, as sums received monies that this or that contributor had in fact not paid and might well never pay. They drew up a separate list of unpaid dues, entered as "expenses" in the same way as were the costs of collecting and the sums handed over to the treasury.

Jean du Bois, a shoemaker, was taxed two ounces of silver in 1421. We read under "receipts" for the district of the local official (*quartenier*) Jean de Vaynes, an area corresponding to the present-day Temple and Saint-Martin-des-Champs districts in Paris: "From Jean du Bois, shoemaker, assessed at two ounces of silver, received from him in silver, for this, silver: 2 ounces."

One would never guess from reading this document that Jean du Bois had paid nothing. And yet, twenty-five pages further on, we find in the "expenses": "Jean du Bois, shoemaker, assessed in the district of Jean de Vaynes in the *dizaine* [district] of Pierre Pasquier at two ounces of silver, released from this due since no one knows him and he cannot be found, and for this sum: 2 ounces."

The tax collector of 1438 was less concerned about formulae of this kind. He quite simply kept two lists: "receipts" and "parts of debts." We find a poultry seller owing 40 sous of which he had paid only 24. Folios 3 and 21 of the tax roll read:

> From Arnoulet Maschecol, poulterer: 40 s.
>
> . . . .
>
> Arnoulet Maschecol, poulterer, remains: 16 s.

Tuscan merchants had been following this practice since the beginning of the thirteenth century. In the 1300s it was adopted in Antwerp, and in Toulouse by the end of the century. Known as a "memorial" to the royal accountants, or a "ledger" to businessmen and the commercial and banking companies, the listing of loans to be recovered and debts to be settled became the daily affair of all management in all short- or medium-term business. The Italians sometimes gave an indication of the importance of such a book, having it sumptuously bound between two wooden boards (*assi*), hence the name *Libro dell'Asse*. Such a book was made to last, one account opening before another had closed, for continuity in business was essential.

This method imposed a chronological order on the opening of accounts. The entry for a new partner would follow an entry inscribed for the first time the day before. In practice it would have been impossible to keep them in alphabetical order after the initial census or even the periodic census conducted in the 1400s by the merchants of Toulouse. The latter could find no better way to list their clients than alphabetically—by first name!

The "ledger" was in fact a list of all the third parties having commercial or financial dealings with the company, and each day that passed added another name to the list. Accounts were entered consecutively and to find a particular entry it was necessary to leaf through the pages. In the fifteenth century, the Venetians came up with the idea, as did also the Genoese of the *Casa di San Giorgio,* of using a separate page for each new client. Even so, when that page was full and further entries had to continue on the next available page, it would be necessary to hunt through the book to find that page.

The Hanseatic merchants of Lübeck or Hamburg did not use this method until later, since they balked at wasting paper by leaving spaces blank: entries for new clients were inserted in any gaps.

Whatever method was used to record debts owed and paid, the merchant was familiar with his own system and understood it. A merchant from Languedoc, for example, recorded "Peyre owes me two écus." When Peyre had paid, he crossed out the entry. But this was not true of all clients. For every one who understood accounting, there were ten who did not, however much they would have liked to be able to interpret the accounts they were shown and the reasons advanced. A cleric depositing his money; a mason who had repaired a wall hoping that his employer would not forget to pay him; a fuller waiting for his salary; a burger taking a piece of cloth, a ewer, or a belt and promising to pay what he owed in a few weeks: all these would have been easier to deal with, when it came to the settling of their accounts, if they could have understood that account without needing a lengthy explanation. Matters got even more complicated when the "bank transfer" came into use as a means of payment between people who were not professional traders: the third parties must have been very confused as to what was happening in their account, now in credit and the next minute in debit. They demanded to see the books.

Thus the custom arose among accountants, in Italy as early as the beginning of the thirteenth century, of putting themselves in the place of the client to whom the account would be presented. A credit of ten ducats on Giovanni is thus entered as what it represents for Giovanni—a debt: "Giovanni must give ten ducats." The merchant or banker who lends ten ducats to Giovanni or who sells him a piece of cloth on credit will record: "Giovanni must give [*deve dare*] . . . ," eventually simplified to "Giovanni must," meaning "Giovanni owes [*deve*]."

Looked at from the other side, the twenty florins lent by Pietro are the accountant's debt, since he has received and thus owes them. But he enters them as credit to Pietro. On the page headed with Pietro's name, he enters: "Pietro must have [*deve avere*] twenty florins." Later the accounts would speak simply of his "*avere*," or "have."

When Giovanni comes to pay off his loan or pay for his cloth, it will be noted down: "Giovanni has given." Thus, logically, "has given" should be the opposite of "must give." But, in fact, in the meantime Giovanni has sold, bought, lent, and borrowed. Business is complicated and the various operations overlapped. What was clear, however, was that these operations always flowed in one direction or the other: debit to credit or credit to debit. Why not, then, collect together on one page all the same type of operations: credits on one page and debits on another? Giovanni's repayment would thus be entered as equivalent to a credit. In the final balancing of the ledger, everything that reduced the debit side increased the credit. So when Giovanni finally decides to pay, it is recorded as: "Giovanni *deve avere*." The very words used for Pietro.

The formulae used by businessmen for their "ledgers" were thus fixed early on, in a manner that was both logical and convenient. Giovanni and Pietro knew what they should have [*devono avere*] and what they should give [*devono dare*] and they knew how to distinguish between the two. They certainly would not dispute the matter. The accountant was sufficiently familiar with his book to know that a "*deve*" ["owes," or debt] page in the account of a third party meant credit for himself and his company; and that entries in the "*avere*" section were all debts. If it was an inversion, it was one of words only. The third-party, or "ledger," account was created so that the client could read it.

The Ugolini of Siena are quite explicit in their book of credit and debt for the Champagne fairs for 1255 onward:

These are the *deniers* that Ghino Ugolini *has paid* in Siena for the French account.

First, he *must have* [*deve avere*] 6 *livres* in *deniers provinois* at the fair of Lagny in 1261, which he *owed* [*doveva*] in Siena in Sienese *deniers* to the wife of Bernardino Ranieri.

Two centuries later, the Florentines Antonio della Casa and Simone Guadagni note in their Geneva company's "yellow book"—so called because of the color of the binding of this and successive books—their debt to the Strozzi for a bill drawn on Rome:

> Carlo della Luna and Francesco degli Strozzi and partners in Rome, according to their account here, *devono avere* [must have] at the August fair 1453 the sum of 20 old écus 1 sou 4 *deniers* that we *have had for them* of Messer Mandone, prior of Valleschuxa, by the hand of Messer Roberto Adimari, remaining from 55 old écus that he owed them: 20 écus 1 sou 4 *deniers*.

Even the merchant of Montauban Barthélemy Bonis, who kept his ledger in 1344 without borrowing this Italian vocabulary—there are no "to give's" or "to have's"—expresses credit and debit in simple terminology easily understood on both sides of the counter. Thus when he sells spices on credit, the sale is the client's debt, the payment the equivalent of the merchant's debt. The verb *dovere/devoir* is used in both cases, but the subject of the verb changes:

> Estève Dannac, of Catalonia, *deu* [owes] by an account in Book B, page 125, and that was for spices, sugar, and other things that we sent him via Durant Turen with his letter which comes to: 5 sous 1 *denier tournois*.
> . . . And we *devem a lhui* [owe to him], that he lent to us on 14 May: 5 sous 1 *denier tournois*.

So *devem a lhui* or *E nos a lu* [and us to him] is the opposite of *deu*. The opposites "to have" and "to give" are not used here. But the two words appear in all the accounts kept in Avignon in 1377 by Francesco di Marco Datini's agent in France. Here Italian usage was already followed:

> Gianino Lorancho, who sells salt in Orange, *must give* [*doit donner*] by the agreed day [that is, 15th July 1377] the salt delivered to him for us in Orange by Giovanni Bontesone of Beaucaire: 50 barrels and 1 quintal, Orange measure, of salt.

The Orange retailer is in debt. He "must give." This is clear enough. As for the suppliers of Datini and company, they "must have" [*devono avere*]:

> Gili Bresc and Piero and Gabriello Vadini, brothers, residing at Aigues-Mortes, *must have* [*devono avere*] on the said day.

Even the least expert salt merchant could understand this at first sight.

Value Accounting: The Cash and Goods Accounts

At the same time, the cashier had begun to keep a separate and impersonal cash account, entering all receipts and expenses. A shopkeeper would have found no need for such an account book. But he would have changed his mind when it came time for the cashier, like any other employee or partner, to render his accounts. In other words, as in the case of the "memorials," the institutions had adopted such measures before the merchants. As soon as there was a treasury, there had to be a treasurer who had to be able to say what he had done with the money. As early as the thirteenth century, the cashiers of the *Biccherna*, which managed the finances of the Commune of Siena, and of the *Opera del Duomo*, which managed the finances of the cathedral chapter of Pisa, knew that they would be expected to account for every *denier* received or spent. Merchants did not follow suit to any extent until the fourteenth century, which saw the proliferation of joint stock partnerships.

The "cash account" thus acquired an autonomy with respect to the entire business. It and the cashier became a "third party," like the clients and suppliers. A payment made from the cash account is money that no longer belongs to the cashier, since he has spent it. He does not owe it any more. Using the same vocabulary that applies to clients, the accountant enters the sum thus paid on behalf of the business as credit to the cashier. Of course, viewed from the perspective of the head of the business, such an entry might seem paradoxical: his own books show as credit (*avoir*) what he has paid out and as debit (*doit*) what he receives, since the cash account owes it to him. It seems like a paradox only if one takes the cash account as recording money belonging to the company or the head of the company. If we remember that it is, in fact, the cashier's account, the paradox disappears.

The reasoning behind this new inversion of signs, or rather, of the books, was quite simple, the result of practice rather than theory. The two basic operations of trade are receiving and making payments. From the moment that a payment made to the cash account by the client Jacopo was entered in Jacopo's third-party account, that is, in the ledger's credit (*avere*) column, it would have become difficult to enter the same payment as credit to "cash" that had received it. If "paid" is expressed as "credit" for the third person, then "received" ought to be expressed as "debit." Otherwise, if the same word changes its meaning according to which book it is in, things would become very confused. The accountant's aim was to keep things clear. The meaning of a verb should not change just because its subject did. Although the merchant from Montauban came to terms with this concept, the Tuscans and Genoese would have none of it.

The cash account owed the head of the business the money it had received. In order to explain the inversion of signs, which was simply an expression of the coherence—albeit still relative—of the system, in future centuries theoreticians would invent the concept of the "master of accounting." The cash account owed this, the client owed that: soon, and well before an absolutely fair and coherent system was created, it was understood that the identical commercial or banking operation would have to be expressed as two entries in two different books: what left one account would be entered in the other. This was the logic behind the keeping of two parallel accounts, one for "cash" and one for the third party. But double entries for the same operation could only reflect the flow of money in opposite directions: credit and repayment, debt and repayment, purchase and payment, sale and payment. Two-way bookkeeping had come about. Jacopo's credit (*avere*)—what he paid to the cash account—could only be a debit (*deve*) for the cash account.

It was simply a matter of words, not of strategy, as some modern scholars would maintain. The first person in the thirteenth century to reverse these words in order to follow what was going on in the cash account was not yet concerned about keeping his books and accounts entirely balanced. He was merely using professional jargon, and the words "*deve avere*" and "*deve dare*" still kept their literal meaning in thirteenth-century Italy. The deal itself was not in any way different, even if the locutions referred logically to the cash account in its impersonal relation to the company.

Things changed and the matter became more complicated with the involvement of the French at the dawn of the modern period. Less familiar with the capitalist structure of the great Italian companies, they often had difficulty in distinguishing between the head of the company and his cashier. Instead of opposing "*deve dare*" (must give) and "*deve avere*" (must have), they used "*doit*" (must, or owes) and "*avoir*" (have). Of course "*deve*" and "*deve dare*" meant the same thing, with one simply a contraction of the other. But rendering "*deve avere/ doit avoir*" as "*avere/avoir*" resulted in a misunderstanding of the phrase. French accountants during the fifteenth century were not, however, perturbed; here, as so often elsewhere, they simply borrowed an Italian practice rather late in the day without properly understanding it.

The cash account and the third-party account balanced properly only in the case of a financial operation. A loan made to Dino was a debt for Dino and an "*avere/avoir*" for the cash account. But things were different in the case of a sale. The stock account resulted as much from this need to balance the books as from a real management necessity. Where business was expanding and diversifying, it was vital to know what one had and what was needed.

At first it was no more than a simple stock book, but quite soon the goods account became the third constituent book in a coherent system of accounting. From the early fourteenth century, in the industrial companies, it integrated the elements that determined approximate production costs. It then became a book of purchases and sales, of *comprevendite*, recording the purchase of raw materials and sales of the finished products. Added to it were wage costs and other expenses, including taxes. This system of calculating production costs, perfected by the Florentine companies during the second half of the fourteenth century, was to be copied, in part and imperfectly but in awareness of the advantages it could offer to commercial management, by French and English manufacturers during the following century.

A cloth merchant active in Toulouse around 1435, Jean Lapeyre, methodically recorded each purchase and sale in this way. He even calculated the profit derived from the operation, anticipating the theory of profit and loss, which would not be fully developed until it entered into the process of balancing the three different accounts. It seems at least that Lapeyre was able to manage his purchases, estimate the likelihood of profit, and evaluate suppliers and clients. In this way he could avoid restocking with goods that might have to be sold off at cost price:

ENGLISH CLOTH

Andrieu del Portz: 7 *canne* of blue-green cloth.

Cost	1 écu 10 *gros*
Sold 8 September 1436, in gold	2 écus 1½ *gros*
Profit	9½ *gros*

Johan de Cassals: 1 *canna* 3 *palmi* of red cloth.

Cost	2 écus 9 *gros*
Sold 1 *canna* 3 *palmi* 2 March 1435	2½ écus
No profit.	

The écu was worth 18 *gros d'écu*. Lapeyre would have understood that he should no longer order red cloth from Johan de Cassals.

A century earlier, we find the Florentines Duccio di Banchello and Banco Bencivenni going much further in their analysis of the receipt of fourteen loads of English wool bought in Milan on 20 March 1339 from Niccoletto Lioni:

9 loads of English wool. The 9 sacks weighed in Bruges: 11 *kiovi*. At 15 marks a bag, they were worth 91 *livres* 16 sous 8 *deniers* sterling, or in *livres de gros* of account the sum of:

£58. 13s. 8d.

5 loads of English wool, from Charchamono, marked K. The 5 sacks weighed in Bruges: 6 *kiovi*. At 13½ marks the sack, they were worth 45 *livres* 18 sous sterling, or:

£29. 6s. 7d.

The 14 loads cost, in expenses incurred in Bruges until the time of loading 15 sous 3½ *deniers de gros*, or:

£1. 9s. 4d.

Cost of expenses between Bruges and Milan 13 florins, or:

£19. 15s. 3d.

Total sum: 1076 gold florins 10 Venice *gros*, or:

£109. 4s. 10d.

Cost, that we have given for the 16 for 100 at the end of four months:

£17. 1s.

In total: 1244 gold florins 10 *gros,* or:

£126. 5s. 10d.

Entered on page 131 that he *deve avere* (must have):

In Milan, for:

    toll at Como: £22. 15s. imperial.

    transporting the wool from the Borgo to the City: £5. 5s.

    the "chain" and putting the wool under cover: 9s. 4d.

    accommodation in Milan: £1. 8s.

    weighing the bales in Milan: 7s.

    transport from Milan to Lodi: £7

    child who looked after the bales from Milan to Lodi: 12s.

    toll at Lodi: £7

    note and loading at Lodi: 16s.

    hire of boat from Lodi to Venice: £15. 8s.

    toll at Pizzighettone: £13. 10s.

    toll on bridge at Pizzighettone: 6s. 8d.

    note: 2s. 8d.

    toll at Cremona at 10s. a load for 14⅔ loads: £7. 6s. 8d.

    weighing and note at Cremona: 6s.

    toll on bridge at Cremona: 7s. 6d.

    toll at Bresello: £2. 2s.

    toll at Borsello: £1. 8s.

    toll at Guastalla: £4. 4s.

    toll at Isollo: £3. 9s.

    toll at Borgoforte: £1. 6s.

    toll at Mantua: £5. 13s.

    Total of all these expenses: £91. 17s. 8d. imperial, or:

£5. 14s. 11d.

And the cost of the expenses incurred by Ambrogio between Venice and Bologna, for:

    return trip to Modena: 10 *gros.*

    six sacks in which to pack the bales: 2s. 3d. in *gros.*

    guide and pilot: 2 *gros.*

    wine for the packers in Bologna: 1s. 4d. in *gros.*

    journey from Bologna to Venice: 1s. 1d. in *gros.*

    and given to Bartolo as commission on the wool: 2s. 4d. in *gros.*

    Total: 9s. 10d.

    Sum total: £132. 10s. 8d. in *gros.*

Or: £133. 1s. 9d.

    We state that Duccio di Banchello and Banco Bencivenni and associates *devono dare* to the order book:

£133. 1s. 9d.

When it came to settling with the two Florentines to whom the stock account *"deve dare"* (must give) 133 *livres* for wool bought for 88 *livres* in Bruges, it is easy to see how useful such an analysis could be for businessmen having to choose markets for supplies and routes to transport them. To transport the wool from Bruges to Milan by the overland route—across passes through the middle of the Alps that directly linked the Rhine and Lombardy—it had cost some 22 percent, to which had to be added the agio charges of 16 percent over four months. By the time it got to Milan, the wool cost 138 percent of its purchase price in Bruges. It cost another 6.5 percent to get it from Milan to Venice. Leaving aside the transport costs from England to Flanders and the profit to intermediaries in the two countries, the cost of the wool had risen by 45 percent in its coast-to-coast journey across the Continent.

If he was to avoid arriving at his final destination with goods made unmarketable by their high cost in a particularly competitive market, it was vital for the merchant to stick rigorously to this analytical accounting. His future fate depended on making the right decisions.

The merchandise itself thus quickly acquired a book, in parallel to the cash account. Like the latter, it assumed an autonomy with respect to the business and was soon treated in the same way as the suppliers and clients. Balancing the books followed the same pattern, and before long it was difficult to conceive how a piece of cloth sold on credit could be entered in the "*deve dare*" column in a customer's account without also being entered in the "*deve avere*" column in the merchandise account. Here again, there was no wish to perform an illogical inversion. Instead we have a thoroughly capitalistic view of the merchandise, now no longer identified with the physical person of the merchant, but instead having to submit its own accounts to the group of partners.

The "yellow book" of Geneva thus makes the company's reserves of silk an accountable individual. Just as Della Luna and Strozzi "*devono avere,*" so the "silk cloth" "*deve avere.*" This means that some of it had been sold:

> Silk cloth from our account "*doit avoir*" at the August fair 1453, 4 florins 3 *gros* in coin since there has been deducted from it 4½ ounces of the black taffeta that we sell at 7¾ écus a pound to Stefano Acaradi and associates: 2 écus 4 sous 6 *deniers.*

This practice of distinguishing between accountant and owner—stemming from the capitalist structure and leading to a situation where "silk cloth" can owe the company four florins—also led to rather surprising statements in opening accounts. Thus the ledger of the Farolfi company records, in 1300, the costs in food incurred by their agents in Salon-de-Provence as follows: "The expenditure in food and drink *doivent donner* from 20 January 1299, where they are entered in the *devaient donner* in the notebook of expenses: £49. 6s. 6d. *tournois.*"

In other words, the reserve of food is counted as a debt to the stock, much like goods received. This entry replaces a similar record of these provisions as receipts in the cash book. The parallel operations of the two accounts are very clear here, and the allocation quite logical:

OPERATIONS	MUST GIVE	MUST HAVE
Purchase of provisions	Cash account (provisions received)	Cash account (money spent)
Subsequent sale	Merchandise	

Toward a System

The partner was a creditor of the company. This was recognized from the outset, and the idea would go very far. Thus, although he was the chief capital investor in his various companies, Francesco di Marco Datini was scrupulous in drawing up, almost every month, an account of his financial participation in the Datini companies. But there was one essential difference: creditors expected nothing more than the restitution of what they had deposited, entrusted, or lent, or payment for what they had sold or provided. At the most, they had a right to a repayment of their money in one form or another. Partners, on the other hand, also had a right to see the books and receive a share of any possible profits.

At those times when the accounts were settled—normally when a company underwent its normal and periodic "renewal"—an overall assessment was obviously called for. But business did not cease at such moments, and it would have been difficult for the company to interrupt all commercial and banking operations in order to distribute among its partners any gold pieces that might have accumulated over many years of trading. At such times, new partners were taken on, bringing in new capital. All or some of the old partners were retained, with their assets and liabilities. Some left, taking with them their capital and their share of the realized profits, or, in other words, a dividend. A company that came to the end of its existence and closed its accounts left behind a complex tangle of credit and debit. It would have been unreasonable to expect that matters would be sorted out instantly for all those involved; instead, the company simply became one of the third-party creditors or debtors of the new company. When the accountant opened a ledger for the sixth Peruzzi company in 1335, he carried over the outstanding credits and debits of the fifth company into an account that he logically enough described as that of the "old company."

A few decades later, toward the end of the fourteenth century, this public display of the resources of some of the important banking families in a single ledger to which even the humblest depositor had access began to seem unwise. A special book was therefore opened, a "secret book" intended for the company accounts. The legally witnessed constitution of the company appeared in this book, together with those accounts which a third party did not need to know, such as staff salaries and the dividends reserved for the partners.

We should not imagine that all systems of accounting worked out in fourteenth-century Italy, and perfected there in the fifteenth century before spreading northward over the Alps, were equally complete or well organized. Well into the fifteenth century, many Tuscan and Venetian accounts consisted only of a ledger in which the individual accounts gave no more than an approximate picture of the state of the business and were, furthermore, inclined to be inconsistent. Double-entry bookkeeping was not appropriate unless the business involved the flow of money in the two directions of receipts and expenditure. The more demanding businessmen, however, felt the need for a systematic form of bookkeeping whereby a static inventory could become an immediate indicator of changes in data and circumstances. They realized that it was pointless, without such an inventory, to attempt to determine the long-term direction of an economic policy or to manage any kind of short-term speculation.

Attempts to find a more rigorous analysis first appear among the Italian companies, where structure and scale made such a need more acutely felt. The first systems of this kind seem to have been used, or at least hinted at, in Florence before 1300, if we can draw such a conclusion from a page preserved from the Peruzzi books for the year 1292. Ten or twenty years later, the usage was becoming widespread in Tuscany, though with much hesitation and very little rigor. Pisa and Genoa followed suit, and then Venice, where the arrangement of accounts on juxtaposed pages or columns—rather than in clauses superimposed at the end—became so common that, before long, all double-entry systems were known as accounting *alla veneziana*.

In the fifteenth century, the whole of Europe began to adopt the use of parallel and complementary accounts. From London to Constance and from Bruges to Lübeck, account books proliferated. But the unifying factor that could have made them a system was only glimpsed. It was usual to keep both a cash account and a client account, and sometimes a merchandise book. The parallelism of the books lay largely in their independence, but this could sometimes lead to incompatibility, when, for example, a single account mixed the schematic arrangements of the ledger and the chronological arrangement of the cashier's day book.

Such a separation of accounts, a result of the different economic activities rather than a search for consistency in the accounting system, could at times be less than revealing. In 1407, the Veckinchusens of Lübeck divided the book kept at their Venetian branch into an account of outgoing goods—Eastern products such as spices, silk, and cotton—and an account for receipts to the cash account and incoming merchandise—products from the North such as cloth, amber, and furs. In Danzig, around 1430, the merchant Johann Piesz kept a ledger where equal place was given to separate accounts for sales, purchases, and current business.

Such arrangements did not easily provide an immediate analysis of the economic health of the concern. Although accounting methods became ever more complex, businessmen were still inclined to follow their own instincts when making decisions. Despite a multitude of contacts in different markets, and despite all the Italian companies now installed north of the Alps, the rest of Europe once again hesitated to follow Italy's lead. As with the move from the contract of exchange to the letter of credit, they could not see the point.

Thus it was not until the sixteenth century that the rest of Europe adopted systematic accounting. The success of the manual published in 1494 by Luca Paciolo da San Sepolcro was ensured, as merchants from every country rushed to buy this guide to accountancy. The system it describes would be followed for almost half a millennium.

The Italians had early on agreed on a very simple principle, which was enunciated in Paciolo's manual. Any economic operation involves a change in the financial status of an enterprise. By its nature, it has two applications, one positive and the other negative. One piece of cloth more is two florins less. One pound of pepper less is five florins more. Every operation has to be recorded, in the parallel books that were born of necessity, by two entries, one showing money or goods coming in, the other those going out. The total sum of these entries had to balance, whichever way they were read.

EXAMPLES OF ACCOUNTING OPERATIONS		
OPERATION	MUST GIVE	MUST HAVE
Purchase of goods on credit	Merchandise (stock account)	Ledger (vendor's account)
Payment of the purchase to the seller	Ledger	Cash account (daily book)
Purchase for cash	Stock account	Cash account
Credit sale	Ledger	Stock account
Payment by the buyer	Cash account	Ledger
Sale for cash	Cash account	Stock account
Loan or deposit received	Cash account	Ledger
Credit given or repayment	Ledger	Cash account
Transfer from client A to client B	Ledger (A's page)	Ledger (B's page)

Transfers between accounts, though maintaining the banker's same overall debit, increased the credit of a third party, reducing by the same amount that of another. The two entries are thus made on two different pages or in two different columns in the same third-party account. The matter is confined to these third parties, the company having merely changed creditor. Everything is balanced in the one ledger.

It was still necessary to balance the figures. There was much hesitation before arriving at a method of balancing them over a period of time, giving a final and overall total. Where should one place the difference between sale price and purchase price? Where should profit go? Or loss (which while rare in commerce was quite frequent in exchange and credit dealings)? Where should the interest concealed within the changes in exchange rates go? In the mid-fifteenth century, many merchants still confined themselves to an internal balancing of each separate operation, made possible by a book of *Avanzi e disavanzi*, where a record of surplus and deficit was kept, too often, and wrongly, interpreted by historians as a fully fledged profit-and-loss account.

The majority of merchants in fourteenth- and fifteenth-century Europe, and even some of the most advanced Tuscans, were content simply to note down a sale for twelve sous of something they had bought for ten. In Toulouse in the fifteenth century, even the most able were content to note the profit made, without trying to incorporate it into an arithmetical balancing of the books. Similarly, in the middle of the same century, the Della Casa and Guadagni companies granted the castellan Giovanni Falconieri a loan of 12 ducats to be repaid at the August fair in 1453. This was noted down in the "white book," which was the ledger, or third-party account of the company that matured at the beginning of that same year.

The renewal of a company meant the opening of new books. A "yellow book" succeeded the "white book." The accountant had to enter all the credits relating to the assets transferred from one company to the next. Thus we find Falconieri's credit entered as follows on the very first page of the "yellow book":

> The white book *deve avere* by the following debtors:
> —Giovanni Falconieri: 12 ducats.

This did not mean that they did not also recopy the said credit into Falconieri's account, entered there in the *deve dare* (debit) column. When he paid off the sum, the amount was entered in his account in the *deve avere* (credit) column, and counted in *deve dare* in the temporary book of receipts from the fair during which he had made his repayment, and then carried over in the same way to the permanent cash book.

But Falconieri also paid 2 sous 9 *deniers*, the barely disguised interest on his loan. The accountant entered this in his account in the ledger, immediately after the mention of the repayment of the capital: "Giovanni Falconieri *deve avere* 14⅙ new ducats worth 12 ducats. And *deve avere* 2 sous 9 *deniers*."

The entry had to balance, so we find the 2 sous 9 *deniers* in the *avanzi e disavanzi di banco* account. If we are to avoid the misleading "profit and loss," it could be described as interest received and paid out: "The *disavanzi devono dare* to Giovanni Falconieri: 2 sous 9 *deniers*."

The accountant has created a considerable distance between his accounting and the company. The interest received is a liability, a "*disavanzio*" of exchange. It was not the company that had received the interest, but the profits account book, which it would then owe to the company. The administrators had been paid, and the realized profit remained owing to the shareholders, partners, and others involved. The capitalist structure is clearly apparent.

The system was, however, less rigorous than it appeared. It had not yet managed an effective analysis of an enterprise's financial state of health. The "fair book" or the "cash book" and the "book of *avanzi e disavanzi di banco*" could only fragment the notion of receipts. The 2 sous 9 *deniers* paid in interest by the castellan Falconieri are entered only in order to prevent them from having to appear right from the start in the real credits, since, legally, interest was not a due; it remained uncertain, and depended on the rates of exchange. In 1453, Della Casa and Guadagni had not yet invented the true profit-and-loss account, which would balance the sum initially lent against that which would settle the deal, and where *avere* would mean profit and *deve*, loss.

By contrast, some accountants in Florence, Siena, and Lucca in the 1300s seem to have adopted accounting methods that were genuinely inclusive and systematic, as seen in the books kept by the *Massari* (stewards) who managed the finances of the Commune of Genoa. The same system can be found a century later in Venice in the accounts of the Soranso brothers, where a real profit-and-loss account balances operations according to a logical scheme that later would be codified by Paciolo:

OPERATION	MUST GIVE	MUST HAVE
Transaction Purchase of cloth at 30 sous	Stock: cloth at 30 sous Cash account: 35 sous	Cash account: 30 sous
Sale of cloth for 35 sous		Stock: 30 sous cloth Profits and losses: 5 sous
Bank Loan or deposit received	Cash account: 10 sous	Ledger (lender's account): 10 sous
Repayment	Profit and loss: 2 sous	Cash: 12 sous

So profit and loss are to be found somewhere between the opening of an account and its successful or unsuccessful settlement. Profit is entered on the same side as credit, but as an *avere* (credit) of the company, not as the debt of a third party or of the company's cash book. Like that of the registered capital, this account is intended for presentation to shareholders or partners, or investors who were not specialists in the financial world and its methods of keeping accounts. They simply wanted to know how much money had been earned on their behalf. *Deve avere* meant one thing to them and one thing only: what they would get when it came to liquidating the company. Once again, logic triumphed. Profit balances sales, on a par with purchase.

This time the system was consistent. This can be seen clearly when a depositor converts his credit or joint deposit and puts this money into the social capital of the company. The social capital is increased at the expense of the client's credit account, which has been integrated into the company by conversion into shares.

OPERATION	MUST GIVE	MUST HAVE
Credit	Cash account	Ledger
Conversion of credit into shares	Ledger	Capital

It is now clear that the significance of these entries—of the headings *doit donner* (must give) and *doit avoir* (must have)—evolved pragmatically. They are tacitly understood as conventions. People needed to know what they were talking about and with whom they were dealing. Businessmen understood this well, since they were quite capable of counting as credit to their company both money incorporated into the capital and money earned, and as credit belonging to the client's account or cash account the money that was owed to either of them and that would no longer be requested from the cashier.

By the fifteenth century, accountants had effectively mastered the system, which would be quite sufficient for economic analysis until late into the twentieth century. Everything was entered into their books that could account for fluctuations in the social capital and the ongoing changes in daily business. Above all, they demonstrated the economic results achieved by the business during a fixed period.

Businessmen now could see where they were going because they had at last gotten their bearings. They could estimate their costs. And they knew the return on yesterday's decisions.

FIFTEEN

The Power of Business

*P*erhaps because they had been created by businessmen, some towns seemed to be made for them. Such were the towns in the Empire where the sovereign authority of the emperor was distant and scarcely noticeable, when it was not actually rejected. Such were the towns of northern and central Italy where the imperial party—the Ghibellines—did not necessarily support the emperor, and where alliances between towns were often more significant than the periodic affirmations of imperial unity. Such were the German towns where the struggle for the imperial crown was considered an issue for princes and archbishops, and of little concern to the townspeople.

At Florence and Lübeck, at Genoa and Hamburg, the real political power lay with the people. In Italy this was sometimes the financial and merchant aristocracy, the *popolo grasso*, at others, the *popolo minuto* of the shop or workshop. In the Hanseatic towns, it was the League's council which solely represented, in theory at least, the merchant class.

Even before the emergence of the bourgeoisie in the eleventh and twelfth centuries, there were towns over which a sovereign power had asserted its authority. The new powers in the towns, businessmen and tradesmen, although initially unsure, soon associated themselves with this convenient ally—convenient because distant—against the more local powers—the count or the lord, the bishop or abbot—inherited from Carolingian times. Whether it was townspeople involved in dispute with a castellan, or the common people with a business patriciate inclined to confuse its own interests with those of the town, all appealed to the sovereign—the king of France, of England, or of Aragon. The patricians of Ypres, playing a subtle but often improvised game, even went so far as to appeal to the king of France over the head of the count of Flanders. Similarly, the guilds of Ghent, in an apparently nationalistic gesture, declined to rally to another count of Flanders who was eager to pay homage to the king of France.

In short, there were businessmen throughout Europe who were fully aware of the political power they possessed or might possess. Some also knew what they could expect from political powers based elsewhere. From the Florentine *arti* that chose their *priori* to govern the city and formulate its policies, to the European horizon of the Parisians who elected *échevins* (municipal magistrates) to watch over the privileges granted to the town and negotiate local taxes with royal officials, the pretensions and real power of businessmen were strikingly varied. The Parisian's view of his role in the politics of his city was very different from that of the Florentine.

Trade and Political Advancement

In the course of the thirteenth century the towns of the Empire seized rights left unclaimed when sovereign power weakened. Even before 1250, the great Italian towns to the north of the papal state usurped one after another a variety of royal prerogatives, ranging from justice, to minting of money, to diplomatic relations. Practically independent as early as 1167, Milan became its own master in 1225. Emancipated in 1114, Bologna followed Milan in 1230. Next to come were Siena shortly after 1240—certainly no later than 1277—and Florence in 1250, when, under the slogan "Long live the People!" the bourgeoisie rose against the control of the old aristocracy, which was finally swept away with the defeat of the last great Hohenstaufen, Frederick II.

The rise of personal lordships in northern Italy posed a threat to such middle-class autonomy. The Este, Visconti, and Malatesta families were to frustrate for many years any hopes of a merchant republic in Ferrara after 1240, in Milan after 1277, or in Rimini after 1295. All these were towns where there did not yet exist a well-established and well-connected merchant class strong enough to stand up to the political schemes fabricated here by the Ghibellines, who found it convenient to rely on the power of the emperor, and there by the Guelphs, who were no less opportunist in their alliances with the papacy and the Angevins in Naples.

At the price of many highly contrived alliances, the power of the people, with all that such a word can embrace in the way of political and social diversity in both time and space, was preserved in those towns where business circles were already asserting their power in foreign relations and where the strength of the guilds was already giving urban society its professional cohesiveness. The great ports—Pisa, Genoa, and Venice—soon became merchant republics in all but name. Siena and Florence became independent political forces at the very heart of the struggle between parties and factions that occupied the princes, without, for all that, succeeding—except perhaps in the case of the Guelphs at the time of Robert of Anjou (king from 1309 to 1343)—in mastering it. While changes in political loyalties might temporarily allow a lord to rule in Florence or, later, in Genoa, the political structure of the great merchant towns would, nevertheless, remain unchanged in its broad outlines until the modern day. The same was true in reverse for Milan, where industrial and commercial development was to come too late.

Things were very different in Germany, where the merchant towns, long defended against feudalism by the Hohenstaufens of the twelfth century, were able to keep their autonomy in the thirteenth century. This was in spite of violent opposition from Frederick II, who was concerned to win the princes over to his side. Here again, it was a series of alliances—and a common policy of political and commercial relations—that protected the quasi independence of the urban patriciates. Leagues of Westphalian towns, of the towns of Lower Saxony, and of the Rhine around 1250 were a clear demonstration of this determination, when royal power, on the eve of the Great Interregnum, was up for auction to the highest bidder. Towns set themselves up as local capitals, Dortmund for Westphalia and, later, Brunswick for Saxony. In the majority of cases, this involved guaranteeing the reciprocal freedom of regional markets and a fair system of common justice. They were, in other words, protecting their economic space.

An alliance of this kind, concluded in the 1230s between Lübeck and Hamburg, would lead to the benefits of a common monetary system—both towns minting the same pfennig—and a shared network of diplomatic relations before expanding, between 1265 and 1280, into the vast complex of Wendish towns—Lüneburg, Stralsund, Wismar, Rostock—and to the new towns and markets on the Baltic that would form the Hanseatic League. The member towns agreed to conduct the same economic policies, confronting together the problems involved in sharing commercial areas and dealing with external competition. Each town, like a miniature republic oblivious of the Empire, maintained its own autonomy.

Fully formed by the mid-fourteenth century, the League formalized its hierarchical structure in 1356. Despite many underlying tensions, this structure benefited Lübeck in particular, because of its central position as much as its economic preeminence. But though the General Diet of the League was held three times out of four in Lübeck, it should be noted that all the member towns participated—in practice, absenteeism was soon to become a common problem—and Lübeck could impose its will only at the cost of interminable negotiations. Whatever its internal problems, the League was, and remained, an organization of and for the merchant classes.

Germany had no objections—quite the reverse. The Great Interregnum and its aftermath meant that, during the second half of the thirteenth century, towns were left with considerable responsibility for keeping the public and private peace. Diplomatic alliances were established, making individual towns the new pieces on the European chessboard. Princes themselves dealt with the towns as with fellow princes. The "Golden Bull" of 1356, in which the emperor Charles IV laid down for a long time to come the procedure for election to the Empire, recognized the right of the towns to special alliances. This was tantamount to saying that they could form leagues.

Of course, the towns continued to pay taxes. Paradoxically, this had the effect of reinforcing their autonomy, since it gave yet another prerogative to local government: by negotiating the overall sum and taking on the task of collecting it, the town became an indispensable intermediary. When Rudolph of Habsburg attempted to go directly to the taxpayers, the towns rose up in protest.

It was as an independent body that, in 1414, the town of Cologne, with a loan of 25,000 florins and a gift of another 5,000, bought the support of the future emperor, Sigismund, against the new archbishop. The latter having offered 18,000 florins, Cologne was forced to find another 9,000 to beat his bid.

The merchant class had been able to take advantage of the increasing remoteness of sovereign power to establish for itself, in both Germany and Italy, a position of political autonomy that was strongly to influence both the structures and the attitudes of society. The town had become prince, but it was a bourgeois prince. However involved he was in the governing of the town, the principal role of the citizen or burger continued to be in economic life.

The regal image of the doge of Venice and his symbolic marriage with the sea in the presence of the assembled consuls did not, despite appearances, mean that the doge's government was a royal government served, as in France and England, by career officials, drawing their livelihood from public service in the short term and, in the long term, the means to their advancement in society. More than once, in the fourteenth century, the Forty asked the Grand Council to remind the magistrates of the limits on their right to demand a salary or to mortgage the revenues in their care—in other words, to restrain the possibilities they might have to derive personal profit from that aspect of public power entrusted to them. At the same time, this same Grand Council was involved in the wheat and wine trade with Crete, was supplying the famine-stricken Negrepont with provisions, fixing the price for the transport of Cypriot salt, guaranteeing the city's trading monopoly in pepper, supervising shipbuilding and controlling the movement of the galleys, when it was not involved in some deal involving usury. Even if the captains, rectors, castellans, and other officials were professional civil servants, the policies they enforced were those of the merchant class.

In this world where even justice had to give way to the merchant's yardstick, the only one to pursue a profession entirely in the public service was the notary. Florence would even rather belatedly make the profession one of the "Major Arts." But there was another world that remained very much apart—that of the clerics. It should be noted, of course, that many merchant families placed some of their members in the church: thus we find an Angelo Acciaiuoli on the bishop's throne in Florence and a Bartolo Bardi as bishop of Spoleto.

The army, too, did not escape the influence of the business world. Created in Italy to ensure that the military power and its role in political government remained outside the internal squabbles of city life, the *podestà* saw its function progressively reduced. The army by now consisted of companies led by captains from outside the town and without a role in municipal society. These were the forerunners of the *condottieri*. The choice of such captains, however, was a matter for the citizens, the businessmen who ran the city and fixed the salaries of the armed services. Supreme command remained with the political power, the counselors of Lübeck or the *priori* of the guilds in Florence. It was the *gonfaloniere di giudizia* (gonfalonier of justice) himself, the merchant Niccolò di Jacopo degli Alberti, of a great business family, who, in 1363, at the head of the Florentine army, won a decisive victory over the Pisans after a war where the stakes were entirely economic. Niccolò Alberti had been shrewd enough to see that the defense of Florence's access to the open sea was, like so much else, good commercial sense.

A political post thus seemed to be the reward for a successful career in trading and banking. Public office in the Hanseatic towns went to the heads of rich families when it came time for them to retire from their commercial travels. Born around 1420 and living in Lübeck in 1450, Heinrich Castorp was a town counselor at the age of forty-two and burgomaster at fifty-two. In 1474 he took part in the Utrecht conference where the Hanseatic League negotiated a peace with France and England.

The same for a Florentine, who took on this or that public post between two voyages in his life as a merchant; his highest responsibilities awaited him when he returned home to grow old in the *palazzo* bearing his family name. After thirty-two years of traveling with spells living abroad—in Antwerp and London as well as in the distant East—Francesco di Balduccio Pegolotti, author of the *Pratica della Mercatura* (A Merchant's Guide), returned to Florence to be a district gonfalonier in 1331 and 1340, *priore* of his guild in 1346 and, in the same year, *gonfaloniere di giudizia*. During the following century, on his somewhat ignominious return at the age of seventy-one from Bruges in 1496, Tommaso Portinari would be ambassador, *Capitano del Popolo*, and judge at the *Mercanzia*.

Lesser merchants contented themselves with positions that may have been less prestigious but that, in a small town, left their mark. Francesco di Marco Datini was a counselor in his hometown of Prato and played an active role in the financial duties of the commune. He was effectively the banker—or, more accurately, creditor—of the municipal treasury. He it was who, in 1388, advanced the funds for the wheat needed to supply the local population. For two months he was even *gonfaloniere di giudizia*—for Prato, needless to say. In this small industrial town within the sphere of Florence, a man like Datini, returning home to the fold, could become, over a period of almost thirty years, a figure of considerable stature.

The Oligarchy

Although the political structures retained for many decades the appearance of democracy, in reality they were all pure oligarchies. As time went by, and despite some popular uprisings such as that of the *popolo* in Florence, power increasingly belonged to a handful of families who held the economic reins in town. It is true that all citizens had the right to attend the assemblies, all counselors were elected as were all the magistrates, unless they were chosen by lot. Nevertheless, reality lay elsewhere.

The political framework of the Florentine government consisted of three distinct bodies. Established originally after the revolt of 1250 and reinstated in 1284, the *popolo* was originally a military institution and civic body intended to keep out the nobles. With its hierarchy of twenty districts commanded by elected gonfaloniers, the *popolo* would have been a democratic government but for the fact that it had to compromise over every matter with all the other bodies in the bewildering political complex that ran Florence. There was the Commune, the long-established municipal body that, as early as the twelfth century, shared power with the military *podestà* and, in the fourteenth century, was being closely watched by the Guelphs, anxious to see how Florence would act in relation to other powers in the Italian peninsula. And then, most importantly, there was the *Signoria,* whose proud buildings and high towers dominated the city. This body was to establish, in the course of the thirteenth century, a truly professional government to which all economic hierarchies aspired.

The *arti* elected the consuls while the *priori* were chosen by lottery. But the lottery was carried out under the auspices of the *Arti Maggiori* ("Major Guilds"), and it was no secret that the only names put into the leather bag were those of members of the most important merchant families. As for the *gonfaloniere di giudizia,* elected by the *priori* and the de facto master of the *Signoria,* he emerged increasingly as representative of the financial interests of the merchant oligarchy and its descendants. It was a group of these families, the Pitti, Salviati, Acciaiuoli, Tornabuoni, and Albizzi, that would form the

Council of a Hundred thanks to which Cosimo de' Medici—the Great, *Pater Patriae*—was able to hold the reins of political life. When, in 1471, Lorenzo de' Medici—the Magnificent—cynically reduced the number of *Arti Minori* (minor guilds) from fourteen to five, abolished the office of *capitano del popolo,* and reduced the role of the *podestà* to the most humble duties, he was doing no more than enacting the political realities of a power that was concentrated entirely in the hands of the *Signoria.* Throughout the 150 years preceding Cosimo's rule, democracy would not have been possible had it not been for the political exclusion of the nobility and the few ancient families that, having made their fortunes in the twelfth century, were regarded in the thirteenth as "magnates."

Similar results were achieved elsewhere by simpler methods. After the *Serrata* of 1297 was drawn up, no new families were allowed to participate in the Venetian Grand Council. Some thousand important citizens governed the town of Venice and its empire that stretched from Crete to Rhodes and as far as Phocaea in Asia Minor. This same Grand Council, within whose walls the chief merchant families conducted their business among themselves, elected the 120 members of the Senate, the Council of Ten, and the doge. The doge was the personification of Venice. Standing on the balcony over-looking the Lagoon, he presented a magnificent and ceremonious figure, but he was in reality a monarch without power, controlled by the Ten and closely watched by the six counselors elected by the *sestieri* (districts). Any suggestions he put forward were usually opposed because of an understand-able suspicion of his lifelong term of office. Whatever his position, every patrician had a role in political power. No aspect of the city's policies escaped the notice of the business patriciate that mingled fiscal matters with opportunities in maritime armaments, mixing salt and grain in a diplomacy that operated on a scale encompassing the length and breadth of the Mediterranean.

Things were very different in Genoa. Here the 300 members of the Grand Council included artisans. Above all, elected by a special assembly and not by the Grand Council, the successors of Simon Boccanegra—the first doge, elected in 1339 following the Venetian example—were in no way beholden to those who sat with them in the council. The doge of Genoa was thus able to enjoy a genuine freedom of action at times of internal peace. By contrast, he had only very minimal civic support in times of difficulty. The high turnover in doges is an eloquent indication of the instabil-ity of the institution. Forced in practice to remain on good terms with the Council of Ancients and, in the fifteenth century, with the protectors of the *San Giorgio,* the doge held power only insofar as he was able to use it for the best economic interests of the city. The business oligarchy was, however, less obviously in charge in Genoa than was the case in Venice or Florence.

The individualism of the Genoese was not helpful to the union of political government and economic initiatives. Nevertheless, the fortunes of the city lay in the hands of those who gave it life.

In Germany, the towns tended to be dominated by a business patriarchate consisting of rich merchants, *rentiers* from the merchant classes, shipowners, and even prosperous artisans. The upper echelons of this patriarchate began to be defined by family—the *Erfsaten* in Dortmund for example—or by pretensions to the military nobility—the "cavaliers" and "maidens"—as well as by a demonstration of wealth. The basis of this oligarchy was quite straightforward, as can be seen from the political influence, in Cologne, of the *Reicherzeche,* or "Circle of the Rich," that governed the town until the end of the fourteenth century.

After a crisis of the patrician regime in the period 1408–16, Lübeck reserved half the seats in the Council for humbler representatives of the business community, for artisans, particularly the brewers, and small tradesmen. A number of uprisings—as in Cologne in 1364, 1370, and 1396, or in Lübeck in 1383—and some temporary concessions in response to popular movements did little to change a political structure from which the majority of Hanseatic towns never departed. The town belonged to its merchants. Professional guilds—often that of the cloth merchants—acted as a kind of institutional broker between those active in the economic world and the organs of municipal government, the Burgomaster and the Council. Such a body was that in Lübeck, founded in 1379 and first meeting in the chapel of the convent that gave it its name of "The Society of St. Catherine." Consisting of some fifty families by the fifteenth century, its members represented all the heads of the business patriciate. In other words, the town councils, regional diets, and, obviously, the general Diet of the Hanseatic League, where each member town had two or three representatives, were composed solely of this patriciate.

The political autonomy of the towns of the interior had been won at the expense of the nobility, that is, the military aristocracy and the landed nobility. The ports, by contrast, had had little difficulty in shaking off a yoke of nobility that had rarely become firmly established in those regions which had seemed to be of no great geographical interest before the economic renaissance of the eleventh and twelfth centuries. Although the Venetians dated the history of their doges back to a military leader of 697, Venice was not sufficiently unified before the beginning of the eleventh century to have established the basis of any kind of feudal power. The ports, therefore, were able to remain untroubled by the problem that was to plague so many small merchant communities that, between the eleventh and thirteenth centuries, had turned their towns into something more than ancient bishoprics with a count or a lord in his castle. They had made town society into something other than a replica of the feudal hierarchy created by the imposition of rights over men and land. They had made something important of the town, which landowners continued to view, even in regions long ago urbanized, as an aberration on the margins of rural society.

Although the evolution toward bourgeois society was often hastened by a period of crisis, breakdowns of society were in reality less common than it might seem. After the upheavals of the thirteenth century and two periods of government by the *popolo*, Florence firmly banished from political life anyone who could possibly be a member of the nobility. Cleverly embracing in a single decree of 1293 both the old landed nobility and an already well-established business oligarchy, the "Ordinances of Justice" deprived the magnates of any political role. A list of 147 families was published and a special unofficial law was applied to them. In some cases even their houses were torn down.

Unmindful of the role played by aristocrats like Corso Donati in the defense of the republic in 1289 at the battle of Campaldino, and above all aware of the cost in taxes of the victory over Arezzo, the *popolani* rejoiced at the takeover of the town's business affairs by the *popolo grasso*, the middle classes. Inevitably these moments of excess calmed down. Retreating to their estates, the nobility would scarcely put in an appearance in a town where, after all, the communal preoccupations were not theirs. They were tolerated in the *arti*, but they were left standing outside the doors of the councils. The language being spoken inside was becoming increasingly foreign to them. Compromised by his leadership of the "white" Guelphs, and then by a marriage of convenience with the Ghibellines, and defeated and executed in 1308, Corso Donati is condemned by Dante in his *Divine Comedy* to be dragged endlessly by his bolting horse toward Hell.

Elsewhere relations were better. The German towns allowed a number of unthreatening nobles to sit in their councils. In fact, the nobility had no more interest in the sea than the townspeople had in the land. Genoa allotted half of its public offices to the *alberghi*, descendants of the most ancient families. Thanks to the campaign long waged by the Boccanegra family, the doge was always chosen from the ranks of the common people. Nevertheless, it was invariably the richest members of the group who monopolized the position. Whether in Genoa or Florence, "popular" did not mean poor. Neither the Fregosi nor the Adornos were anything but great lords, rich, in the Genoese manner, in both estates and ships.

The situation in Venice presented a paradox. Not only was their power not feared, but the nobility was even given a privileged position. This may be explained by the fact that the Venetian nobility was, more than any other, an urban nobility. Landowners from the moment Venice expanded onto the mainland, officials and settlers during the period of colonization, shipowners and merchants at all times, the nobility did not lay claim to either an origin or a function different from those of the middle-class citizens.

These old families, which, according to tradition, had taken part in the election of the first doge, were perceived more as a legendary bourgeoisie than as a military aristocracy. Their members enjoyed in practice, though not in law, a preeminence in all spheres of political life. They dominated the commissions that chose the doge, leaving to others only the privilege of acclaiming the newly elected leader. Some dozen families, closely linked by the matrimonial alliances so essential to the perpetuation of this power, legislated in both the Grand Council and the Senate. It would have been hard to find a Venetian in the latter body who was not a patrician. There was nothing surprising about this. The Venetian aristocracy considered itself the aristocracy but behaved no differently from the bourgeoisie. Here no legal distinction was made between classes, those ruling in La Serenissima being simply the richest and oldest families.

If the business world differed from place to place in its relations to the old nobility, it had, nevertheless, one thing in common: every instance saw the triumph of the merchants. They had been successful everywhere in eliminating those artisans who had once been their companions in arms in the now distant struggle—during the eleventh and twelfth centuries—for urban emancipation. Society was beginning to exclude those at the bottom. Underpinning the political system were the socioprofessional bodies: the guilds, crafts, or *arti*—and they were in agreement on the need to exclude outsiders. This they did by imposing legal and economic conditions, by co-optation, subscriptions, even the *numerus clausus*.

Small co-opted groups, the merchant guilds in the German towns were less prepared to accept as a member an artisan or shopkeeper than a rich foreign merchant who had married and settled in the town. All these groups, the cloth merchants' guilds in Bremen or Magdeburg, the "Circle of the Rich" in Cologne, the "Society of the Circle" in Lübeck, the "Confrérie of St. George" in Danzig, set themselves up as political filters controlling entrance to the councils. Family connections played the same important role in appointments to positions in government bodies as they did elsewhere in certain royal institutions—as in France, for example, for the *Parlement* or the exchequer. Nowhere is it put down in writing, but the lists of members speak volumes: in Lübeck, around 1380, all the counselors were related.

The *Serrata* of 1297 in Venice had closed the list of those eligible for the Grand Council, restricting it to the counselors allowed to participate in the lottery and those citizens declared eligible by the Forty. In fact, for more than a century there had been no one on the Grand Council who was not a descendant of a counselor. This situation was made official in 1322. The official list, kept since 1315 and known from 1506 as the *Libro d'Oro* or

Golden Book, contained, in the fifteenth century, some 1,200 to 1,300 names representing not more than two hundred families of great merchant patricians. In order to be included on the list, it was necessary to prove one's noble birth. The election of the doge was, more often than not, as in 1476 for Andrea Vendramin, an illustration of this monopoly of political power held by the most successful businessmen on the Grand Canal.

In Florence the system was quite straightforward. There had not been, since the thirteenth century, any real power in the *Signoria* other than for the seven *Arti Maggiori:* the *Calimala* (at first known simply as the "Guild of the Merchants"); the Guild of Moneylenders; the Wool Guild, where merchants had very quickly ousted any artisans; the *Arte di Por Santa Maria,* later to become the Silk Guild; the Guild of Haberdashers, Spice Merchants, and Doctors, which controlled much of the luxury trade with the East; and the Furriers and Fur Traders, who ensured the import of luxuries from northern Europe. The seventh and rather different body was that of the Guild of Notaries. Only the *Arti Maggiori* could take part in the Council of Priors, and only they could sit on the bench of the *Mercanzia*.

The five *Arti Mediocri,* which consisted of the master craftsmen and their associates—the clothes dealers and linen merchants, the shoemakers and hosiers, masons and carpenters, metal workers and butchers—were allowed to participate only in strictly local matters, such as the supplying of provisions and game. They were rigorously excluded from anything affecting the economic and foreign policies of the *Signoria*. As for the *Arti Minori,* which included anything from wine merchants and innkeepers to locksmiths and bakers, they confined themselves solely to matters concerning their own trades. They were able to elect a consul representing the *popolo;* but it was well known that, although he could make a lot of noise, this representative was not in a position to affect decisions.

As in Venice, the important thing was to have a fortune and influence. Political power was earned and justified by economic power—unless of course it was bought. The Medici owed their rise in the fifteenth century to a fortune acquired through their commercial and banking success.

The dominant group kept power within its own hands; at the very least it expected to exercise it. All contemporary political regimes revealed the same preoccupation with power, resolved with varying degrees of success, as the accession of the Medici in Florence would demonstrate. There was a need to curtail the threat of a monopoly, to avoid one-man rule. The sole raison d'être of the Council of Ten in Venice was to limit the powers of the doge. Similarly, in Florence, the numerous councils and the collegial structure of the *arti* with their *priori* had the effect of parceling out authority. There were very few examples, in any city, of appointments for life, the only exceptions being the doges of Venice and Genoa as well as a few administrative appointments, as of the procurators of St. Mark's in Venice. *Priori* and *gonfalonieri di giudizia* were elected to serve for no more than two months at a time. Even Cosimo de' Medici held the latter office only three times in thirty years of "government"—a total of six months. In the German towns, it was usual to elect the council for one year. Only rarely were people allowed to stand for election after having just completed a term of office.

Such precautions, while effective in Germany, were virtually useless in Italy. Influence, used in the interests of the dominant families, undermined any facade of egalitarianism erected by the ruling group. Continuity, absent from the fortunes of individuals, became firmly established in the great families. The lists of doges of Venice and Genoa show the same names recurring and alternating. In Genoa, the Adorno and Fregosi families competed for a century and a half as they succeeded each other and advanced their sons and nephews. This rivalry became overt in 1363 with the election of Gabriele Adorno, the immediate successor to Simon Boccanegra. Eight years later, Domenico Fregosi succeeded him. In 1390 another Fregosi replaced an Adorno. After eleven Fregosi and six Adorno doges, the monopoly of power was given a further twist when, in 1483, the archbishop, Paolo Fregosi, by now a cardinal, deposed his nephew Battista Fregosi and had himself proclaimed doge.

No family reclaimed power so often in Venice, where the rule of the doge was more stable. Nevertheless, besides the five Candiano doges of the ninth and tenth centuries, there were four Orseolo doges in the ten and eleventh centuries, three Contarenos from the eleventh to the fourteenth centuries, three Dandolos between the twelfth and fourteenth centuries, two Tiepolos (father and son) in the thirteenth century, three Gradenigos in the thirteenth and fourteenth centuries, and three Mocenigos in the fifteenth century.

Such things were less immediately obvious in Florence, because the names varied. Nevertheless, no one failed to notice that those who succeeded to the highest offices were all Medici protégés. From 1434, Cosimo became "first citizen of Florence." Everything was done openly according to his advice.

Business in Politics

This domination by the business world was to have far-reaching consequences. Never absent, but of secondary importance for a long time, economic concerns now largely determined political decision making. The opening up of trade, and the need for sea transport, led to the establishment of territorial states. It was the need for a route or access to the sea, or for space as the basis of economic independence, that stimulated the territorial ambitions of Florence, Lucca, or Siena. When Venice effectively colonized parts of Romania, the first thought was of the opportunity for new food supplies and then of the possibilities for trade offered to the city of the doges. The Venetian territory on the mainland—the terra firma—had been established with the sole intention of balancing the economic zones of the peninsula against the economic forces at the heart of the Venetian empire.

In the same way, the Casa di San Giorgio determined Genoa's colonial policies in the fifteenth century. This is no surprise, since profits from overseas trading represented a sizable portion of the income used by the commune to service the public debt—in other words, for interest payments made by the *San Giorgio*. Already in the fourteenth century the commune had signed a treaty with the king of England agreeing to reciprocal military and economic assistance: the Genoese needed royal protection for their business in England while Edward III needed the naval strength of the Genoese fleet.

Economic arguments were so powerful that political alliances could be broken as a result of shifts in the map of trading relations. Florence, finally a maritime power and at last in a position to rival Venice on the sea, turned to Milan, for example, making common cause with the Sforza family at the conference at Lodi in 1454. From this time, Florence was able to assess the success of her policies and alliances as much on the sea as within Italy.

The merchant was ready to fight for his routes, his ports, and his markets, whether close at hand or far away. If necessary, he was prepared to drag his city into war. But first he would try the subtle art of negotiation. Thus we see the Hanseatic patriciates doing everything possible to avoid war. However late in the day, concessions in the name of diplomacy were always preferable to even the most just wars.

Economic objectives thus dominated both the domestic and the foreign policies of the city-states that never forgot that they were first and foremost merchant cities whose independence depended entirely on their prosperity. All the prerogatives of sovereignty found in a monarchy—taxation, the right to coin money, diplomacy—were here the undisputed prerogatives of those who watched over both the greatness and wealth of the *res publica*.

The municipal oligarchies understandably attempted to establish and maintain a fiscal system favorable to business—a system that would support collective expansion and protect the inheritance of the dominant families. The greatest enemy to this aim was direct taxation, which struck the rich in proportion to the wealth of their current enterprises and accumulated profits. Even a town like Bruges, which had to compromise with the demands of a prince, was able, in the fourteenth century, to abolish all taxes on estates. The time of the poll tax, where the rich man paid no more than the poor man, had long gone. Now, rather than a tax of "so much in the pound" on land and possessions, or a proportional tax based on wealth, a tax of "so much in the pound" on sales and purchases was deemed preferable. Although it hit trade, it was ultimately the consumer who paid. In Bruges, indirect taxation raised 80 to 90 percent of the town's revenues. In effect, the foreign merchants were being charged for their trade and the local population for their consumption.

The impact of these public charges on the lower classes was felt even more strongly in the merchant republics. Direct taxation represented some 10 percent of the revenues of fourteenth-century Florence, including a poll tax that, giving a nod in the direction of the civic fiction that "everyone pays," taxed the rich in a manner that was little more than symbolic. When Florence was forced in 1494 to reintroduce direct taxation, the method chosen was a tax on land that spared both business and income. Smaller cities acted similarly: direct taxation in Pistoia, at the peak of its prosperity in the fourteenth century, provided no more than 5 percent of the communal revenues.

In these circumstances it is not surprising that changes in taxation often provoked social upheaval. French taxpayers complained bitterly about the poll tax that favored the richest, demanding, often with violence, a tax where "the strong carried the weak." Similarly, citizens of the independent towns of Germany and Italy rose up periodically against the distribution of taxes and the excessive use of borrowing that meant good business in merchant circles, but not to artisans and small shopkeepers. When the people in Nuremberg rose up in 1348, or in Frankfurt in 1364, it was due in large part to a tax system that too obviously served the oligarchy.

The people of Rouen in the "Harelle" uprising of 1382, like the Parisians in the "Maillotin" revolt, had a similar grievance. The reimposition of an indirect tax on retail trade was seen as a victory for the richer merchant classes, formerly in power under Charles V and believed by the common people to have been removed. The circumstances of the "Maillotin" uprising are well known, the rioting having been sparked in the Halles district by the introduction of a few *deniers* in tax on a bunch of watercress.

It was not only the big metropolitan centers that got their towns into debt, imposing heavy communal taxes on the common people and putting substantial amounts of interest into the pockets of the merchants in power. While such indebtedness was endemic in the towns of France before the intervention of St. Louis and Alphonse of Poitiers, and later Philip the Fair, it seems to have been regarded as perfectly normal by the local oligarchies dominating even the most modest German towns. In 1408, a very ordinary man like the burgomaster of the small town of Rotenburg in Hesse, Heinrich Topler, was the creditor in some hundred and twenty municipalities.

Indirect taxation lent itself to tax-farming, and, as a consequence, to discounting: the man who took on the farm of a *gabelle* was making an advance by paying for his lease. The preferential treatment given to him by the merchant governments thus led to public borrowing and to that system of financing adopted by all the republics governed by the merchant milieus and so closely dependent on expectations of growth. As early as the end of the thirteenth century, the entire financial structure of Venice depended on loans that were guaranteed and repaid from revenues of the *dazio,* the indirect tax on the movement of goods—a tax ultimately paid by the consumer. In fourteenth-century Pisa, compulsory borrowing became established as a regular government practice. Repayment came partly from taxes and partly from state exploitation of the iron mines on the island of Elba. Genoa did the same, making compulsory lending the basis of the system managed in the fourteenth century by the *compere* of creditors of the commune and, in the fifteenth century, by the Casa di San Giorgio.

Paying close attention, from the thirteenth century onward, to that essential requisite of economics—a sufficient supply of the means of payment—monetary policy began to move in the direction favored by the interests of the dominant commercial groups. In Metz, a bishopric where the municipal magistrates—the *échevins* and the "Thirteen Jurors"—legislated endlessly in the matter of obligations, all monetary decisions were influenced by this one preoccupation: the need to maintain the intrinsic value of the loans.

The weak relationship between gold and silver owed nothing to the Aristotelians and theologians who expounded on the subject of money in the king of France's Council. In a city like Florence, it was a matter of giving the advantage to the great entrepreneurs who paid their workers in silver but who were themselves paid in gold for their wholesale sales in the markets both near and far. A piece of cloth costing twenty or thirty florins was thus worth more days of work by the fuller or dyer earning four or five sous. Genoa went further: from 1447 onward, all deals struck in major commerce would have to be settled in gold.

The result of all this was a diplomacy of business. Not a treaty was signed where the merchant republics did not insert preferential clauses, giving them freedom of commercial access or preferential customs duties. The treaty negotiated in 1369 between Pisa and Florence provides for free access for the companies at Porto Pisano and furnishes a list of 108 Florentine companies that benefit from tax exemptions in Pisa. It was all too clear that the *Signoria* was entirely subservient to the merchants' interests. It became the official duty of the protectors of San Giorgio in Genoa to determine a customs policy that would result immediately in revenue from *gabelles,* industrial exploitation and commercial monopolies that could ensure the interest for the public debt.

At the same time, the economy became a political instrument. The

Venetian banks had only one important client, La Serenissima, and they refused credit to any other states, whether city-states or monarchies. The Hanseatic League was capable of imposing an embargo on any power it wished to cripple: Bruges twice had this unpleasant experience when the Hanseatic merchants transferred their staple to Dordrecht in 1358–60 and again in 1388. The League suffered from this move, but not as much as Bruges, which lost the essential advantage of its position along with the other Flemish towns. Deprived of Prussian grain, particularly in a year when the harvest in Flanders had failed, deprived also of the taxes they normally levied—as a port of call—on all trade on the North Sea, and with their continental trade threatened by Cologne's intransigent support of the blockade, the Flemish were forced to back down in 1360. The Hanseatic merchants were able to recover and even increase the tax privileges that Bruges, hard pressed by difficult times, had wanted to reduce. After another crisis during the years 1388 to 1392, yet more concessions—and an indemnity—were needed to persuade the Hanseatic merchants to return.

This subordination of the affairs of state to the imperatives of the economy turned out to have an unexpected advantage for the governments of the communes, as emphasized, none too subtly, around 1339, in Ambrogio Lorenzetti's fresco in the *Palazzo communale* of Siena, called "Good Government." Leaving aside the idyllic view of the social harmony ensuing from prosperity that the Sienese merchants wished to portray here, one has to admit that a concern for the interests of the merchants certainly led, if not to equality, then at least to a high level of expertise in management and financial administration. The cities dominated by trade were those where the most accurate municipal accounts were kept.

Naturally, even those business circles familiar with double-entry bookkeeping did not dream of introducing it into the account books of public finances, but this was because many years of experience in cost assessment had led them to believe that cities had nothing to do with a systematic method of accounting with concepts quite foreign to public finance. If Florence did not adopt the double-entry system for its accounts, it was because there did not seem to be any point in including in an analysis of the commune's property the value of the *palazzo del podestà*—known to us today as the Bargello. It would have been useless to enter such virtual capital in the accounts as an asset. A decree issued in Genoa in 1327, however, orders that the commune's accounts be kept "like those of a bank." This seems to imply some analysis of real and potential resources and a distribution of the receipts and expenses among these records of property—the treasury account books—and the third-party accounts—the creditors' account books.

Elsewhere, where the businessman's technical mastery had not attained the systematic rigor of the Italians, the merchant and the municipal accountant were inspired by similar practices. In southwest Germany, public and private account books were kept in the same way. The chief concern was generally, as in Constance, to analyze receipts and expenses, in their separate, but parallel, registers. During the same period, the clerks of the Apostolic Chamber also kept accounts of the pope's revenues and expenses. Financial analysis was becoming more sophisticated, but no one sought to follow the Italian accountants in their move, in the management of private business, toward books that balanced by means of double-entry accounting.

The merchant circles who controlled municipal finance and provided for the treasurers and the accountants understood this principle: their stock of cloth was an asset balanced by expenses from the "cash" account, while loans drawn on a commercial partner had to be entered in the opposite column from the debt, in favor of the depositors. The *Palazzo communale* and its contents, on the other hand, in no way balanced the cost of a war that it was sometimes possible to see as an investment. Similarly, the capacity of taxpayers to eat or drink—thereby paying a tax—could hardly be entered opposite the salary of the sergeant who kept order in the streets. The clear-sighted realism of the businessman demonstrated at all levels that one could govern a city as a businessman managed a business. Government could play a part in business, but for all that a city was not a business.

SIXTEEN

The Businessman and the Prince

*I*t was possible to be a loyal subject to one's king without renouncing one's aspirations to a place, and a role, in politics. Whether French or English, Castilian or Portuguese, businessmen knew that in their towns—unlike Genoa or Lübeck—power did not come from economic strength. The *res publica* sprang from different sources, and its definitions were different. For all that, business clearly could not be indifferent to the implications of fiscal policy or diplomacy.

It was well aware that it could realistically influence political economy only if it had a foothold in the various layers of political society. Although, in London or Lisbon, it was not the businessman who decided on war or peace, he could still listen to what was being said in the council and make his voice heard in financial negotiations between the sovereign power and parliament, the states general or provincial, or the Cortès. It was as important for him to determine the common stance of the town or region toward the monarchy's demands as to the competition with other economic powers.

Business in the City

Even in the heart of town, sovereign power greatly inhibited the activities of municipal bodies. Insofar as they were a social group, the middle classes had less and less autonomy. From England to Sicily, they saw their freedom of action restricted to the defense of their economic interests and, particularly, to the discussion of their contribution to the kingdom's financial burden. The monarchies, for their part, actively discouraged these urban leagues, the alliances that gave the Italian and German towns their strength. It was rare for relations to be established between towns; and they were more often the result of shared problems than deliberate initiatives. The relationship of the town to the sovereign could be conceived only in terms of submission—though that did not necessarily exclude discussion about matters of limited significance—or of rebellion.

The urban uprisings in Paris, Rouen, Ghent, and Reims during the fourteenth century were more the result of imitation than coordination. The insurgent Florentines had no idea of what was happening in Paris. At the peak of the riots of 1382, Parisians may have shouted "Long live Ghent," but those in Ghent knew nothing of this, and benefited not at all. In the end, these uprisings brought the towns nothing but the loss of their privileges—after the "Maillotins" incident it was thirty years before Paris was again allowed to elect échevins—and the imposition of crushing new taxes and indemnities. The lessons bore fruit in the fifteenth century: the middle classes were careful to steer clear of major political movements that had been introduced by the princes for their own benefit. In this matter the business community was at one with the small shopkeepers. In neither the Prague uprising of 1439 nor the League for the Public Good of 1465 did the economic powers in the towns support the uprising against feudalism. The businessman knew quite well that things always ended up with the prince making his peace and the towns begging his forgiveness. For some the end meant banquets and celebratory Te Deums to the accompaniment of pealing bells; for others it spelled ruin or the gallows.

There were thus two different political forces at work, each with its own objectives, in the two nonhierarchical spheres of town and kingdom. Unlike a duchy, composed of a pyramid of counties and estates, a kingdom did not consist of a hierarchy of towns. Within the confines of the state, the individual could be employed only for the common good—or "Common Profit," as it was called in medieval France—and could profit from it personally only within the framework of public service, which meant, above all, in the service of the prince.

These offices should not be confused with the municipal posts held in cities like Florence or Genoa. In the town, the burgess—in his role as citizen and not because he was a businessman or tradesman—took part in a form of municipal government whose aims and powers were limited by the presence of royal judges, royal administrators, and royal tax collectors.

Municipal government, thus, remained under the supervision of the sovereign and his bailiffs and sheriffs. It was essential for the conduct of business, but not in a position to make policy decisions. Although merchants were to be found among the London aldermen and the Toulouse capitouls, they never achieved the preeminence, even in the town halls, of their counterparts in the city-states.

It was the state that was preeminent, its power manifested even at the very heart of the town's institutions by the presence of representatives of the crown. In Toulouse, between 1380 and 1420, a quarter of the *capitouls* were drawn from the merchant classes—cloth merchants, money changers, and spice merchants. But there were an equal number of nobles and almost as many members of the legal profession—judges, lawyers, and notaries.

In Paris, where businessmen and tradesmen—clothiers, butchers, and money changers—had been in the majority among the *échevins* up to about 1450, for the simple reason that this body was not a municipal government but rather an organization of the "Guild of Water Merchants." But elections after the war suddenly resulted in provostships going to the merchants, while the *échevins* were increasingly composed of magistrates, lawyers in Parliament, officials in the exchequer or the *Chambre aux deniers,* and people from the Court of Aids. The provost of the merchants was one Denis Hesselin, provisions officer to the king, while the *échevin* was one Jean de Harlay, a man known to all as the *chevalier du guet,* or, in other words, the chief of police. The inspector at the Châtelet, Jean Colletier, would hold the office of *échevin* six times—a post supposedly held for a term of two years—from 1471 to 1485. No merchant was ever again to hold the position of provost of the merchants after the money changer Pierre des Landes, who was replaced in 1444 by a counselor in the Parlement. The legal profession had, until the time of Bedford, held on average one place in five at the Hôtel de Ville. By the mid-fifteenth century, they held two or three out of four. Only the City of London was to retain, until the end of the Middle Ages, an authentic merchant presence in its Guild Hall: the aldermen were all members of the merchant guilds.

It all came down to influence, and also to profits. Real power lay elsewhere. The jurisdiction of the municipal bodies was, and continued to be, limited. The City Hall dealt with matters such as the policing of the town, public health, transportation of goods, the town watch, and defense. As soon as trouble loomed and some specific danger threatened, the royal administration took over. It was the royal provost of the Châtelet, Hugues Aubriot, who organized the new defenses required for a Paris rendered vulnerable by its increasing size. The Bastille was a royal fortress; and when, in the time of Charles V, it came to building new surrounding walls, the Parisians had only the right to contribute to the cost.

This is not to say that the middle classes did not discuss municipal finances among themselves. Maintaining the city walls or repairing the paving stones, paying the sergeant or the person who looked after the water supply, was the responsibility of the inhabitants, and the notables among them would speak for all. Similarly, they would bargain with the king's men over the amount of the tax before deciding on how it should be allocated and collected. This was a matter, however, where in order to ensure not only a successful collection but also social peace in terms of public order, the royal officials were not prepared to yield an inch. Their task was greatly assisted by the cooperation of the majority of taxpayers, who were not inclined to divide the tax burden in favor of the merchant oligarchies.

Even where it was a matter of defending the economic interests of the town or the region, the municipal institutions could not, unlike governments of the independent towns, negotiate face to face—whether as friends or as enemies—with their competitors. Florence could negotiate with Siena, or Lübeck with Hamburg, but Lille could not negotiate with Amiens, nor Madrid with Cádiz. Everything had to be negotiated directly with the king, with his Council, or with the influential people in his entourage. Thus the importance of petitions delivered each year by town representatives at the assemblies and of the ambassadors dispatched to the court.

Tact and diplomacy were all-important. It would have been inconceivable to conclude a piece of business without allies in the marketplace and without making presents to those on the spot. When Louis XI made his triumphant entry into Lyons in 1476, the town was prepared:

> Alardin, treasurer, has supplied by command and written instruction of the town counselors, both to Monsignor d'Argenton, counselor and chamberlain to our lord the king and to Monsignor the bishop of Évreux, counselor of the said lord, for certain entertainments and services performed by the said lords on behalf of the said town, 63 royal écus of gold to the lord Argenton and 43 gold écus to the lord bishop of Évreux.
>
> The said Alardin has furthermore given, as mandated and ordered as above, the sum of 50 gold écus at a rate of 35 silver *gros* per écu, which sum has been given, supplied and delivered on behalf of the town to Madame du Bouchage for certain entertainments and services provided by M. du Bouchage, her husband, to the said town.

The assemblies did not have a truly political role except during times of crisis. The States General were able to take advantage of John II (the Good)'s financial problems to recast the system of taxation in the kingdom of France:

> It is ordered that from the three estates certain good, honest, solvent, loyal people, and above suspicion be directed and deputed, to arrange the things mentioned above throughout the country, appointing collectors and agents according to the directions and instructions that will be made on this matter.
>
> And, in addition to the individual commissioners and deputies for the different regions and counties, there shall be ordered and established by the three estates mentioned above nine good and honest people, that is to say, three of each estate, who will be generals and superintendents over all the others, and who will have two trustworthy and solvent general collectors.

Control from above became more oppressive, first with the defeat at Poitiers and then with the stormy sessions—this was the moment when the provost of merchants, Étienne Marcel, made his brief but dramatic appearance on the political scene of the kingdom—in a Parliament brought into disrepute by the volatile mood of the people. The alliance of interests between the reformist middle classes, who had risen up against the speculators on the Council and against a nobility incapable of translating their financial efforts into victory, and the peasants in the surrounding countryside, who had risen up against the landowners, was compromised. As the danger receded, royal absolutism hardened. Representatives were retained and described as "elected," but in reality it was the king who now nominated them.

It was in one such period of crisis that the English Parliament began to take action that could properly be called political. When it deposed Richard II in 1399 because of his too obvious enthusiasm for an entente with France, Parliament must also have kept in the back of its mind the problem of economic competition with Flanders.

Normally, when Parliament or, in France, the States General and States Provincial (for Languedoc, Normandy, and so on) discussed the total sums to be raised by taxation, they were skilled at getting their message through to the king and his representatives in the different economic domains. In this way the business world was able to pass on the benefits of its experience, often lacking in the king's officers, who were unfamiliar with the region or the business world, although many had recently emerged from it. The king of England was prepared to listen to the wool merchants in Parliament, for he knew that the royal finances were largely dependent on the volume of wool exports. The king of France was equally attentive to what deputies from the towns of the south had to tell him about the region's prosperity or poverty, essential knowledge when fixing the taxation rate.

Although well represented in the English Parliament, the businessmen's role was unobtrusive. It was the petty nobility, rather than the commoners, who were more inclined to intervene in the matter of the allocation of taxes. The merchants were more occupied with their own particular concerns, which were not necessarily those of their towns. Londoners often represented rural boroughs in Parliament, and their involvement in the political life of the kingdom generally followed a similar track to that of an aristocracy interested in the prosperity of the counties where they were landowners. This meant that the broadest and most effective pressure group was connected with the production and export of wool. Landowners who possessed flocks thus found common cause with wool merchants.

The situation in France was different. Elected in the towns along with notaries and lawyers, equally eminent representatives of the middle classes, merchants played an essential role in the provincial assemblies. It was in these assemblies, as we have seen, that contributions to the financial revenues of the state were fixed; and these negotiations gave local representatives an opportunity to influence policy, using as bargaining points their local trading privileges, particularly relating to the fairs, and tax exemptions. The nobility often tired of these assemblies in which it took little interest, since it enjoyed its own special rights, thus allowing the merchant classes to make the best use of their influence in establishing tax rates. This is particularly evident in Montpellier, where the first consul—usually a money changer—was invariably appointed as delegate to the assembly. The assembly was the place to talk figures.

This representation of regional interests varied in effectiveness according to place and time. Nevertheless, it was through such institutions that the business world was able to influence the allocation of taxes, particularly with regard to indirect taxes that benefited local commerce. Using the same channels, they also were able to press issues with long-lasting consequences. The Languedoc assembly persuaded Louis XI in 1471 and Charles VIII in 1484 to agree to limit the economic expansion of Lyons by prohibiting the import by land of spices into France. The Provence assembly got King René to regulate the enclosure of land, a measure consistently opposed by the graziers and farmers.

There were times when a delegation took on a legal aspect. In the late fifteenth century the Languedoc assembly petitioned the *Parlement* in Bordeaux, then that of Paris, finally the Grand Council, to allow the wine growers of Gaillac and northern Languedoc to sell their wine on the Quai des Chartrons from the day after St. Martin's Day (11 November). The people of Bordeaux objected, claiming a privilege permitting them to sell without interference from competitors until after Christmas.

The matters at stake impinged at times on the rights of the king himself. The same Languedoc assembly fought, session after session, for a repeal of the ban on payment in foreign coin—sensible enough in theory, but in practice causing all kinds of problems. In 1424, the *capitouls* instructed their delegates to the assembly in Le Puy to raise the issue:

As divers foreign merchants and others buy cloth, oils, honey, and other merchandise and foodstuffs and make other contacts and various deals, and for this reason carry with them different coins of gold and silver, let it be authorized to accept these for a value to be agreed by the parties involved, without any blame. . . .

As the city of Toulouse is situated close to different kingdoms and counties, such as those of Aragon, Navarre, Béarn, Foix, Armagnac, and to other lands and estates whence come many merchants to trade, bringing different gold and silver coins, let the aforementioned suppliants be authorized to accept the said coins for the value on which the parties agree, without any blame.

Perhaps the public confrontation of local interests built into the structure of the English Parliament made the vision of a common interest in the kingdom more of a reality than in France, where the notion of the *res publica* was torn between the practice of sending representatives to petition the king and that of strictly local negotiations. Whatever the case, the decrees of the English monarchs outdid one another in emphasizing the profound unity of the island's economy. The notions of the kingdom's common good and common profit took on, in the English tongue, resonances that the same words never acquired in France. On the Continent they were simply ready-made formulae and justifications for custom, not the expression of a genuine vision of the national economy.

Serving the Prince

Many merchants aspired to municipal office, and it was by way of this path that the Italian or German businessman managed to influence the affairs of state. Where policy was decided by the sovereign, a post in the prince's service was rarely accessible to merchants. Such offices were full-time posts, and it was not possible to be both cloth merchant and *bailli,* as one could be, in Italy, a money changer at the same time as *priore* of the guilds, or a shipowner and senator. Those who held high office were professionals; at this level the amateurism of annual appointees would not have been tolerated. A career in public service had to be orchestrated, involving as it did a move up the social ladder, the first step of which was the hardest to reach.

Though it was unlikely that the businessman would take up office in the royal administration, it was quite possible for his sons or nephews, who already were beginning to distance themselves from trade. They might have studied law and might be gradually moving away from those temporary appointments, in which the interests of business and public service coincided, such as taxation and local tax-farming. Whereas the older generation might remain money changers all their lives but also got themselves appointed collectors of one particular tax, a person of the next generation might effectively devote all his time to the collection of a variety of distinct duties or taxes that were assigned on a yearly basis, eventually winding up as permanent collector for an entire district.

If he intended to remain a merchant or money changer, the businessman was called to the prince's service only to perform occasional, vaguely defined, duties, outside the regular administrative framework and without prospects of a career in public life. A few exceptional figures, whose business interests were tightly interwoven with those of the prince, rose to the very top. Businessmen needed the prince. It was in their interest to gain a position in which they could influence policy. At the same time, they were too prominent to avoid notice, nor could they refuse to provide services or credit. The more business prospered, the more it seemed to be influenced by political factors.

Ideally, businessmen did not want administrative duties that would monopolize their time. What they coveted were positions of influence that opened the way to a network of useful contacts. The Italians, welcomed as counselors by princes all over Europe, were past masters at this game. Biche and Mouche were at one and the same time advisers, businessmen, and well-rewarded diplomats to Philip the Fair. Edward I, during this same period, admitted his banker Berto Frescobaldi to his council. Conte Gualter-otti was counselor to the count of Flanders, Louis de Nevers, who eventually made him his chancellor. In Bordeaux the *connétable* in charge of the financial policies of the duchy of Guyenne was Amerigo Frescobaldi. The queen of Naples, Jeanne I of Anjou, made Niccolò Acciaiuoli her counselor and subsequently her chief seneschal. Nor should we forget Dino Rapondi, coun-selor and banker to the duke of Burgundy at the end of the fourteenth century.

A century later, Tommaso Portinari, as the head of the Medici branch in Bruges, was not merely banker to Philip the Good and Charles the Bold, but he also had a seat on their council. In 1468 he participated in negotiations for the marriage of Duke Charles to Margaret of York, sister of the king of England, Edward IV. In 1487 he was in Milan as the ambassador of Maximil-ian of Habsburg, and in 1496 he was Philip the Fair's ambassador in London.

French businessmen were, in turn, accepted into the royal council, and some were already established in the chamber of accounts. In the fourteenth century, the father-in-law of Étienne Marcel, Pierre des Essarts, both cloth merchant and banker, became one of the principal merchants in the Paris market. But he was also banker and adviser to the throne. Although ennobled in 1320, he remained at heart a businessman, in defiance of the regulations. As the conclusion of this ambiguous career, in 1336 he replaced his younger brother Martin, who had long since given up trade, as Master of the Excheq-uer. In the fifteenth century, Jacques Coeur managed to combine the activities of merchant with those of counselor to the king, royal commissioner to the Languedoc assembly, and inspector general of taxes.

The middle classes were already represented in the council of John the Good. These were the Parisian families—Poilevilain, Lorris, Des Essarts, and Braque among others—long active in those areas touching both the king's service and the world of business and now making their way to both fortune and nobility. A century later, under Louis XI, they were present in sufficient numbers to provoke the sarcasm or jealousy of the nobles. The names that appear most frequently at this period are from Berry and Toura-ine—Beaune and Briçonnet. Raoulet Toustain, an important salt merchant on the Loire and the Seine, acted as agent, if not spy, to Louis XI at the time of the League of Public Good. In fact, there was no less mixing of careers in trade and public service than before. Michel Gaillart of Blois was, in 1463, farming the salt taxes in Poitou, Aunis, and Saintonge. In 1473 he became the chief official in charge of finances. By 1476 he was also the principal owner of the French galleys, bought from Jacques Coeur's successors. Learning from the painful experiences of his father and grandfather, Louis XI mistrusted the capital and its inhabitants, but not the business world whose style of dress he was notorious for adopting together with, more importantly, their political views and calculating realism.

No contemporary was as successful in achieving fortune and position through a combination of service to the prince and trade as Jacob Fugger, the Augsburg merchant who became banker and counselor to the Habsburgs. In the years before 1485 the Fugger family had established itself in the German market and in Venice, forging contacts but limiting its speculative activities. They had a position in mind, but it remained a local one. It was at this time that they came into contact with the count of Tyrol, a Habsburg.

The election of Maximilian as emperor and the speedy elimination of the dukes of Bavaria opened up new perspectives, guaranteeing to the Habsburgs the profits from the Tyrolean mines. Jacob Fugger knew how to make himself indispensable to this prince with so promising a future. It was a gamble, but a sure one: Maximilian continued to rely for advice on this man, who was now acting as his banker.

While financing the emperor's policy on a European scale, Fugger did not neglect his own economic aims. When, in 1493, the Fugger family bore the cost of the Habsburg embassy to the conference of Senlis that was to reward Maximilian with Artois, the Franche-Comté, and the Charolais, they took advantage of the result to open a branch in Antwerp, thus consolidating their position in northern Europe. For his bankers, Maximilian's triumph meant above all opportunities for new establishments in Hungary, Carinthia, Thuringia, and even the papal court in Rome.

When it came to financing the wars of an ambitious prince who was perfectly capable of finding credit elsewhere, Fugger showed himself to be extremely shrewd: he offered cash advances to be paid back at a later date in metal ore. Acting more with the instincts of a businessman than a speculator, he obtained between 10 and 20 percent on a more or less guaranteed profit from production. But Jacob "the Rich" was not content to stop there. The emperor's ambitions forced him ever more frequently to go cap in hand to Fugger. One war followed another, and the banker became more necessary than ever. Maximilian borrowed more than two hundred thousand florins from him in 1491. Not surprisingly, rates went up. The new emperor did not question the conditions that allowed Fugger, who had become a great capitalist and backer of the mining industry, both silver and copper, to take control of the Hungarian metal industry. By the beginning of the sixteenth century, Jacob Fugger and his partners were sole masters of the money market in the young Habsburg state. On the threshold of the modern age, the Fuggers had done what Biche and Mouche had first attempted in the 1300s and Jacques Coeur had tried a century and a half later: in a political regime that reserved for others the prerogatives of power, they had expanded the power of business to reach the level of the state.

A Clash of Interests

Businessmen derived primarily personal advantages from their involvement in political life. Each man acted for himself, and a seat in the royal council chamber had more to do with competition than mutual cooperation. Those who got close to the throne were chiefly concerned to promote deals, adjudications, privileges, and monopolies that touched them personally. Jacques Coeur took advantage of his influence over Charles VII to ensure the safety of his business in both Lyons and Languedoc. Palamèle Forbin, the viceroy of Provence and son of the most prominent businessman in Marseilles, used his position to control the farming of taxes. Each and every one made use of privileged access to information to manipulate the market. What more reliable basis for speculation than to be privy to the latest news about fiscal trends?

Although business deals might be large or small, there was no such thing as small news. The Parisian Bertrand Rournet, who farmed the dues on logs, discovered this to his cost when he had already successfully bid for and obtained the lease for the year 1426–27, only to find that the owners of the bathhouses—major consumers of firewood, needless to say—were once again trying to obtain a tax exemption. The previous year he had managed to get them to pay. This time he had misjudged the situation and got his fingers badly burned. The government had sided with the bathhouse proprietors. Even in such a modest speculative venture, it was advisable to know in advance whether wood for the public baths was likely to be taxed.

Public opinion was to prove very sensitive to such abuses of political position that could so easily influence affairs. Whoever had advance information was in a better position to influence decision making. Even if this were not the case, it was certainly what people thought, and a deep mistrust of speculators was one of the most constant grounds for the revolutionary rumblings in medieval towns. Taxes, changes to the currency, even defeat in war—for military setbacks always prompted taxpayers to wonder why they were paying taxes—could all be explained by the fact that the prince was governed by the speculators.

Some saw this desire to do away with speculators as nothing but jealousy. Those who were quick to condemn when outside the council were ready to seize on any advantage once inside. A rebellion like that led by Étienne Marcel was not so much the reaction of the common people to the bad government of John the Good, but rather that of the upper bourgeoisie cheated by one of their better informed fellows. Marcel made the worst mistake of his life when he turned down the chance to succeed his father-in-law Pierre des Essarts, who had been accused of fence-sitting by the angry reformists of 1346, following the defeat of Philip VI at Crécy. His brother-in-law Robert de Lorris, on the other hand, was only too pleased to step into des Essarts' shoes despite being saddled with an enormous fine. Whether or not Lorris knew that Pierre des Essarts' sentence would be revoked, Marcel certainly thought he had known when he saw the fine of 50,000 écus being returned to des Essarts' daring heir. His angry condemnation of speculators did him no good; he had simply been outwitted.

The sovereign found himself pulled in every direction by the conflicting interests among his entourage and by the many pressure groups that were constantly changing in contour and objective. He was also at the mercy of the generally contradictory demands of the business classes and a nobility all too often inclined to denounce speculators who aroused in them a dual hostility: toward the king and his abuse of the customary prerogatives of the feudal lords; and toward the bourgeoisie and its creation of a society removed from the seigneurial and landowning foundations of the feudal system.

The king was at a loss on how to satisfy the landowners—the old nobility whose wealth lay in land as well as the new *rentier* class that had moved out of trade—with their impossible dreams of a return to a strong currency, in other words, of a revaluation of duties, credit, and rents, and, at the same time, the businessmen worried about having the market supplied with sufficient means of payment. Both sides were very vocal in their demands, even if, in the eyes of specialists in the money market, they were deluding themselves about the merits of a coinage that might circulate well enough, but only because it was inferior. It was left to the money changers, consulted by Philip the Fair at the end of his reign, to defend the introduction of "black money":

> It seems to us that it would be a good thing, if it pleased the king our good lord and his noble council, to make black coins at a particular rate, that could circulate freely among the people. . . .
>
> The kingdom would be at peace, for there would be only two kinds of coin: the gold "lamb" *denier* and the black coins. All others would be converted, and thus the people would be rich. And if the people are rich, the lord is rich also.
>
> Trade, which is dead and reduced, will be entirely recovered because of the black coins and the wide distribution there will be of them.

The response was the usual chorus of protest from the proprietors and creditors who had an equal presence on the council. The king, unable to give them satisfaction, nevertheless promised them the earth:

Having heard the complaints of our subjects and other interested parties and inhabitants of our kingdom, on the matter of trade and many other matters, on the troubles and injuries that they suffer, without number or estimation, increased by the changes to and weakening of the currency, and the great danger of losing body and property in which they have been and still stand on account of the bad, false, and counterfeit coins that have been made and introduced in the past by covetous and avaricious counterfeiters, and are still being made even in our said kingdom, and produced and spent as genuine, so that one does not recognize their counterfeiting and falsity,

We have had our old accounts and registers searched and investigated for the orders, statutes, and commandments on the matter of the coinage by Monsignor St. Louis, our predecessor and king of France, who, with his great excellence, held his kingdom in great peace and tranquillity and governed it wisely.

The return to the good money of St. Louis was to be the ideal and standard for two or three generations. For those who received land rents paid in *deniers,* and were thus seeing the collapse of the buying power of their estate, a return to a strong currency was the obvious way to put the kingdom in order. In the council, the loudest voices were those of the aristocracy of barons and prelates.

And what of the "small people," tenants and debtors? In the councils of government there was no one to represent the clientele of usurers, but their angry presence was felt by those who had to maintain public order. The king's officials and the merchant classes were well aware of the costs of an ill-considered revaluation such as that in September of 1306, when Philip the Fair was forced to back down after massacre and pillaging in his capital.

The consequences of this continuous war of attrition were serious. The spectacle of a king such as John the Good in France or Henry IV of Lancaster in England attempting first to satisfy one group, in order to ensure their service, and then another so they would continue to pay and then yet others so that they would not cause trouble, and trying too rapidly to compensate for the effects of a decision with measures favoring those whom it had injured, revealed their lack of a coherent policy. The people were confused by this continual vacillation in which they detected the influence of the speculators. In reality, it was simply the hybrid offspring of conflicting pressure groups and the king's own uncertainty.

Any measures taken in these circumstances were rarely effective. They were too often short-lived; and businessmen, having become accustomed to these contradictory policies, were inclined to adopt a policy of wait-and-see, since speculation was, after all, based on anticipation of the inevitable reversal of policy. This is how it went when a sovereign sought to listen to everyone, because he needed them all.

From 1420, Charles VII, and then Louis XI, had established and developed the fairs at Lyons, thus setting themselves against a faction of finance officers convinced that such fairs, so close to the borders of the kingdom, would encourage the export of precious currency. This was a matter in which Jacques Coeur had displayed his acumen, deliberately playing off the expansion of the Lyons fair against the competition from Geneva, despite the views of more cautious businessmen who were nervous at the idea of making Lyons a stopping-off place on the road to Geneva. Coeur's gamble seemed to have paid off, for, in October 1462, a decree closed all access to the Geneva fairs and gave the monopoly to Lyons. Three years later, a rumor began to circulate along the Rhône:

> Those of Geneva and certain others have boasted and have let it be heard that, with the help of some lords of noble blood, they will have the king break and abolish the decree.

These "noble lords" were the duke of Savoy, the duke of Burgundy, and a few others who were upset by the concentration in Lyons of a sizable flow of trade, reducing that to other markets where they had an interest. In the spring of 1466, the count of Bresse, Philip of Savoy, was trying to persuade Louis XI to return to a fairer balance between the two rival markets, Lyons and Geneva. At the same time he was reassuring the people of Lyons and forming a commission of royal officials and businessmen charged with proposing a solution.

In fact, the core of the problem lay elsewhere. As long as relations with Burgundy continued to deteriorate, the king could not afford to fall out with the Swiss cantons. In September 1466 an agreement was reached: two annual fairs in Lyons and the same number in Geneva. The Lyonnais were furious, but would not declare themselves beaten.

During this same period, Louis XI was having to deal with the report of the commissioners who had presided, in his name, over the session of the Languedoc assembly. And he was listening to Jacques Coeur's successors, Guillaume de Varye and Pierre Doriole; the spice trade was making the fortune of the "French galleys" based at Montpellier and Marseilles. In November, a royal decree banned imports of spices by any other route but the sea. For Lyons, crossroads of several transalpine routes to the Italian ports, it was another severe setback.

An international conference was organized, meeting in Montluel in April 1467. Here the different points of view engaged in close combat, noted by Louis XI's representative, none other than that selfsame official in charge of finances, Guillaume de Vayre, Jacques Coeur's onetime right-hand man. The consuls from Lyons argued that they should at least be allowed the two best fairs, but could not agree on whether these were the Easter and All Hallows fairs, or Easter and Assumption Day. The Italians were drawn into the argument, as were the Germans. The representative from the *Rav-*

ensburger Gesellschaft was heard. Giuliano del Zaccheria, with Francesco Nori, one of the two directors of the Lyons branch of the Medici company, emphasized the inconvenience of the division:

> It is neither expedient nor profitable that the said fairs be separated or divided. If it pleased the king to separate them, it would be, for those merchants attending the fairs, too crowded, involving expense and loss, both for the vehicles they would have to procure and the storage of their goods as for the renting of houses and other costs and expenses that they would be forced to make on account of the said separation.

The decision satisfied no one: there was to be a division, with the freedom of two fairs out of four, but no one yet knew which. Lyons sent a deputation to the royal council. The embassy had a powerful argument: an offer to the king to finance the purchase of two hundred sets of harness that he badly needed for his next campaign. On 14 November, Louis XI reversed the Montluel agreement.

The king of France still needed the Swiss as much as ever. They were granted privileges that gave them a special status in Lyons.

The royal officials, meanwhile, turned a blind eye to the overland import of spices. The people of Languedoc, keeping a close watch on the trade, reported that some 18,000 gold marks had left France in this way for the purchase of spices in Venice. In April 1471, Louis XI reiterated the ban on imports by land. Five years later he lifted it.

Charles VIII was no better. In 1484 he quite simply stopped the Lyons fairs all together and confirmed the monopoly of the maritime ports for the import of spices. Delegations flocked to Paris, scheming together or arguing. In 1487 the king reestablished two out of four fairs. Once again, no one was satisfied.

If there was one result of the presence, permanent or episodic, of the business world in the heart of government, it was mercantilism, and particularly a policy aimed at encouraging exports over imports.. Encouraged in the late thirteenth century by the monetary policy of Philip the Fair or Edward I's policy on wool and, at the end of the fourteenth century, by the intricate play of alliances formed by Philip of Burgundy, it exploded into life in the 1460s. The king of France prohibited his merchants from attending the Geneva fairs; the king of England banned, in quick succession, imports of silks, exports of raw wool, and imports of woolen cloth; and the duke of Burgundy, as much by way of reprisal as to save the textile industry of the Brabant, closed the ports of the Netherlands to English cloth.

The same protectionism incorporated industrial initiatives derived from economic theories that a country should have its own resources, producing for itself to satisfy its needs and importing as little as possible in order to avoid losing precious metal. Another mercantilistic concept was added to this balance sheet: the idea of a global amount of work, which had to be protected from the covetous eyes of outsiders. As England's industrial power developed, Richard III was to return to this idea several times: anything that threatened employment had to be rejected, from a fulling mill that deprived artisans of their work to the immigration of specialists who stole jobs from from the English. The prosperity of English industry depended on the working of wool in England by the English.

Hostility to immigrants might have been less pronounced if they had not been associated with the most lucrative activities:

> They do not want to take on themselves any laborious occupation, such as that of carter, laborer, or other such work, but rather become involved in the manufacture of cloth and other manual trades and comfortable occupations.

Louis XI similarly sought to free France from Italian supplies of silk by encouraging, rather unsuccessfully, the development of the silk industry in Tours and giving considerable privileges to that of Lyons. But he was a realist and was well aware that the kingdom lacked specialists. In contrast to what happened in England with regard to the development of a trade in the manufacture of woolen cloth, French manufacturers sought to attract Italian artisans skilled in working silk. The cities of Tuscany did the same when, in the fourteenth century, they welcomed the influx of weavers forced to flee Flanders by premonitions of crisis. Whereas immigration led to creativity, a policy of protectionism made for local expansion.

It was similarly to limit imports from central Europe that Louis XI tried to increase, in difficult circumstances and at unreasonable cost, production in the Lyonnais and Roussillon mines. In September 1471 he was forced to call on the state for funds for these ventures:

> We have been reminded that if we want to make things go well in the mines, as they do in several other kingdoms and parts of Christendom, as in the country of Germany, in the kingdoms of Hungary, Bohemia, Poland, England, and elsewhere, and make decrees and constitutions to set up and manage such work as is done in the above mentioned kingdom and countries, great good could come of it, useful and profitable to us, to our kingdom and the Dauphiné and to the subjects of these places.

The entry of businessmen into the sphere of political decision making thus drew them into the economic functioning of the state. Policies originally conceived and carried out at the local level during the thirteenth century had grown, on the eve of the Renaissance, to the dimensions of the state.

SEVENTEEN

Social Aspirations

*E*ven though as a group merchants were inclined to keep to themselves and, jealous as much of their markets as of their privileges, were unwilling either to share the first or to allow the second to be diluted, they always left open the possibility of penetration from outside. Both at the margins of the group and within its inner divisions, there was in effect a two-way process of osmosis unimaginable in the hidebound world of the shop and the workshop. If we look at the destinies of some exceptional figures in this world, it is tempting to imagine a genuine fluidity among social classes. But in reality, all social developments reflect a balance between the natural ossification of all social structures and the dynamism inherent in individuals or the economic climate.

The Paths to Fortune

The structural constraints that confined and divided the petite bourgeoisie were not there simply for protection. Because the closing of ranks was seen by those who were the first to be established as an appropriate response to the threats posed by newcomers, the weaver, pewterer, or baker took refuge in a social rigidity that eventually overcame his whole outlook. An inscription scratched with a knife point on the wall of the Palais de la Cité, under the portrait that Enguerran de Marigny, Philip the Fair's minister, had painted of himself on the stairway leading to the great hall, draws the moral from the too rapid rise and subsequent spectacular fall of the great:

> *Chacun soit content de ses biens,*
> *Qui n'a suffisance n'a rien.*

> Let each man be content with what he has
> He who is never satisfied has nothing

The moral of this sad story of a favorite who had recently been hanged because he had grown too rich would have been appreciated by the ordinary Parisian. The baker stayed a baker, and his son would be a baker after him. If he changed trade, it was by choice, talent, or convenience. There was not always room for another hand around the forge or the kneading trough. Although welcome in those trades requiring a large work force, the son was sometimes surplus to requirements when technical production capacities could not expand or when the market was saturated. An anvil could be used for only one job at a time, and villagers were not going to eat more bread just because the baker had his son working alongside him.

Among the Parisians living on the right bank of the Seine near Rue Saint-Martin in 1421, we find a reference to a certain "Jean Saintot, known as Le Barbier [French for Barber], baker." It would appear from his name that he had changed trades without an apparent improvement in his social standing. Those cloth merchants who became manufacturers, or goldsmiths who turned to banking, had not, in reality, changed their status: the lower stratum of the bourgeoisie remained within its bounds.

Paradoxically, it was the poor relations of the merchant world who proved better equipped to deal with the vicissitudes of life. These were the people who, unable to set up for themselves or succeed on their own, were obliged to become employees. More than the shopkeeper, with his restricted intellectual and economic horizons, the agent or *garzone* was in a position to see where—or how—he could direct his ambitions. He might be poor, but in the practice of long-distance trading he had developed initiative; he might have no capital, but he knew how to take advantage of the distinct functions of finance and management that emerged with early capitalism. Furthermore, he could seize the opportunities offered by the great companies encountered at the many fairs, trading posts, banking centers, and political capitals, all requiring the presence of branch companies or partnerships, agents and correspondents. For many, the chances were there for the picking.

Such was the story of Boninsegna di Matteo, a Florentine of modest family who joined the Avignon company of Francesco di Marco Datini as a *garzone* in 1372, when he was still very young. Quickly showing an aptitude for managing affairs, he was put in charge of the accounts. He then mastered the intricacies of commerce and banking. Francesco di Marco became fond of his young employee and paid off his debts. On 1 December 1382, the day before he returned to Prato, he altered the statutes of his office in Avignon, making his two agents partners. In this way Boninsegna di Matteo and Tieri di Benci put their work and their savings into the company. Years went by. Despite the fact that Tieri di Benci was the elder and had brought in more capital, it was Boninsegna di Matteo who held the position of *procuratore,* or representative, of Francesco di Marco. He was, in fact, the director of the Avignon company. The *garzone* had turned into a business-man. With his premature death on Christmas Day 1397, the Avignon business community lost one of its most important figures.

Along with the sons and nephews sent off to Venice, Ancona, or Rome to get to know the world and the family business, the Medici similarly appointed directors of humbler origins whose abilities had been demonstrated in a career of ever-increasing responsibilities. The future head of the Bruges branch, Tommaso Portinari, had come to Flanders in 1437, at the age of twelve, to work under the supervision of his cousin Bernardo. In 1465, at the age of forty, he became director.

Especially favored by the Venetians, and preferred by the state, the individualistic contracts of *commissione* and *comandata* allowed many merchants lacking fortunes to enter the market and increase their business dealings. Even when buying or selling for someone else, the *commissario* was still able to keep 1 or 2 percent of the total sum of his transactions to put in his own pocket. Even more important, over the years he acquired capital in the form of information, contacts, skills, and perhaps reputation. Sooner or later he would risk his own capital in trade.

Outside Italy, where social advancement existed only within the local framework of the city and its economic empire, many fortunes depended on the expansion of a small town into a medium-size town, or a medium-size town into an economic metropolis or political capital. Inhabitants of Dieppe advanced a rung up the social ladder when they set up in Rouen. Inhabitants of Rouen had a choice of paths to fortune: Rouen and the sea, or Paris and the kingdom. Merchants and artisans flocked to Paris from the surrounding small towns, just as the English were drawn to London from the towns and villages of the "Home Counties." Hans Fugger, father of Jacob "the Rich," left his village of Graben where, like his ancestors before him, he had cultivated the land and moved to Augsburg in 1367 to become a weaver. A merchant who was reluctant to make such abrupt changes in horizons and habits could always send his son or nephew as an apprentice to the big city. There the younger man could seize his chance.

This fluidity in society was often furthered by marriage. In helping to bring about or to consolidate the crossing of barriers, it was often the best means of getting around the law or integrating into those societies that tried to exclude outsiders. Almost the only way of penetrating the Hanseatic League was through the bonds of marriage: the people of Nuremberg were well aware of it, and marriage into the patriarchal families of Lübeck became the object of a veritable merchant diplomacy. Hans Fugger was able to acquire citizenship of Augsburg only at the price of two successive marriages, which eventually brought him a place on the council of his profession. In the same way, the former peasant was able to acquire, along with an improved social status, enough capital to start out as a haberdasher. He had become a merchant.

In the closed world of the French or English artisan guilds, marriage was similarly the principal route to promotion for a journeyman wishing to rise to the rank of master craftsman. Plenty of widows of established artisans were able, by taking such a man as a second husband, to buy themselves relative security for the future. The important thing was to ensure the survival of the workshop.

As a group became more accessible, and initiative and talent were rewarded with increased responsibilities, marriage came to be seen as a natural progression rather than a factor in promotion. Above all, it was viewed as an instrument of social cohesion: marriages within the merchant classes were generally arranged between equals, with those instances where marriages were made to promote a career being considered as "good marriages" for one party as much as misalliances for the other.

Eight times out of ten, the municipal authorities of the city of London, who were involved choosing a husband for the daughters of deceased merchants, gave these orphans in marriage to husbands of the same economic status as the dead fathers. A document of 1360, recording a total of sixty-three marriages, shows that fifty-three were between equals, while, of the other ten, five girls married nobles and five married merchants belonging to inferior companies. Clearly the ideal was to find a son-in-law on a par with the son.

A century later, we learn from the marriages of young London merchants that the balance was still much the same. Six percent of merchants took wives from the ranks of the nobility, 27 percent married daughters of merchants from lesser companies—but who seem, coincidentally, to have been the richest of their company—while 64 percent married widows or daughters of colleagues of the same rank.

In Paris, advocates married daughters of the legal profession, butchers married among their own group, while the professionally rather indeterminate group of cloth merchants and money changers practiced an endogamy that reduced business rivalry to a family dispute. All the genealogies of the rich merchant families show links through marriage with other important families. Rivals could become allies.

The Tuscans elevated the practice to the level of a strategy. The structure of the *compagnia* had, of course, always depended to a large extent on family ties. In Lucca, the Cenami family intermarried with the Guinigi and Rapondi. In Florence, the Medici took as wives or husbands members of the Bardi, Capponi, Gianfigliazzi, Strozzi, Cavalcanti, and Gualterotti families.

This would have meant an end to any upward social movement, were it not for the biological effects of such intermarriage. The merchant classes, though less inclined than the feudal aristocracy to dispatch their younger sons to the Church or the army, nevertheless applied a similar Malthusianism to those who could not hope to have a share in either the estate or the tools of the trade. In London, wills dating from the fourteenth century mention on average just one male heir still living at the time of the death of the father. At times of epidemic, the survival of the line was anything but secure. The problem was even greater in the small towns depleted by migration to the metropolis. Demographically speaking, cities like Paris, Genoa, Florence, or Cologne were as bottomless pits. Merchant dynasties ruled over the towns for two or three centuries, to the detriment of the small reservoir of people remaining in the neighboring smaller towns.

To this should be added the effects of an average life expectancy that was particularly detrimental to the continuity of business. Children rarely had to wait until adulthood to inherit, and the number of octogenarians that we find mentioned in some family histories should not deceive us: those who died at twenty simply did not merit an entry.

Based as it was on lineal inheritance, the feudal world united to ensure the protection of an heir who was still a minor. Guardians and trustees watched over the fief. An estate could run itself without the personal expertise of a child heir. In the same way, a lord would consider himself responsible for the children of one of his vassals who had died prematurely. It was, in any case, in the lord's interests, for he was thereby ensuring the continuity of the generations of vassals capable of assuming the duties of service to the fief.

None of this was applicable to the world of business. Here all enterprise was personal, and all that was established contingent on the individual. A market stall rented for a year was not much use if the cloth merchant was no longer there. A money changer's bench could not be employed if the son of the money changer was not yet old enough to count. There was little in the way of continuity to offer to the youthful son of an agent, a *commissario*, or a "merchant adventurer," and no clientele. And if continuity disappeared in the conduct of business, how much more true was it of capital, which consisted of merchandise that had to be sold without delay and of debt that would have to be settled.

Group solidarity supported the son of an artisan as he progressed toward the same rank of master craftsman that his father had attained. In a business world that was continually in flux, there was no such framework for looking after the orphans of the rich merchant classes—except for the babies. Inherited capital was used to bring up such orphans, and the moral code of the group ensured that it was well used to that end. Later on, the young merchant's son would be found a job among the young men of his generation. But others, in the meantime, would have been running the business in his place. Inherited capital could be used for the upbringing of future merchants but not for the conduct of business. The orphan would start out in life with a real advantage—an apprenticeship and contacts. But in the future he would have to make his own way.

Sometimes one person's promotion would provide an opportunity for others. A taste for the duties of public service, or even the aristocratic life that often followed on from them, soon lured certain merchants' families away from the trade they had once practiced, particularly in the capitals and regional metropolises. In London, one sheriff's son out of two abandoned the world of business. This movement began to accelerate: out of 26 sheriffs' sons listed in the fourteenth century, 16 were merchants (62 percent); 10 out of 17 in the fifteenth century (59 percent); and 26 out of 52 in the sixteenth century (50 percent). Some important merchants in the London market must have been the only businessmen left in their families. The quicker the success in trade, the sooner it came to an end.

This phenomenon caused unrest in the upper bourgeoisie in Paris. Although one might have expected the opposite, things even got significantly worse as a result of the political upheavals during the years 1400 to 1436. The civil war had exposed the fragility of trade. Many faced ruin in 1418 because they had lent or sold on credit to apparently creditworthy Parisians who, because they happened to support the Armagnacs or were simply on bad terms with an enthusiastic Burgundian, suddenly disappeared from the marketplace. At best the debtor, tenant, or even trading partner might reappear some twenty years later. The majority of debts of Louis of Orleans, assassinated in 1407 at the Porte Barbette, were never repaid, any more than were the forced loans extracted by his son-in-law Bernard d'Armagnac, who ruled over Paris from 1413 to 1418.

Still others faced ruin in 1436, as they watched the English—few in number but greatly loaded down with debt—leave with the loans that had seemed so safe in the time of Bedford, Henry V's regent in France. Some were quick to realize that, for a period of twenty years, all they had to do to escape their creditors was to reach Étampes or Arpajon, where the justice of the French king was powerless to arrest the supporters of another.

During this terrible period of the Hundred Years' War, the Seine and its tributaries were clogged with sunken boats, ports were deserted, roads threatened by bands of robbers, fairs suspended or inactive, and the currency completely out of control. At the end of the conflict, those who survived were the lucky ones, but they had paid a terrible price. Whether or not they were inspired by xenophobia, the massacres and banishments had not only affected their victims; they had brought about the departure of all who felt threatened, because of their wealth, by the people's desire for revenge. The Parisian marketplace was virtually paralyzed. It would not recover fully until modern times.

How did the stunned middle classes react? In these difficult times it seemed better to serve a "bad" king than to sell cloth honestly.

This was the second result of the policies of the duke of Burgundy, Philip the Good. Cheated in the alliance with England, in which all the advantages, including the govenorship of Paris, seemed to have gone to Bedford, he realized that he could at least maintain a balance in the West. The final outcome of a hard-won peace was the Treaty of Arras, finally negotiated in 1435. This gained him the neutrality of Charles VII, against the hostility that he was provoking in the East with his all too obvious desire to rebuild a state following the lines of ancient Lotharingia.

Thus, without for one moment forgetting it, it was possible to silence the resentment. One of the clauses imposed by Duke Philip was that his old supporters keep their posts. Those who had served Anglo-Burgundian France in Paris were thus able to remain in their positions alongside supporters of Charles VII coming from, or coming back from, Bourges or Poitiers. Regardless of which king they had served for the past twenty years, they now sat together in the Parliament, the exchequer, the Court of Aids, the treasury, and the law courts in the Châtelet.

Their presence was very apparent in this capital city so badly shaken by the events of the previous years. The *lieutenant civil* at the Châtelet—the king's ordinary judge for Paris, called a provostship and viscountcy but in fact a bailiwick—Jean de Longueil had been appointed in 1431 by the English regent, Bedford. Longueil would preside over civil hearings at the Châtelet until 1461. In the Parliament, a certain Arnaud de Marle, who was made counselor in September 1413 at the height of the Armagnac counterattack and had sat in Charles VII's Parliament in Poitiers, would pass his last years as president of the reunited Parliament in Paris. One of his colleagues was Robert Piédefer who had been appointed a counselor in 1410 when the duke of Burgundy, John the Fearless, dominated the government and the capital. Piédefer had been *maître des requêtes,* presenting petitions to the councils, and then presided over the Paris Parliament under Anglo-Burgundian rule; he too would conclude his career as president of the Parliament reunited under Charles VII.

All these officials had assuredly suffered as a result of the upheavals. During the war—and this was particularly true for the Parisians—their employers had frequently neglected to pay their salaries. They were fortunate, at least, to emerge from this period with their capital intact.

We can imagine the thoughts of the Parisian merchants about such careers, exceptional for the extent of their responsibilities but not for their stability. While merchants suffered a loss of trade, or even bankruptcy, for having done business with the Parisians under the Bedford government, the former servants of the English rulers were still ruling the roost. It was no wonder that business seemed to be the least secure investment in the Paris of 1440.

The more astute had understood this as early as the fourteenth century, a time when the reformers had aligned themselves against the speculators and when Charles V's counselors, the Braques and the Bureaux, had started to penetrate the ranks of the nobility. Arnoul Braque, a money changer until the 1340s, officially renounced his bourgeois status in 1346, announcing that he was now a member of the nobility. His sons were still money changers, but none would remain so for long. Robert de Lorris, son of an innkeeper, was notary and secretary to the king in 1339. In 1346 he was *maître des requêtes* and a nobleman. Jean Le Mercier, still referred to as being of humble origins in 1358, was a noble by 1374, and his origins were no longer publicly acknowledged.

With the Hundred Years' War over, uncertainty receded as the capital reestablished its position in the 1440s. However, the economic market did not recover with the same speed. Of the great families who had dominated the maritime trade through the Marchandise de l'Eau 150 years earlier, few now sat in the Hôtel de Ville. Two exceptions were the Gencien and the Pizdoe families, who were still found in public service at the time of Charles V until their banishment in 1418. The time had come to make way for others. Certain families, like the Arrode or Dammartin, became part of the legal establishment; soon they would play the gentleman. The majority, like the Marcel or Coquatrix families, lost much of their influence, and names like Augier, Barbette, and Saint-Benoît returned to the ranks of the bourgeoisie. Here there were positions to be filled.

Whereas promotion to a political career left gaps in the ranks of the merchant classes, it did little to prevent demographic extinction or economic ruin. In every town there were examples of these municipal success stories, a shining star one day only to disappear the next. A modest merchant family from Cordes called Najac provides a good illustration. Arriving to seek their fortune in Toulouse around 1375, their rise was meteoric. After two generations, we find the Najacs, important cloth merchants in the Languedoc market, sitting among the *capitouls*. A Najac was *maître des monnaies*, in charge of the mint. When Toulouse sent representatives to Paris or elsewhere to discuss affairs of the town, one of the ambassadors was usually a Najac. Fortune seemed to smile on the family. But shortly after 1450, the very name Najac had virtually disappeared from municipal documents. The family was ruined and had disappeared. This sort of mobility, as fortunes rose or fell, would ensure that society remained fluid.

The Businessman and the Gentleman

Naturally, the moment he had success in his grasp, the businessman aspired toward the aristocracy. Here we must distinguish between those countries where the nobility could legitimately take part in commerce and countries where such activity would be enough to banish them forever from the ranks of the aristocracy. In England, business was considered quite respectable, which explains the relatively high number of marriages between the nobility and middle classes, principally between young noblemen and daughters of merchants: at a later date many members of the European nobility restored their family fortunes by marrying money. Although in theory mutually exclusive—one could not simultaneously be noble and bourgeois—the two notions were not contradictory in practice, either in everyday life, where the two classes met in the course of business, or in the broader destinies of families who often intermarried over a period of several generations.

While it is true that the ennobled merchant generally gave up commercial activities, it was not so much for legal reasons but because he intended to profit fully from his new status, so laboriously acquired. On his path to social acceptance he would have taken considerable pains to allow himself the eventual pleasure of living like a nobleman. In the mind of the English businessman, ennoblement was simply a bridge to be crossed, a reward for an industrious career.

There are other, even more clear-cut examples. The Venetian patriciate remained a merchant class at heart, even after it had taken over the government of La Serenissima and made the Venetian empire into one large trading company. Naturally the old nobility did not want to be excluded from politics and took to trade without the slightest embarrassment.

The situation was the reverse in France. Taxation weighed heavily on the middle classes, the future third estate. The nobility was exempted only for the reason that it traditionally defended the country in time of war: nobles fought while the others paid. It is true that, from the fourteenth century, the nobility's exemption from taxes was principally justified by the fact that it fell to the same person, the king, to tax the lords but allow them in turn the right to raise part of the revenue demanded by taxing their own people; or to tax the common people directly, although with consent of the agreement of the nobility. In either case, it was the peasants who paid. A direct levy had the advantage that tax revenues would more likely end up in the royal treasury.

There were a number of consequences. The king would be unlikely to let a merchant fortune escape tax on a plea of nobility; the public would find it hard to understand how a merchant's activities could be allowed to escape taxation; the nobility, aware of the taxes levied on the raw products of landed estates through taxes on their inhabitants, was not prepared to accept the exemption of certain kinds of revenue from taxes. Finally, the business community itself would have been loath to accept a fiscal privilege that could upset the market's equilibrium, as well as the structure of commercial costs. There could be no equality of opportunity for one merchant who paid taxes and another who did not.

In the theological separation of functions, there were those who prayed, those who protected, and those who provided by working. As late as the twelfth century, St. Augustine's *De Civitate Dei* reproduces the old tripartite structure of Indo-European societies. The simultaneous development of urban societies and mercantile fortunes, on the one hand, and the state with its distribution of responsibility through taxation and the financing of social services, on the other, put up new barriers between the legally defined social strata, in which each person sought his own advantage. The nobleman of ancient lineage, last remnant of the age of chivalry, viewed with disgust the rise to the nobility of parvenus who combined the noble's privileges and the merchant's wealth. It seemed that the cards had been—and would continue to be—reshuffled within the very heart of the aristocracy; and the new hand did not favor those whose ancestors had fallen in the Crusades at Jerusalem or Acre. The merchant, for his part, would not tolerate competition in the marketplace from a colleague privileged by his social status. The idea of the noble businessman was roundly rejected by all, save for the few who found themselves in that ambiguous position.

In reality, things were much less clear-cut than it would seem from the ritten legislation. One Guillaume Sanguin, a money changer like his father and the possessor of a comfortable fortune, was ennobled by Charles VI in 1400. He took the title of *écuyer* (esquire) and had himself called "noble man." He gravitated toward the entourage of the duke of Burgundy and was appointed *échanson*, or cupbearer, to the duke, John the Fearless. In 1412 he commanded a company of soldiers. He became a *rentier*, with houses in Paris and estates in the region. He was seen in Parliament, where Philip the Good entrusted him with an important task—asking the court to send a representative to the negotiations for the Treaty of Troyes, which in 1420 made the king of England the son-in-law and heir to the king of France. Like a prince, Guillaume had his bastard son ennobled. The latter would count among his descendants a cardinal and several counselors in Parliament.

But, meanwhile, the former money changer had not been neglecting his business. In 1412, the same year that he played the soldier, he sold the duke of Burgundy a ruby and a silver chain—presented by John the Fearless, respectively, to the king and the future Philip the Good—as well as another silver necklace that the duke wanted to ornament his armor. Along with Dino Rapondi he stands out among those who advanced the largest sums to finance Burgundian policies. In 1429 he was elected provost of the merchants.

Three years later, he was still trading in sapphires, rubies, and other gems. His patron the duke also bought from him a piece of jewelry as a New Year's gift for the duchess.

It is hard to tell whether or not the body buried in 1441 in the Church of the Holy Innocents (where a boss carved with his arms was found in 1974) could be that of a merchant. Perhaps he resembled Molière's Monsieur Jourdain in *The Bourgeois Gentilhomme,* an "obliging friend" who, not only knowledgeable about jewels but also acquainted with important people in society, could supply their needs. We are a long way from the shop counter and the money changer's bench. But business is business.

In short, many noblemen got involved in business, and plenty of ennobled merchants continued to pursue their lucrative enterprises for some time. The king's tacit agreement had been obtained. We find systems that combined tax-farming—from the mint to the tax on the consumption of wine—and the designation of a special collector for each tax, even when directly levied, who was expected to advance a percentage of the revenues to the king and to ensure the flow of funds and payments into the treasury. The king had some excellent servants, rewarded for their excellence with ennoblement, who moved gradually toward other types of service, without any abrupt interruption of their trading activities in which the state participated.

At the threshold of nobility, it was necessary to consider its potential rewards. In Italy, from the end of the thirteenth century, a rise to the ranks of the nobility had ceased to be of interest. For a Florentine it would mean exclusion from political society. And there would be no advantage for a Genoese: nobles and commoners had the same privileges, with the distinctions between families by now entirely historic. In Venice, as we have seen, the patriciate was closed, so there was no point in trying to enter it. The advantages of nobility were more obvious in England, but its essential privileges were of a feudal nature and would be of little value to a merchant disinclined to venture into landowning.

The German merchant saw other advantages in nobility, given the role of the knights at the side of their prince. The attraction was proportional to the importance of the political influence of the prince. The Lübeck merchant could not care less about nobility, but it was a different story for the Augsburg merchant. Hamburg and Bremen were practically republics, but, in Augsburg, Andreas Fugger received from Frederick III in 1452 his coat of arms "azure and checky or" (blue and gold checks). In the following century, Jacob Fugger would finance the election of the emperors Maximilian and Charles V. His nephew Anton would become a count. And eventually the Fuggers would become princes of the Holy Roman Empire.

And then there was France. Despite setbacks during the Crusades and the defeats of the Hundred Years' War, the nobility maintained its role, its prestige, and its prerogatives. Sufficiently removed to keep its distance but close enough not to be strangers, the nobility with the most ancient pedigree lived on its estates outside the town without, for all that, having any less presence in the town. The expansion of public service had sufficiently swelled the ranks of the legal profession—drawn from the nobility—to accustom people to the idea of a nobility that was not in any way inferior even though it did not take up arms and that would not see its fortunes collapse even if it did not indulge in trade. A new intermediate class emerged in the thirteenth century as the "king's knights" and, in the fourteenth century, as presidents and noble counselors of the Parliament. Bailiffs and seneschals were normally knights, or at least squires.

The living proof was there for all to see: the path to fortune and position was through service on the councils, study of the law, and oratory. Between the soldier knight and himself, the French businessman saw a social class that was well off, esteemed, and, in many ways, very accessible. Although the jurist turned royal judge was not the same as the merchant turned royal financier, the only real difference between them lay in the means of their ascendancy. Once arrived, the presidents of Parliament and the Court of Aids were equals. Marriage wove alliances. The nobility was not, as in England, a world apart.

The advantages of nobility were obvious to the businessman. With his fortune made and his position as a noble consolidated, he also acquired tax privileges and estates. The privileges that accompanied a jurisdiction were not insignificant, acting as they did as protection from legal surprises. In a country where the judge in a civil court was above all an arbitrator, there was much advantage in being assured of the best judges and most favorable laws. The nobility, which forbade basic commerce and placed limits on the pursuit of business, would be seen as nothing less than the final goal, the crowning achievement. But it would be a mistake to evaluate nobility entirely in terms of material advantages: it is clear from the behavior of the press of people who sought entry to the ranks of the nobility that the prime advantage was social position and the esteem that went with it. The honor of being noble could not be measured, but it counted for much and many would seek it, regardless of the financial cost involved. After all, in business, it is worth something to make one's neighbor jealous.

If the pursuit of ennoblement varied from country to country, it was partly because the relationship between civic and economic matters differed from place to place. There were countries—and marketplaces—where because of the nature of the regime, the municipal administration of the city was closely linked to commerce. In the great city-states of Germany and Italy, the art of dominating the market fused with that of managing the state. This fusion is most apparent in the Venetian Senate, where the same people made decisions about both alliances and seagoing convoys. And there were still other countries where the emergence of a state distinct from the aristocracy, but symbolized by the Crown and represented by a king, gave rise to a public service whose functions were clearly delineated, along with a career structure. France, England and, to a lesser degree, the Iberian kingdoms thus offered ambitious individuals new paths to success. Though they often passed through a commercial phase, they emerged to leave it behind them.

The Path to Aristocracy

From the moment that ascent into the nobility was seen as deserved promotion and the crowning of a career, as something desirable, two routes—dependent on political opportunity, local conditions, and personal talents—opened up. The first was the economic path, which harmonized with habits already established by the businessman. The second was the political path, which depended to a large extent on the goodwill of the prince. The greater accessibility of one or the other of these two routes varied from one town to the next.

Paris offered ambitious people paths to social advancement that they could not have found in the provinces, however good the opportunities for making one's fortune offered by the princely courts in the fifteenth century. A person became rich and important through service to the king, or even the princes, which brought proximity the royal throne, and a seat in the great councils and courts of law. The great Parisian merchant families found their way into the legal profession and were on the edges of the nobility by the time of the first Valois kings. Braque, Malet, Lorris, and Le Mercier were nobles under John the Good or Charles V. They demonstrated their nobility in their lifestyle, building magnificent *hôtels* in the fashionable streets and gaining an entrée into the houses of the great. This was power enough in itself. Moreover, there were the landed estates. Arnoul Braque bought a few pieces of land and some woods, but it was his son Nicolas who bought, on a single occasion, the entire estate of Châtillon-sur-Loing, paying 7,700 écus. Ennobled in 1374, Jean Le Mercier was already the king's counselor when, around 1380, he began to invest the sums he received from the treasury of Charles VI, as a gift from the king and his uncles, in landed estates.

Things worked rather differently in Dijon, Rouen, and Toulouse. The Crown had not yet thought of ennobling the lower judges [*greffiers*] and consuls. The route to nobility in the provinces more commonly passed by way of a fortune invested in the lifestyle of the traditional nobility, in the purchase of estates, in a particular manner of passing leisure time, and in a certain kind of aristocratic idleness. Nobility could be achieved and could prove its credentials, provided that one conformed with the time-honored formula "who has always lived nobly." In these circumstances, it would have been a mistake to have continued trading.

Many families, in the short term at least, were able to plan their future. The eldest would establish the family's rank and ascend the ladder to future greatness. A younger member of the family would stay in business, securing the family against the possibility of future economic upset. By the next generation the two branches of the family would have little in common. As recently ennobled lords began to take the name of the land they had acquired, they conveniently forgot the family name they had borne in common, and which too blatantly recalled their origins.

An important trader, not only in exotic products but also in herring, between Rouen, Paris, and Lyons, just after the Hundred Years' War, Cardin Le Pelletier was well known in these towns as a significant figure in the Rouen market. His son Richard, pursuing and expanding his father's trade, began in the 1450s to acquire investments in rents and lands. In 1471 he took advantage of the decree concerning frank-fees and became, overnight, one of the nobility. He had, nevertheless, married into the solid, rich bourgeoisie of Rouen, and he chose similar spouses for his children. For all that they were now nobles, Richard and Jacques Le Pelletier were happy to continue trading in pewter with England, cloth with Lyons, and grain with Portugal. Naturally they both had seats in the town hall. Their reputations began to spread abroad. In Venice, Jacques Le Pelletier backed one of Charles VIII's loans. But, at the same time, he continued to build up an estate, carefully selected from the best wheat-growing lands in the Caux and Bray countryside. In 1486 he was lord of Martainville. Time passed; he lived as a nobleman and played at patronage. By now he was known as Sire de Martainville. His grandson obtained letters patent in 1571, granting him the right to call himself Richard de Martainville. As Parliament kept him waiting for the registration of his change of name, Richard explained away the delay as a consequence of the legal profession's jealousy of the old aristocracy of the sword. Whether this was self-deception or a deliberate lie, it was certainly no dream when his own son married into the Montmorency family.

Whatever the case, the businessman could not aspire to the acknowledged aristocracy unless he had already achieved a certain economic status in which his wealth and success were socially conspicuous. Whether or not living an aristocratic style of life was a means to reaching the aristocracy, it was certainly the result. Neither the prince nor the social class would have allowed a family to establish itself in such a position unless it had a large enough fortune to maintain that status.

Social position was, of course, a relative notion, as was that, so closely linked to it, of poverty. The fall in seignorial revenue had, since the fourteenth century, multiplied the number of "poor knights," who were often richer than many a well-off peasant but found keeping up the appearances that went with the status of knight well-nigh impossible. To be poor was relative, and its opposite was not "rich" but "comfortable." The same income could make the laborer content with his plow and the country squire ashamed of being unable to fulfill his obligations. The rich merchant who needed to continue with trade in order to maintain his position in the bourgeoisie was scarcely standing at the threshold of nobility. In order to cross this threshold, the businessman had to demonstrate that his descendants could be guaranteed to maintain the status of gentleman.

Thus the public display of merchant wealth was more than mere showing off. At the dawn of modern banking, the Florentine *palazzi* symbolized the solidity of the bank's credit. In London or Paris, the grand houses of the wealthy merchants signified the secure foundations of their respectability. Tapestries, paintings, collections of *objets d'art,* musical instruments, and even samples of the goldsmith's craft—all were evidence of the lasting nature of the family's fortune. Acceptance into the nobility was an acknowledgment of de facto status. Tidemann Limberg, wanting to do things propery, even obtained from Clement VI in 1351 the right to have a portable altar. This indicated a certain style of daily life and meant that his personal chaplain could say mass for him at home and wherever he traveled. But we should not have any illusions: this type of display caused many to fume and rage; and the ancient nobility sneered all the more at the ostentation of these nouveaux riches because they themselves could rarely afford the luxury of even a part-time chaplain.

The real proof of one's fitness for the noble life was the possession of a country estate. Living like a lord proved that one ought to be a noble, and living like a *seigneur* often meant the possession of a *seigneurie.* The business world had been able to take advantage of sales and mortgages forced on those impoverished nobles who had seen their income, entirely dependent on land rents, whittled away by inflation. As we have seen, wealthier merchants began, in the thirteenth century, to invest in fiefs. Eager to encourage this development while still controlling it—he was, after all, king of the bourgeoisie as much as of the nobles, and he could see an advantage to himself in granting such acquisitions—the king of France did not hesitate to put pressure on the often reluctant aristocracy. Thus, in 1328, he compelled the abbot of Saint-Germain-des-Prés to receive the homage offered by a bourgeois for a recently acquired fief.

The nobility was quick to respond. In 1275, for the royal domain of the Capetians, it was made quite specific: the purchase of a fief was not a sufficient reason to ennoble the buyer. Paying for the entitlement of frank-fee authorized someone to hold a fief even though he could not fulfill the chief service required, which remained, in theory, that of providing an army. It was possible to pay for not giving such service, but that was then not serving. Whether a person had in fief entire estates or, as they said in Normandy, nothing more than a quarter of a coat of chain mail, it made no difference. However nobly one lived, one was still not a nobleman. The frank-fee was only an indemnity, and a very poor compensation for the replacement of a knight vassal by a bourgeois vassal. And yet the king and the upper aristocracy accepted such substitutions: it was not so easy to find another knight prepared to buy up the fief of a ruined knight; and there was a risk that, if everyone were turned down, succession dues might not be paid. It therefore seemed better to add the frank-fee to the succession dues on the fiefs—known as the *relief*—and do without the services. It was important to safeguard the cohesion of the group.

In the fourteenth century, the old aristocracy resisted the newcomers for quite other reasons: the need to protect the social class and avoid a dilution of their privileges. The artisans had done the selfsame thing by opposing the promotion of journeymen and the acceptance of outsiders. The struggle found its justification in the idea of the "three estates": the fief had never been intended for the investment of merchant profits; it was there to support the defenders of the kingdom. The king and the clergy, agreeing that this semblance of nobility should be restricted, found a solution in the purchase of a "noble fief." Thus the king was the chief beneficiary, becoming the sole dispenser of nobility.

The wealthy bourgeois who had planned their path to nobility through the acquisition of land thus found themselves relegated to a position inferior to that of some of those who had made their way through the royal entourage. Such was the case of those businessmen under John the Good and Charles V who had become counselors. For those who reached the top only to find that the door had just been slammed in their faces, the feeling of bitterness was great. One such was Étienne Marcel.

Nevertheless, the enthusiasm of the merchant classes for landed property did not show any signs of diminishing. It seemed the obvious direction to take, because of both the desire for safe investments and the need for raw materials. Still exploiting their skills in trading, these men could at the same time demonstrate their status as landowners: the Londoner bought pasture lands to raise sheep for wool; the merchant from Bordeaux invested in vineyards; the Venetian, like Benedetto Zaccharia, took over an alum-producing fief in Phocaea; another, like Federigo Corner, might obtain sugar-producing land in Cyprus. The effect on his guests when the Parisian or the Dijon merchant served wine from his own vineyards was not to be underestimated. If he was not yet a noble, at least he began to resemble one.

In the France of the period following the Hundred Years' War, rural reconstruction favored and accelerated this trend. Only those with enough capital to be unconcerned about an immediate return on their investment could begin to restore the estates, install new tenants skilled in farming, and purchase new tools or seed with the knowledge that the first harvest would not be for another three years, or seven in the case of vineyards. Businessmen knew how to invest their money elsewhere if they wanted to make money quickly, but financial security and social position were worthwhile long-term investments.

Merchants of merely average wealth, whose political horizons were relatively modest, were inspired above all by economic motives. The ambition of the honest merchant who wished to establish himself, slowly but surely laying the foundations of a secure future, was for a sure supply of wool and a security that was easily acquired but not too easily realized in case of sudden need. The bigger businessman was slower to become involved in such enterprises. His sights were aimed higher, and he wished to see his ambitions rewarded with speedier results. If he bought land, it was through social ambition and not economic calculation: he wished to play at the landed gentry, or at least enable his son to do so, and endow his daughter as befitting the manners and customs of the old aristocracy.

We are now moving out of the sphere of economic rationalism and its measurable parameters into that of the psychology of the ambitious man, the illusions of the parvenu with dreams. Thus we find sometimes quite considerable differences within the same social group. Some of the wealthiest London merchants had no estates at all, while others of their less well-off colleagues spent a third or half of their fortunes on land.

A political post often consolidated promotion acquired through wealth. We come across this situation in Italy with the appointments made by governments of the city-states. The head of the richest family—and of the biggest company—in Lucca, Paolo Guinigi, became the lord of Lucca in 1400. Franco Sacchetti, son of a Florentine merchant, made a dazzling career as a professional *podestà*, or mayor, in several Italian towns. Neither Guinigi nor Sacchetti could, however, be taken as typical.

In those countries where posts in public service were more individualized, on the other hand, such careers provided a genuine political path to the aristocracy. More than any other, the administrative and judicial bureaucracy of the kingdom of France and its great principalities offered a wide range of careers where the businessman or his family could easily apply their abilities, whether in accounting, the treasury, or the mint. On a lower level, for those just starting out, there were the counselors, masters of the mint, and tax collectors. Nor should we forget the courts and councils that offered posts to their offspring, who had studied a little law and could call on useful family contacts, pulling strings as any nephew of a counselor in the Parliament would naturally do.

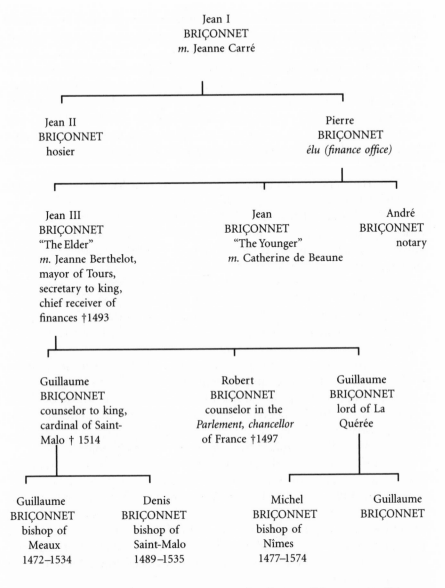

Jean I
BRIÇONNET
m. Jeanne Carré

Jean II
BRIÇONNET
hosier

Pierre
BRIÇONNET
élu (finance office)

Jean III
BRIÇONNET
"The Elder"
m. Jeanne Berthelot,
mayor of Tours,
secretary to king,
chief receiver of
finances †1493

Jean
BRIÇONNET
"The Younger"
m. Catherine de Beaune

André
BRIÇONNET
notary

Guillaume
BRIÇONNET
counselor to king,
cardinal of Saint-
Malo † 1514

Robert
BRIÇONNET
counselor in the
Parlement, chancellor
of France †1497

Guillaume
BRIÇONNET
lord of La
Quérée

Guillaume
BRIÇONNET
bishop of
Meaux
1472–1534

Denis
BRIÇONNET
bishop of
Saint-Malo
1489–1535

Michel
BRIÇONNET
bishop of
Nîmes
1477–1574

Guillaume
BRIÇONNET

The astonishing rise of the Briçonnet family is well known. It all began
in Tours with a successful local merchant, Jean Briçonnet, known later in
the genealogical tables as Jean I. In the 1390s he was trading in salt. He
married the daughter of a money changer. They had two sons: Jean II was
a merchant hosier, while Pierre was a notary. Very soon the notary had
moved into a career in the royal finances with a post overseeing the collection
of "aids," a form of levy on tenants or boroughs. These appointees had been

quite openly nominated by the king for at least three-quarters of a century. When his son, called Jean the Elder since two of his sons were named Jean, succeeded him in the same post and married the daughter of an important money changer who had become Master of the Bedchamber in the service of the queen, the Briçonnets were well embarked on their way to power.

Jean the Elder, or Jean III, by now one of Charles VII's right-hand men, took part in sequestration of the goods of Jacques Coeur. In 1462 he became the first mayor of Tours and a man of standing. At that time his brother André was still a notary. No Briçonnet had, as yet, open pretensions to the nobility.

The friendship of Jean Bourré, secretary to Louis XI, led to the appointment of Jean the Elder as chief tax collector for northern France and treasurer to the king. Louis XI placed such trust in him that he even used him at times as a political agent. Thus in 1469, he was given the task of keeping an eye on the activities of Louis's troublesome brother Charles of France. In other words, Jean Briçonnet III had left behind his role as a businessman.

His brother Jean the Younger, known as *patron* (head or boss), was to go even further. First, he married the daughter of the great financier of the court at Tours, Jean de Beaune. Next, he entered his father-in-law's company. Soon he was in charge of the head office in Tours. He was still a businessman, but a long way from the shop counter.

The two brothers were now on the very top rung of business, one in charge of the royal finances and the other at the head of a commercial and banking company unequaled at the time in France, and whose only real nearby rival was the Medici representative, Lorenzo the Magnificent's agent Giannetto Ballerini.

Time passed, and with it the period of hegemony enjoyed by Tours. Others moved into the market. But the Briçonnet family had been launched. When Jean the Elder died in 1493, his son Guillaume already had made a tidy fortune in trade and had married into the Beaune family. Now he was a widower. He entered holy orders and that same year was created bishop of Saint-Malo. A year later he was a cardinal and, while retaining his bishopric in Saint-Malo, procured the administration of that of Nîmes. With influence at the papal court, he was to remain the much valued counselor of Charles VIII and Louis XII.

The cardinal left the bishopric of Saint-Malo to his son Denis and that of Nîmes to his nephew Michel. As for his son Guillaume, in 1489, at the age of seventeen, he was bishop of Lodève. Ambassador of Louis XII to Italy, bishop of Meaux, and reformer of his abbey of Saint-Germain-des-Prés, he was to be remembered above all as the man who, having sided without hesitation with the reforming faction of the Church, was to bring together in Meaux a group of humanist scholars that barely escaped accusations of heresy.

The cardinal had two brothers. One, Robert, was president of the Chamber of Accounts and then chancellor of France. The other, Guillaume, was known as the lord of La Quérée. He would be the founder of a noble family that had entirely forgotten its origins in salt, money changing, and hosiery.

Ennoblement, it is clear, could happen at any time. Though still close to their bourgeois origins, Pierre des Essarts was ennobled in 1320 and Guillaume Sanguin in 1400. Others waiting their turn, like the Briçonnet family, found other routes to the aristocracy. The letters patent sometimes arrived before permanent appointment to public service, more often afterward. They did not, in any case, prevent the individuals involved from pursuing lucrative business deals, as long as it was clear that their domain was broader and more elevated, and far removed from the world of the shop.

For those with the best contacts, who might reach nobility in one generation, it was not necessary to first establish country estates. First they made their mark, and then they legitimized their promotion with massive purchases of land. This was not the method of a Le Pelletier who slowly accumulated one piece of land after another, one rent and then another. In the years following his ennoblement, Guillaume Sanguin bought no fewer than seven large estates in the environs of Paris, including Meudon, Malmaison, and Ormesson. Pierre d'Orgemont bought Thoiry in 1376 and Chantilly in 1386.

The length of time elapsing between the ennoblement of the Bureau family and their acquisition of an estate was even more notable. Members of this family had served John the Good and Charles V. Ennobled in 1361, they were regarded as parvenus, rich in bonds, gifts from the king, and a few small pieces of land bought at random. The brothers Jean and Gaspard Bureau served the king in their turn, first Henry VI and his regent Bedford and then Charles VII. They improved the French artillery, making it into a useful arm of battle. It was only then, after 1440, that they became obsessed with the idea of becoming landowners. It had taken more than a century for the Bureau family to join the ranks of the landed aristocracy.

Although ownership of land did not assist these high-ranking public figures up the social ladder, a time would come when to be without land would raise eyebrows. A person's way of life had to correspond to his importance. In all probability, it was simply a matter of fashion. At the end of the war, when, in the face of the new artillery, the fortified castle lost part of its raison d'être and the French aristocracy discovered the charms of the country château and its pleasure gardens, there emerged a new criterion of respectability: it was not proper to spend the summer season anywhere but beneath the leafy bowers of a country estate that bore the name of its owner.

EIGHTEEN

Fortune and Conscience

*A*n orderly world is necessary in business. Safe deals and a good yield on investments depended on present certitudes, while future uncertainty could be mastered through the businessman's skill. The mercantile mentality shunned both adventurism, seen as foolhardiness, and anything resembling an asceticism that seemed to smack of impracticality. The moral code of business was that of the happy medium.

Profit and Salvation

Profit is a means, but it is first and foremost an end, and in no way shameful. The remarks in the Gospel of St. Matthew (19:23–24) on the difficulties awaiting the rich man seeking to enter heaven did not in any way upset the self-confidence of the business world. Though the profits from usury were certainly rather hard to justify, those from commercial and banking activities had more to do with God's words in Genesis (3:19): man shall earn his bread by the sweat of his brow ("in the sweat of thy face shalt thou eat bread"). The merchant and banker had no doubt that they had perspired sufficiently, and the Bible did not say anything about how much bread. Ecclesiastes (1:3) appears to encourage us to resignation: "What profit hath a man of all his labor which he taketh under the sun?" This was not taken as a condemnation of paid effort but rather as a reminder of what man is in the face of God's power. By the same token, the parable (Matt. 6:26) of "the fowls of the air" that "sow not neither do they reap" would have to be taken as condemnation of agriculture. It had long been customary to take from the Holy Scriptures what one wanted to hear.

Usury was the object of the fiercest condemnation, no exceptions or attenuating circumstances being admitted. St. Thomas Aquinas, in the thirteenth century, notes that usury is a sin "because one is selling that which does not exist." This is to imply there is no sin in selling—with profit, naturally—real goods. The preacher Jacques de Vitry, in the collections of exemplars that he compiled for the use of his brotherhood, reserves his harshest words for the usurer:

> God has ordered three types of men: peasants and other workers to ensure the survival of all, knights to defend them, and clerics to govern them. But the devil has ordered a fourth: the usurers. They do not participate in the work of man. They will thus not be punished with men, but with the demons.

The preacher had put his finger on it: the activities of the usurer were characterized by the absence of work. Money can work on its own, given time. We will ignore his suggestion that the cleric is to "govern." St. Augustine and the eleventh-century theologians who followed were content to confine the role of the clerics to praying for humankind. It is significant that, in the thirteenth century, after two centuries of commercial expansion and the emergence of an artisan class concerned with much more than merely local work, he does not limit the world of work to the peasantry alone. The merchant is implicitly included in the words "other workers." But the usurer is not among them:

> The amount of money they receive from usury will correspond to the quantity of wood sent into Hell to burn them.

Dante went even further, seeing usury as a crime against nature. He places in his *Inferno*, along with the usurers proper, all those who dealt in money: businessmen, merchants, and bankers:

> *Ma io m'accorsi*
> *che dal collo a ciascun pendea una tasca.*
> About the neck of each a great purse hung (XVII.54–55).

But Dante was neither a theologian nor a moralist. He was a polemicist who rarely moderated his harsh words. It was easier, however, to thunder against usurers from the pulpit or at one's desk than to manage without one in daily life. The nub of the problem, for the Christian usurer as for the Christian who required his services, lay in making the price of money appear to be something else. If they were forced to call it by its real name, if profit from money fell without an escape clause within the category of canonic condemnation, then the usurer had no choice but to resign himself to being a poor sinner.

But we should not judge reality by sermons. The usurer could find some comfort in the knowledge that this was not his only sin. He, like any other man, might deceive his wife or get into a fight with his neighbor. The necessary connivance between the Church and the sinner—for religion was not intended to lead to despair—gave rise to the notion, entirely absent in the fundamental theological texts, of Purgatory. This convenient place became, toward the end of the twelfth century in a time of economic growth, the natural and right home for anyone forced to live in the everyday world: neither a saint nor an enemy of God. Humankind had become fallible and had to take the consequences, but did not see itself as rebellious or doomed to damnation.

It was above all the notion of the happy medium that inspired the search for moderation of the rates that would make usury bearable. The greatest sin of all, in this matter, was excess. Just as the Bible does not condemn the wine from the vineyards of Canaan but rather emphasizes the social consequences—shown in the attitude of his sons—of Noah's drunkenness, so the canonists and theologians denounced above all the involvement of usury with excessively high rates of interest, from which the debtor could never manage to disengage himself. With the application of the happy medium, things would balance out: the usurer would be able to emerge from his exile in Purgatory just as his debtor had been able to free himself of the debt that had held him prisoner. It was when there was no hope for the unfortunate debtor that there could be no remission for the usurer. The man who gave no hope to his neighbor would find that his own family had been abandoned by the Supreme Judge. Hell was reserved for those unmoved by pity.

A businessman would have lived his entire life on credit and the receipts of credit. It was a common view, therefore, that Paradise could be obtained by notching up credit in good deeds. In the next world, in the final balancing of the books that governed relations between man and God, time spent producing money would be set against time used to procure salvation.

The humanity of the Earthly City provided a justification for the aims of profit. It ensured security; it freed people from anxiety. It allowed for the enjoyment of temporal goods that no one would suggest were intrinsically evil. The luxurious villa of the Florentine banker Niccolò di Jacopo degli Alberti was known as the Villa del Paradiso, with no hint of irreverence. The humanism of the late Middle Ages frequently identified Beauty with Goodness. To live in gorgeous surroundings, if acquired by virtues of work and intelligence, could not be seen as an offense to God.

Profit was also linked closely with man's fate as the means to social and political advancement. This advancement was enough to justify the profit, for it was part of the "good government" of the commonweal, something that the merchant world knew all about. Success in business opened the way to civic honors for the Florentine, involving service and duty as much as the objects of their ambition. The rich were useful to the city. It was, of course, hard to convince the poor of this, but the rich never doubted it.

For the French or the English, wealth offered visions of social mobility, a rise up the rungs of a ladder embedded in the natural fabric of society and established by God. With the exception of a few shows of revolutionary resistance, limited in both time and space—the Jacquerie of 1358 in France, the "Peasants' Revolt" of 1381, and even the preaching of the Franciscan Spirituals at the beginning of the fourteenth century or those of Savonarola at the end of the fifteenth—medieval man was no more scandalized by the fortunes acquired by the merchant than by the inherited wealth of the old aristocracy or the power, equally inherited, of the princes. The English preacher John Ball, following the Spirituals, was to ask: "When Adam delved and Eve span, who was then the gentleman?" Savonarola attacked luxury, women, and money changers. To the merchant trying to live at peace with his conscience, all this seemed a little excessive. In troubled times one kept one's head down, and there was no need to go so far as to overthrow the state.

Besides, there were plenty of pious works available that could justify profit. Who would give to the poor if there were no rich people? Religious foundations and other charitable works were the legitimate final repository of the accumulated wealth of a merchant like Datini, who had no legitimate heir and saw no reason why he should make his nephews' fortunes for them. City dwellers almost by definition, merchants were on relatively good terms with those essentially urban phenomena, the mendicant friars, the Dominicans, and particularly the Franciscans.

As he was nearing the end of his life and settling his affairs, it was to their monasteries, symbols of evangelical poverty, that the merchant made his largest donations. It was for the chapel of the Bardi family of bankers in the Franciscan monastery church of Santa Croce in Florence that Giotto in about 1317 painted a *Life of St. Francis,* as he had done earlier for the monastery in Assisi. The funerary chapel of the banker Francesco Sassetti in the Santa Trinità church has several scenes from the life of the same St. Francis of Assisi, his patron saint, painted in 1485 by Ghirlandaio.

Profit was not the be-all and end-all of the Christian obliged to live in the world. It was, rather, a gift from God, even regarded sometimes as a loan, as in the formula that either Dino Rapondi or his Parisian lawyers thought up for his will: "Desiring, for the salvation of his soul, to settle and dispose of the worldly goods that God, in his goodness, has lent to him on this pilgrimage through life."

Wealth remunerated a merchant for his virtues. Morelli went further, saying it was the reward for piety. In his *Libro della vita onesta,* Paolo da Certaldo asserts that wealth achieved through personal effort is legitimate. Inherited money was something extra and it was fitting to thank God for it, not refuse it. But it was important not to count on such legacies. Echoing Paolo da Certaldo, many businessmen were careful to specify in their wills that the money they left was earned through their own efforts.

San Bernardino da Siena, mouthpiece for the very genuine religious sense of the Tuscan business world, found a formula to legitimize interest through its usefulness to trade: it contributed to the orderliness of Christian society. Man does not live by bread alone, say the Gospels, but he needs bread to live. At the end of the fifteenth century, the Dominican cardinal Giovanni Dominici managed to argue that economic profit was part of the Divine Plan, a daring thing to do in the light of Savonarola's preaching. God had chosen certain people for wealth, thereby giving them a particular mission to fulfill.

From this period, the virtues of trade begin to be formulated. They were those same virtues found in any honest man and good Christian who dutifully pursued his allotted path. For some they reflected God's share of an inevitable world, for others man's share of a necessarily temporal Creation.

The first of these virtues was the respect due to God—the "first to be served," as Joan of Arc put it, though it was not a new idea—and a respect for one's portion in life that derived from one's success. For many this was merely a manner of speaking; for others it was such an integral part of their lives that it is difficult to distinguish between sincerity and superstition. It was always wise to head a contract with an invocation to the deity; the notary took care of it, just as he added a pious preamble, written with flourish, at the top of a will. With the passing of time these formulae became ever more elaborate, though two lines were thought quite sufficient. Far more tangible, however, was the share of capital that many entrepreneurs apportioned "in the name of God" to benefit the poor.

It was considered a pious deed to register 1 percent of a business deal in the account books in the name of God. For some merchants, at least, it was a way of involving God in business. If the unfortunate man's ship sank, that was too bad. It was the will of God. Thus the insurance premium was supplemented by divine insurance. After all, the businessman knew that everything had its price, and that he could only count on those friends in the council or senate whom he rewarded. Like any other form of cooperation, that of God and his saints did not come free.

Everyone knew that all business was an adventure; and adventure was one and the same thing as Providence or, to use its classical name, Fortuna. The ambiguity in these words reflects an ambiguity of attitude.

There was a price list for religion. This was an age of arithmetical piety, when a vow to go on a pilgrimage or to the Crusades could be converted into alms and indulgences, and accumulated by repeating certain prayers: the saying of the hundred and fifty *Ave Marias* of the rosary or the cycle of thirty requiem masses, the trental, repeated through the months of the year. Then there were the "Seven Joys" and "Seven Sorrows" of the Virgin, that were carefully worked through and meditated upon. It comes as no surprise to find the cost of salvation estimated in a will.

Though it can be seen as a deplorable product of the mercantile mind, such an attitude was no different from the idea of replacing service in arms by taxation; it was merely a naive expression of the merchant's need for security. Naturally he needed to know what it would cost and what he would be getting for his money. One had to pay for eternal salvation, and the mathematics of the wills reveals a concept of insurance through the sharing of risks not unrelated to the allocation of assets favored in nascent capitalism. Even with regard to the next world, one never put all one's eggs in a single basket.

Having recommended his soul to God and specifically mentioned the names of the Virgin, St. Michael the Archangel, the apostles Saints Peter and Paul, St. Merry, St. Nicholas, and St. Anthony, the Genoese goldsmith Nicolas Pigasse goes on to invoke more generally "all the saints, confessors, martyrs and all male and female saints, and all the blessed court and company of Paradise." This smacks of a chancellery clerk multiplying the legal formulae to be quite sure of getting it right. But Pigasse, who had become one of the richest men in Paris business circles, was now settling his accounts with his protectors in Heaven. He starts with the Cordeliers (Franciscans), the poor medicant friars, in whose monastery he hoped to be buried:

> To the monastery of the Cordeliers of Paris, to be buried in the said place, to say offices and be included in the prayers and blessings of the said monastery: 100 *livres tournois.*
> To his confessor in the said order of the Cordeliers: 25 *livres.*
> To the companion of the aforementioned confessor: 4 *livres.*
> To the priest of Saint-Merry, to bury the body: 60 *sous tournois.*
> To the canons, chaplains, and community of the said church of Saint-Merry, for the same reason: 6 *livres.*
> To two clerics of the said church: 20 *sous.*
> To the work of the said church: 100 *sous.*
> To the Augustinians, Carmelites, and Jacobins, to each order for the saying of offices: 60 *sous.*
> To the Hospital of the Holy Ghost of Grève: 40 *sous.*
> To the Hôtel-Dieu of Paris: 100 *sous.*
> To the Hospital of Haut-Pas: 40 *sous.*
> To the work of Notre-Dame de Paris: 40 *sous.*
> To the Quinze-Vingts de Paris: 20 *sous.*
> To the good ladies of Sainte-Avoie: 20 *sous.*

This was God's share. But for someone who was accustomed to divide up his business so as to spread out the risks, to give a lump sum of 167 *livres* to the Cordeliers would seem rather unwise.

Few saw any contradiction here between money and the Gospels. The words "Blessed are the poor" were viewed more as words of consolation for the unlucky. "No man can serve two masters" did not present problems either: there seemed to be no incompatibility between wealth in this world and salvation in the next. But this did not mean that merchants shrank from their charitable obligations, even if, for the wilier members of their class, the obligation to fulfill this duty was bequeathed to their heirs. The merchants were simply following a precedent set long ago by the nobility, who did not always follow the example of the count of Anjou, Foulque Nerra, or the king of France, Philip I, who founded a new monastery in reparation for each one they burned down. Jean Boinebroke, for instance, left the problem of making good his sins in a life as a usurer to the executors of his will.

Though less engaged in the quest for profits, the Florentine notary Ser Lapo Mazzei had close links with the world of trade. He reveals in his correspondence an ascetic turn of mind, inclined even toward mystical outbursts in which he places himself in the hands of Providence. It was Providence that had given him his honest and comfortable living. While creating obligations, it was not a matter for metaphysical agonizing.

Others, higher up the ladder of success, like Francesco Sassetti or Cosimo de' Medici, put on a public show of self-mortification that was not free of a hint of personal vanity. When, for the salvation of his soul, Sassetti commissioned Ghirlandaio to paint frescoes in the chapel he had built at the church of the Holy Trinity in Florence, it was also with the intent to use the chapel as a family tomb that would demonstrate to future generations the wealth of the Sassetti. As painted by Ghirlandaio, the family lined up behind its head hardly resembles a group of penitents.

It was with the same idea in mind that Datini, in the absence of a legitimate heir, bequeathed on his death his entire fortune and house—with the garden and the loggias, he specifies—to a hospital that he had founded in Prato. The one condition—for which historians will be eternally grateful was that this Casa del Ceppo de' poveri preserve in perpetuity the entire archive of his business. Without this business it would not have been possible for this merchant of Prato when thinking about his final demise, but no less about his jealous nephews and compatriots, to exercise the charitable work of a rich man. Lest there should be any misunderstanding, Datini makes sure that his gift is not anonymous: "Unlike the other Houses and the Hospital within the territory of Prato, this one will be called *The Francesco di Marco Home for the Poor.*"

Datini's wishes were fully understood. Scarcely had he died when his friends had the facade of the house painted with frescoes and thus converted into a work of piety and a memorial. It was not enough that the house go to the poor, it also had to be worthy of Datini.

It would be easy to mock this "portion for God" that hurt only the pockets of the descendants, but it would be wrong to do so. The same Francesco di Marco, like so many others, was capable of bringing all his business to a halt for ten whole days in order to go on a pilgrimage, all the while, ever the prudent businessman, keeping careful accounts both spiritual—the "pardon" or indulgence—and temporal:

> A record that on 28 August 1399, in the name of God and the Virgin Mary, I, Francesco di Marco, through the inspiration of God and His Mother, our Lady Holy Mary, resolved to go on pilgrimage, dressed in white linen cloth and shod as the majority of people go on these occasions.

Datini makes it clear in his account that it is forbidden to remove this garment for the nine-day pilgrimage (or novena) or to sleep in a bed.

Rising early, the seventy-year-old Datini set off across Florence. From Piazza Tornaquinci he reached Santa Maria Novella, the Dominican church where he took communion, without apparently hearing mass. Then he left the town proper and met up with other groups of pilgrims, one bringing the crucifix from the Santa Maria district and another that from Santa Croce. He joined the other pilgrims, all similarly dressed in white. All were barefooted, as our man does not omit to point out. They next went to Santa Croce and then to San Niccolò. They followed along the bank of the Arno as far as the abbey of Ripoli, where the bishop of Fiesole awaited the pilgrims and celebrated a solemn mass for them.

After mass there was a break. Everyone went into the fields to eat their bread, fruit, and cheese. Meat was forbidden for the duration of the pilgrimage.

They set off again in the midafternoon. By evening, at Ruballa, the pilgrims were already tired: "There, we spent the evening, feeling great consolation, that all the things we were lacking were for the good of our souls and bodies."

The pilgrimage continued. The second evening was spent at Figline, the third at Castello San Giovanni, the fourth at Montevarchi, the fifth at Quarata, and the sixth at Arezzo:

> We arrived there about midday and heard mass said by the bishop of Fiesole, outside in a meadow. Then the sermon. Then we went to eat. Our lodgings were with the brothers of the Minims of the monastery of St. Francis, and we spent the evening there very well.

On the seventh evening they arrived at Laterina, where the bishop of Fiesole again said mass, then on to Leona where they stayed in the inn. On the eighth day they reached Castelfranco and on the ninth Pontassieve, where the innkeeper turned out to be a friend of a Pisan haberdasher of Datini's acquaintance. Meat was still forbidden and, besides, it was Friday. Nevertheless, the friendly innkeeper regaled the pilgrims with a feast of fish. On Saturday, at the hour of Vespers, they were passing through the Porta Santa Croce. By evening Francesco di Marco was back home. It was 6 September:

We did not undress to go to bed, and we did not remove the white robe before the Sunday morning when the Crucifix was returned to Fiesole with those who followed it. On the square in Fiesole the bishop said a solemn mass. Then there was a sermon and a benediction for all.

Each person returned to his home, and the journey and pilgrimage were thus completed. May God make it profitable to our souls, if such be His will. Amen.

Our pilgrim had not forgotten to be a merchant all this while, counting and taking notes. On the evening before his departure he bought a hundred biscuits, a brooch to attach his rosary, and a cord to belt his white robe. He had his two mares and mule reshod, so they could carry the provisions that Datini intended to share with the twelve companions—friends and some of his employees—that he had persuaded to come with him to obtain the "pardon."

Everywhere they went he paid for everything—wine, salad, eggs, beans, straw and hay. He had even brought a supply of watermelons. He did not forget to write down the 3 *soldi* paid to the innkeeper in Montevarchi "for cooking what was needed" or the 18 *soldi* paid to the landlord in Pontassieve "for his work in cooking, the oil and the vinegar." It is hard to believe that the thirty fish, for which he paid 1 *soldo* 8 *denari* on the last day in Rovezzano, were for the supposedly frugal last meal of the journey that he shared with his companions; he may well have been taking advantage of a bargain to bring some home to Florence for the next day's meal.

The total cost was small. The nine-day pilgrimage had cost 35 *lire*. But here was an eminent and wealthy merchant of considerable years walking nearly two hundred kilometers in ten days, on the first day barefoot, and sleeping rough every night. It was not done with an eye to self-aggrandizement or publicity; Francesco di Marco was thinking very seriously about his soul. He could not be other than he was; so he noted down everything and had the healthy satisfaction of a duty accomplished. He conducted his pilgrimage with the same efficiency as his business.

Giovanni Colombini of Siena went further. In 1360 he gave away all his money and set off to preach throughout the country, eventually founding the small religious order of the Jesuates. The majority preferred to confine themselves to promoting such work, initiated by St. Francis of Assisi, through contributions to the Franciscans. St. Francis was greatly venerated by the merchant community during the fourteenth century. By the fifteenth century, many businessmen were more inclined to display their knowledge of quotations borrowed from Seneca and Cicero.

Good Government

Another virtue prized by merchants relating to men rather than God made all the difference between the businessman rewarded by God and the miser—or usurer—portrayed in depictions of the Last Judgment on many a church tympanum as a hanged man with his purse round his neck. This was respect for the just price, the price that, according to St. Thomas Aquinas, results from legitimate remuneration for any kind of work, including that of the merchant who has his role to play in the Earthly Jerusalem. It all depended, however, on what the entrepreneur thought was a fair reward for his effort.

It was always possible to stand aloof from inconvenient definitions. The guilds' regulations constantly reiterated their ban on games of chance, both for moral and for employment reasons: a guild member who was gambling was not at work and in danger of wagering jugs of wine that could keep him from doing his job. This did not prevent many people from indulging in gambling, and indeed, in many towns, dice makers were an officially recognized trade. There were, as we have seen, ways of getting around the ban on money that bred money. The just price was a philosophical idea, the object of endless treatises by theologians who attempted to calculate what it could be. For the businessman it was quite simply the price that, less able competitors notwithstanding, he could obtain through his talent, his position, and his daring.

The good merchant set great store by other virtues, that the merchant classes regarded as ideals here on earth: good manners, good appearance, and a good upbringing. Giovanni di Pagnolo Morelli moralizes on the subject at great length for the benefit of his children and successors in his memoirs. These were recommendations intended for young people or for the instruction of wives. But the astute businessman was well aware that such virtues were as useful in building a good reputation during one's life and good business in the market as in guiding the soul to Heaven:

> Have nothing to do with someone who has changed his work, partners, or masters. Be careful not to entrust your money or your business to a man who gambles, lives a life of debauchery, dresses too richly, or is forever feasting—in short, to a man who lacks a brain.

Prudence, one of the "moral virtues" of the theologians, was always praiseworthy. This was a virtue that protected as much against bankruptcy as against eternal damnation and, as such, fit neatly into the picture that the merchant liked to paint of himself. Order, prudence, and security were all one and the same thing, even when the moment came for daring. Prudence led to caution, to discretion, and to secrecy. The greatest sin for a businessman was careless talk.

Good faith was another virtue that was as much a necessity of life in society as a moral affirmation. A prerequisite of all forms of payment and credit, it formed the basis of all written documents and, in particular, account books. Although it was necessary to hedge it around with a precise framework of evidence and witnesses, that was done only as protection against emergencies or court cases. It would have been impossible to conceive of a world of economic relations in which this legal system was always brought into play.

This array of virtues defined a merchant morality in which the word *profit* equaled *goodness* and the advantage of each individual contributed to that of the commonweal. When the Commune of Siena commissioned Ambrogio Lorenzetti in 1337 to decorate the hall of the *Palazzo Communale,* where the government of the Nine met, it chose "Good Government" as theme for the fresco. Naturally, they were referring to government by businessmen, and the impact of such government on urban and rural society. How could it be otherwise in a city-state where the Nine, drawn from its financial aristocracy, had ensured the town's prosperity since the overthrow of the old nobility half a century earlier?

Lorenzetti designed a bipartite composition, each section dominated by a central allegorical figure: on one side Good Government and on the other Securitas. Seated like a court around the old man, who represents the power of the commune of Siena, are the six virtues of Good Government: Peace, Fortitude, Prudence, Magnanimity, Temperance, and Justice. Seven years later, Lorenzetti would paint this same hieratic figure of the old man on the covers of the account book for the Biccherna, the finance department of the Commune. Here was the sort of government that merchants and bankers could understand.

The second section of the fresco portrays *The Effects of Good Government.* In a double scene, showing both the town and countryside, and painted with consummate skill in perspective and trompe-l'oeil, Lorenzetti has fulfilled his commission with a realistic depiction of a society in which work guarantees prosperity. Everything is peaceful harmony and diligent activity. The shepherd leads his flock with a quiet modesty. The donkey waits patiently to receive its load. No one rushes, but no one is idle. There are no beggars in the roads. Very few faces look out from the windows, for in this well-regulated world everyone is in his place and at his work.

Prosperity is apparent from each person's fitting occupation, but this busy world is not without its joyful touches: in the foreground, girls are dancing to the sound of a tambourine.

On the right-hand side of the composition, rural occupations provide balance to this global view. Seen from the top of the tall *campanile* of the *Palazzo Communale,* the countryside is nearby and, as it still does today, reaches deep into the town. The fields are neatly hedged, the peasants busy bringing in the harvest and taking it to be sold in the town market, secure in the knowledge that it will be fairly regulated. The noblewoman riding through the countryside encounters a population that is nothing but industrious and respectful. Even the pig being led to eat acorns seems well disciplined.

Of course, the material world depicted by Lorenzetti is seen through a poetic veil whereby naturalistic observation of everyday life and work is transposed into a hymn in praise of prosperity through honest toil. Movement in the scene is created by the pack animals, loaded with bulging bales. There are no stray dogs or idle hands. The city walls enclose empty space and guarantee peaceful tranquillity.

In a second fresco, Lorenzetti shows *The Effects of Bad Government*. What he shows, in a word, is war.

The allegorical figure who sums it all up is the winged woman with the attributes of Fortune who is seen hovering over *The Effects of Good Government* fresco and is called Securitas. She holds a banner over the neat fields inscribed with the moral of the scene:

> *Sença paura ognuom franco camini*
> *elavorando semini ciascuno*
> *mentre che tal comuno*
> *manterra questa donna in signoria*
> *chel alevata arei ogni balia.*

> Let each man walk freely without fear,
> and everyone work and sow,
> As long as such a Commune [Siena]
> Keeps this Lady under its sway
> for she will keep away every tyrant.

Success can more easily be integrated into patriotism than into religion. That the commonweal was due its share seemed perfectly natural to the businessman for whom the size of his enterprise was closely dependent on the success of the state. A Florentine gained every time Florence's reputation increased, and a man like Jacques Coeur, always ready to imitate the Italians whom he hoped to beat at their own game, was thinking along these lines when he attempted to make France, whose financial reins he had firmly held in his hands, the new economic power in the Mediterranean world. Italian or German, the merchant never missed an opportunity to sing the praises of his town. Furthermore, he did everything in his power to beautify it. A love of one's native soil chimed in very well with a concern for good publicity.

Thus, despite the fierceness of competition, one virtue became increasingly important. Almost definitive for the middle classes in the distant days of the struggle for the autonomy of the city-state, it was appreciated once again after the collapses of the great banks and the first signs of economic depression. This virtue, inscribed on the cover of a Biccherna account book for 1385, was solidarity.

The anonymous artist has borrowed the symbolic figure of the old man from Lorenzetti. But there had been a change in political regime since the days of *Good Government* by the merchant class. The events of 1355 had brought to power a strange alliance of the old nobility and the lower classes. There was no more talk of prosperity in a town that was beginning to feel its decline. The Black Death had caused great losses in Siena. The town lost its commercial and banking influence in Europe. In the face of this crisis, unity was even more important than it had been at the time of Siena's greatest glory. Around the old man, members of the Council of Ten are linked in a circle one to the other, united by the cord they hold and enclosing Good Government. The image is clear: all are united by solidarity in the same movement.

Their civic sense did not, however, go so far as to eradicate fraud. Local governments and their policing agents spent their time seizing false measures and burning them in the public square, destroying inferior goods, and ripping off dubious labels. Letters from Bruges to Danzig and Torun are filled with complaints about deliveries of furs, which did not match in quality what had been promised. It even happened that samples were returned with accusations of cheating. The response was, naturally, an affirmation of good faith and reputation. Nevertheless, many deals ended up in the courts. In Paris, they complained of chalk in the wine. In Harfleur the weight of some overdamp salt was disputed. And the innkeeper who never watered down his wine was regarded as a paragon of probity.

There were disputes about the conduct of the slightest operation. A fisherman from Épernay, Jean Chaillot, who in June 1462 delivered more than two thousand carp and pike to the Parisian fishmonger Jean Chastriet, was unconcerned that his client had sold the fish at a loss and thought that he, Chaillot, should share in the loss. The fishmonger swore in court that they were partners, while Chaillot said that he had simply sold some fish and ought to be paid for it.

Tax fraud was widespread in every market. It is hard to find a merchant who does not appear, at one time or another, on the list of those fined by the royal courts. Fraud found ways to get around the law. Keen to make the fairs he had established in Lyons attractive to merchants, Charles VII exempted all merchandise sold there, and there only, from the *rève*—the tax on transactions. The response of the merchants was to offer for sale in Lyons huge quantities of merchandise, quite disproportionate to the small number of clients in these newly established fairs. They then took the goods to Geneva where the volume of trade was much greater. Since the goods had apparently been bought at the Lyons fairs, they could be traded tax-free. The king was forced to modify his decree, applying the *rève* to any goods leaving before the end of the fair without having been expressly part of a transaction. But it was impossible to prove whether or not such a transaction had taken place; the merchants stood together against the king.

In many cases, it was impossible to tell from decrees or court cases who was wrong and who right. The line between the suppression of fraud and fiscal persecution was a fine one. The system of tax-farming, whereby the tax collector took a share of the sum he had levied in the name of the king, led inevitably to an excess of zeal. Disputes multiplied, brawls were not uncommon, and the parties usually ended up in court.

An innkeeper, exasperated—and perhaps with reason—by the tax-farmer who called several times a day to check that his barrels were not being secretly refilled in order to cheat on the actual quantities of wine being sold over the counter, one day roughly pushed the tax collector into the cellar, locked the door, and went off to the country for a few weeks' holiday.

When tax officials caught up with a student who was supplying the entire district of Paris that would later be known as the Latin Quarter with wine sent by his father, officially for his son to drink during the year but in reality to help him pay for his studies, the university rose up in the student's defense. All testified to the student's good intentions. He had never dreamed of engaging in commerce; he had merely sold a little of his extra wine. Fraud on a larger scale can be found in Francesco Sassetti's last words to his children. Quite openly, this agent of the Medici advises them to put the Villa de Montughi, the most significant portion of their inheritance, in the name of his son Federigo: Federigo was a priest.

With regard to the roles of tax-farmers, agents of the public authorities, and the world of commerce in organizing and suppressing fiscal fraud, it was never entirely clear who did what. In Nîmes, a royal judge by the name of Jean Tiray had several of his cattle slaughtered in 1447. This would not have been of any significance were it not for the fact that he had taken advantage of his official position to ban all other butchers in the town from slaughtering any other animals until all his own meat had been sold. Naturally, the other cattle breeders protested at this unfair competition. Things began to turn nasty when the tax-farmer who collected the dues on butcher's meat appeared to make his collection. Tiray gave him a dressing down, saying that the animals belonged to the king. The tax-farmer, having heard this one before, was not deceived for a moment. He knew how to distinguish between the king's cattle and those belonging to one of the king's judges. Heated words were exchanged and tempers lost. Tiray grabbed the account book that the tax-farmer always carried with him when going about his work and ripped out several pages. The tax-farmer raised his hand to hit him and Tiray seized him by the collar, attempted to knock him onto the ground, but eventually settled for throwing him out into the street. Needless to say, the matter went to court, and the judge of Nîmes was not presiding.

If civic rectitude was fallible in the matter of taxation, it was rigorous when it came to law and order, without which there could be no economic life. And if there was one word businessmen feared above all it was *war*. Above all, they knew that any armed conflict reminded society not only of the valuable services of the aristocracy, who fought on horseback, but also those of the foot soldiers with their knives and axes, and of the "specialists"—the professional archers and crossbowmen. It was the merchant's money that paid for all this, but the glory went to others. Even if businessmen cared little for this glory, they would certainly suffer its repercussions.

War meant a lessening of their influence, despite a few famous exceptions to the contrary. One of these, the *gonfaloniere di giustizia*, Niccolò di Jacopo degli Alberti, led the Florentine army against the Pisans in 1363, at a time when the fortunes of the Alberti bankers were at their height. Heinrich Castorp fought bravely against England in 1470, in the war he had tried so hard to prevent. On the whole, however, businessmen left the job of representing their towns in battle to the artisans.

This quickly became apparent when Charles VII came up with the idea of granting an exemption on imports to those "free archers" chosen from the middle classes: the businessmen would join their ranks for the sake of the exemption and then pay a cheap replacement to go in their place, the latter running off at the first opportunity. For the important merchant, even more than for his more modest counterpart, time was money. Although a tiler could make as much money being a soldier as tiling roofs, a cloth merchant or money changer could not say the same. As for the banker, there was no question of comparison.

This hostility to war had other, and deeper, roots. However righteous the cause, armed conflict upset economic life. It impeded communications and discouraged investment. It made it difficult to obtain credit and caused a loss of faith in the currency. "Peace!" was always the slogan shouted by the merchants when they joined the protests on the streets. And it was not because they were cowards.

The attitude of the Parisians during the civil war and English occupation is a good illustration of this hostility to war. Each time peace was made or a treaty signed that seemed likely to bring an end to the turmoil, they lit celebratory bonfires, with shouts of "Noël!" and the ringing of church bells. Processions were organized and Te Deums chanted. Gates that had been sealed were reopened and the river trade reinstalled. The fairs started up again.

Not the least bothered about loyalty to the old dynasty, Parisians adapted fairly readily to Lancastrian rule, since it seemed likely to bring peace. When, around 1425, it appeared that Bedford's regime had been consolidated, confidence was also restored in the ports of Argenteuil and Neuilly. Merchants were again traveling to the Lendit fair, held in June on the plain of Saint-Denis. Paris might now be English, but at least it was at peace.

But just how English was it? If Joan of Arc was not welcomed in the merchant circles of the capital, it was not because she talked of "chucking out" the occupier but because she was reviving war in a region that had begun to believe in peace. Whether it was an English peace or an Anglo-Burgundian peace, it mattered little: it was peace. In 1419, a tax-farmer collecting dues on merchandise entering the gates of Paris—land-based trade, in other words—declared that he was losing money, not collecting enough to cover what he had paid for the lease. In short, merchants were staying away from Paris. In 1424 they were back again—from Rouen, Dieppe, Caen, Bernay, and Saint-Quentin. The Lendit fair, suspended since 1418, reopened in 1426. The bids for tax-farms began to rise. While the merchants may not have been supporters of Charles VII, there was nothing wrong in dreaming of a return of prosperity.

When Joan of Arc appeared on the scene, for the Parisian of 1429 it initially meant hope, swiftly followed by disillusionment. But by 1430, once again there was no fair, and no merchants passing through. The archer who aimed his crossbow at Joan from the top of the Porte Saint-Honoré was not an Englishman but a Parisian. When the time came, he would not refuse to "chuck out" the English; but for the moment he could do without this renewal of hostilities provoked by the Maid of Orleans.

And what of these English "occupiers"? In this capital city, defending itself against Joan of Arc, the captain of the Saint-Antoine barracks, the future Bastille and the largest fortress in Paris, was Sir John Fastolf, Shakespeare's and, later, Verdi's Falstaff. Fastolf had, to help him hold the Bastille, eight swordsmen and seventeen archers: including the squires and servants, a total of some thirty-five soldiers. When his successor Thomas More took over the garrison, he had nine swordsmen and twenty-eight archers: in all, between forty and fifty soldiers. Between 1430 and 1436 there were, at most, two hundred English in the entire city.

This hardly sounds like an occupied town. Even if the population of the capital had fallen, at this dramatic moment in its history, to something less than fifty or eighty thousand (depending on which figures we follow), two hundred foreign soldiers do not constitute an occupation. In fact, if Paris was English, it was because it was resolutely Burgundian.

Neither the middle classes nor the clerics had forgotten the proposed reforms of John the Fearless, and they had had plenty of time too to think about the promises—unfulfilled—of a reduction in taxation made by Duke Philip the Good. By now, people hardly believed this old rhetoric. Paris judged the Bedford regime by the yardstick of its demands for taxes, and its celebrations paid for by the taxpayer. As for the duke of Burgundy, he was almost always away.

The economic realities remained. In peacetime, the major part of the capital's trade was conducted with the lands around the lower Seine and those to the north, which from 1418 meant, in effect, the Anglo-Burgundian kingdom. A third of river trade took place with Rouen, Elbeuf, Nantes, Vernon, Dieppe, and Louviers. From these towns came provisions of wheat, fish, fruit, wood, and hay. French and Burgundian wines also traveled this route. They were exchanged for cloth and metalwork. Another 40 percent of the total river trade was with Picardy, Artois, and French Flanders. Of the overland trade, less well documented and so more difficult to measure, more than half must have been with the north, for the Parisian the most politically important region.

Thus one can imagine the emotions felt on the reconciliation, in 1435, of the Valois king Charles VII and the duke of Burgundy, count of Flanders. It is easy to understand what it meant for the Parisian businessmen to regain Pontoise in 1441 and Rouen in 1450. With the return of peace, trade with those regions to the south of the Loire made up less than 1 percent of business passing through the Parisian ports. When it came to choosing, the Parisian might prefer one king or another, but with his eye on the routes to Lille, not Bourges.

When it came to fighting, businessmen preferred to choose their own weapons: economic diplomacy and the money market. They could adjust prices to deprive their enemy of the means to prosperity. Mercantilism ruled here, and with it the firm belief that one person's riches were gained at the expense of another's ruin. When forced, they would fight for economic concessions that gave some meaning to treaties: they were prepared to sacrifice immediate peace for a lasting advantage. But the stakes were not measured in the language of honorable chivalry. Even if it meant paying heavily for the cost of defeat, merchants preferred to pay. All agreed that captains should be paid wages like soldiers. Thus the prince or the town could hire professional soldiers, the nobleman could gain a new income, and the merchant new markets: victory, with its profits in peace, could be bought.

NINETEEN

The Merchant and the Arts

*T*he businessman lived with a pen in his hand. Though a product of secular education and unfamiliar with the clerical culture acquired by those of the bourgeoisie who aspired to a profession in the law, he handled a pen every bit as frequently as money. He had sufficient time for leisure and reflection to allow him to become quite a book lover and sometimes even a writer on professional subjects.

A pragmatist in his business affairs, he showed little inclination for vain philosophical or political speculation. He had little enthusiasm for the generally inelegant Latin used in the universities and still, very often, by lawyers. Nor was he impressed by the contrived Latin used by the humanists trying to rival Horace or Cicero. He used the everyday language of commercial correspondence, the down-to-earth prose of the account book. When he took up his pen to describe or relate something other than a newly discovered marketplace or his recent experience of the rates of exchange, he used his mother tongue or sometimes, as in the case of the notary Rusticello of Pisa who recorded Marco Polo's memoirs in French, another language commonly used in the place where he lived.

In turning their backs on the Latin culture of the clerics brought up on Boethius, businessmen sometimes drew near the secular humanists, whose accurate descriptions of the world, combined with a revival of interest in antiquity, had a vitality that had quite vanished from the minute dissections of old texts practiced by generations of scholars in the universities. A number of these businessmen would take their studies to a high level. Palla Strozzi, the richest man in Florence, according to the 1427 census listing taxable wealth, read Greek and had secretaries with the unusual names of Argyro-

349

poulos and Callixtus. The majority stopped short of Greek, confining themselves to travelers' tales and chivalrous romances that fired the imagination,
as well as bourgeois comedies that poked fun at their neighbors.

Account Books and Journals

The context of the businessman's intellectual life remained, nevertheless,
the world of trade. The town lay at the heart of this world, providing both
the stage and the object of bourgeois literature. The merchant's year, the
chronological framework of his narrative, was the commercial year of 365
days, which began on 1 January. Even when telling a story, the merchant
rejected the chancellery calendar, which began sometimes at Christmas,
sometimes at Easter, and which, given the frequent changes in the date of
Easter in the West, might one time run for eleven months and the next for
thirteen. The merchant liked to be precise, and could give the price of beans
or cheese to the nearest *denier*. His narratives crammed with figures were,
whether he realized it or not, statistics, his preference being for fixed coordi-
nates. Both accountant and citizen, he lived according to the rhythm of
hours struck on a public clock—there were such clocks in Florence, in
Milan, in Padua from the first half of the fourteenth century, and in Paris
from about 1370—and his mind did not readily conform to the ecclesiastical
calendars or the agricultural seasons. It was no use calculating something
down to the last sou and then dating it "from the Thursday that follows
the Sunday when the *Oculi* is sung," which was 4 March in 1350 and 24
March in 1351.

Initially businessmen preferred those types of literature which related
to their professional activities and were inspired by preoccupations of the
business world. In other words, they particularly enjoyed description of
human societies, whether in the past or in other parts of the world. When
writing themselves, either to inform a partner about changes in the market
or to keep journals noting financial institutions or commercial trends, businessmen constantly added notes in the margins or the text, details making
them historians of their own businesses as well as the social milieu in
which they lived and worked. Merchants' letters are packed with fascinating
information about the daily life of the city and the state, as well as events,
however serious or trivial, that were the topics of gossip that week. Such
accounts captured the texture of the times, from war and peace to pilgrimages
and the successful birth of a son.

As historian of his world, the merchant did not hesitate to make the
kind of value judgments typical of the commercial world. It was part of
the merchant's professional duties to evaluate people and events, and he
performed the role of chronicler as naturally as he made decisions based
on the assessment of partners or opportunities.

As long as such account books were restricted to a size that one person could write up on his own, they remained a mix of business and family memoirs. These became known in French as "*livres de raison*" ("books of reason"), as a result of a misunderstanding of the Italian word *ragione* with its two meanings, "account" and "reason." The important moments of private life entered here in chronological order, with marriage really "counting" for what it was—a family event but also an estate matter—while births and deaths appear in the entries as so many profits and losses affecting the structure of the family business, its dynamics and its future. Anything that might be useful is noted down, and it was a foolish merchant who failed to record external events that might influence the family's affairs. As in all the businessman's assessments—and even more so for the speculator's—a noble marriage, war, or peace, even a heat wave or excessive rainfall had their place in an account of risks and opportunities.

For the merchant whose business had grown so large that others had to help with the bookkeeping, there seemed to be no harm in keeping a separate book for recording a random collection of things seen or heard, descriptions of places visited or phenomena encountered. Some of these books became the works of true chroniclers. Giovanni Villani paints a history of the world between 1336 and 1341 from the viewpoint of a Florentine merchant. He also works out the figures:

> After careful enquiry, we have found that there are at this time in Florence some twenty-five thousand men between fifteen and seventy, all citizens and capable of bearing arms. Of these, there are one thousand five hundred nobles and rich citizens, who, as magnates, give the Commune its security.
>
> There are also in Florence about seventy-five knights fully equipped with arms. Before the second government by the *popolo*, presently in power, there were certainly two hundred and fifty knights. But since the time that the *popolo* has taken government, the magnates have not kept their status and their authority, so that few people now set themselves up as knights.
>
> Judging from the quantity of bread regularly needed for the city, it was estimated that there were some ninety thousand mouths to feed, including men, women, and children.
>
> It was estimated that there were always in the city about one thousand five hundred outsiders, travelers or soldiers, not including in this total clerics or cloistered monks and nuns.
>
> Then eighty thousand people were counted in the territory and district around Florence.
>
> According to the priest who baptized the children and put down a black bean for each boy baptized in the church of San Giovanni and a white bean for each girl, so that he could be certain of the number, we know that there were at that time between five thousand five hundred and six thousand baptisms a year, the boys generally outnumbering the girls by between three and five hundred. And we find that there were between eight and ten thousand boys and girls learning to read, between one thousand and twelve

hundred children learning the abacus and algorithms, and between five hundred and fifty and six hundred learning grammar and logic.

Clearly Villani wished to boast of his city's achievements, particularly in the old days. In the following century, around 1423, Marin Sandro gives us an outline of the history of Venice from a merchant's point of view. Buonaccorso Pitti shows himself to be more ambitious, producing nothing less than a chronicle of the Western world, though naturally featuring Florence as its center. The majority of these merchant historians confined themselves, however, to their own cities, or even just their own families, as did Jacob Lubbe for Danzig in the late fifteenth century or Hans Vessel for Stralsund in the early years of the next century.

Reading these chronicles written by men more used to handling figures, one is tempted to take the precision of the medieval merchant for that of the historian or the modern economist: population figures, monetary rates, or the price of cochineal. Everything is counted, dated, and measured. But that would be a mistake.

For these figures do not stand up to comparison or analysis. Population figures, particularly, are inflated, as we can see from contemporary tax rolls. The businessman seems to draw a distinction between numerical data with a personal significance derived from professional sources, and data that—lying outside his own domain and so, for him, unquantifiable—are significant only as superlatives. When Francesco Datini notes down the price of a pound of pepper, he knows what he is talking about. When Bonvesin della Riva evaluates Milanese society in 1288, he indulges in a taste for large round numbers:

> In the town and its county, more than a thousand people can easily keep war horses at the disposal of the Commune. . . .
> The notaries number more than one thousand five hundred, among whom there are many who excel in the drawing up of contracts.

Bonvesin would have been hard put to say how he had counted these hordes of notaries. It is clear that many different factors, notably patriotic and psychological, contribute to this exaggeration: it is easy to round up a figure to inflate the standing of one's hometown, as it is to sacrifice truth in describing faraway lands, the better to amaze those who stayed at home. From Bruges to China, descriptions of the worldly Italian businessmen combined in an unverifiable proportion the art of astonishing with the failure of medieval people to estimate crowds and measure phenomena. In his narrations of other people's tales Guillebert de Metz, probably a professional scribe, used figures in this vague way in his famous description of Paris:

> It was estimated that in Paris there were more than four thousand wine taverns, more than eighty thousand beggars, more than sixty thousand scribes. The same of scholars and tradesmen without number.

Such figures could not possibly refer to a town whose population at that time, as estimated by even the most generous historians, was some 200,000. They mean only that in Paris, in the 1400s, there were a lot of taverns and a lot of beggars and scholars. And yet we find the same Guillebert de Metz, in the same text, giving us an apparently precise record of the food supply:

> They ate in Paris each week, taking one thing with another, four thousand sheep, two hundred and forty cattle, five hundred calves, two hundred salted pigs, and four hundred unsalted. Similarly, there was sold each day seven hundred barrels of wine, for which the king received his quarter, without counting the wine for the scholars and those who did not pay, like lords and several others who harvested their own on their estates.

If we take the highest estimated figure for population—and the one generally accepted today—that makes one cow a week per 800 inhabitants, one sheep per 50, one calf per 400, and one pig per 500. That would mean one serving of meat a *day* for the rich and one a *week* for the poorer people. These figures would be plausible.

An explanation of the discrepancy is hinted at in the matter of the wine. Guillebert mentions the number of barrels for which dues had been paid—a quarter—and is well aware that he is leaving out the wine consumed by those exempted from tax, as well as that used by scholars and nobles. He also does not know how much wine the owners of vineyards in the region around Paris brought into their cellars in the autumn. In other words, his figures for consumption were obtained from the tax-farmer, who collected the dues, who would have scrupulously counted each barrel and every cask of wine. The animals providing meat had no doubt been counted in a similar way by the tax-farmers collecting dues paid at the gates of Paris and in the pig market at Porte Saint-Honoré.

To the merchant's way of thinking, what could be counted should be counted. A person involved in business knew how to count heads of cattle. Whatever could not be counted had to be invented, and the large figures are no more than superlatives. Everyone understood this. The reader knew very well that it was easy enough to count cattle at the city gates or in the market, but that it was impossible to count the number of taverns when every house opened onto the street and had a table and a counter. No one could accuse the narrator of being a liar when he enumerates the beggars: it was simply a manner of speaking. But to make a mistake about the number of wine barrels was quite another matter and would be taken for incompetence.

Merchant Literature

The observations, information, and instruction that could be passed on through travelers' tales made them the preferred literary genre of merchants who had traveled in foreign parts in order to learn about the world and who still maintained conections in far-flung places to keep themselves up to date. Part wide-eyed adventurer and part hard-headed expert in his field, he revealed himself as both witness and analyst. Buonaccorso Pitti was much read by those who were to follow his routes in the West. Boccaccio made his talents available to a simple merchant from Ravello who was better at telling a tale over dinner than writing down his memoirs in a book. It is well known that it took the combined talents of the notary Rusticello and the merchant Marco Polo to write down the often embroidered tale of Polo's travels. Christopher Columbus used it when seeking information about the East that he hoped to reach by the opposite route.

Many businessmen knew what there was to be gained by acquiring accurate information about the world. Geography already was viewed as a science necessary for economic policy. Knowledge about resources, clients, distances, and customs might all come into play one day in making the right choice or a costly error.

As the fifteenth century progressed, economic circles began to realize the need to support scientific research, both theoretical and practical. In the previous century, studies that had led to the creation of the so-called Alphonsine astronomical tables had not had any practical effect on the daring voyages of the navigators. Now the merchants of Nuremberg offered to finance research into astronomy, with the intention of improving mercantile communications and safeguarding the profitability of sea voyages. Martin Alonso Pinzón, a navigator and shipowner from Palos in Andalusía who provided Christopher Columbus with ships and himself captained the *Pinta* on the voyage to what would be America, was a keen astronomer. Amerigo Vespucci, one of the Medici agents in Cádiz and later in Seville, and an enlightened cosmologist, would give his name to the new continent. He was not the first to set foot on the land across the Atlantic, but he had a better understanding than Columbus of what had been discovered.

Yet another characteristic of merchant literature stemmed from the merchant's realism. There is an obvious concern with handing down—to those who had a right to it, not to the competition—useful tricks of the trade. Underlying all the treatises on morality and good housekeeping—one and the same thing in the rhetoric of the good bourgeois—we feel the anguished knowledge of the fragility of personal fortunes, and the fear that everything might collapse the moment one died. How to make money and how to earn and maintain a good reputation, how to live happily and esteemed by others—this is the advice that the merchant neatly set out for his widow, his children, and his partners. The pleasure in being able to cite himself as an example is barely concealed.

Two things above all seem to have preoccupied the mind of the advice giver: the importance of instilling in the minds of his partners and family the principles of professional life that made it possible to make one's fortune without going to Hell or to prison, and the need to supervise the education of his children. His morality was pragmatic and, as we have seen, that of the golden mean, of prudence, even suspicion. Money was not only the key to everything but also the supreme reward here on earth. Whether sought or guarded, it was deserved. As for education, this was very much more—according to the moralizer at least—than mere professional training. There were other things to know, not least the tricks of the trade. There was the art of forming a character capable of mastering both happiness and success. There was even an art in knowing how to reprimand servants and how to pay suppliers:

> Always remember to say to your people that they should deal only with reasonable people, that they should bargain before doing anything, and that they should pay frequently, without waiting for debts to mount up on the tally stick or on paper, though it is better to use a tally or written entry than to rely on one's memory, for creditors always believe a sum is more and the debtors less, and from this are born quarrels, hate, and ugly reproaches.

Realism in business did not exclude works of the imagination. Thus the merchant favored literature that drew its themes from his intellectual and social world. He liked to see mirrored his neighbors and colleagues, and his life as a citizen, successful businessman, husband, and trader. Needless to say, the middle classes particularly enjoyed the satire of other social groups that gave them a chance from time to time to take their revenge. Here imagination extended, and corrected, the real world. A common target was the priest, the eternal rival, in the lives of his female parishioners, of the husband too busy with his work. Satire was also aimed at the peasant whose rustic boorishness reassured the middle classes of their superiority. Nor was the legal profession spared—for the judges and lawyers who grew fat on trials had ruined many a merchant—nor the nouveaux riches, those recently ennobled merchants who had too quickly and conveniently forgotten their origins. The only figure never ridiculed in bourgeois literature was, of course, the merchant.

The literature produced by ecclesiastics provided a counterweight to this type of comedy, with its procession of boorish bourgeois and half-witted aristocrats. If the pathetic hero of *The Fifteen Comforts of Marriage* gives us a picture of the "good citizen," self-satisfied to the point of blindness, it was because the author, a cleric, wished to amuse his peers with a portrait of the stupidity of the shopkeeping classes.

The merchant's sense of humor was not always the most subtle, but at least it was not bitter. Shopkeepers enjoyed a good laugh but were not inclined to indulge in a serious critique of social or political life. Novels and plays were for amusement, not reform.

There was also a more escapist genre of literature that allowed the merchant's imagination to turn away from the grayness of everyday life and the narrow horizons of his world. Aside from those few great merchants who traded with Alexandria in Egypt or speculated on the arrival of caravans from the Sudan, there were many ordinary shopkeepers who pored over these books to expand their perspectives, which had contracted, over time, to the dimensions of a market stall.

In these books businessmen found stories of heroism that were totally different from the professional risk taking of a cautious speculator. After a day's work, our merchant also liked his share of epic, chivalrous, or simply tall stories. He was receptive to noble self-denial and fine sentiments. The imagination of the money changer or cloth merchant was fed by novels and plays inspired by the Arthurian legends. It was heady stuff and some were intoxicated: the burgomaster of Lübeck, Johann Roseke, liked to be known as Johann Perceval. In many German towns, merchants met in what they liked to call "the court of Arthur," where they escaped the dullness of their daily lives in dazzling feats of the imagination. The French world of the counter or the workroom sought pleasure in the platitudes of works like *Amadis des Gaules, Petit Jehan de Saintré,* or *Jehan de Paris:*

> The heralds of Jehan of Paris entered the room where the king of Spain sat, surrounded by several other kings, barons, ladies, and knights, to ask the king for lodgings for their master.
>
> "Your majesty, king of Spain, our master Jehan of Paris greets you and the noble company.
>
> "Will it please you to provide him and his followers with suitable lodgings in a separate part of the town. And he will come and see you, and the ladies. Otherwise he will not come!"
>
> "In good faith, my friends," said the king, "he shall not wait for a matter of lodgings, for I shall provide him with them."
>
> "Sire," said the heralds, "will it please you to show them to him now, to see if he can lodge there."

This is what pleased the merchants. They knew all about the problem of finding lodgings. And they were even more interested in Jehan's tour of Europe since the character is an impostor, a rich trader who makes a big display of his wealth to deceive the courts so that the king and his courtiers fear a diplomatic incident if they do not receive such an apparently important man and his train with due ceremony. The reader could enjoy the banquets and ceremonies that he would never see, and at the same time laugh at the trick played by a merchant on a gullible aristocracy:

> Jehan de Paris took up his cup and commanded that two others be given to the two queens, saying: "Let us three drink, to start with. The others will

drink when they will." And he drank without further ado. Then he gave his cup to the maiden before him, saying: "There, my darling, I have drunk to you. I think now you will never fear me."

"By God," said the maiden, "there is no reason for it. And I thank you heartily."

The kings and the other lords and ladies drank, much amazed that Jehan de Paris had taken it upon himself to drink before all the kings, who were his elders.

A blend of the fantastic and the ribald, a happy juxtaposition of sense and silliness, went to make up the popular literature of the late fifteenth century. It was at the same time imbued with the epic and chivalrous vein taken from the chansons de geste and the Arthurian romances. The new possibilities of mass production meant that these novels, which laboriously reworked ideas originally brought to life by Chrétien de Troyes, knew a great vogue. Precisely this type of literature, from 1480 onward, was produced annually by the first Parisian printing presses.

For the printer had to make a living too, and it was not Gasperin de Bergamo's *Latin Letters,* the works of Sallust, the letters of Bressarion, or Cicero's *Tusculan Disputations* that kept the press going. While the invention of movable type was significant to the Humanists for its ability to revise and edit texts, thus opening the way to a revival of the study of philology and rediscovery of ancient languages and ideas, the thirst for culture in the solid bourgeois, whether lawyer or merchant, was slaked by the presses' capacity to print multiple copies and at a reasonable price. Along with Cicero and the *Grandes Chroniques de France,* the presses produced works such as the *Farce de maître Pathelin,* which amused audiences with a debtor's attempt to avoid paying what he owed by bleating like a sheep. Villon's *Testament* was most appreciated for the humor of a situation where the author ironically has an inn of dubious repute bequeathed to the captain of the watch and a diamond he does not own to one of the richest jewelers on the Pont au Change. Editions of *Fierabras, Merlin l'Enchanteur,* and *Amadis des Gaules* stirred the imaginations of those who dwelled on the *piano nobile* (main floor) of the merchants' half-timbered houses.

A century later, Cervantes was to paint a dramatic portrait of a well-intentioned man driven almost to madness in his attempt to re-create the chivalry of the past. *Don Quixote* owed much to *Amadis des Gaules.* Don Quixote's extravagant imagination was a response to the harsh, stony plateaus of the Castilian *meseta.* At lower altitudes, and with a less violent clash of imagination and reality, more than one such Don Quixote could be found on the Pont au Change.

Primary expression of the cultural life of the middle classes, the theater offered its fictional world as a form of communal escapism. The towns of Germany rivaled one another in the production of plays whose plots were derived from ancient mythologies, both Greek and Germanic. One town presented a *Judgment of Paris*, introducing the beautiful Helen of Troy who was to loom so large in the work of later German poets. In another, one might see *Frau Krimhilt*, which reduced the cosmic story of the Nibelungen to the dimensions of a domestic drama and the tragic fate of the Valkyrie to the story of a *ménage à trois*. France, too, delved into its ancient history, producing incidents from the lives of St. Louis and Joan of Arc that could be fitted into the comfortable mold of the mystery play.

The *Vrai Mystère de la Passion*, written in 1452 by the organist of Notre-Dame in Paris, Arnoul Gréban, took four days to tell the story of the Redemption, the words of the Gospels enriched by every allusion in which the New Testament is prefigured by the Old. The play is full of the details of daily life, down-to-earth characters, attitudes, and language. Gréban's intention is clear: to help the ordinary person understand the essential truths of the holy story. The way to do this was clearly to use language and references that such people would understand.

Just as there was more than one kind of trade, so there was more than one type of bourgeois. A rich merchant did not see things in the same way as a seller of swords or a butcher's assistant. In an enterprise as expensive—in time more than money—as public theater, the major part of the work was done by the poorer classes, glad of both the change and the chance to appear on stage. But we should not suppose, for all that, that they made any artistic choices. That was a matter for the powerful classes. The city oligarchies managed the stage just as they kept an eye on the bookseller.

New Princes, New Patrons

Businessmen never neglected to calculate costs. Just as they measured the cost of eternal salvation, so they were not unaware of either the price of or the profit to be gained from a culture that was part of their public image. Although of no obvious direct benefit, culture was an expression of fortune and the achievement of success. It emphasized the blessings of Heaven as much as it stemmed from them. When Tommaso Portinari commissioned the Flemish Hugo van der Goes to paint a triptych for Sant'Egidio in Florence, he was proclaiming his arrival to the whole city. He was now one of those eminent figures who could afford to offer Christian society a setting for life and prayer.

There could be no better evidence of a newly acquired dignity and social worth than this availability—or even this waste—of both time and money reflected in the chivalrous fantasies of the German Johann Perceval or the healthy self-satisfaction of the Arnolfini couple that Van Eyck, with a clever trick of the mirror, portrays majestically, in both front and rear view.

The Florentine businessmen won over to Platonic humanism in the

1450s were altogether different. Palla Strozzi supported various scholars, including Tommaso Parentucelli, the future Pope Nicholas V. Cosimo de' Medici founded the Platonic Academy, a gathering of learned minds that met for erudite discussion. It was the same Cosimo who would give an oportunity to his doctor's son, whose name was Marsilio Ficino.

We should be clear, however, that by this time someone like Palla Strozzi or Cosimo the Great had very little to do with business affairs. Nevertheless, they brought to bourgeois society the idea of the conscientious, impartial, and, indeed, secular patron. This was something very different from the pious patronage that had, two centuries earlier, provided Chartres Cathedral with forty-two stained-glass windows paid for by the guilds, alongside the forty-four paid for by the sovereigns and barons. Merchants and artisans can be seen in the windows at Chartres and elsewhere, proudly displayed with the tools and activities of their trades. Families like the Medici and the Bardi, whose generosity would be manifested in a funerary chapel for their dynasty, were unlikely to reveal the origins of their wealth in trade in such a way. We are now also a long way, though not so long in time, from the self-promoting patronage of Jacques Coeur who displayed his maritime ambitions in the decoration of his house in Bourges.

The patronage of these new Tuscan patrons and their imitators was of a new sort, inspired by a new attitude toward accumulated wealth, perhaps even a new vocation for the rich in the world. "The gift of spending well is a virtue," wrote Giovanni Ruccellai, son-in-law of Palla Strozzi, in his *Zibaldone*.

Extending its desire for entry into aristocratic society even to philanthropy, the business world now laid claim to a function that had hitherto been the preserve of princes and barons, cardinals and archbishops. Like Charles d'Orleans in his court in Blois—reminiscent of the "competition" illustrated by François Villon—or René of Anjou in Naples and in Provence, the princes of trade and banking now took part in giving commissions to artists and hospitality to poets and philosophers. "God's share" of a merchant's wealth was now destined for art and charity.

In fact, one did not exclude the other, and many commissions for paintings and *objets d'art* continued to be inspired by religion, even if literature was pursuing other paths. Orders for a "Madonna and Child" or a favorite saint flooded in. Other popular subjects were the Nativity, Wise Men, Passion, and Deposition from the Cross. Francesco Sassetti and Giovanni Tornabuoni both turned to Ghirlandaio for the decoration of their funerary chapels, just as the Bardi and Peruzzi families had looked to Giotto a century earlier, or the Strozzi and Acciaiuoli families to Orcagna. Having failed to come to an agreement with the friars of Santa Maria Novella, Sassetti had the chapel he was preparing for himself in Florence decorated in the nearby church of the Trinità. Tornabuoni wanted something better. When in Rome, he had commissioned Ghirlandaio to paint the tomb of his wife, a member of the Pitti family, in the church of Santa Maria sopra Minerva, built on the foundations of what had originally been a Roman temple to Minerva. Now, in 1477, he had the same Ghirlandaio paint the chapel he had reserved for himself in Santa Maria Novella.

Cosimo de' Medici commissioned from Rogier van der Weyden, then in Italy, a retable—part of the decoration standing above and behind an altar—of the Madonna with Saints Cosmas and Damian. Lorenzo de' Medici asked Botticelli for an Adoration of the Magi.

Collecting art, once associated only with princes, now became part of the life of the merchant who had started out in a shop. Such a collection was put together for his own pleasure and that of his family and came to include such things as manuscripts and, in due course, early printed books. By the beginning of the fifteenth century, even men of very moderate education like Datini owned copies of Livy and Seneca. Whether he read them or not, he must certainly have enjoyed having them in his library, every bit as much as Jean de Berry at the same period prized his jewels and illuminated manuscripts. At the very least he recognized that one could not be a businessman rewarded by Fortune if one did not have at hand the classical foundations of the new culture. The ornate frame of the mirror in Jan van Eyck's portrait of the Arnolfini is adorned with a crown of lapis lazuli as well as ten enamels showing the Stations of the Cross.

This new mercantile patronage marked art with its own stamp, that of realism. It was an economical realism to start with, for the businessman knew how to strike a good bargain. He knew what the work would cost and what he would get for his money. For the doors of its Baptistery, the city of Florence organized a competition, won by Lorenzo Ghiberti. A desire for greater realism in religious painting led the world of trade to favor the experiments of artists like Giotto and, later, Uccello. Artists who knew how to observe and measure could give a more precise representation of the world, making it not simply a reflection, but the image of life itself. Similarly, a greater realism in portraiture was sought by men who rejected ideal or hierarchical representation, preferring to know whom they were dealing with and judging individuals for what they were, for their personal qualities and not for their place in the divine plan.

It comes as no surprise, then, to find that the greatest master of perspective was a merchant's son, Leone Battista Alberti, or that the first realist painter of portraits was Jan van Eyck, a native of Flanders where economic realities were so natural a part of daily life. In business it was wise to know and be known.

Two ambitions converged in this new taste for portraiture, the product of the two social tendencies in the businessman: individualism, linked to his search for profit; and his sense of group solidarity formed in the face of markets and privileges. A good example was set, from above, by the papal court where that old adversary of the Medici, Sixtus IV, found space for portraits of his entire entourage in murals painted by Perugino, Signorelli, Rosselli, and Ghirlandaio in the new chapel—the Sistine Chapel—consecrated on 15 August 1483. The director of the Medici office in Rome, Giovanni Tornabuoni, appears in one of Ghirlandaio's works, the *Vocation of Saints Peter and Andrew*. A few years earlier, as we have seen, Tornabuoni had already employed Domenico Ghirlandaio, the son of a goldsmith, to decorate his wife's funerary chapel.

The individual portrait, an outward representation of the success and refinement of a personality, placed the merchant on the same footing as the prince. In the early fifteenth century, van Eyck had already painted a less than flattering portrait of an unknown goldsmith (in the Bucharest Museum) before producing, in 1434, the Arnolfini portrait (in London's National Gallery) with its more sensitive attention to the conventional demands of respectability, and, in 1436, a portrait of the head of the goldsmiths' guild in Bruges, Jan de Leeuw (in Vienna's *Kunsthistorisches Museum*). Cosimo de' Medici had his bust sculpted by Donatello, Sassetti by a pupil of Rossellino. At the end of the century, Tommaso Portinari had his features and those of his wife Maria immortalized by Hans Memling (in New York's Metropolitan Museum of Art), an artist who had already proved his worth with his portrait of the Florentine merchants of Bruges in his *Last Judgment* (in the Gdansk Museum).

With Arnolfini, as with Portinari, we approach a dynastic view of art, viewed as a representation of success. When he offered the church of Sant'Egidio—attached to the Hospital of Santa Maria Nuova—an *Adoration of the Shepherds*, still in existence today in the Uffizi Galleries in Florence, Portinari went further: he asked Hugo van der Goes to depict, behind his own portrait as the donor, his entire family including his youngest children, in an attitude of humble seriousness fitting for the heirs to a great name. Francesco Sassetti similarly had the shepherds in the *Nativity* portrayed with the faces of his own family, while his son Teodoro features in the foreground of the scenes depicting the *Life of St. Francis of Assisi* that he commissioned from Domenico Ghirlandaio circa 1483 for Santa Trinità.

In the choir of Santa Maria Novella, Ghirlandaio places in the foreground of his major frescoes *Life of the Virgin* and *Scenes from the Life of St. John the Baptist*—finished about 1490—the entire Tornabuoni family and almost all of the immediate entourage of Tornabuoni's nephew, Lorenzo de' Medici. Here we see, of course, Lorenzo's mother, Lucrezia Tornabuoni. Perhaps more surprisingly, given the evident rivalry between the two men in business, we find Francesco Sassetti, who is included in a spirit of group solidarity.

Framing the frescoes, amid the classicizing trompe l'oeil friezes, are the personal symbols chosen by the Tornabuoni: a leafy branch and a centaur. Here the businessman has laid claim to a princely insignia. Philip the Good had had his bed hangings embroidered with an eagle. Within a few years the porcupine of Louis XII was to be found everywhere. Anne of Brittany would decorate every wall with representations of an ermine—the animal as well as the black-and-white ermine fur of the Breton coat-of-arms—and a twisted cord or cordeliere. François I made the salamander his heraldic beast.

The Medici family acted no differently from their faithful Tornabuoni when they chose to be represented in the flesh by Sandro Botticelli in the *Adoration of the Magi* (in the Uffizi Galleries), painted at about the same time—a little before 1480, and certainly before his work on the Sistine Chapel—as he painted the *Primavera* for the Medici villa at Castello.

Botticelli was more audacious in his double portrait (c. 1486, now in the Louvre) when he shows the beautiful Giovanna degli Albizzi Tornabuoni as a character in an allegory of *Venus and the Graces*, while her husband, Lorenzo di Giovanni Tornabuoni, first cousin to Lorenzo the Magnificent, blends unobtrusively into the background group of conversing figures representing the *Seven Liberal Arts*. Here it was no longer a matter of simply making a likeness of a man or woman, identifying them, and dating the picture. Rather, the painter wishes to express the deeper sentiments of his characters apart from any reference to their wealth. The place in an ideal society claimed by the Tornabuoni, and bestowed on them by the genius of Botticelli, was not found in the world of profit but in that of the spirit.

The social process was complete. Lorenzo di Giovanni Tornabuoni was a banker. He was the son of the Medici's agent in the Naples branch. He himself had founded and managed, rather inefficiently, two banking companies, in Naples and in Rome. And now here he was shown discoursing with the Liberal Arts, the pillars of all learning, in the place that had formerly been reserved, among the learned and wise of the Palatine Academy, for no less a personage than Charlemagne.

CONCLUSION

*W*e have come a long way from the "dusty-footed" merchant. There were still peddlers selling sewing thread and trinkets, knife sharpeners and water carriers, *hénouars* and dealers to provide salt or shallots to stay-at-home housewives. Along the roadside the blacksmiths' counters were still a common sight, selling the products of their glowing forges, along with glove makers and dressmakers offering the latest fashions, cloth merchants selling measures of cloth, and innkeepers selling wine by the jug.

The first dusty-footed traders bore little resemblance to the first merchants who emerged to satisfy the needs of the resurgent towns of the eleventh century. The small worlds of the peddler and shopkeeper had nothing in common with that of the big businessman, or the trader whose cargo, sailing between distant ports, was never simply the piece of cloth that one could rub between one's fingers; or the banker for whom transfers, reports, and accounts represented values and not objects; or the speculator who regarded the economic climate in Alexandria as a matter for European politics and considered the taxes on an industrial or commercial monopoly fit remuneration for loans extended to the papal state or the Habsburgs.

Cosimo the Elder, who died in 1464, was still involved in managing his wealth. Lorenzo, born in 1449, lived in another world, one in which his son and then his nephew would become popes. Grandson of a Bardi, son of a Tornabuoni—names that ring like florins in the world of business—Lorenzo the Magnificent married an Orsini, a name that in Rome evoked five hundred years of feudal lordship. His great-granddaughter Catherine would become queen of France as would, after her, Marie, granddaughter of Cosimo I, who had been crowned grand duke of Tuscany by Pius V.

By this time the grandnephews of Jacob the Rich were counts of the Holy Roman Empire. Their descendants would be the Fugger princes.

Their posterity was long-lasting, and included the Parisian financiers and farmers-general to whom we owe some of the most beautiful *hôtels* of the Marais and Île Saint-Louis districts in Paris.

Not far from the City of London, the seat of the Lord Chancellor in the House of Lords has always been the Woolsack, an apposite reminder of how much England's fortunes and trade with the furthest corners of the world was owed to the humble sheep.

During the course of these three centuries, we have seen how the merchant—worried about the bales of cloth that he himself transported to the Champagne fairs—developed into someone who could manage a complex, multidimensional organization. The businessman had emerged, defined by the intellectual tools that, vanquishing time and space, he himself had created to expand the horizons that now opened up for him.

He had discovered the art of uniting capital and energy. He had found new ways of creating wealth. He had found a means—fragile and always dangerous—of transcending the material dimensions of money.

The businessman had created the science for the systematic analysis of economic structures and operations, which survived almost intact well into this century until the advent of new business technology. He had invented methods of assessing the necessary balance between risk and security, contingency and certitude. He had carved out a niche in a society that gradually was acknowledging the reciprocal influences of politics and economics. He thus brought to the intellectual world an understanding of the levers of economic policy, rooted in the laws and practice of political economy.

A new class had taken its place among those who ruled, acted upon, and interpreted the world.

By the time of the early Renaissance, the businessman had become established; he was no longer the dusty-footed traveler, the explorer of distant places and peoples. Now that it was possible to insure against the risks of the "great venture"—long-term trade—the businessman left the adventure to others. The Atlantic was regarded as nothing more than an investment.

Gold and spices: there would come others for whom these words could still conjure a world beyond the known horizons.

BIBLIOGRAPHY

Additional works for this edition (1998) appear on pages 372–75.

Author's Note

A single author cannot deal with a subject as vast as that of business in the late Middle Ages. During the last fifty years, understanding of economic and social history has been greatly advanced by a number of detailed monographs. These studies are limited in perspective, based as they are on documentary sources and archival material bearing on specific subjects. Most of them treat particular towns or types of merchandise.

This means that, in the following bibliographical guide, any form of classification is misleading. A book on Bruges may include an analysis of European monetary phenomena; a study of Toulouse may provide unique insights into the origins of small-scale capitalism; a dissertation on the fur trade may shed new light on a possible relationship between business and fashion. In such cases it is difficult to distinguish between what bears on general history and what has more limited significance.

To make consultation easier, I simply list the works in alphabetical order by author. For editions of primary sources other than those long published under the name of their medieval author, it has become customary to list anonymous works by their titles. However, for the sake of convenience, I prefer to list them by the names of their modern editors.

This bibliography is limited to generally available works that themselves contain useful bibliographies. Because of the breadth of the subject it is impossible to list the hundreds of fundamentally important articles I have consulted, which are often difficult to obtain outside of research libraries. Generally the major insights and conclusions drawn in such articles are incorporated into more general works.

Primary Works

Balard, Michel. *Gênes et l'Outre-Mer., vol. I. Les actes de Caffa du notaire Lamberto di Sambuceto, 1289–1290.* Paris/The Hague. 1973.

Bastian Franz. *Das Runtingerbuch 1383–1407 und verwandtes Material zum Regensburger-Südostdeutschen Handel und Münzwesen.* 3 vols. Regensburg, 1944.

Bensa, Enrico. *Francesco di Marco da Prato. Notozie e documenti.* Milan Treves, 1928.

Borgia, L., E. Carli, M. A. Ceppari, U. Morandi, P. Sinibaldi and C. Zarrilli. *Le Biccherne. Tavole dipinte delle magistrature senesi (secoli XIII–XVIII).* Rome, 1984.

Bougard, Pierre, and Carlos Wyffels. *Les Finances de Calais au xiiie siècle.* Ghent, 1966.

Brereton, Georgine E., and Janet M. Ferrier. *Le Ménagier de Paris.* Oxford, 1981.

Casini, Bruno. *Il catasto di Pisa del 1428–29.* Pisa, 1964.

Cassandro, Michele. *Il libro giallo di Ginervra della compagnia fiorentina di Antonio della Casa e Simone Guadagni, 1453–1454.* Prato, 1976. (Istituto internazionale di storia econòmica F. Datini, Prato, I, 3).

Chiarini, Lorenzo. *El libro di mercatantie et usanze de paesi.* Edited by F. Borlandi. Turin, 1938.

Cobb, Henry S. *The Local Port Book of Southampton, 1439–40.* Southampton, 1961.

Day, John. *Les douanes de Gênes. 1376–1377.* 2 vols. Paris, 1963.

Dini, Bruno. *Una pratica di mercatura in formazione (1394–1395).* Florence 1980. (Istituto internazionale di storia econòmica F. Datini, Prato, I, 2).

Doehaerd, Renée. *Études anversoises. Documents sur le commerce international à Anvers.* 3 vols. Paris, 1962–1963.

Fagniez, Gustave. *Documents sur l'histoire de l'industrie et du commerce en France.* 2 vols. Paris, 1898–1900.

Favier, Jean. *Les contribuables parisiens à la fin de la guerre de Cent ans. Les rôles d'impôt de 1421, 1423 et 1438.* Paris, 1970.

Fedou, René. *Le Terrier de Jean Jossard, co-seigneur de Châtillon-d'Azergues, 1430–1463.* Paris, 1966.

Forestie, Édouard. *Les Livres de comptes des frères Bonis, marchands montalbanais du xive siècle.* 3 vols. Paris/Auch, 1890–1894.

Guasti, Cesare. *Lettere di un notaio a un mercante del secolo XIV.* 2 vols. Florence, 1880.

Heers, Jacques. *Le Livre de comptes de Giovanni Piccamiglio, homme d'affaires génois. 1456–1459.* Paris, 1959.

Le Roux de Lincy, Antoine, and Lazare-Maurice Tisserand. *Paris et ses historiens aux xive et xve siècles.* Paris, 1867.

Lopez, Robert S., and Irving W. Raymond. *Medieval Trade in the Mediterranean World.* New York, 1955.

Machiavelli, Niccolo. *Opere.* Milan, 1969.

Malden, H. E., *The Cely Papers. Selections from the Correspondence and Memoranda of the Cely Family, Merchants of the Staple.* A.D. *1475–1488.* London, 1900.

Melis, Federigo. *Documenti per la storia econòmica dei secoli XIII–XVI.* Florence, 1972. (Istituto internazionale di storia econòmica F. Datini, Prato, I, 1).

Michaelsson, Karl. *Le livre de la taille de Paris l'an 1296.* Göteborg, 1958.

Mollat, Michel. *Les affaires de Jacques Cœur. Journal du procureur Dauvet, procès-verbaux de séquestre et d'adjudication.* 2 vols. Paris, 1952–1953.

———. *Comptabilité du port de Dieppe au xve siècle.* Paris, 1951.

Pampaloni, Guido. *Firenze al tempo di Dante. Documenti sull'urbanistica fiorentina.* Rome, 1973.

Pegolotti, Francesco di Balduccio. *La pratica della mercatura*. Edited by Allan Evans. Cambridge, Mass., 1936.

Pryor, John H. *Business contracts of medieval Provence. Selected Notulae from the cartulary of Giraud Amalric of Marseilles*. 1248. Toronto, 1981.

Rigaudière, Albert. *L'Assiette de l'impôt direct à la fin du xive siècle. Le livre d'estimes des consuls de Saint-Flour pour les années 1380–1385*. Paris, 1977.

Sapori, Armando. *I libri della ragione bancaria dei Gianfigliazzi*. Milan, 1947.

———. *I libri di commercio dei Peruzzi*. Milan, 1934.

Stieda, Wilhelm. *Hildebrand Veckinchusen. Briefwechsel eines deutschen Kaufmannes im 15. Jahrhundert*. Leipzig, 1921.

Thiriet, Freddy. *Délibérations des Assemblées vénitiennes concernant la Romanie*. 2 vols. Paris/The Hague, 1966–1971.

Tuetey, Alexandre. *Journal d'un Bourgeois de Paris. 1405–1449*. Paris, 1881.

———. *Testaments enregistrés au Parlement de Paris sous le règne de Charles VI*. Paris, 1880.

Uzzano, Giovanni da. *El libro di mercatantie a usanze de' paesi*. Edited by Franco Borlandi. Turin, 1936.

Villain-Gandossi, Christiane, ed. *Comptes du sel de Francesco di Marco Datini pour sa compagnie d'Avignon. 1376–1379*. Paris, 1969.

Villani, Giovanni. *Cronica*. Edited by Magheri. Florence, 1823.

Wolff, Philippe. *Les "estimes" toulousaines des xive et xve siècles*. Toulouse, 1956.

Secondary Works

Abrams, Philip, and E. A. Wrigley, eds. *Towns in Societies. Essays in Economic History and Historical Sociology*. Cambridge, 1978.

Ariès, Philippe. *L'homme devant la mort*. Paris, 1977.

Astuti, G., ed. *Il libro dell'entrata e dell'uscita di una compagnia mercantile senese del secolo 13.1277–1282*. 2 vols. Florence, 1995.

Baldwin, John W. *Masters, Princes and Merchants. The Social Views of Peter the Chanter and His Circle*. 2 vols. Princeton, 1970.

Baratier, Édouard, and Félix Reynaud. *Histoire du commerce de Marseille. vol. 2. From 1291 to 1480*. Paris, 1951.

Barbali Bagnoli, Vera, ed. *Domanda e consumi, Livelli e strutture (nei secoli XIII–XVIII)*. Florence, 1978. (Istituto internazionale di storia economica F. Datini, Prato, II, 6).

———. *La moneta nell'economia europea. Secoli XIII-XVIII*. Prato/Florence, 1981.

Bec, Christian. *Les marchands écrivains. Affaires et humanisme à Florence, 1375–1434*. Paris/The Hague, 1967.

Bergier, Jean-François. *Genève et l'économie européene de la Renaissance*. Paris, 1963.

———. *Une histoire du sel*. Paris, 1982.

Bernard, Jacques. *Navires et gens de mer à Bordeaux (vers 1400–vers 1550)*. 3 vols. Paris, 1968.

Bigwood, Georges. *Le régime juridique et économique du commerce de l'argent dans la Belgique du Moyen Age*. 2 vols. Brussels, 1921.

Billot, Claudine. *Chartres à la fin du Moyen Âge*. Paris, 1987.

Blumenkranz, Bernhard, ed. *Histoire des Juifs en France.* Toulouse, 1972.

Boissonnade, P. *Le socialisme d'État. L'industrie et les classes industrielles en France pendant les deux premiers siècles de l'ère moderne (1453–1661).* Paris, 1927.

Bolton, J. L. *The Medieval English Economy, 1150–1500.* London, 1980.

Brandi, Cesare., ed. *Palazzo pubblico di Siena. Vicende costruttive e decorazione.* Milan, 1983.

Braudel, Fernand. *Civilisation matérielle, Économie et Capitalisme, xvᵉ–xviiiᵉ siècle.* 3 vols. Paris, 1979. Available in English as *Civilization and Capitalism, 15th–18th Century.* 3 vols. New York, 1981–4.

Braunstein, Philippe, and Robert Delort. *Venise, portrait historique d'une cité.* Paris, 1971.

Bresc-Bautier, Geneviève. *Artistes, patriciens et confréries.* Rome, 1979.

Bridbury, A. D. *England and the Salt Trade in the Later Middle Ages.* Oxford, 1955.

Brucker, Gene A. *The Civic World of Early Renaissance Florence.* Princeton, 1977.

Carrère, Claude. *Barcelone, centre économique. 1380–1462.* 2 vols. Paris/The Hague, 1967.

Carus-Wilson, E. M. *Medieval Merchant Venturers.* London, 1954.

Cazelles, Raymond. *Paris de la fin du règne de Philippe Auguste à la mort de Charles V.* Paris, 1972.

———. *La société politique et la crise de la royauté sous Philippe de Valois.* Paris, 1958.

———. *Société politique. Noblesse et Couronne sous Jean le Bon et Charles V.* Geneva/Paris, 1982.

Chevalier, Bernard. *Les bonnes villes de France du xivᵉ au xviᵉ siècle.* Paris, 1982.

———. *Tours, ville royale. 1356–1520.* Paris/Leuven, 1975.

Chevalier, Bernard, and Philippe Contamine, eds. *La France de la fin du xvᵉ siècle. Renouveau et apogée.* Paris, 1985.

Chiffoleau, Jacques. *La comptabilité de l'Au-delà. Les hommes, la mort et la religion dans la région d'Avignon à la fin du Moyen Âge.* Rome, 1980.

Cipolla, Carlo M. *The monetary policy of Fourteenth-Century Florence.* Los Angeles, 1982.

———. *Studi di storia della moneta. I movimenti dei cambi in Italia da secolo XIII a XV.* Pavia, 1948.

Cloulas, Ivan. *Laurent le Magnifique.* Paris, 1982.

Coornaert, Émile. *Les corporations en France avant 1789.* Paris, 1941.

———. *Dawn of Modern Banking.* New Haven and London, 1979 (Center for Medieval and Renaissance Studies, University of California, Los Angeles).

Day, John, ed. *Études d'histoire monétaire.* Lille, 1984.

Delaruelle, Étienne, Edmond-René Labande, and Paul Ourliac. *L'Église au temps du Grand Schisme et de la crise conciliaire, 1378–1449.* 2 vols. Paris, 1962.

Delort, Robert. *Le commerce des fourrures en Occident à la fin du Moyen Âge.* 2 vols. Rome, 1978.

Delumeau, Jean. *L'alun de Rome. xvᵉ–xixᵉ siècle.* Paris, 1962.

———. *Le péche et la peur. La culpabilisation en Occident (xiiiᵉ–xviiiᵉ siècle).* Paris, 1983.

De Roover, Raymond. *The Bruges money market around 1400.* Brussels, 1968.

————. *Business, Banking and Economic Thought in Late Medieval and Early Modern Europe*. Selected Studies, edited by Julius Kirshner. Chicago/London, 1974.

————. *L'évolution de la lettre de change, xive–xviiie siècle*. Paris, 1953.

————. *The Medici Bank: Its Organization, Management, Operations and Decline*. New York, 1948.

————. *Money, Banking and Credit in Mediaeval Bruges*. Cambridge, Mass., 1949.

————. *La pensée économique des scolastiques. Doctrines et méthodes*. Montreal, 1971.

————. *The Rise and Decline of the Medici Bank, 1397–1494*. New York, 1966.

————. *San Bernardino of Siena and Sant'Antonio of Florence: The Two Great Economic Thinkers of the Middle Ages*. Boston, 1967.

Desportes, Pierre. *Reims et les Rémois aux xiiie et xive siècles*. Paris, 1979.

Dollinger, Philippe. *La Hanse (xiie–xviie siècle)*. Paris, 1964.

Dubois, Henri. *Les foires de Chalon et le commerce dans la vallée de la Saône à la fin du Moyen Âge*. Paris, 1976.

Dufourcq, Charles-E., and Jean Gautier-Dalche. *Histoire économique et sociale de l'Espagne chrétienne au Moyen Âge*. Paris, 1976.

Edler, Florence. *Glossary of Mediaeval Terms of Business. Italian series. 1200–1600*. Cambridge, Mass., 1934.

Espinas, Georges. *Aux origines du capitalisme. I. Sire Jehan Boinebroke, patricien et drapier douaisien*. Lille, 1933.—*II. Sire Jean de France, patricien et rentier douaisien. Sire Jacques Le Blond, patricien en drapier douaisien*. Lille, 1936.

————. *La draperie dans la Flandre française au Moyen Âge*. 2 vols. Paris, 1923.

Fagniez, Gustave. *Études sur l'industrie et la classe industrielle à Paris aux xiiie et xive siècles*. Paris, 1977.

Fanfani, Amintore. *Le origini dello spirito capitalistico in Italia*. Milan, 1933.

Favier, Jean. *Les Finances pontificales à l'époque du Grand Schisme d'Occident. 1378–1409*. Paris, 1966.

————. *Paris au xve siècle*. Paris, 1974.

————, ed. *La France médiévale*. Paris, 1983.

Favreau, Robert. *La Ville de Poitiers à la fin du Moyen Âge. Une capitale régionale*. 2 vols. Poitiers, 1978.

Franklin, Alfred. *Dictionnaire historique des arts, métiers et professions exercés dans Paris depuis le xiiie siècle*. 2 vols. Paris/Leipzig, 1905–1906.

Fryde, E. B., *Studies in medieval trade and finance*. London, 1983.

Gandilhon, René. *Politique économique de Louis XI*. Paris, 1941.

Garin, Eugenio. *L'Éducation de l'homme moderne. 1400–1600*. Paris, 1969.

Gutkind, Curt S. *Cosimo de' Medici, Pater Patriae, 1384–1464*. Oxford, 1938.

Heers, Jacques. *Christophe Colomb*. Paris, 1981.

————. *Gênes au xve siècle. Activité économique et problèmes sociaux*. Paris, 1961.

————. *Le Clan familial au Moyen Âge*. Paris, 1974.

————. *L'Occident aux xive et xve siècles. Aspects économiques et sociaux*. Paris, 1963.

————. *Marco Polo*. Paris, 1983.

Hilaire, Jean. *Introduction historique au droit commercial*. Paris, 1986.

Hocquet, Jean-Claude. *Le sel et la fortune de Venise. Production et monopole*. Lille, 2d ed., 1982.

————. *Voiliers et commerce en Méditerranée. 1200–1650.* Lille, 1979.

Huisman, Georges. *La Juridiction de la Municipalité parisienne, de saint Louis à Charles VII.* Paris, 1912.

Johnstone, Mary A. *Life in Florence in the Fifteenth Century.* Florence, 1968.

Kaeuper, Richard W. *Bankers to the Crown: The Riccardi of Lucca and Edward I.* Princeton, 1973.

Kedar, Benjamin Z. *Merchants in Crisis: Genoese and Venetian Men of Affairs and the Fourteenth-Century Depression.* New Haven/London, 1976.

Klapisch Christiane, and David Herlihy. *Les Toscans et leurs familles.* Paris, 1978.

Klein, Julius. *The Mesta: A Study of Spanish Economic History, 1273–1836.* Cambridge, Mass., 1920.

Lacroix, Jean-Bernard. *Les Fermiers fiscaux parisiens de la seconde moitié du xvᵉ siècle.* Dissertation for l'École nationale des chartes, 1973, unpublished.

Lane, Frederic C. *Andrea Barbarigo, Merchant of Venice, 1418–1449.* Baltimore, 1944.

————. *Venice: A Maritime Republic.* Baltimore/London, 1973.

La Roncière, Charles de. *Un changeur florentin du Trecento: Lippo di Fede del Sega (1285 env.–1363 env.).* Paris, 1973.

————. *Prix et salaires à Florence au xivᵉ siècle, 1280–1380.* Rome, 1982.

Laurent, Henri. *Un grand commerce d'exportation au Moyen Âge. La draperie des Pays-Bas en France et dans les pays méditerranéens (xiiᵉ–xvᵉ siècle.).* Paris, 1935.

Le Goff, Jacques. *La Bourse et la vie. Economie et religion au Moyen Âge.* Paris, 1986. Available in English as *Your Money or Your Life: Economy and Religion in the Middle Ages.* Translated by Patricia Ranum. New York, 1988.

————. *La Naissance du Purgatoire.* Paris, 1981.

Lopez, Roberto S. *La Révolution commerciale dans l'Europe médiévale.* Paris, 1974.

Lorcin, Marie-Thérèse. *Façons de sentir et de penser : les fabliaux français.* Paris, 1979.

Maffei, Domenico. *Il giovane Machiavelli, banchiere con Berto Berti a Roma.* Florence, 1973.

Magalhães Godinho, Vitorino. *História económica e social da expansão portuguesa.* Lisbon, 1947.

Mallett, Michael E. *The Florentine Galleys in the 15th century.* Oxford, 1967.

Malowist, Marian. *Wschód a zachód Europy w 13–16 wieku. Konfrontacja struktur spoleczno-gospodarczych.* Warsaw, 1973.

Melis, Federigo. *Aspetti della vita econòmica medievale (Studi nell'Archivio Datini di Prato).* Siena, 1962.

————. *Origine e sviluppi delle assicurazioni in Italia (secoli xiv–xvi).* Rome, 1975.

————. *Storia della ragioneria. Contributo alla cognoscenza e interpretazione delle fonti piu significative della storia econòmica.* Bologna, 1950.

Michaelsson, Karl. *Études sur les noms de personne français d'après les rôles de taille parisienes.* Upsala, 1927.

Miskimin, Harry A. *The Economy of Early Renaissance Europe, 1300–1460.* Englewood Cliffs, 1969.

————, David Herlihy, A. L. Udovitch, eds. *The Medieval City.* New Haven/London, 1977.

Molho, Anthony. *Florentine Public Finances in the Early Renaissance, 1400–1433.* Cambridge, Mass., 1971.

Mollat, Michel. *Le commerce maritime normand à la fin du Moyen Âge.* Paris, 1952.

———. *Genèse médiévale de la France moderne.* Paris, 1970.

Moranvillé, Henri. *Étude sur la vie de Jean Le Mercier.* Paris, 1888.

Munro, John H. *Wool, Cloth and Gold: The Struggle for Bullion in Anglo-Burgundian Trade, 1340–1478.* Toronto, 1973.

———, ed. *Le Rôle du sel dans l'histoire.* Paris, 1968.

North, Douglass, and Robert Paul Thomas. *The Rise of the Western World: A New Economic History.* Cambridge, 1973.

Pampaloni, Guido. *Firenze al tempo di Dante. Documenti sull'urbanistica fiorentina.* Rome, 1973.

Petry, Ludwig. *Die Popplau. Eine schlesische Kaufmannsfamilie des 15 und 16 Jahrhunderte.* Breslau, 1935.

Pirenne, Henri. *Histoire économique de l'Occident médiéval.* Paris, 1951.

Postan, Michael M. *Medieval trade and finance.* Cambridge, 1973.

———, and E. Rich, eds. *The Cambridge economic history of Europe.* vol. 2, *Trade and industry in the Middle Ages.* Cambridge, 1952.

———, E. E. Rich, and Edward Miller, eds. *The Cambridge economic history of Europe.* vol. 3, *Economic organization and policies in the Middle Ages.* Cambridge, 1963.

Power, Eileen. *Medieval English Wool Trade.* London, 1941.

———, and Michael M. Postan. *Studies in English trade in the 15th century.* London, 1933.

Renouard, Yves. *Études d'histoire médiévale.* 2 vols. Paris, 1968.

———. *Les hommes d'affaires italiens du Moyen Âge.* Paris, 1968.

———. *Les relations des papes d'Avignon et des compagnies commerciales et bancaires de 1316 à 1378.* Paris, 1941.

Rubinstein, Nicolai. *The Government of Florence under the Medici (1434 to 1494).* Oxford, 1966.

Sapori, Armando. *Le Marchand Italien au Moyen Âge.* Paris, 1952.

———. *Una compagnia di Calimala ai primi del Trecento.* Florence, 1932.

Schick, Léon. *Un grand homme d'affaires du début du xvie siècle, Jacob Fugger.* Paris, 1957.

Schneider, Jean. *La Ville de Metz aux xiiie et xive siècles.* Nancy, 1950.

Schulte, Aloys. *Geschichte der grossen Ravensburger Handelsgesellschaft. 1380–1530.* 3 vols. Stuttgart/Berlin, 1923.

Sicard, Germain. *Aux origines des sociétés anonymes. Les moulins de Toulouse au Moyen Âge.* Paris, 1953.

Société Jean Bodin (Recueils de la), vol. 5. *La Foire.* Brussels, 1953.

———. *vol. 10. L'Étranger.* 2 vols. Brussels, 1958.

Sombart, Werner. *Der moderne Kapitalismus.* Berlin 2d ed., 1928.

Spufford, P. *Monetary problems and policies in the Burgundian Netherlands. 1433–1496.* Leiden, 1970.

Tenenti, Alberto. *Florence à l'époque des Médicis. De la Cité à l'État.* Paris, 1969.

Thrupp, Sylvia. *The merchant class of medieval London, 1300–1500.* London, 1948.

Touchard, Henri. *Le commerce maritime breton à la fin du Mo, :n Âge*. Paris, 1967.

Transports au Moyen Âge, Les. *Actes du VII⁰ congrès des médiévistes de l'Enseigne-ment supérieur*. Rennes, June 1976. *Annales de Bretagne*, 85:2 (1978).

Trocmé Étienne, and Marcel Delafosse. *Le commerce rochelais de la fin du xv⁰ siècle au début du xvii⁰*. Paris, 1952.

Usher, P. *The Early History of Deposit Banking in Mediterranean Europe*. Cambridge, Mass., 1943.

Van der Wee, H. *The Growth of the Antwerp Market and the European Economy*. 3 vols. The Hague, 1963.

Vannini Marx, Anna, ed. *Credito, banche e investimenti, secoli XIII–XX*. Florence, 1985. (Istituto internazionale di storia econòmica F. Datini, Prato, II, 4).

———. *Trasporti e sviluppo econòmico, secoli XIII–XVIII*. Florence, 1986. (Istituto ... Datini, Prato, II, 5).

Wolff, Philippe. *Automne du Moyen Âge ou printemps des temps nouveaux. L'économie européenne aux xiv⁰ et xv⁰ siècles*. Paris, 1986.

———. *Commerces et marchands de Toulouse (vers 1350–vers 1450)*. Paris, 1954.

Additional Primary Works for the English Edition

Arbel, Benjamin, ed. "Venetian Trade in Fifteenth Century Acre: The Letters of Francisco Bevilaqua 1471–1472." *Asian and African Studies* 22 (1988): 227–288.

Goldthwaite, Richard, Enzo Settesoldi, and Marco Spallanzani, eds. *Due libri mastri degli Alberti: Una grande compagnia di Calimala, 1348–1358*. 2 vols. Florence, 1995.

Zibaldone da Canal. *Merchant Culture in Fourteenth-Century Venice*. Edited and translated by John Dotson. Binghamton, 1994.

Additional Secondary Works for the English Edition

Abulafia, David. *A Mediterranean Emporium: The Catalan Kingdom of Majorca*. Cambridge, 1994.

Angermann, Norbert, ed. *Die Hanse und der deutsche Osten*. Lüneburg, 1990.

Ashtor, Eliyahu. *Levant Trade in the Later Middle Ages*. Princeton, 1983.

———. *Technology, Industry, and Trade: The Levant versus Europe, 1250–1500*. Edited by B. Z. Kedar. Aldershot, 1992.

Assis, Yom Tov. *Jewish Economy in the Medieval Crown of Aragon, 1213–1327: Money and Power*. Leiden, 1997.

Attman, Artur. *The Bullion Flow Between Europe and the East, 1000–1750*. Göteborg, 1981.

Bautier, Robert-Henri. *Commerce méditerranéen et banquiers italiens au Moyen Âge*. Aldershot, 1992.

Borsari, Silvano. *Una compagnia di Calimala: gli Scali (secc. XIII–XIV)*. Macerata, 1994.

Brennig, Heribert. *Der Kaufmann im Mittelalter: Literatur, Wirtschaft, Gesellschaft*. Pfaffenweiler, 1993.

Britnell, R. H. *The Commercialisation of English Society, 1000–1500*. Cambridge, 1993.

Britnell, Richard, and Bruce Campbell, eds. *A Commercialising Economy: England, 1086 to c.1300.* Manchester, 1995.

Chiapelli, Fredi, ed. *The Dawn of Modern Banking.* New Haven, 1979.

Childs, Wendy. *Anglo-Castilian Trade in the Later Middle Ages.* London, 1978.

Cipolla, Carlo M. *Before the Industrial Revolution: European Society and Economy, 1000–1700.* 3rd ed. London/New York, 1994.

———. *La moneta a Firenze nel Cinquecento.* Bologna, 1987.

———. *La moneta a Milano nel Quattrocento: monetazione argentea e svalutazione secolare.* Rome, 1988.

———, ed. *Banchieri e mercanti di Siena.* Rome, 1987.

Commerce, finances et société (XIᵉ–XVIIᵉ siècles). Recueil de travaux d'histoire médiévale offert à M. le professeur Henri Dubois. Paris, 1993.

Constable, Olivia Remi. *Trade and Traders in Muslim Spain: The Commercial Realignment of the Iberian Peninsula, 900–1500.* Cambridge, 1994.

Contamine, Philippe et al. *L'économie médiévale.* Paris, 1993.

Day, Gerald. *Genoa's Response to Byzantium, 1155–1204. Commercial Expansion and Factionalism in a Medieval City.* Urbana, c.1988.

Day, John. *The Medieval Market Economy.* Oxford, 1987.

———, ed. *Etudes d'histoire monétaire, XIIᵉ–XIXᵉ siècles.* Lille/Paris, 1984.

Dufourcq, Charles-Emmanuel. *L'Espagne catalane et le Maghrib aux XIIᵉ et XIVᵉ siècles.* Paris, 1967.

Elbl, Ivana. "Nation, Bolsa and Factory: Three Institutions of Late-Medieval Portuguese Trade with Flanders." *The International History Review* 14 (1992): 1–22.

Elbl, Martin. "The Portuguese Caravel and European Shipbuilding: Phases of Development and Diversity." *Revista da Universidade de Coimbra* 33 (1985): 543–572.

English, Edward. *Enterprise and Liability in Sienese Banking, 1230–1350.* Cambridge, Mass., 1988.

Felloni, Giuseppe, and Dino Puncuh, eds. *Banchi pubblici, banchi privati e monti di pietà nell'Europa preindustriale: Administrazione, tecniche operative e ruoli economici.* 2 vols. Genoa, 1991.

Furió, A., ed. *València, un mercat medieval.* Valencia, 1985.

Galassi, Francesco. "Buying a Passport to Heaven: Usury, Restitution and the Merchants of Medieval Genoa." *Religion* 22 (1992): 313–326.

Gerkens, Gerhard, and Antjekathrin Grassman, eds. *Der Lübecker Kaufmann: Aspekte seiner Lebens- und Arbeitswelt vom Mittelalter bis zum 19. Jahrhundert.* Lübeck, 1993.

Goldsmith, Raymond. *Premodern Financial Systems. A Historical Comparative Study.* Cambridge, 1987.

Goldthwaite, Richard. *Banks, Palaces and Entrepreneurs in Renaissance Florence.* Aldershot/Brookfield, 1995.

Grierson, Philip. *Later Medieval Numismatics (11th–16th Centuries). Selected Studies.* London, 1979.

Gucciardino, Marianna. *Trasporti e commerci nel Medioevo.* Rome, 1987.

Harte, Negley B., and Kenneth G. Ponting, eds. *Cloth and Clothing in Medieval Europe. Essays in Memory of Professor E. M. Carus-Wilson.* London, 1983.

Heeres, W. G., L. M. J. B. Hesp, L. Noordegraaf, and R. Voort, eds. *From Dunkirk to Danzig. Shipping and Trade in the North Sea and the Baltic, 1350–1850.* Hilversum, 1988.

Hendy, Michael. *Studies in the Byzantine Monetary Economy, c. 300–1450.* Cambridge, 1985.

Hodges, Richard. *Dark Age Economics: The Origins of Towns and Trade, A.D. 500–1000.* London, 1989.

Hunt, Edwin. *The Medieval Super-Companies: A Study of the Peruzzi Company of Florence.* Cambridge, 1994.

Jenks, Stuart, and Michael North, eds. *Der Hansische Sonderweg? Beiträge zur Sozial- und Wirtschaftsgeschichte der Hanse.* Cologne/Vienna, 1993.

Kermode, Jennifer, ed. *Enterprise and Individuals in Fifteenth-Century England.* London, 1991.

Kowaleski, Maryanne. *Local Markets and Regional Trade in Medieval Exeter.* Cambridge, 1995.

Lane, Frederic. *Venice and History. The Collected Papers of Frederic C. Lane.* Baltimore, 1966.

―――, and Reinhold Mueller. *Money and Banking in Medieval and Renaissance Venice.* London/Baltimore, 1985.

Langholm, Odd. *Economics in the Medieval Schools: Wealth, Exchange, Value, Money and Usury according to the Paris Theological Tradition, 1200–1350.* Leiden, 1992.

Le Goff, Jacques. *Pour un autre Moyen Âge: temps, travail et culture en Occident.* Paris, 1977. Also available in English as *Time, Work and Culture in the Middle Ages.* Translated by Arthur Goldhammer. Chicago, 1980.

Lewis, Archibald, and Timothy Runyan. *European Naval and Maritime History, 300–1500.* Bloomington, 1985.

Lloyd, T. H. *England and the German Hanse, 1157–1611: A Study of Their Trade and Commercial Diplomacy.* Cambridge, 1991.

Lopez, Robert. *I monetieri del primo medioevo: la più antica aristocrazia professionale laica che la storia recordi.* Milan, 1991.

―――. *The Shape of Medieval Monetary History.* London, 1986.

Mackenney, Richard. *Tradesmen and Traders: The World of the Guilds in Venice and Europe, c.1250–c.1650.* Totowa, N.J., 1987.

Magalhães Godinho, Vitorino. *Mito e mercadoria, utopia e prática de navegar: sécolos XIII–XVIII.* Lisbon, 1990.

Mainoni, P. *Mercanti lombardi tra Barcellona e Valenza nel basso medioevo.* Bologna, 1982.

Marx, Anne Vannini, ed. *Trasporti e sviluppo econòmico: secoli XIII–XVIII.* Florence, 1986.

Mazzaoui, Maureen. *The Italian Cotton Industry in the Later Middle Ages, 1100–1600.* London, 1981.

Melis, Federigo. *I mercanti italiani dell'Europa medievale e renascimentale.* Florence, 1990.

Miller, Edward. *Medieval England. Towns, Commerce and Crafts, 1086—1348.* London, 1995.

Miskimin, Harry. *Cash, Credit and Crisis in Europe, 1300–1600.* London, 1989.

Munro, John. *Bullion Flows and Monetary Policies in England and the Low Countries, 1350–1500.* London, 1992.

———. *Textiles, Towns and Trade: Essays in the Economic History of Late-Medieval England and the Low Countries.* London, 1994.

Nicholas, David. *Trade, Urbanisation and the Family: Studies in the History of Medieval Flanders.* Aldershot, 1996.

North, Michael. *Das Geld und seine Geschichte: vom Mittelalter bis zur Gegenwart.* Munich, 1994.

———, ed. *Geldumlauf, Währungssysteme und Zahlungsverkehr in Nordwesteuropa, 1300–1800. Beiträge zur Geldgeschichte der späten Hansezeit.* Cologne/Vienna, 1989.

———, ed. *Kredit im spätmittelalterlichen und frühneuzeitlichen Europa.* Cologne/Vienna, 1991.

O'Neill, Timothy. *Merchants and Mariners in Medieval Ireland.* Dublin, 1987.

Petralia, Giuseppe. *Banchieri e famiglie mercantili nel Mediterraneo aragonese: l'emigrazione dei pisani in Sicilia nel Quattrocento.* Pisa, 1989.

Pryor, John. *Commerce, Shipping and Naval Warfare in the Medieval Mediterranean.* London, 1987.

———. *Geography, Technology and War. Studies in the Maritime History of the Mediterranean.* Cambridge, 1988.

Reyerson, Kathryn. *Society, Law, and Trade in Medieval Montpellier.* Aldershot, 1995.

Richards, John F. *Precious Metals in the Later Medieval and Early Modern Worlds.* Durham, N.C., 1983.

Sánchez Benito, José María. *La corona de Castilla y el comercio exterior: estudio del intervencionismo monárquico sobre los tráficos.* Madrid, 1993.

Sayous, André-Emile. *Commerce et finance en Méditerranée au moyen âge.* Edited by Mark Steele. London, 1988.

Schatzmiller, Joseph. *Shylock Reconsidered: Jews, Moneylending and Medieval Society.* Berkeley, 1990.

Schonfelder, Alexander. *Handelsmessen und Kreditwirtschaft im Hochmittelalter: die Champagnemessen.* Saarbrücken, 1988.

Spufford, Peter. *Money and Its Use in Medieval Europe.* Cambridge, 1988.

Strassle, Paul. *Der internationale Schwarzmeerhandel und Konstantinopel, 1261–1484: im Spiegel der sowjetischen Forschung.* New York, 1990.

Tracy, James, ed. *The Political Economy of Merchant Empires: State Power and World Trade, 1350–1750.* Cambridge, 1991.

———, ed. *The Rise of Merchant Empires: Long-Distance Trade in the Early Modern World, 1350-1750.* Cambridge/New York, 1990.

Unger, Richard. *The Ship in the Medieval Economy, 600–1600.* London/Montreal, 1980.

Van Cauwenberghe, Eddy, ed. *Money, Coins and Commerce. Essays in the Monetary History of Asia and Europe (from Antiquity to Modern Times).* Leuven, 1991.

Vilar, Pierre. *Oro y moneda en la historia, 1450–1920.* Barcelona, 1969. Available in English as *A History of Gold and Money, 1450–1920.* Translated by Judith White. London, 1976.

Italicized page numbers indicate maps.